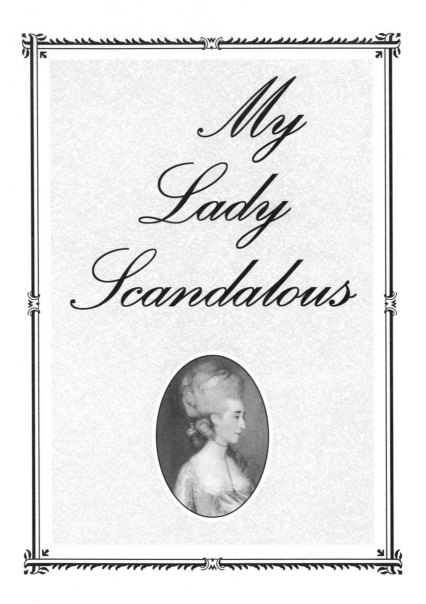

My Lady Scandalous

SIMON & SCHUSTER

New York   London
Toronto   Sydney

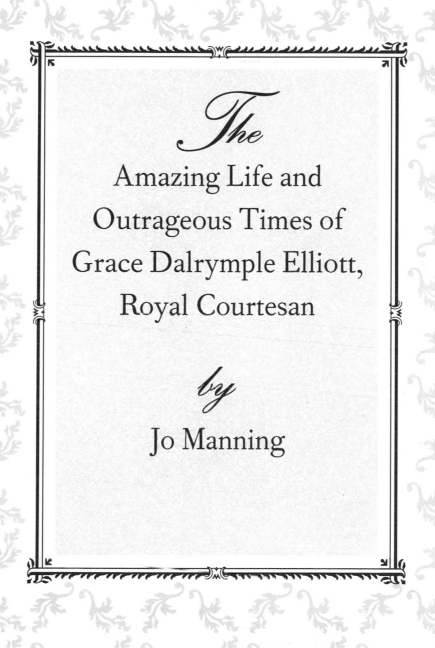

The Amazing Life and Outrageous Times of Grace Dalrymple Elliott, Royal Courtesan

by

Jo Manning

SIMON & SCHUSTER
Rockefeller Center
1230 Avenue of the Americas
New York, NY 10020

SIMON & SCHUSTER and colophon are registered trademarks
of Simon & Schuster, Inc.

For information regarding special discounts for bulk purchases,
please contact Simon & Schuster Special Sales at 1-800-456-6798
or business@simonandschuster.com

Designed by Jeanette Olender
Genealogical tables prepared by Shyamali Ghosh
Frontispiece: *Mrs. Grace Dalrymple Elliott* (detail), by Thomas
Gainsborough (The Metropolitan Museum of Art)

Manufactured in the United States of America

1   3   5   7   9   10   8   6   4   2

Library of Congress Cataloging-in-Publication Data
Manning, Jo
My lady scandalous : the amazing life and outrageous times of Grace
Dalrymple Elliott, royal courtesan / by Jo Manning.
p.   cm.
Includes bibliographical references and index.
1. Elliott, Grace Dalrymple, d. 1823.   2. Great Britain—History—
George III, 1760–1820—Biography.   3. George IV, King of Great Britain,
1762–1830—Relations with women.   4. France—History—Revolution,
1789–1799—Biography.   5. British—Fra..e—History—18th century.
I. Title.
DA506.E44 M9   2005   941.07'092—dc22   [B] 2005049035

ISBN-13: 978-0-7432-6262-0
ISBN-10: 0-7432-6262-X

Oct 2005

DEDICATION

*T*his book is dedicated to the following individuals, whose inspiration provided moral support during the several years it took to research and write it: Eric Rohmer; Lucy Russell; David Cholmondeley, seventh Marquess of Cholmondeley; and the late Hubert von Sonnenburg.

To the venerable French director Eric Rohmer, for rescuing Grace Dalrymple Elliott from the dustbin of history—where too many women are sent—and for bringing her dramatic story to the screen; to the excellent and lovely actress Lucy Russell for portraying this extraordinary woman in a nuanced, memorable performance; to the Most Honorable David George Philip Cholmondeley, seventh Marquess of Cholmondeley and Lord Great Chamberlain of England, for his interest in this project; and to the late Hubert von Sonnenburg, the distinguished art historian and conservator and Chairman of the Paintings Conservation Studio at the Metropolitan Museum of Art.

Dr. von Sonnenburg, who passed away on July 16, 2004, kindly showed me the beautiful Joshua Reynolds portrait of Georgiana Elliott as a baby, a painting rarely on display, and offered to photograph it so that I would have it for this book. Lucy Russell took three hours out of her busy schedule between films to tell me what it was like working for Eric Rohmer and how she felt about Grace Elliott. The Marquess of Cholmondeley has always been gracious and kind in response to inquiries about his family. I never met Eric Rohmer face to face; I know him only through his films. Generous individuals such as these make the dark side of a researcher/writer's job—having to deal with the realities of closed or relocating archives, unavailable books, blurry microforms, nonexistent documents, ineffectual information providers, and uncooperative sources—a lot more bearable.

I also want to thank my agent, Jenny Bent, of Trident Media Group, who has been with me since the idea for this project first interrupted the writing of my third historical novel and who encouraged me to follow this dream, and to my incredibly hardworking editor, Denise Roy, who's had to deal with the hard-to-break habit of this lifelong researcher to give just a teensy bit more information than necessary. As my old boss Jack O'Hara, the former CEO of *Reader's Digest*, once advised concerning the decision to include or exclude a piece of information, the key question always has to be, Is it nice, or is it necessary? Merely "nice" never made the cut.

Miami Beach

ACKNOWLEDGMENTS

I want to acknowledge the help of the following researchers and others who contributed to the making of this book:

My primary researchers and translators were Colette Pozzi-Barsot, whose knowledge of the area in and around Meudon, France, proved immensely valuable in tracing Grace Elliott's later years; Colette would not give up until she located Grace's final resting place at Père Lachaise. Kristina Hickey and Daniele Perez-Venero provided quick and intelligent French-to-English translations; Daniele did a superb job on the Sainte-Beuve appreciation of Grace's *Journal*, and Kristina accompanied me on my trip to Paris and to Ville d'Avray, where we found Grace's death certificate exactly where we thought it would be. Colette and Kristina also took many of the photographs in France and England.

Barbara Rosenbaum did a masterful job of plowing through the Bentley Archives at the British Library to get an answer for what had happened to Grace's original manuscript of the *Journal;* Richard Grenville Clark of Guildford was a vast fount of information on Lady Seymour Dorothy Fleming, Grace Elliott's good friend; in Scotland, genealogist Alison Mowat tried valiantly to locate records of Grace and her family.

Various librarians, archivists, curators, historians, genealogists, writers, and others took time to assist me in what often was a frustrating undertaking. David Yaxley, historian at Houghton Hall, Norfolk, found letters pertaining to Grace in an old trunk of assorted financial documents and was a wealth of information on the history of the Cholmondeley family; art historian Charlotte Crowley suggested portraits of the first Marquess of Cholmondeley for use in this book; Susan Cleaver, Houghton Hall administrator, also provided assistance; the Frick Collection's Margaret Iacono and Patrice Mattia, in the European Paintings Department at the Metropolitan Museum of Art, graciously allowed me to use the curatorial files pertaining to the two Gainsborough paintings of Grace in their collections; various librarians at the Frick Art Reference Library were extremely helpful; law librarians Andrea Longson at the Faculty of Advocates Library and Audrey Walker at the Signet Library, both in Edinburgh, and Stuart Adams at London's Middle Temple Library explained the Scottish legal system to me; Stephanie Tarot of Pathé, Paris, kindly supplied images from the film *L'Anglaise et le Duc;* Christine Wollett of the Royal Society of Arts, Simon Chaplin of the Royal College of Surgeons, and Natasha McEnroe, curator of Dr. Johnson's House, all led the way to additional materials and information on the period. Henry Gray of St. Etheldreda's Church in Hertfordshire took the photograph of Sir John Eliot's memorial tablet and contacted his colleague P. L. Dickinson, the Richmond Herald at the College of Arms, for Eliot's pedigree; James Strachan and Hugh Alexander at the National Archives, Kew, were helpful in securing the Eliot/Elliott wills; Miss Pamela Clark, registrar at Windsor Castle, verified the payment of Grace's annuity from King George IV and provided photocopies of original documents in the collection of Her Majesty Queen Elizabeth II. I want to acknowledge the help and support of my fellow Regency buffs and writing colleagues Emily Hendrickson, Margaret Evans Porter, Victoria Hinshaw, Rosemary Stevens, Nancy Mayer, Mary Jo Putney, and Lynne Connolly; thanks go to my Miami friend Walkyria Batista, who tried to find Grace's gravesite early on. Phyllis Robarts and Margaret Borgeest of the University of Miami and Rita Cauce and Joan Bueter of Barry University helped me find books.

Very special thanks go to the artist Francis Farmar, whose late father Hugh Farmar's marvelous book, *A Regency Elopement,* filled in so many gaps in the life of Georgina Cavendish Bentinck; Francis showed interest in this project from the first when a strange lady he did not know approached him via cyberspace. Curator Derek Adlam at Welbeck Abbey was gracious and generous beyond measure and greatly enriched this book. I am grateful to the twelfth Earl of Portland, actor Tim Bentinck, for making this contact. To the two Mikes, Paterson and Powazinik, and to genealogist Margaret Greenwood of Australia, thank you so much for everything you did.

Picture research and photographs were so important to this book. I want to thank the British Museum, especially Sheila O'Connell, assistant keeper, Prints Department; Tom Schaefer, of the Helen Allingham Society; Lesley Hodgson, Bridgeman Art Library; J. Pitcher, British Library Newspaper

Collection; Helen Trompeteler, National Portrait Gallery; David Beevers, Royal Pavilion, Brighton; Julie Cochran, Museum of London; Laura Hitchcock, Empics; freelance picture researcher Kate Pink; my colleague and fellow Regency author Candice Hern for images from her fabulous Web site; Jean-Robert Durbin at the Huntington Library in California, who provided an engraving of Grace from a publication the British Library no longer owns (the Huntington is a great resource); Steve Bartrick at Steve Bartrick Antique Prints & Maps; and others for their alacrity in dealing with frantic last-minute requests from someone who'd done a lot of text research but never picture research, and had to learn fast. Alun Ford, University of London and Rory Lalwan at the Westminster City Council were both immensely helpful, as was Mark Annand, Bath Spa University College. I am grateful to Dr. Steven Greenberg, National Library of Medicine, Washington, D.C.; Paul Garner at John Garner Antiques; Caroline Benson, Museum of English Rural Life, University of Reading; Audrey Hall, Lady Lever Art Gallery, Liverpool; Susan Odell Walker, Lewis Walpole Library, Yale University; Eileen Sullivan and Eva Peters, Metropolitan Museum of Art; Mark Vivian, Mary Evans Picture Library. If I have omitted anyone inadvertently, I apologize.

Ray Wadia took my photograph and well as many other photos for the book and did a magnificent job; Simon Tibbs took most of the other photos of London sites. Thanks to David Vaughan, who provided crucial computer advice and to the very kind Paul S. Smith, who supplied photos from his Grangerised edition of the *Journal*.

Finally, but not least, family, whose moral and emotional support is always there: I want to express my thanks to my daughter, art conservator Tracy Manning, for dealing with payments in pounds sterling and exchange rates that kept going up, up, up, and to my talented daughter-in-law Shyamali Ghosh, for the excellent genealogical charts that reunited natural children with their rightful families at long last. My son-in-law Mark Winterbotham's patience in putting up with a madly rushing about mother-in-law in residence for an inordinate period of time was extraordinary. My editor/writer son Matthew Manning knew a too-long Introduction when he read it and offered the good suggestion of cutting it back mercilessly; my husband, Nick Manning, provided many other good ideas. I cannot wait until my grandchildren,

Julian, Zoë, William, and Esme, who love words and reading as much as I do, are old enough to read Grace's story. There are many stories still to be told, and I hope that they will be among the tellers of such tales in the future; so far, their fledgling literary efforts are most promising.

My agent, Jenny Bent, at Trident Media and my editor, Denise Roy, cannot be thanked enough for their guidance, editorial sense, and faith in me to see this project through. Annie Orr, editorial assistant to Ms. Roy at Simon & Schuster, handled the picture traffic and all the complications connected with this often tedious and details-heavy task with good humor and skill.

CONTENTS

GENEALOGICAL TABLES

The Dalrymple Family

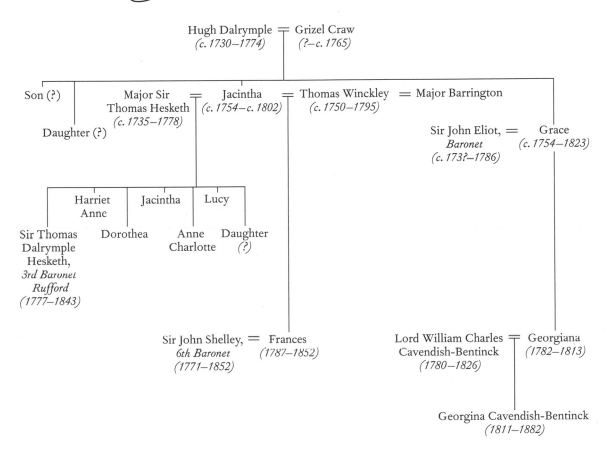

Hugh Dalrymple = Grizel Craw
(c. 1730–1774) (?–c. 1765)

Son (?)

Major Sir = Jacintha = Thomas Winckley = Major Barrington
Thomas Hesketh (c. 1754–c. 1802) (c. 1750–1795)
(c. 1735–1778)

Daughter (?)

Sir John Eliot, = Grace
Baronet (c. 1754–1823)
(c. 173?–1786)

Harriet   Jacintha   Lucy
Anne

Sir Thomas   Dorothea   Anne   Daughter
Dalrymple   Charlotte   (?)
Hesketh,
3rd Baronet
Rufford
(1777–1843)

Sir John Shelley, = Frances
6th Baronet (1787–1852)
(1771–1852)

Lord William Charles = Georgiana
Cavendish-Bentinck (1782–1813)
(1780–1826)

Georgina Cavendish-Bentinck
(1811–1882)

THE ELIOT FAMILY

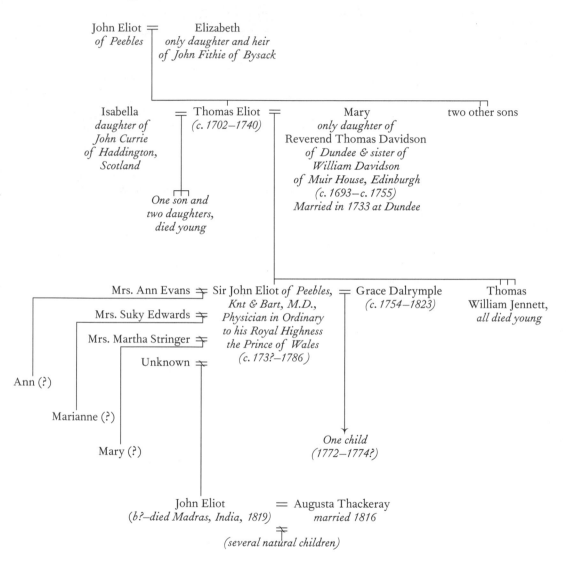

John Eliot = Elizabeth
of Peebles *only daughter and heir*
of John Fithie of Bysack

Isabella = Thomas Eliot = Mary two other sons
daughter of *(c. 1702–1740)* *only daughter of*
John Currie *Reverend Thomas Davidson*
of Haddington, *of Dundee & sister of*
Scotland *William Davidson*
of Muir House, Edinburgh
(c. 1693–c. 1755)
One son and *Married in 1733 at Dundee*
two daughters,
died young

Mrs. Ann Evans = Sir John Eliot *of Peebles,* = Grace Dalrymple Thomas
Knt & Bart, M.D., *(c. 1754–1823)* William Jennett,
Mrs. Suky Edwards = *Physician in Ordinary* *all died young*
to his Royal Highness
Mrs. Martha Stringer = *the Prince of Wales*
(c. 173?–1786)
Unknown =

Ann (?)

Marianne (?) One child
(1772–1774?)
Mary (?)

John Eliot = Augusta Thackeray
(b?–died Madras, India, 1819) *married 1816*

(several natural children)

The Cavendish-Bentinck and Cholmondeley Families

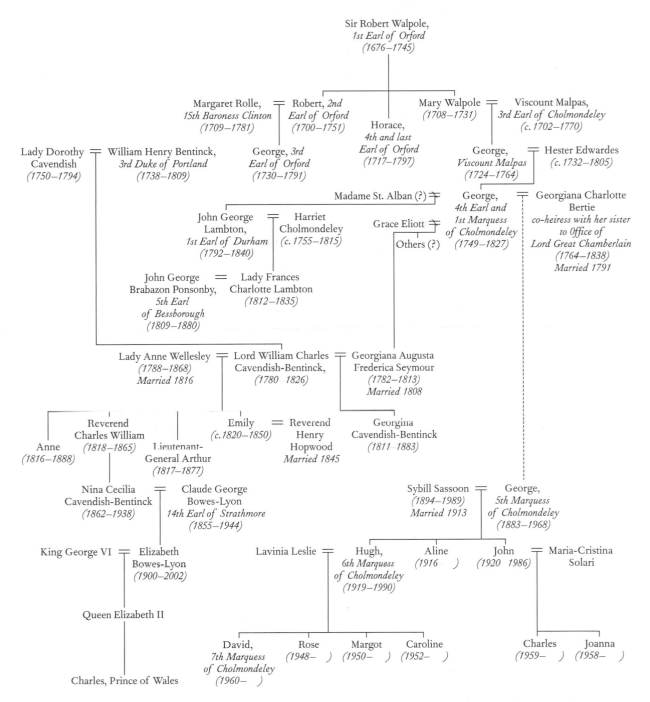

Sir Robert Walpole,
1st Earl of Orford
(1676–1745)

Margaret Rolle, = Robert, *2nd*
15th Baroness Clinton *Earl of Orford*
(1709–1781) *(1700–1751)*

Horace,
4th and last
Earl of Orford
(1717–1797)

Mary Walpole = Viscount Malpas,
(1708–1731) *3rd Earl of Cholmondeley*
(c. 1702–1770)

Lady Dorothy = William Henry Bentinck,
Cavendish *3rd Duke of Portland*
(1750–1794) *(1738–1809)*

George, *3rd*
Earl of Orford
(1730–1791)

George, = Hester Edwardes
Viscount Malpas *(c. 1732–1805)*
(1724–1764)

Madame St. Alban (?) = George,
4th Earl and
1st Marquess
of Cholmondeley
(1749–1827)

Georgiana Charlotte
Bertie
co-heiress with her sister
to Office of
Lord Great Chamberlain
(1764–1838)
Married 1791

John George = Harriet
Lambton, Cholmondeley
1st Earl of Durham *(c. 1755–1815)*
(1792–1840)

Grace Eliott =

Others (?) =

John George = Lady Frances
Brabazon Ponsonby, Charlotte Lambton
5th Earl *(1812–1835)*
of Bessborough
(1809–1880)

Lady Anne Wellesley = Lord William Charles = Georgiana Augusta
(1788–1868) Cavendish-Bentinck, Frederica Seymour
Married 1816 *(1780–1826)* *(1782–1813)*
Married 1808

Reverend
Charles William
(1818–1865)

Emily = Reverend
(c.1820–1850) Henry
Hopwood
Married 1845

Georgina
Cavendish-Bentinck
(1811–1883)

Anne
(1816–1888)

Lieutenant-
General Arthur
(1817–1877)

Nina Cecilia = Claude George
Cavendish-Bentinck Bowes-Lyon
(1862–1938) *14th Earl of Strathmore*
(1855–1944)

Sybill Sassoon = George,
(1894–1989) *5th Marquess*
Married 1913 *of Cholmondeley*
(1883–1968)

King George VI = Elizabeth
Bowes-Lyon
(1900–2002)

Lavinia Leslie = Hugh,
6th Marquess
of Cholmondeley
(1919–1990)

Aline
(1916   )

John = Maria-Cristina
(1920 1986) Solari

Queen Elizabeth II

David,
7th Marquess
of Cholmondeley
(1960–   )

Rose
(1948–   )

Margot
(1950–   )

Caroline
(1952–   )

Charles
(1959–   )

Joanna
(1958–   )

Charles, Prince of Wales

Mary Robinson (Perdita), Gertrude Mahon (the Bird of Paradise), and Grace Elliott (Dally the Tall) getting dressed for their dates. Frontispiece from *The Rambler*, January 1783. (Reproduced by permission of the Huntington Library; San Marino, California)

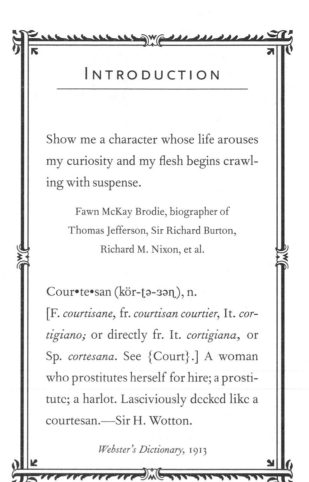

INTRODUCTION

Show me a character whose life arouses my curiosity and my flesh begins crawling with suspense.

Fawn McKay Brodie, biographer of
Thomas Jefferson, Sir Richard Burton,
Richard M. Nixon, et al.

Cour•te•san (kör-ţə-ɜəŋ), n.
[F. *courtisane*, fr. *courtisan courtier*, It. *cortigiano*; or directly fr. It. *cortigiana*, or Sp. *cortesana*. See {Court}.] A woman who prostitutes herself for hire; a prostitute; a harlot. Lasciviously decked like a courtesan.—Sir H. Wotton.

Webster's Dictionary, 1913

Grace Dalrymple Elliott was a courtesan, a celebrated courtesan who attracted attention from starstruck admirers and held her position at the top of a slippery pyramid for many years, a woman who chose her lovers well—and not that often—and lived a life of luxury well out of the reach of most inhabitants of late eighteenth- and early nineteenth-century England. In her day, she found only two serious rivals: Mary Darby Robinson, the actress known as Perdita, and Elizabeth Armistead, who became the wife of the statesman Charles James Fox.

Courtesans tended to the flamboyant—it was in the nature of their business to make a showing and be noticed—but not all courtesans became household words. Such is the nature of notoriety that very few people now know of Grace Elliott—"the fair Elliotina."

It was not, however, until the French director Eric Rohmer came upon Grace's memoir (serendipitously, by all accounts) and made his critically acclaimed movie *The Lady and the Duke*—starring the English actress Lucy Russell as Grace—that this woman's story came to the attention of a more general public.

Let us discuss what a courtesan is—and isn't. In her insightful book *Courtesans*, Katie Hickman provides a good working definition:

Part of the allure of the courtesan . . . is that she has always been an ambiguous figure. She is not a mere prostitute, although she is unequivocally a "professional" woman who accepts money in return for sexual favors. Neither is she a mistress, who usually considers herself the lover of just one man—although many courtesans . . . were much-beloved mistresses at some point in their careers. Unlike a prostitute, prepared to sell her favours to all comers, a courtesan always chose her patrons, very often for her own pleasure as well as theirs. Her gifts—of company and conversation as well of erotic pleasure—were only bestowed upon a favoured few, who paid fabulous—sometimes ruinous—sums for them. . . . [Courtesans were] fabulous, semi-mythical creatures.

A Peep at Christie's,—or—Tally-ho, & his Nimeney-pimeney taking the Morning Lounge, by James Gillray, September 26, 1796. The Earl of Derby, a follower of horse racing and fox-hunting, is Tally-ho; Nimeney-pimeney refers to a stage role of his longtime actress girlfriend Elizabeth Farren. They're at Christie's exhibition rooms, and Derby is intent upon a fox-hunt painting, *The Death*, while Farren is gazing at another, *Zenacrates and Phrynne*, showing a Greek philosopher dallying with a courtesan. Derby's wife is ill and will die in early 1797; he will marry Farren within two months' time. The print's symbolism is clear. It was not the norm for an aristocrat to marry his mistress, but it did happen, giving hope to courtesans everywhere. (National Portrait Gallery, London)

ᴀ Glossary of Terms for Courtesans and Prostitutes, and Related Jargon

Bachelor Fare; Barque of Frailty; Bit o' Muslin; Blows-abella / Blowse; Bunter; Buttock / Buttock and Twang; Cat; Chère-Amie; Come-at-able; Concubine; Convenient; Covent Garden Nun; Crack; Curtezan; Cyprian; Cytherean; Dell; Demi-Mondaine; Demi-Rep; Dirty Puzzle; Dollymop; Down Buttock and Sham File; Doxy; Draggle / Draggle-Tail; Drury Lane Vestal; Dulcinea; Fancy / Fashionable Woman; Fen; Fille / Fille de Joie / Fillette; Grizette; Harlot; Haymarket Ware; Hedge Whore; Half-Timer; High-Flyer; Horizantale; Impure / Fashionable Impure; Inamorata; Incognita; Jilt; Kept / Kind Woman; Laced Mutton; Lady of Easy Virtue; Ladybird; Letting Out One's Room / Room; Light-Heeled; Light o' Love; Light-Skirt; Member of the Cyprian Corps / Covey / Family of Love / Linen-Lifting Tribe / Muslin Company; Mab; Madam; Magdalen; Miss; Mistress; Mob; Moll; Natural; Nightwalker; Odalisque; On the Town; One of Us / One of My Cousins; Paphian; Paramour; Peculiar; Posture Moll; Prime Article; Prime Piece; Public Ledger; Quean; Receiver General; Rep; Ruin; Seven-Dials Stroller; She-Friend; Short-Heeled Wench; Slattern; Slut; Squirrel; Stroller; Strumpet; Sweet-Heart; Tackle; Tail; Tart; Tavern Player; Thais; Town / Woman of the Town; Trapes; Trollop; Trull; Trumpery; Unfortunate; Votary of Venus; Wagtail; Wanton; Ware; Wasp; Whore; Wife in Water Colors; Woman of Pleasure; Woman of the People.

The language of the times offered colorful and graphic descriptions of lower-end women of the street who sold their favors cheaply, as well as of women who were longtime mistresses or courtesans kept in high style by men of means, and who might be accepted at court (more so in laissez-faire, sophisticated Paris than in uptight London during the reign of King George III). Such females were not to be confused with one another or lumped together; even courtesans had their distinctive differences.

Some whores had specialities. The "posture moll" was skilled in flagellation and also played the "chuck game," an entertainment that involved imaginative insertion of coins and other objects into private parts. There were terms for amateurs, too, like "barber's chair" (where everyone has sat at one time or another); "Athanasian wench" or "quicunque vult," for a forward girl ready to oblige any man who asks; "thorough-good-natured-wench," for a girl who, being asked to sit down, will lie down. "Half-timers" were married women who walked the streets only occasionally, for household money. A "ruin" was a good girl soiled by a rake.

The going rate for a streetwalker was about ninepence. A courtesan's rates could be fabulously high, upwards of many, many thousands of dollars in today's U.S. currency. A married man who kept a mistress was said to be a "dark cully," since he visited his lover only at dusk for fear of discovery. A "whore-monger" was a man who kept more than one mistress at the same time. One made an "honest woman" of his mistress by marrying her. To "slice" was to intrigue with a married woman, the logic here being that one slice off a cut loaf is not missed.

A cuckolded man was said to be wearing horns, or "hornified." A man who was "horn mad" was extremely jealous of his wife; "horn work" was making a man a cuckold. A "keeping cully" was one who may have thought he was keeping a mistress for his own exclusive use, whereas the lady's uses tended to be more public. A "rum cull" was a rich man easily cheated by his mistress.

A "whore's curse" was a gold coin valued at 5 shillings, 3 pence, frequently given to women of—or on—the town. A "whore's pipe" was a penis. Men kept by women were said to be "petticoat pensioners"; men kept by old women were "stallions." One of the terms used to describe a debauched man was "whore's bird." The union of a whore and a rogue was a "Westminster wedding." A "nugging dress," or a "slammerkin," was loose garb of the kind worn by loose women. A "covey" was a collection of whores.

A word about bawdy houses: Brothels were referred to as "nunneries," the prostitutes as "nuns," and the madams of such establishments as "mothers" (as in mothers superior) or "abbesses." When Hamlet told Ophelia "Get thee to a nunnery," this was what he meant, the pig. Other words for whorehouses: "bagnios," "nugging houses." A procuress was called a "bawd." As most men understood that the lower-class brothels were to be found in the Covent Garden area, there were many phrases with "Covent Garden" as a prefix: "Covent Garden abbess" (a bawd); "Covent Garden ague" (venereal disease); "Covent Garden nun" (a prostitute). Covent Garden was also vulgarly referred to as "Common Garden." "Drury Lane" (the name of the theater that was close by) was often substituted for "Covent Garden," as in "Drury Lane ague."

Grace Dalrymple was not a prostitute, never a streetwalker ("Haymarket ware," in the parlance of the times), but a sophisticated, cultured, polished woman who selected her lovers—drawn from the peerage and royalty, i.e., the pinnacle of society, familiarly known as the ton—and tended to engage in long relationships with them. The world of "high harlotry," according to the biographer I. M. Davis, "reached its zenith in the late eighteenth century." In *The Harlot and the Statesman: The Story of Elizabeth Armistead and Charles James Fox* (1986), Davis writes:

> *The great courtesans were public figures. . . . Their dress, the decoration of their coaches, even the flowers adorning the window-boxes of their elegant houses, were matters for chronicle. . . . This age, that still took pleasure in draping its frivolities with the shreds of classical imagery, liked to deem these women the votaries of Aphrodite: they were Impures, but they were also Cythereans, Paphians, Cyprians. This last was the preferred designation, and collectively the leading harlots of the 1770s and 1780s were the Cyprian corps.*

How did a courtesan kept by a wealthy, important man spend her day? After a long night of partying into the wee hours, perhaps at the assembly rooms, a gaming hell for ladies, or a masquerade, she would rise at noon or 2 P.M. in her love nest—in the Piccadilly area (Half-Moon Street or Clarges Street), St. John's Wood, or Queen Anne Street, all popular areas for these homes away from home, perfect to store one's "ladybird." She would drink her morning chocolate—brought to her, in a pot specially made for the purpose, by a housemaid, one of the many servants in her well-staffed household.

She'd bathe, have her hair dressed by a professional hairdresser as she sat *en déshabillé*, decide on her costume and have her person dressed by her abigail (lady's maid), have breakfast brought to her in the morning room, and eagerly read the latest *on-dits* in the *Morning Chronicle*, the *Oracle*, the *Morning Post*, or the *Morning Herald*. She'd search for her name and the names of her friends, reviews of the latest plays, and accounts of balls at Carlisle House, the Pantheon, the Argyll, and other fashionable assembly rooms.

She'd scan the personal ads, see if her name was again mentioned under the column "Cytherian Intelligence," note what new books were available at Hatchards bookstore, and perhaps decide to attend the opera that evening. Her lover had spent hundreds of pounds for a box, and she really must use it some of the time. Was there an exhibit at the Royal Academy? Would her

Stage of Drury Lane Theatre, from
The Microcosm of London (1808),
by R. Ackermann.

portrait—painted by the most sought-after portraitist of the day—be on display? Perhaps there'd be an amusing exhibit in town of exceptional creatures, such as the Irish Giant (over eight feet tall!) or that woman from Africa called the Hottentot Venus, whose private parts were said to be most unusual. There was always something taking place in London, to which the whole world seemed to come.

But time was wasting and she had to get to her mantua maker's on Conduit Street. Madame Blanche was a busy woman, but her lover's name would gain her immediate entrée; unlike many aristocrats who lived on credit, he always paid her millinery and modiste bills on time. The latest Parisian fashion magazines would be in! She had to be fitted for a new riding costume (military-inspired riding habits, à la Lady Worsley's portrait by Reynolds, were all the crack these days), as befit the spirited white mare—"a sweet goer"—His Lordship had bought for her at the last Tattersall's horse auction. If there was time before tea, her coachman could drive her through Hyde Park at the appointed hour—4 P.M.—to see and be seen. Her new carriage and her superb pair of matched grays were the talk of the bon ton, or ton. Keeping one's name and face in the public eye was essential to those in her profession, but it was important to present oneself properly. Those who made scenes—she'd heard, but not seen, incidents of women who screeched and spat at their rivals like cats when they encountered them on the drive— were vulgar and common.

Tattersall's Horse Repository, from *The Microcosm of London* (1808), by R. Ackermann.

One or two of her friends—they were always, alas, the same friends, women of her ilk, courtesans, divorcées, friends and rivals both—might drop in for tea, or she could meet them at Gunter's for pastries and ices. Then it was dressing for the evening, remembering to wear her lover's latest bauble, bought from Rundell & Bridge, the fashionable jewelers His Lordship favored; then a light supper, champagne, and the night's event, probably the opera, perhaps the playhouse, maybe—a pleasant thought!—the pleasure gardens at Ranelagh or Vauxhall. It was a lovely warm day and should be a lovely evening as well. She had a box at the theater and could afford the best of the boxes at Vauxhall. The thin sliced ham there, she had to admit, was delicious; the concerts were jolly; and there were amorous possibilities to be had in all those secluded walkways and shaded groves of trees. . . . It all depended on her mood. Indoor entertainment . . . or outdoor? A flirtation with a handsome man, so long as she was discreet, was certainly not out of order. But he was such a thoughtful gentleman, His Lordship! She had to mind her step, but she had no concern for access to ready cash and she'd signed the annuity agreement at his solicitor's at the very beginning of their relationship, as an older, more experienced courtesan had advised her.

Love, lust, beauty faded; money retained its value. As that quaint character Signor Casanova was reputed to have said, "In London, everything is easy to him who has money and is not afraid of spending it." She was spending it— that is, she was spending His Lordship's—but putting her annuity away for

her old age and investing a portion of it in bonds, on her lawyer's advice. An annual £500 for life was handsome indeed, and it would keep her secure when she was no longer the toast of the town, with gallants eager to fill His Lordship's shoes. Woe to those of her sisters who'd eschewed this basic and important consideration for their future, those silly, flighty grasshoppers who thought life would be one endless summer! She would rather be the homely ant of that Greek fable.

And, afterward, when he was through dutifully squiring his boring heiress wife (the mother of his spoiled, disagreeable children) to the musicale at the rich and unpleasant Lady Jersey's home, why, then he was all hers—until the next morning, of course. Was it beyond the pale to imagine that one day the bore would meet her demise—perhaps in childbed, like so many wives—and that he'd marry her? A few had crossed that bar over into respectability, why not she? How lovely it would be to affix "Lady" before her name. *Pah!* Romantic nonsense, shame on her! She'd be much wiser to settle for his money here and now rather than indulge in such fantasies. She was nothing if not a realist, and being one had taken her quite far already.

She'd be old and rich, for sure, saving what she could from the almost £3,000 a year her protector was freely allowing her to spend and having that annuity secured for her future; she would not squander her fortune as that silly goose the actress Sophia Baddeley—she of more hair than wit—had done. (And what of poor "Perdita"—Mrs. Robinson, another actress—angling for £20,000 from the fickle Prince and having to settle for only £5,000 from his father the King?)

Although some of her frail sisterhood (as the gallants referred to her and her kind) had succeeded where she had so far failed and she was not yet, and might never be, a titled "Lady," she would shed no tears. Yes, Kitty Fisher married Lord Maynard; Emma Lyon, Lord Hamilton; Elizabeth Farren, the Duke of Derby. Elizabeth Armistead wed Charles James Fox; Harriet Powell snared the Earl of Seaforth; even Harriette Wilson's younger sister, that little whore Sophia Dubochet, became the wife of Baron Berwick. True, several of these gentlemen were in their dotage, and Berwick smelled to high heaven, but a title made up for a great deal that might otherwise be lacking.

It was not impossible to marry one's protector, though whether former courtesans who married into the ton were accepted by the ton and had easy entrée into society was debatable. High society's ranks could slam closed on those deemed inferior . . . or worse. Poor Mrs. Elliott never got Lord Cholmondeley to say "I do," not with that family of his aghast at her notoriety. (*His* notoriety, of course, was another matter entirely.)

Meanwhile, in case His Lordship's interest flagged and another "fashionable impure"—there were so many!—caught his eye, she'd better see to cultivating possible replacements. 'Twas always wise to have another protector or two waiting in the wings, as it were. . . . Or should she leave off her herbal draughts and postcoital washes and mayhap become pregnant by His Lordship before the inevitable end transpired? A brat or two would bring additional annuities. She'd farm 'em out in the country for a modest fee and keep the rest. Ah, the possibilities!

Courtesans are fashioned by circumstance, not born, despite the charges of Grace Elliott's most serious detractor, the biographer Horace Bleackley, who included Grace in his 1909 compendium of courtesans (a work several times reprinted) entitled *Ladies Fair and Frail: Sketches of the Demi-Monde During the Eighteenth Century.* Bleackley asserts with great confidence:

> *Nature intended her to be a courtesan, and she reveled in the power and the risk and the freedom of her adventurous life.*

How absurd! Bleackley is judgmental to an amazing degree. He's a typical late Victorian male, and his biased comments are outrageous to contemporary readers. He categorizes females as either good (wives, mothers) or bad (courtesans, prostitutes). What he had to say about Grace Elliott has, unfortunately, obscured the truth and been repeated as fact for almost a hundred years.

Until now, no one has questioned Bleackley's research into Grace Elliott's life nor disputed his statements. Unfortunately, the insufferable biographer does not stand alone. John Goldworth Alger, another Victorian male, the "J.G.A." who penned the article on Grace in the prestigious *Dictionary of National Biography*, is also opinionated. His piece borders on the snide and it also contains factual errors. (The *DNB* article appeared not long after the publication of Grace's memoir in 1859.)

Going to the other extreme is Richard Bentley, who published Grace Elliott's memoir, *Journal of My Life During the French Revolution*, after her death. Bentley supplies anecdotal rather than verifiable accounts and persists in giving wrong, even ludicrous, dates for events in Grace's life. Chief among these whoppers is the statement that Grace Dalrymple was born in 1765, which would have made her six years old at the time of her marriage to Dr. John Eliot. The esteemed publisher clearly did not bother to check the facts. That process would have taken time, and Bentley was in a great hurry to market this memoir. His business was to sell books—something at which he excelled—and that was uppermost in his mind, especially as he had recently suffered a serious business reversal.

Bentley's prime source of information was Grace's beloved granddaughter, Georgina Cavendish-Bentinck, who was twelve years old when Grace died and a long-in-the-tooth spinster of forty-seven when—over the objection of family members—she brought the manuscript to the attention of this publisher. Georgina may not have had much physical contact with her grandmother at all.

Where, then, is reliable information on Grace Dalrymple Elliott to be found? The outline of her life may be gleaned from the tabloids and magazines of the day, but the discerning reader will not mistake everything that was written in those publications for truth. As a celebrated demimondaine (the wonderfully evocative word comes from "demi-monde" and is attributed to Alexandre Dumas *fils*), Grace saw her every move become fodder for the scandal sheets, and the more tantalizing the tidbit, the better.

Grace's tabloid fame proved fleeting, as happens today. Her direct line died out in three generations. Grace's letters, the original manuscript of her

Journal, and any diaries she may have kept were most probably burned, forgotten, or discarded as being of no consequence after her death and that of her granddaughter. Grace's notoriety could have been another incentive for a straitlaced family member to get rid of what she left behind, just as the eminent Victorian art critic John Ruskin, the painter J.M.W. Turner's executor, fearing that the artist's erotic drawings were pornographic and would tarnish Turner's reputation, supposedly took it upon himself to destroy them.

When King George IV died in 1830, all the personal letters and tokens he'd received over the years from the many females who'd shared his bed were burned immediately, without a thought of preserving them. (The Duke of Wellington was put in charge of this destruction.) George was an unpopular king, no hero to his valet, not liked by those who surrounded and served him and who might have pretended to be his friends. His intimate leavings were considered trash and were treated as such. According to Charles Cavendish Fulke Greville, his clerk of the council and definitely not a friend to the monarch, George IV was a pack rat. He saved anything and everything, every scrap of paper, every piece of clothing, each bit of stuff. There can be no doubt that letters and tokens from Grace Elliott were among the articles consumed in that great bonfire of lost love and lust. It was probably as huge and unmourned as fat old King George IV himself.

All that *stuff*, lost! And bear in mind that he was a man, and a king. What could a mere woman with no power leave behind that anyone would care to save? Apropos of this, the historian Laurel Thatcher Ulrich comments:

> *My connection to the past, like any historian's, is through the stuff that's left behind. It's not an imaginative connection, although imagination is part of it. It's about documents, it's about sources, it's about clues, it's about the leavings, the shards, the remnants of people who once live[d] and don't live anymore. Without the documents, there's no history. And women leave very few documents behind.*

Grace Elliott, however, did leave behind a memoir, and in it her voice is clear and present. It's a strong, literary voice and the closest thing one has to Grace herself. She may not have ruled a nation or an empire, discovered the cure for a rare disease, created great works of art (though she inspired some), educated the multitude, or accounted for much in the matters that have always concerned men and by which men are measured, but she did make a contribution, however small and unheralded, to her society and times.

There is a strong possibility that Grace Elliott spied for England when she lived in France during the French Revolution. England was at war with France for much of this period, and Grace was able to move easily among those at the highest levels of French society. At the very least, we know that she acted as a courier between the French and English monarchs. There are passages in her *Journal* in which it is clear that she passed on information from Queen Marie-Antoinette to the Austrians and to Whig politicians like Charles James Fox. Grace was closely watched, and for a long time the only thing that kept her from arrest and incarceration was her intimate relationship with the Duc d'Orléans, King Louis XVI's cousin. And it is a fact that she put her own life and her personal safety in danger several times to save individuals from arrest and from the guillotine.

Beautiful, witty, and charming, Grace Elliott was a glamorous figure much admired by rich and powerful men, but there was far more to her than the mere good looks and surface glitter that attracted such men and kept them interested. Her life was scandalous to many, but she remained true to herself, showed integrity, courage, and intelligence, and never wavered in her deeply held beliefs. All this has to count for something in the final analysis of her character and life.

Arthur James Balfour, the nineteenth-century philosopher and statesman, wrote, "Biography should be written by an acute enemy." This viewpoint finds a reflection in the negativism of those who have offered critical commentary on Grace Elliott's life.

This was an exceptional woman, and her life deserves to be told by someone with a sense of fair play, a freedom from gender bias, and a balanced perspective of the times and the mores of those times. So here, then, is Grace Dalrymple Elliott's story, and it's about time it is told.

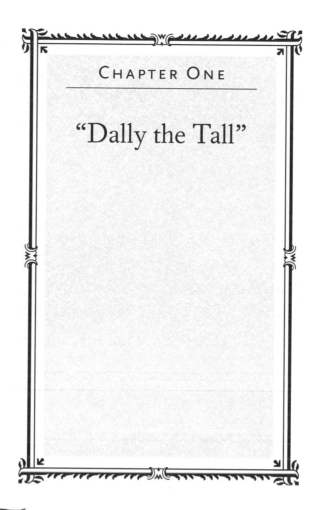

CHAPTER ONE

"Dally the Tall"

*T*he romantic adventures of Grace Dalrymple Elliott began at a masked ball at the Pantheon, a venue long known as a place where titled or wealthy men could meet loose women loosely attired in dominos—voluminous, tantalizing costumes cum face masks that hid all but promised much. There could be a prim and proper lady under that flowing, hooded robe, or someone vastly more interesting. Pantheon balls were advertised in the newspapers, and it was at the Pantheon on the night of January 24, 1776, that Grace Elliott's longest-lasting liaison was to commence.

Grace, about to be divorced by her cuckolded husband and despairing of ever marrying the gazetted rake who'd ruined her reputation, was there with

A masquerade at the Pan-
theon.
(*Tom & Jerry: Life in London*,
by Pierce Egan, © London,
John Camden Hotten,
Piccadilly)

a coterie of Cyprians and other fast women trolling for their next protectors or one-night stands. Arm in arm with other ladies of tarnished reputation, divorcées and celebrated ladybirds—among them Gertrude Mahon (the "Bird of Paradise") and Seymour Dorothy, Lady Worsley—she was to meet George James, Lord Cholmondeley, aka "Lord Tallboy."

Love? Lust? After more than two centuries, does it matter?

There was an instant, passionate physical attraction—these were two beautiful people at the height of their good looks—and the liaison, however it morphed over the years, lasted for some fifty of them. Few marriages have that impressive a track record. Unfortunately, no love letters between Grace Elliott and Lord Cholmondeley appear to have survived, and the newspaper and magazine accounts of their relationship have to be taken with more than a bit of caution. But one can safely say that these two individuals became part of each other's lives and stayed in touch with each other until Grace's death, which was only four years before Lord Cholmondeley himself passed away.

Obligations on each side were met, debts were paid, and mutual concerns —especially those having to do with Grace's daughter and granddaughter, who could have been Cholmondeley's daughter and granddaughter—were handled in an amicable and conscientious manner. Though there were rifts and separations, arguments, and certainly despair, the tie, the bond, the friendship endured. And it could have been made flesh more than once, in the person of one or more children who may have been born to the lovers. There were rumors over the years of other children of Grace and Cholmondeley, but if any did exist, their fate is unknown.

WAS GRACE ELLIOTT BEAUTIFUL?

Is beauty merely skin deep? Or is the well-worn phrase merely facile? True, there is such a thing as inner beauty—a component of which is charm— meant to compensate those whose outer trappings don't quite pass muster. And, granted, renowned great beauties may not really be, on an objective scale, the most beautiful creatures, but their ability to convince their admiring audience that they *are* the fairest of them all is what sets them apart from other good-looking women and puts them into the ranks of the incomparables.

That was one of the period's names for great beauties: "incomparables." There were also "diamonds, from "diamonds of the first water," and "toasts," as in all the toasts—champagne, of course—smitten, besotted men made to their beauty. Just as the legendary Helen of Troy's face "launched a thousand ships," beautiful faces in the eighteenth century launched many a career. But there was more to the story than those often very lovely faces, for some of the most successful courtesans of the time were not conventionally beautiful.

Harriette Wilson, née Dubochet (1786–1846), stands out as the most obvious example of the latter case; her wit, vitality, sharp tongue, and, yes, very large breasts, shown to advantage in high-waisted Regency-era décolletage, compensated for what anyone would agree was a rather plain and uninteresting face. (Sir Walter Scott went further, calling her "ugly," though agreeing, in a letter to Lord Montagu dated February 17, 1825, that she was "remarkably witty.")

Then, too, notions of beauty shift and change over the ages and from culture to culture. The shape of a woman's body, for example, is either pleasing to the eye or not. The fleshy pink supersize females beloved of the

Dutch painter Rubens do nothing for aficionados of twenty-first-century supermodel-thin, long-legged bodies. African women with large buttocks were considered a curiosity in Georgian England—as witness the Hottentot Venus—and still do not fulfill European notions of what constitutes a beautiful body. Even Marilyn Monroe, that curvaceous American film icon whose name is synonymous with sexiness, is today dismissed as fat by many critics.

The eighteenth century's standards of beauty were undoubtedly influenced to some extent by the craze for classical Greek and Roman statuary brought on by a wave of archaeological discoveries (e.g., Pompeii, where excavation began in 1748) and what pieces of art young lords brought back from their grand tours. The white marble body of a statue depicting the goddess of love, found on the Aegean island of Melos in 1820 and named the Venus de Milo (Venus of Melos) by the French, epitomized female beauty in the ancient world.

The English—with the much-earlier importation (many say theft) of the Parthenon Marbles by Lord Elgin—found these Hellenistic bodies to be perfection. This was a form with gently rounded curves and a graceful symmetry that served as an admirable model of womanly loveliness for the period. No excess poundage; smooth, willowy limbs; and, ah, that white marble skin!

What kind of looks, then, were considered beautiful in the eighteenth century? Though there are certain characteristics of feminine loveliness that never seem to vary much from century to century—such as a fine, clear, unspotted complexion—there are others peculiar to time and

Harriette Wilson, alas, not a face that would ever have launched one ship, much less a thousand of them . . . and this is one of the more flattering images of her. On the plus side, Harriette's chestnut brown hair was said to be thick and glossy, and her mischievous, devil-may-care, tomboy personality appealing to men. (National Portrait Galley, London)

Lord Elgin and the Parthenon Marbles

Thomas Bruce, the controversial seventh Earl of Elgin, was the British ambassador at Constantinople in 1799 when he fell in love with the exquisite bas-relief friezes around the Parthenon, on the Acropolis

Venus de Milo. (Bridgeman Art Library)

in Athens. In 1801 Elgin obtained permission from the Turkish sultan—and overlord of Greece—to strip these sculptural elements from the fifth-century BC temple. Between 1802 and 1811 the marbles were shipped to England. They were stacked haphazardly

in the open about Lord Elgin's Park Lane mansion in London and exhibited to the ton and any other interested parties, while the peer tried to sell them to the government. Their classical perfection profoundly influenced the art and architecture of England, as many churches, public buildings, and private homes came to be designed in the neoclassical style. In portraiture, ladies were frequently depicted as ancient goddesses, clad in rippling togas and draped around Ionic columns.

In 1816, the government purchased the marbles for the British Museum. A special gallery was built to display them. There was criticism from concerned contemporaries who'd been to Greece and seen the friezes in place at the Parthenon of the destructive methods used to strip the temple. Writers, statesmen, politicians, and clergymen were appalled at this brutal pillage. George Gordon, Lord Byron—who died for the cause of Greek independence, albeit not on the battlefield—chimed in for the ages in his magnificent epic poem *Childe Harold's Pilgrimage.*

Among those calling for the repatriation of the friezes in the twentieth century was Philip Sassoon, MP and later private secretary to Prime Minister Neville Chamberlain. Sassoon's sister Sybil was married to the fifth Marquess of Cholmondeley, the direct descendant of Grace Elliott's lover, the first Marquess. Lord Cholmondeley may have viewed the Parthenon marbles with Grace one fine day at the dawn of the nineteenth century; he also may have seen them earlier on his grand tour.

place. Sixteenth-century Venetian women, for example, plucked back their hairlines for a coveted highbrow look, and in certain African tribes and Pacific cultures large facial tattoos are thought to enhance beauty.

Beauty was captured for posterity in an official portrait by a prominent artist of the day. Among courtesans, a commissioned portrait was a mark of rank. Only for the most beloved mistress would a lover go to the trouble and expense of having her portrait painted by a noteworthy artist, preferably a member of the prestigious Royal Academy, in order to show his pride in her and his appreciation of her beauty and style. It's interesting that no portrait of Harriette Wilson exists, only an amateur drawing or two and a number of cartoons. Grace Elliott, meanwhile, was painted at least twice by Gainsborough (she may have sat for him a third time, but that portrait was either unfinished or lost), and several times by the eminent miniaturist painters Richard and Maria Cosway.

It can be seen from the smaller Gainsborough portrait that Grace had the celebrated "Dalrymple brow, so well known in Scotland," that is, a rounded brow with a widow's peak, that dip at the hairline that forms the curves at the top of a heart-shaped face.

A good complexion in Georgian times meant a smooth, flawless, white-skinned complexion, not freckled, certainly not suntanned, and definitely not one marred by smallpox scars. Eloquent, speaking eyes, a long white neck, elegant rounded white shoulders, tiny feet and hands, and innate grace and poise, plus what the French called *tournure,* were all recognized as hallmarks of great beauty.

This is a fascinating word, *"tournure."* Not only can it mean a graceful figure and pleasing contour of body, but it is also the word for bustle, the device used to expand the skirt of a dress below the waist. Late eighteenth-century female costume was dependent upon the graceful set of this *tournure.* The taller the woman, too, the more elegant the bustle appeared. On a tall woman with good posture and a straight back who moved well, the effect could be striking, the kind of effect that turned heads.

Grace Elliott was a striking, head-turning woman. Evarts Seelye Scudder, the British biographer of Louis-Philippe-Joseph, fifth Duc d'Orléans (later called Philippe Égalité), did not miss an opportunity in his book *Prince of the Blood* (1937) to praise her beauty. Scudder writes of her, "This young

Those Coveted White Complexions . . .

They held a deadly secret: ceruse. Not all women had naturally pale, ivory-colored complexions. Nature could be assisted by the use of a mixture of white lead and vinegar, a thick paste that was applied as foundation to the face, neck, and bosom. The first record of its use was in Tudor times, the 1500s. Not only was a desirable white complexion achieved, but this concoction successfully hid what smallpox left behind: pits and scars. (Acne would also be covered.) Unfortunately, white lead was a killer. Mercury, used for facial peels, was deadly as well. Vermilion (mercuric sulfide), used to paint lips and cheeks, was also dangerous. Belladonna, which made the eyes sparkle (it dilated the pupils and whitened the whites), was a toxic hallucinogen. Applied to the cheeks, it was a kind of blusher, as the plant irritated the skin and caused redness. Safer cosmetics were prepared from madder, cochineal, and ochre, for lips and cheeks, and kohl (powdered antimony), to line the eyelids. Overapplication of ceruse would, like today's Botox, limit a user's ability to smile; cracks would appear on the thickly applied base. There was also a good possibility the user would die, as a number of aristocratic women and their demimondaine sisters did. Women of the lower classes, with no money to purchase these artificial aids to beauty, were likely to live longer.

Scotchwoman was as courageous as she was beautiful and she was very beautiful." In her diary, Grace's niece Frances, Lady Shelley, described Grace as simply "the most beautiful woman I had ever seen."

The "Dally" in Grace's sobriquet "Dally the Tall," was taken from her maiden name of Dalrymple. Though she's sometimes referred to as "Dolly the Tall," that is an error, the phrase coming from a letter of Horace Walpole's. It's "Dally," not "Dolly"—there was nothing even remotely doll-like about the statuesque Grace Elliott.

Though we cannot be sure of Grace's exact height in feet and inches, some assumptions can be made. The first Gainsborough portrait, from 1778, shows a slim, willowy woman with a small waist and full, high, rounded bosom. She is striking in looks and appears tall from her erect carriage and bearing, though there's nothing in the background against which her height can be gauged with any degree of precision. Height is relative to the times. What could have been considered tall in the eighteenth century might be dismissed as merely average height today. Horace Bleackley discusses Grace's "lofty stature:"

[Her] nickname—derived from her patronymic and occasioned by her lofty stature—of "Dally the Tall" . . . was elaborated into "Dally the Maypole" and "Dally the Colossus." . . . Many, however, did not admire her, calling her gawky.

How tall, though, *was* Grace?

According to U.S. Department of Health and Human Services statistics, the average height for an American woman now is almost 5 feet 4 inches; the average Miss America contest winner tops out at about 5 feet 7 inches. Studies of bones from the seventeenth and eighteenth centuries exhumed from graves in London—such as the Farringdon Street site—indicate that the average height of men was 5 feet 6 inches and that of females was 5 feet ½ inch, figures that remained constant for the period.

A 2003 study in the *Journal of the Royal College of Physicians of Edinburgh* adds another layer to this elusive question. Grace was Scottish, and Scottish women, on average, were taller than their English counterparts. In the seventeenth and eighteenth centuries, the average height of Scottish females was 5 feet 3 inches, compared to the English average of just ½ inch over 5 feet. (Mary, Queen of Scots, at 5 feet 11 inches, was unusually tall.)

For an eighteenth-century English woman, 5 feet 3 inches would have been considered tall, 5 feet 7 inches would have been substantially tall. Grace's biographer Horace Bleackley states that "her figure was more remarkable than the beauty of her features, for she was uncommonly tall, being far above the ordinary stature of women."

How is one to interpret this? Five foot three, five foot seven, or six feet tall? Five foot three would have been well above average, but "far above"? A woman who was five foot seven or six feet tall in those days could well be described thus, though, and also as "uncommonly tall." Lady Craven—showing not a little jealousy, perhaps, to a possible rival—upon seeing Grace at the Ranelagh pleasure gardens, described her in a catty manner as a "Glumdalclitch," the young giantess in Jonathan Swift's fantasy tale *Gulliver's Travels*. (Bleackley, who rarely has anything good to say about any woman he writes about, gets his digs in about Lady Craven, too, calling her "clever and winsome . . . [but the] most wanton of wives.")

Suffice it to say that Grace was tall—and we have to assume this was upwards of five foot three, even perhaps up to six feet tall. To quote the "winsome" Lady Craven in full:

"Oh, Lord, I know that figure; (cried her ladyship) it is extremely familiar to me; that is GLUMDALCLITCH, the heroine of Gulliver's Travels,— *I have the Dean's works in my private library, with cuts!"* (The Rambler's Magazine, *August 1784*)

The writer of that *Rambler's Magazine* article seems to be obsessed with Grace's height. He (or she) cannot let go! (Hmmm . . . Did Lady Craven—at one time involved with Grace's Lord Cholmondeley—write that piece herself?) A bit later the claim is made that when Grace went to Paris she was

[by] no means an object of general admiration; she was too tall for the standard of Galic [sic] dalliances; and the tonish expression of the Parisians was, that she was a kind of agreeable monster!

Grace's lover Lord Cholmondeley was a big man. Bleackley describes him as "a huge ungainly youth of great physical strength" who was known by various nicknames, including "Lord Tallboy." A tallboy is a tall, substantial chest of drawers whose lower section is slightly larger than the upper section it supports.

That no one ever described the couple as ill suited in terms of size is worthy of note, for no opportunity was ever missed by the tabloids and their paparazzi to demean or satirize the ton and its playmates. A disparity in size would have been noted and remarked upon with glee. The height difference between Grace and Dr. John Eliot (who was said to be barely five feet tall) was certainly noted, to the doctor's detriment. Grace and Lord Cholmondeley were a well-matched pair.

Grace's friend Gertrude Mahon, the flamboyant "Bird of Paradise," was minute, well under five feet tall, a tiny woman of the type known as a "pocket Venus." That is, she was well-formed, in good proportion, but small enough to stash in one's pocket if one were so in-

A tallboy. (Photo by Ray Wadia of a piece belonging to author)

clined. Horace Bleackley quotes from the daily newspapers describing her (omitting, as usual, the exact publication, probably the *Morning Herald* or the *Morning Post,* and the date, probably 1780–1781): "The Bird of Paradise appeared at Vauxhall in glittering plumage, her waist not a span around, her stature four feet one inch." A span, or hand span, was usually measured from the extended tip of the thumb to the tip of the pinky, or nine inches. For the span of a waist, this would be doubled, so about eighteen inches around was probably Mahon's waist size. Gertrude and Grace, arm in arm at a Carlisle House masquerade, must indeed have been a pair to watch—an eighteenth-century version of the twentieth-century cartoon characters Mutt and Jeff, at just over four feet and possibly almost six feet, respectively.

Fair white complexion, eloquent eyes, long white neck, elegant white shoulders, tiny feet and hands, grace and poise, that all-important *tournure*—Grace fit all the criteria the eighteenth century set for female beauty, save that she might have been too tall to suit the times. Her lovely long white neck and rounded shoulders—not to mention her fine bosom in its décolletage—are displayed to perfection in the second portrait that Gainsborough painted of her in 1782, the year she was pregnant with her daughter Georgiana.

It's an oval portrait bust, and the sitter looks directly at the viewer. Grace's hair (dark blond or light brown, apparently, from a lock of hers preserved on the back of a locket-shaped miniature portrait in a private collection) is powdered—white powder was de rigueur for the period—and her face is very white. Her cheeks are heavily rouged, in the French style à la Madame de Pompadour, and her lips are glossed. Her eyebrows are dark and no doubt enhanced by black frankincense, resin, or mastic. These were the three most popular ingredients used to darken eyebrows from blond to black. Rubbing the eyebrows with burnt cork, burnt cloves, or elderberry juice would also darken them.

An unusual earring arrangement is exemplified by this portrait. Grace was typical of the girls of that time in having pierced ears; ears were commonly pierced in young girlhood with a darning needle and a cork. Earrings then were attached with hooks; butterfly/stud fastenings came much later, as did screws and clip-ons. Heavier earrings would have a long hook that could fasten around the top rim of the ear from the back. The usual kind of earring was a girandole—a central jewel with pendants—but the pendants were often re-

Mrs. Elliott, by Thomas Gainsborough, portrait bust painted in 1782. (The Frick Collection, New York)

movable, so the earring could be worn at less formal events. Another way of securing the earring however, was with a ribbon that was tied around the ear, and this arrangement is what's shown in the Gainsborough portrait bust. Grace's earrings are secured by a ribbon tied under the chin and then continuing downward to the dress neckline, where it disappears behind a large carved green gemstone cameo surrounded by seed pearls that is pinned to the middle of the bow just below the bustline.

A description of Grace when she was newly out of her French convent, at fifteen or sixteen years of age, "declared that 'her complexion was clear as the clouds of a May morning and tinged with the roseate blush of Aurora.'" The portraits bear this out. And her eyes!

Grace's eyes, and her sensual stare, the eyes half-lidded, caused consternation among art critics when the portrait bust was first exhibited at the Royal Academy. Too bold by half—that was the opinion of a critic in the *Public Advertizer* (May 2, 1782), who said that the portrait was "not a good moral likeness—the Eyes are too characteristic of her Vocation." In his essay "The Spectacle of the Muse: Exhibiting the Actress at the Royal Academy," Gill Perry makes the following point:

What worried the writer for the Public Advertizer, *paradoxically, was that Gainsborough's picture was* too *close to its subject, inasmuch as it was seen to betray her lack of moral character. The critic found her expression simply too alluring, as evidence of a threatening feminine sexuality that had no right to be seen in respectable society. To be deemed acceptable for public exhibition, portraits of women of dubious repute had to undergo a form of masquerade: such sitters had to be given "polite" masks, even if these made it hard to tell them apart from "proper" members of their sex.*

The eyes are simply beautiful, the expression more serene than come-hither. They are large, dark, and appealing. These are not necessarily the eyes of a whore, but rather the eyes of an attractive woman. Nothing shouts out that this is a demimondaine. It's interesting that Grace's looks would be considered threatening, because, although she is a notorious courtesan, she appears in this painting to be a respectable woman, just like any other respectable woman sitting for a portrait, though perhaps more beautiful than most.

In the 1778 full-length portrait, Grace's hands and feet are small compared to her overall height. Tiny hands and feet—even in men—were thought to be another sign of beauty. In her *Memoirs,* the courtesan Harriette Wilson goes into raptures on the small, white hands of her young lover Meyler, her "little sugar-baker," something that strikes a modern-day reader as odd. Men—if they are at all masculine—are supposed to have large hands, are they not? But Wilson praises him for his little hands.

How a woman moves can be infinitely pleasing. If gawky or ill coordinated, the loveliest woman loses all claims to beauty. The cumbersome costume of the day was not easy to carry off—not until the Regency period were women able to relax in loose, comfortable dress. Grace moved well in bustle and panniers. She had poise and charm, and "her disposition was lively and her temper mild and engaging."

Consider the following assessment of the fashionable looks of a comparable celebrated courtesan, Elizabeth Armistead. Grace Elliott was probably much prettier, but they had some characteristics in common, as may be seen from this description by I. M. Davis:

> *She [Mrs. Armistead] was not a great beauty, but it was her fortune that her*

A Peep into Brest with a Navel Review!

Artist and publisher Richard Newton's July 1794 satire of the plunging-neckline costumes (open almost to the navel) favored by demimondaines and aristocratic ladies. The title *A Peep into Brest with a Navel Review!* is a play on "breast" and "naval"; Brest is a French port. (Library of Congress)

The Women's 'Zines

Though some French and German magazines could be purchased by London's fashionable women, the following were all written in English, published in London, and perhaps the best known of this type of publication from the late eighteenth and early nineteenth centuries: *The Lady's Magazine, or Entertaining Companion for the Fair Sex, Appropriated Solely to Their Use and Amusement*, 1770 to 1837; *Le Beau Monde, or Literary and Fashionable Magazine*, published from 1806 to 1809; it was renamed *Le Beau Monde and Monthly Register*. 1809 to 1810; *The Gallery of Fashion*, 1794 to 1803; *La Belle Assemblée, or Bell's Court and Fashionable Magazine Addressed Particularly to the Ladies*, 1806–1832; *The Lady's Monthly Museum, or Polite Repository of Amusement and Instruction: Being an Assemblage of What Can Tend to Please the Fancy, Instruct the Mind, or Exalt the Character of the British Fair*, 1798–1814, renamed *The Ladies' Monthly Museum*, 1814 to 1832; Rudolf Ackermann's *Repository of Arts, Literature, Commerce, Manufactures, Fashions, and Politics*, a very high-end publication, 1809 to 1829; and the short-lived *La Miroir de la Mode* (1803–1804), published by a fabulous character, the early-nineteenth-century modiste who styled herself Madame Lanchester.

Ball dress from *The Lady's Magazine, or Entertaining Companion for the Fair Sex, Appropriated Solely to Their Use and Amusement*, February 1801. It was copied from a more daring plate in the 1801 Parisian *Journal des dames et des modes*, in which the lady's left nipple clearly showed. The London publication raised the neckline to cover the nipple. (Image courtesy of novelist Candice Hern, from her collection of ladies' fashion magazines at her Web site, www.candicehern.com)

looks entirely conformed with the requirements of current taste. This, while approving girlish freshness, saw nothing to please in girlish slenderness. Fashion in dress favoured maturity of figure: height to carry off spreading hoops and high-piled hair, a bosom to justify deep décolletage . . . a bearing of stately ease despite the weight of hoops, the grip of tight-lacing and the bur-

den of the lofty coiffure. (Small slight girls were in this generation singularly unlucky. . . .) Fashion demanded and fashion displayed the fine woman, and Mrs. Armistead, younger in face than her years but tall, deep-bosomed and superb in bearing, was now reckoned one of the finest women in England.

Grace Elliott's extremely generous lovers allowed her to afford the very latest in style, the "dernier cri," as it was called. And courtesans set style, so whatever she chose then became the style to follow. It was a superior package in every way that mattered, and, as her memoir was later to show, the package was completed by her intelligence, vivacity, and superior conversational skills. Unfortunately, none of the above is easily conveyed by brushstrokes.

Mrs. Grace Dalrymple Elliott, by Thomas Gainsborough. (The Metropolitan Museum of Art)

One more thing: The long-faced, long-nosed physiognomy; the creamy, flawless complexion; the carriage; the height; the long-legged leanness and athleticism combined with the high-bosomed figure, these attributes of Grace Elliott bear no little passing resemblance to those of Diana, the late Princess of Wales, another lovely British female. There is a timeless British beauty exemplified both by the Princess and by Grace that continues to be appealing. Though standards for beauty change and are affected by culture and fashion, their kind of attractiveness does not go out of style, especially in their native land.

Grace Elliott was beautiful then, and would be considered beautiful now, no question about it. Grace Elliott's face and figure on the cover of a modern fashion 'zine like *W* or *Vogue?* Absolutely!

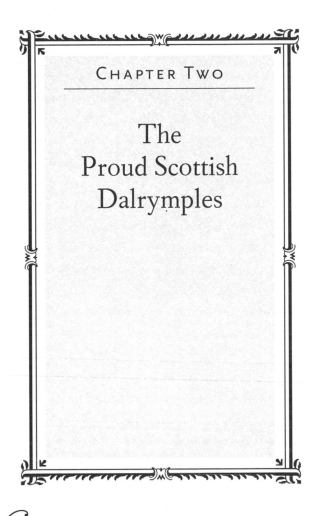

CHAPTER TWO

The Proud Scottish Dalrymples

*N*ot much can be said with certainty about the life of Grace Dalrymple, least of all her date and place of birth. The possible date of her birth ranges wide, from 1750 to 1765. No record is known to exist in any church parish. Working backward from the information appended to the permission for the "Special Licence" issued on the October 19, 1771, when she married Dr. John Eliot, it seems that the most likely date for her birth is 1754. She was seventeen, and subtracting her age from 1771 gives us 1754. (The fact that she was listed as a minor on the marriage registration means that she was under twenty-one years of age.) Her probable place of birth was Scotland's capital, Edinburgh, or its environs.

Going for any further proof is a futile exercise, as eighteenth-century Scotland had no official requirement that births or baptisms be registered. It was not until a hundred years later that such registration was mandated.

It's known from the Faculty of Advocates in Scotland that her father was Hew (Hugh) Dalrymple, a solicitor of good family:

> *Dalrymple, Hew, LL.D., 14 July 1752, . . . son of Robert Dalrymple of Dreghorn, W.S., died 8 March 1774, married Miss Craw. Middle Temple 8 February 1771, Attorney-General of the Bahamas.*

Hew Dalrymple's flamboyant extramarital relationships had estranged him from his wife, Grizel (the name is the old Scottish form of Grace), née Craw, and they had separated and were living apart before Grace's birth; the girl was said to have been born at the home of her maternal grandfather, Craw (or Brown, as the surname of this military family is sometimes given in error). Grace may have had no contact with her father at all until the death of her mother, which occurred when Grace was eleven. What a surprise that must have been!

Along with an elder sister, Jacintha (?–c. 1802), she'd been brought up by a single mother in a household that included maternal grandparents. This is a common enough scenario today, but it was likely not the norm then for a proper middle-to-upper-middle-class household in Edinburgh, Scotland.

Was Grace a lonely child? That she turned out to be quite vivacious argues for a happy childhood. One wonders, though, if she'd had a solid male role model (grandfather, uncle, cousin, brother) in her formative years, and what she might have overheard about her dissolute father from family members. Children are sometimes unfairly burdened with a parent's bitterness or animosity toward an estranged spouse, and this traumatic situation can make them reluctant to marry or can foster hatred of the absent parent. Such a situation may have influenced the choices Grace made, particularly when she willingly married the much older Dr. John Eliot, her father's pick. Was she subconsciously trying to please the parent she never knew, or did she go the other way round entirely and select a man who seemed as unlike her father in personality and looks as possible?

There is a passing mention in *The Dictionary of National Biography* to a son of Hew's—Grace's brother—who is said to have spirited her away to a French convent after her indiscretion with a married man in 1774. The pur-

*C*onvent Schools and the Education of Women

Convent schools for girls were established in England and on the Continent during the Middle Ages by orders of nuns. Here girls could spend their adolescence, leaving to get married, usually at fifteen or sixteen years of age. The curriculum included not only the housewifely arts but reading, writing, and musical training. There were Roman Catholic convent schools for girls in England before the dissolution of the monasteries under Henry VIII and the beginning of the Reformation. English orders of nuns fled to the Continent—to Belgium and France—and there reestablished themselves.

A peculiar thing happened with these Roman Catholic schools on the Continent: not only did the wealthier Catholics in England send their daughters there to be educated, but so did the well-off Protestants. The reputation of the schools was that good. In England there were dame schools, boarding schools run by entrepreneurs. Often these were no more than finishing schools, with emphasis on art and music, singing, dancing, perhaps a smattering of languages. Anyone could open one, and teachers were likely to be unqualified. (In her *Memoirs,* the courtesan Harriette Wilson claimed she'd taught French in one of these schools; the actress Mary Robinson's mother ran one for a short time.) Thomas Jefferson, who served as U.S. minister to France from 1785 to 1789, sent his two daughters, Martha and Mary, to the most fashionable Roman Catholic convent school in Paris, the Abbaye Royale de Panthemont. Jefferson, a Protestant, pulled both daughters out of the school when Martha wrote to him saying that she wanted to become a nun.

The Reverend Robert Cholmondeley, Anglican priest and uncle of Lord Cholmondeley, enrolled his two daughters in a French convent school, on the advice of Horace Walpole's good friend Madame du Deffand.

ported brother seems to be somewhat of a spirit himself, and there's no proof that Grace was sent to a convent at that time. As the *DNB* piece is replete with errors, it's probably safe to say that Grace never had a brother.

Hew, left with a young girl on his hands when his wife died, sent Grace to a convent school in France—or Flanders—until she was fifteen or sixteen. The exact name and location of her school are not known, nor is it known if her elder sister also attended it. These Roman Catholic boarding schools—the majority of them were in France and Belgium—were popular with the Protestant nobility and well-off middle class, and they were not inexpensive.

Did Hew pay for his daughter's secondary school education, or was she accepted as a charity case? These schools prided themselves on their academic rigor and often did take a few promising scholarship students. Were the Dalrymples or the Craws Catholic? The earls of Stair, with whom the Dalrymples claimed relationship, were strongly Protestant and were staunch supporters of the Union with England, but it is interesting to note that Frances, Lady Shelley, the daughter of Grace Elliott's sister Jacintha, mentions in her *Diary* that her mother's family was originally Jacobite, and Jacobites were usually Catholics. Lady Shelley wrote:

> *We were at that time all strong Jacobites. In our old house the Pretender had slept on the night before the battle of Preston [Prestonpans]; and I still possess a bracelet given to him by my ancestor, with a portrait of King Charles [Charles I, who was beheaded on Cromwell's order], made in his own hair, which was cut off on the scaffold and dipped in his blood. I recall the pride with which I wore this bracelet on State occasions.*

She recalled sitting on her mother's knee to "listen to the old Scottish Jacobite ballads."

It's difficult to establish whether or not they were closet Catholics, practicing the old religion in secret, as some in the British Isles still did even after Henry VIII had abolished the religion in the mid-sixteenth century; there is no hard evidence. Grace Dalrymple, by all accounts and by the proof of her *Journal*, was well educated, literate, and fluent in foreign languages, and she was said to be a charming and witty conversationalist. She was probably an exemplary student at her convent school, whether she was there to strengthen the old religious beliefs of her family or not.

At about sixteen years of age, Grace came home, not to Edinburgh but to London, the bustling metropolis where her father now lived. London in the 1770s was fast growing into the city of a million people it would become at the turn of the nineteenth century; it was a diverse, cosmopolitan, and vibrant capital. Hew Dalrymple had made a new life for himself on the fringes of London's volatile political scene, associating mostly with his fellow Scots. Armed with a fresh new LLD, an English law degree awarded after several years of study at the Inns of Court, he was about to embark for a lucrative—but, as it turned out, short-lived—government position in the West Indies.

Grace—Hew's nubile, graceful, and head-turning teenage daughter, who no doubt looked older than her years—was an encumbrance to his career

The "Auld Alliance": The Special Relationship of Scotland and France

There has long been a special connection—called the "auld alliance"—between France and Scotland, dating back to a thirteenth-century Scots king John Balliol, and subsequently to Mary, Queen of Scots, and Bonnie Prince Charlie, Charles Edward Stuart, aka the Young Pretender. There are ancient language ties between the Gaels of Scotland and the Bretons of northern France. Mutual antipathy and hundreds of years of conflict between the English and the French further cemented the relationship, and France offered refuge for Jacobite exiles from the Young Pretender's failed campaigns. Jacobites (from the Latin for James) were followers of James Edward Stuart, the Old Pretender and Catholic son of James II, who was recognized as rightful Stuart king of England and Scotland by France. The failure of either to gain the throne led to the demise of the Jacobite movement after the Battle of Culloden in 1746.

There was a Royal Ecossais (Scottish) regiment in the French army whose motto was *"omni modo fidelis"* (Faithful in every way), and French descendants of Jacobites fought against the English at Quebec. In literature and the arts, the popularity of Sir Walter Scott led to a French craze for tartans, while the Scots Colourists were artists greatly influenced by French painters. In 1942, General Charles de Gaulle, in exile with the Free French, stated, "I do not think that a Frenchman could have come to Scotland at any time without being sensible of a special emotion. . . . Awareness of the thousand links, still living and cherished, of the Franco-Scottish Alliance, the oldest alliance in the world, leaps to his mind."

There's a Web site, Auld Alliance Online, whose goal is "to celebrate the strong bond of friendship between France and Scotland," and there's a thriving Franco-Scottish Society of Scotland.

plans. He was responsible for her, but he had that career to think about, and it—not his lovely girl child—was foremost in his thoughts. Marriage was the logical solution, and the beautiful Grace Dalrymple was eminently marriageable.

What might a suitor have discovered of the background of the Dalrymple family?

According to *Some Old Families: A Contribution to the Genealogical History of Scotland* (1889), by Hardy Bertram McCall, the Dalrymples were a distinguished family from Waterside, in the county of Dumfries. A likely derivation of the family name is from the Old Saxon *"dahl hrympel,"* referring to a rumpled or puckered appearance that is characteristic of this landscape. As for the Dalrymples' place of origin:

The name Waterside is so frequently met with as the name of lands in Scotland that it is necessary to mention that the property here indicated is situated in the parish of Keir, and county of Dumfries, and lies on the right bank of the Scar, just above the latter's junction with the Nith.

The first mention of Dalrymples in this area is of one Malcolm Dalrymple, who "sat on an assize, together with John Dalrymple of Stair." There is an old relationship between the Dalrymples and the earls of Stair, who are powerful Scottish lairds. The seat of the earls of Stair is Lochinch Castle in western Scotland. Lochinch is close by the ruins of Castle Kennedy, near Stranraer, a town at the head of Loch Ryan, an arm of the Irish Sea. According to *Some Old Families*, the Stair-Dalrymple relationship began in the Middle Ages, with the marriage in 1450 of William Dalrymple to Agnes Kennedy:

The Dalrymples of Waterside . . .

The surname of this family is of local derivation, and is taken from the Barony of Dalrymple, co. Ayr, which after being held for at least three generations, was alienated about 1371, by Malcolm and Hugh de Dalrymple, to John Kennedy of Dunure, who, in 1375, had a gift of the relief payable from the lands of the late Arthur de Dalrymple. William Dalrymple acquired the lands of Stair by marriage with Agnes Kennedy, in 1450, and from this marriage, the Earls of Stair are descended.

The Dalrymple pedigree covering the seventeenth and eighteenth centuries supplied by McCall shows a rich mix of lawyers, military men, clergymen, and chamberlains to peers in this Scots family, and includes a woman with the unusual first name of Nicholas, who married a brewer.

The pedigree opens the door to a number of questions, as someone has penciled notations in the copy of *Some Old Families* that was consulted at the Society of Genealogists Library in London. This genealogist added another sibling, a "Margaret D.," who is noted to the left of Hugh Dalrymple and Primrose, his brother. (A woman named Nicholas and a man named Primrose—the mind boggles.)

In this copy of *Some Old Families* there is also an arrow extending the issue of Robert Dalrymple—indicating he had other sons and daughters—and another arrow under Margaret D. indicating issue of hers. Under the

The Curse of Scotland and the Earls of Stair

The playing card the nine of diamonds is known as the "Curse of Scotland." The origin of the phrase is obscure, but one theory is that it comes from the nine red lozenges that formed the arms of the staunchly Protestant second Earl of Stair, who was universally loathed for the part he played in both the bloody Massacre of Glencoe (1692), in which the Clan MacDonald suffered great losses, and the Union with England (1707). The definition in the *1811 Dictionary of the Vulgar Tongue* states:

French playing cards circa 1785—note the nine of diamonds. (Photo by Ray Wadia, collection of author)

Diamonds, it is said, imply royalty, being ornaments to the imperial crown; and every ninth king of Scotland has been observed for many ages, to be a tyrant and a curse to that country. Others say it is from its similarity to the arms of Argyle; the Duke of Argyle having been very instrumental in bringing about the union . . . considered as detrimental to their country.

entry for Hugh, the printed term "d.s.p." has been crossed through, and a notation that looks like "e1779" penciled in. The latter mark is mysterious. There are other minuscule pencil marks on these pages, and "d.s.p." is an abbreviation from the Latin used by genealogists, "decessit sine prole," which means "died without issue."

Nor do the pencil marks end there. On page 31 there is another mysterious addition following a description of the issue of John Dalrymple and Elizabeth Herries, who "had many children"; these would have been the grandparents of Hew Dalrymple. Robert, Hew's father, was their second son. He is described as

a writer to the Signet, *and the law-agent and principal director of the Stair family. He was the father of two sons, who both died without issue, namely,*

Hugh Dalrymple, a celebrated lawyer, attorney-general of Grenada, and author of the political poem entitled "Rodendo," [sic] and of various other pieces; and Primrose Dalrymple, a captain in His Majesty's Service.

The penciled notation asserts that "Hugh had at least 3 daughters and 1 son." This is of prime interest to Grace Dalrymple Elliott's story. According to many sources, Hew/Hugh was the father of Grace, and of another daughter, Jacintha:

Jacintha Dalrymple was the daughter of Hugh Dalrymple. She died on 7 January 1802. Child of Jacintha Dalrymple and Thomas Winckley: Frances Winckley + d. 24 Feb 1873. . . . Children of Jacintha Dalrymple and Thomas Hesketh: Jacintha Catherine Hesketh b. c1776, d. 31 Aug 1801 [and] Sir Thomas Dalrymple Hesketh, 3rd Bt. b. 13 Jan 1777, d. 27 Jul 1842.

Jacintha has to have been the mother of Frances, Lady Shelley (1787–1873), who married Sir John Shelley (1771/72–1852), sixth Baronet Shelley, of Maresfield Park in Sussex, in June 1807. As Lady Shelley narrates in her *Diary*,

I was born at Preston, in Lancashire, in 1787. My father, Thomas Winckley, of Preston, was a direct descendant of the de Winkelmondeleys who, in Saxon times, settled in a corner between the Ribble and the Calder. My mother, who was the daughter of Hew Dalrymple, descended from a kinsman of President Lord Stair, who carried the Union with England. She had previously been married to Major Hesketh, who died young from a severe wound received in the American War of Independence. By her first husband she had one son, afterwards Sir Thomas Hesketh, and six daughters."

Lady Shelley does establish that her mother—whose first name, unfortunately, she does not actually provide—was Jacintha, a daughter of Hew Dalrymple. In a later passage of her *Diary* she goes on to describe the first and last meeting she ever had with her notorious aunt Grace—just before her mother, Grace's sister, died in the winter of 1801–1802—and to supply valuable information about Grace's daughter, Georgiana. There is, alas, no genealogical chart to consult in this published diary.

Who Hew's other two children were, his third daughter and his son, if they indeed existed at all, is a mystery.

What else can we verify about the checkered life of Hew Dalrymple? We have evidence that he was in London for a period of years before being called to the English bar in February 1771, and that he was a witness at the wedding of his minor daughter, Grace, to Dr. John Eliot on October 19 of that same year. The next—and only other thing—we hear about him is the newspaper report of his death in early March 1774.

But there was something else that gave Hew the late eighteenth century's equivalent of the twentieth century's fifteen minutes of celebrity. It was the publication of a poem—not, incidentally, the first of his poems to be printed—"The Rodondo" (sometimes spelled "Redondo") in March 1763. The importance of this to Grace's story is that it is further evidence that he was living in London after 1759, the year he joined the Middle Temple.

"The Rodondo" is a satire, a faux celebration of the three-hour speech attacking the government made to Parliament in the late fall of 1762 by Sir William Pitt the Elder, first Earl of Chatham. Pitt, looking very ill indeed, pale and emaciated, was borne by a servant to the House of Commons to deliver his scathing speech, a tirade against the terms of the Peace of Paris, which had been negotiated by his political rival the Prime Minister, John Stuart, third Earl of Bute. The Earl of Bute, a Scot, was an unpopular politician owing to his espousal of increased (and somewhat curious) taxes to pay for the war with France.

The much-beleaguered Bute was replaced in 1763 by George Grenville, Sir William Pitt's brother-in-law, who remained in office until the middle of 1765. Bute's fall from power was commemorated in 1763 in an unusual double-print political cartoon captioned "Excise—Resignation"; this description is from *The Prime Ministers: An Irreverent Political History in Cartoons* (1995), by Kenneth Baker:

> *The fall of Bute is celebrated in a double print. His Chancellor of the Exchequer had introduced a tax on cider and this . . . precipitated his downfall. It was so unpopular that Bute was physically assaulted and there were riots in the apple-growing areas of the West Country. There was the added twist that the Scots neither made nor drank cider. Within a month Bute resigned and he is shown here as hanging from an apple tree while a decoletee [sic] Princess of Wales weeps. To the right, the Devil tears Bute away by clutching at his private parts, with Bute plaintively pleading, "Oh spare my manhood."*

Hew Dalrymple's poem is pro-Bute and anti-Pitt. It satirizes Pitt's bravery in coming to speak before Parliament despite his marked ill health.

The Inns of Court and the Middle Temple

There are four Inns of Court today in London: Lincoln's Inn, Gray's Inn, the Inner Temple, and the Middle Temple. The Inns of Chancery—among them Clement's Inn and the New Inn—folded for various reasons over the centuries. They were referred to as "inns" because they served as hostels for law students and barristers. The Middle Temple is associated with the Knights Templar; the original Hall dates from 1320 and the present building was completed in 1573. According to *The London Encyclopaedia* (1993), these are some of the prominent men associated with the Middle Temple: Sir Francis Drake, Sir Walter Raleigh, William Wycherley, William Congreve, John Evelyn, Henry Fielding, Edmund Burke, Charles Dickens, and Thomas De Quincey. (Dickens, according to Stewart Adams, a librarian at the Middle Temple Library, was a member there for thirty years but didn't pursue admittance to the bar. He dropped his membership when he became a literary star.)

A Scottish advocate desiring to practice in England has to be admitted to the English bar. To do this, he must train at one of the four Inns of Court. It's a fact that Hew Dalrymple joined the Middle Temple, one of these four, on May 17, 1759; it is so noted in that body's records. After twelve years he was called to the bar; this took place on February 8, 1771. To qualify he'd had to have "kept terms," that is, to have been physically present at the Middle Temple for at least twelve terms, or three years. "Keeping terms" meant that he had to be present during dinner and religious services at the Middle Temple, and that he had to pay for both. In addition, he was expected to receive Communion and this suggests that he was, or had become, an Anglican, a member of the Church of England. He had to attend lectures and intermingle and hobnob—network, to use the modern term—with other students, lawyers, and politicians.

In addition to the fees noted above for keeping terms, there was a fee for joining the Middle Temple. Hew Dalrymple had to be physically present in London for the three years preceding his call to the bar, that is, from at least 1768, but it was more than likely that he'd lived in London for at least twelve years, beginning in 1759 when he'd first applied to the Middle Temple.

Fountain Court, Middle Temple Lane.
(Photo by Simon Tibbs)

Dalrymple hails Pitt as a "patriot," but the sarcasm is blatantly apparent. Dalrymple stood by his fellow Scot, Lord Bute, pronouncing his loyalty:

> The groundlings cry alas! poor man!
> How ill he is! How pale! How wan!
> At length he tries to rise, a hum
> Of approbation fills the room.
> He bows and tries again; but no,
> He finds that standing will not do,
> And therefore to complete the farce,
> The House cries, "Hear him on his arse!"
> He may break off by grief o'ercome,
> And grow pathetically dumb!
> He next may SWOON and shut his eyes;
> A cordial, else the patriot dies!
> The cordial comes, he takes it off;
> He lives, he lives, I hear him cough.

Appropriate declamation of this poem is to elocute while sneering. It's mean-spirited and disrespectful, but, despite its tone, well phrased and even quite witty.

Why "Rodondo"? What is the significance of the title? Is it an allusion to the author of the poem, Hew Dalrymple, and its subject, Pitt, the Earl of Chatham? That is unclear, but Rodondo—or Dalrymple's Rock—is off one of the Galapagos Islands, not far from Chatham Island. These are actual place names, given in the late 1600s by a William Ambrose Cowley, who drew up the first navigation charts for the Galapagos using the names of English royalty and peers.

Dalrymple's Rock is three hundred feet in circumference, nearly round, and high, according to a description by the sea captain Amasa Delano in 1801; it lies four miles distant from Chatham Island. There is also a formation of rocks off New South Wales, not far from Port Dalrymple, named the Rodondo. Was an effort made to connect these dots? Lacking a published exegesis of this poem, one is at a loss to know.

Grace's biographer Horace Bleackley has this to say about the poem and its author's motivations for writing it:

He made an effort to gain the favour of Lord Bute by a trenchant attack upon the enemies of the government. This . . . was a satire . . . in which the writer trounced Messrs Wilkes and Churchill with great severity for their abuse of the Scottish nation. Even the Great Commoner [Pitt] received a full measure of ridicule, for he was made the hero of the poem, being depicted as a "State Juggler" without principle, and it was suggested that a pension and a peerage had been the object of his political career. In spite of the extravagance of the verses, their evidence of prejudice, and frequent vulgarity, the little book caused much amusement even to the admirers of the great Pitt. During the spring of 1763 everyone was laughing over "Rodondo," and all allowed that the young Scotsman had a pretty wit.

Did Hew Dalrymple gain any favour with Lord Bute with his poem? Apparently not, again according to Bleackley, who says that Bute "made no attempt to reward his champion." Bleackley explains this lack of support by asserting that Bute was "said to have objected to his [Dalrymple's] moral character" owing to a scandal with a married woman in Scotland. Dalrymple went on to publish a third canto of "Rodondo," which Bleackley calls "more ribald even than its predecessors."

Hew Dalrymple seems to have moved in fashionable and political circles—if not in the heart of the ton itself, certainly on its influential fringes. But was he a wealthy man? Though Bleackley describes the "worldly-wise" Dalrymple as "rich and famous," this is at odds with his previous description of him as "broken in fortune." Rich? Sans fortune? What was the exact state of his finances? Bleackley can't have it both ways.

Grace's father was living in London, an expensive city, and apparently living well enough to afford the not-inexpensive fees for joining the Middle Temple. He couldn't have been practicing as a lawyer, as he wasn't called to the English bar until early 1771. After that date, however, with his obvious intelligence and his political contacts, he could have been doing very well.

He did succeed in getting an appointment as attorney general to the Bahamas, according to the Faculty of Advocates list and *Some Old Families*, and this foreign service must have been lucrative. But here is where the thread becomes frayed, and nothing can be said with any degree of certainty, as there is no material to back anything up. For example, did Hew provide Grace with a dowry? He should have, but again, there is no way of knowing how much, if he did so.

An explanation of the dowry system is given by Lawrence Stone in his study *Broken Lives: Separation and Divorce in England, 1660–1857* (1993):

> *On her marriage, the family of the bride paid a dowry to the family of the groom, in return for which the latter settled property for the maintenance of the couple . . . and made provision for a jointure, which was a life annuity for the widow if she survived, usually assured by settlement of property. On marriage, the husband gained possession of all the wife's personal property, and control over much of her real property . . . He could do what he liked with the personal estate, including furniture, jewels, and money, and could enjoy the income of the real estate.*

Look at this more closely. Property? Highly dubious that any was settled on Grace. The Dalrymples were not significant landholders. Furniture, jewels? It's doubtful that the young bride had any furniture or jewelry of any worth. Money? A dowry from Hew was all she could possibly expect, and if she received one, it may have been meager.

But there was a flip side to husband-takes-all. Stone adds:

> *[The husband] could use any or all of this property to pay off his own debts, but at marriage he also became liable for all his wife's debts run up before or during marriage. This issue of debt loomed very large indeed in eighteenth-century English life, since the society increasingly depended on credit, and the ultimate penalty for non-payment was arrest and indefinite imprisonment. It is hardly surprising, therefore, that there are many cases of men marrying women merely in order to seize their property and use it to pay their own debts. On the other hand, some women could play the same game.*

Hew Dalrymple probably thought that he'd done the best he could for his daughter and that she would give him no future worry. He passed from this earth just before news of the scandalous doings of Grace and her paramour erupted into the *on-dits* of the bon ton and were plastered across the daily newspapers.

Bleackley seems to lay most of the blame for Grace's immorality and extramarital affairs on her father's nature: like father, like daughter seems to be his judgment. But while he states that "Nature intended her to be a courtesan" and that her father "possessed little strength of character," he also notes that Hew's influence was not entirely negative, by allowing that her *Journal* "shows she had inherited some of her father's talents." Bleackley has to acknowledge that Grace, like her father, was "clever," and, like him, a talented writer as well.

Would Grace's life have been any different if her father had not died in the Caribbean and had come back to sort things out between her and Dr. Eliot? Would this careless man have been concerned enough to intervene? However one might want to speculate in his favor, given what is known of the probable character of Hew Dalrymple, it might not have made one iota of difference in the outcome of Grace Elliott's life if he had lived. He'd cast her off, and it's doubtful he would have been interested in rescuing her from the path she was about to follow.

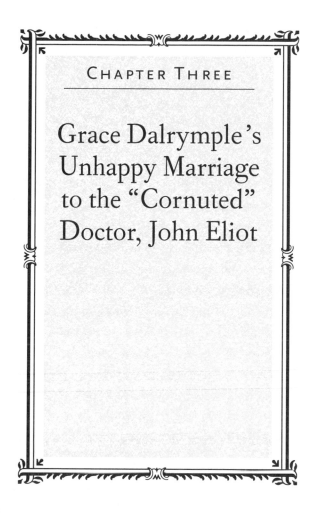

CHAPTER THREE

Grace Dalrymple's Unhappy Marriage to the "Cornuted" Doctor, John Eliot

$\mathcal{G}$olden Grace caught the eye of Dr. John Eliot, a respected Scottish-born physician. Eliot was a colorful character right out of a Charles Dickens novel. He was not in the least attractive physically, as he was "scarce five feet high" and had "harsh, ill favored features" and a "sallow . . . complexion." His many years at sea in the open air, subject to harsh winds and strong sun—no sunscreen available then—had further coarsened his looks.

His "disposition" was said to have had "a natural turn to festivity," and he was described as having the good sense of humor particular to the Scots; he was called "chearful" and "the cause of chearfulness in other men," with "no want of conversation talents." Indeed, he was said to have a "rich" store of "historical anecdote" he loved to relate. But there was a downside to this good-natured aspect; one report had it that Eliot was "trammeled by that superiority which some ability, joined to successful ambition, never fails to inspire."

That report, from *The Rambler's Magazine* of August 1784, was yet another example of the way eighteenth-century journalism seemed to delight in damning people with faint praise and sly innuendo. The picture that emerges is of a fellow full of bonhomie, someone who was physically unattractive but had charm, and who, unfortunately, also had the unpleasant tendency to let everyone know how brilliant he thought he was. In short, the diminutive doctor was a man who was full of himself.

He could be preachy and condescending, as noted in this anecdote from a letter written on March 26, 1786, by a doctor of divinity, Dr. Michael Lort, to the medieval scholar Thomas Percy, Bishop of Dromore. Eliot had just attended the Prince of Wales during an illness no doubt brought on by the young man's usual dissipation, and the story concerned Eliot's advice to Queen Charlotte about the unhealthy life being led by her son. "Sir John Eliot told the queen that he had been preaching to the prince against intemperance as any bishop could have done; to which the queen replied, 'And, probably, with as like success.'" What this illustrates is Queen Charlotte's surprisingly wry sense of humor (she was not known for her wit) in contrast to Dr. Eliot's preachiness and posturing self-importance.

Nevertheless, even with a tendency to be overbearing and looks that could be off-putting, Eliot reportedly had an excellent bedside manner, especially with his female patients. We know, too, that he was a successful practitioner of the medical arts, if income is any indicator. That charm, combined with the aforesaid "chearfulness" and his acknowledged conversational skills, were clearly the keys to his great success. His obituary (written three months after his death) in the *World & Fashionable Advertizer* on January 30, 1787, stated that

> *in address and manner, particularly to women Eliot excelled. He therefore kept, for some time, all the business that he got. He was one of the most conspicuous and busy town-doctors.—None went to more shewy houses; none was more shewy, in the houses he went to. He drove very fast. He went very far;*

with much emolument to himself with as little injury to others, as might be! For to do him justice, he was a very simple practitioner; and free from all hazardous experiments. And he further merited the vogue he had by moderation in medicine, as to quantity; by exactness in little things; and by discipline in diet. . . . His fees amounted to four or five thousand pounds a year."*

Eliot had gotten a good start to his fortune from the days he'd spent as a surgeon's assistant aboard a privateer, amassing enough in prize monies to go to medical school—in both Scotland and England—and to set up a lucrative London practice. A fellow Scots doctor had introduced him to the right people in society—the wealthy and powerful members of the ton—and he became one of the busiest physicians in the city.

The Scots had a powerful network in London and Scots doctors were said to be the best of the profession. Eliot, moreover, had the reputation of never being too busy to see a patient; he never turned anyone down, be she lady, courtesan, or servant. To him, everyone's money was the same. And now he was to put his money to excellent use. He would acquire a young, beautiful trophy wife who would be a social asset and attract even more patients to his practice:

> *[Grace Dalrymple was] a very striking figure, tall and elegantly made, with a beautiful countenance, and an engaging air, [and] she soon attracted the attention of the men, and had many suitors, though she was not yet seventeen years of age. Her prudent kinswoman pointed out to her such as she judged eligible, and those she thought improper. D.E——was among the number of her admirers, and her faithful monitress counseled her to listen to his addresses, as he was at that time in very considerable practice, and was judged to have already acquired an easy fortune.* (The Town and Country Magazine, *August 1774)*

A miniature of Grace from this period—attributed to Richard Cosway and possibly a betrothal miniature or one painted at the time of her marriage—is in a private collection. It previously belonged to a twentieth-century Dalrymple kinsman, the Honorable Hew Dalrymple.

---

*The standard here is to multiply the eighteenth-century figure by 60, then to adjust that sum by the exchange rates of other currencies, so this is equivalent in 2004 British currency to £240,000–£300,000 and in 2004 U.S. currency to $480,000–$600,000.

The following excerpt is from Pierce Egan's classic tale *Tom & Jerry, or Life in London*, published in 1820–1821, which details the adventures of two Corinthian bucks (young sporting types) in London during the Regency period; it may serve to illustrate the particular kind of medicine John Eliot practiced so skillfully and well:

> *Tom . . . finding himself "out of sorts," as the phrase goes, called . . . on the celebrated Doctor Pleas'em . . . [who] cured more persons by his pleasing address than his prescriptions, however skillfully applied. It was said of him that his tongue had been his fortune. He had talked his way through life to a good purpose. He had not only procured himself a practice of ten thousand pounds per annum, from the humble situation of an apothecary; but he had also gained for himself a Title;—not merely that of a "great Physician," yet one that his heir could enjoy without the slightest knowledge of physic.*

This is really very close to the bone, as Egan narrates how "Doctor Pleas'em" mingled with society and royalty with the greatest of ease and lived in a "truly imposing . . . mansion" where he gave "frequent" and "excellent" dinners.

According to his obituary in 1787, Dr. Eliot had risen from humble beginnings—something that may not be altogether true if one digs deeper into the status of his mother's family—to become one of society's darlings, part of the fondly regarded medical staff attached to the insular court of King George III. His personal success supports the tradition that England has always been a country that delights in its eccentrics, especially those who are funny-looking. He served as one of the personal physicians of the Prince of Wales and attended tonnish ladies of fashion as well as ladies of the night.

One of the doctor's many patients was the celebrated actress-courtesan Sophia Baddeley, the beautiful mistress of the wealthy Peniston Lamb, Lord Melbourne. Eliot attended both her and her mother. (Another of his actress patients was Mary Robinson, more familiarly known to the theater-going public as Perdita.)

The selections that follow demonstrate John Eliot's ac-

Grace Dalrymple as a young woman, probably just prior to her marriage. (Private collection)

Sophia Baddeley: One of the Eighteenth Century's Most Beautiful and Celebrated Courtesans

She was born Sophia Snow in London; her father was an army trumpeter. At eighteen she eloped with the well-known actor Robert Baddeley; the marriage failed and husband and wife went their separate ways. Sophia—with her good looks—found rich, besotted protectors who showered her with gifts and money. Obscenely extravagant, she squandered millions of pounds in clothes and accoutrements; she was exceedingly generous to her servants, giving her maids new and costly garments. By all accounts a terrible actress, she had a lovely singing voice and gave memorable vocal performances at the Vauxhall and Ranelagh pleasure gardens. Among her notable songs were "Sweet Willy O" and "My Jockey Is the Blithest Lad." Baddeley made her acting debut as the tragic heroine Ophelia in Shakespeare's *Hamlet* at the Drury Lane Theatre in 1765, and gave her last stage performance in Edinburgh in 1784. Some of her most famous roles were as Clarissa in Charles Dibdin's comic opera *Lionel and Clarissa, or A School for Fathers,* and as Mrs. Strictland in Benjamin Hoadly's comedy *The Suspicious Husband.* She may

have been a much better comic actress than she was a tragedienne. Baddeley eventually had to flee London to evade her creditors. She died destitute in Scotland at the age of forty-one.

Sophia Baddeley (née Snow), mezzotint, 1772, by Robert Laurie, after John Zoffany. (National Portrait Gallery, London)

cessibility to, and popularity with, his patients. The first excerpt concerns Sophia Baddeley's elderly mother, who was residing on Grafton Street. The narrator is Sophia's companion Mrs. Elizabeth Steele, who wrote the six-volume work titled *The Memoirs of Mrs. Sophia Baddeley,* covering the years 1745 to 1786:

> *We then went for Doctor Eliot . . . to attend her, who told me apart, he did not think her so bad, as she thought herself; but that as she was in a deep*

Medical Dispatch, or Doctor Doubledose Killing Two Birds with One Stone, a hand-colored etching (Thomas Tegg, 1810), by Thomas Rowlandson. On the left, a fat old physician feels the pulse of an elderly woman while gazing affectionately into the eyes of her lovely young daughter. On the table sit a Composing Draught and a jar of opium, ready to mix together and dose the old dear. (National Library of Medicine)

decline and dropsical, she could not live for six months; however, he would do all in his power for her. Mrs. Baddeley desired him to attend her daily, and was very anxious to know from me, what the doctor thought of her; I told her in the softest manner I could, and she wept much. We stayed all the night with her, and in the morning took our leave, Mrs. Baddeley giving her mother twenty pounds [£1,200/$2,200], and desiring her not to want for anything, for when that was gone, she should have more, and every thing in her power to give her; and begged, if she found herself worse, to send for her express, and she would fly to her with the utmost speed possible.

At least this Doctor Pleas'em didn't bleed her.

Sophia Baddeley may have been a laudanum (opium) addict. The high-strung actress was subject to devastating headaches, and laudanum helped relieve them. The substance was as freely prescribed then as aspirin is today. Dr. Eliot called on his fragile patient often; note that he does not seem to impress the hard-nosed Mrs. Steele:

Mrs. Baddeley still complained of a pain in her head, and Lord Melbourne requested I would send for Dr. Eliot the next morning to attend her. I did, but he was of little use to her.

In about 1769, Sophia attempted suicide over a love affair that was not going well:

As soon as Mr. Hanger had left the house, Mrs. Baddeley called a hackney-chair, and ordered herself to be let down at an apothecary's in Dean-Street, where she asked for three hundred drops of laudanum. The master of the shop scrupled selling such a quantity, till she informed him who she was, adding at the same time, that she was accustomed to take a dose of it every night, and as she was going into the country, she wished to take as much as would last until her return. The apothecary entertaining no doubt of her veracity, consented to let her have it. On her return home, she discharged the chair, went up to her chamber and swallowed the whole quantity. She then made her servant acquainted with what she had done, assuring her that her Gaby's treatment of her (for so she affectionately called Mr. Hanger) made her life insupportable, and as a short time must now terminate her existence, she enjoined her to bear him the tidings of her fate.

The maid, alarmed at what she heard, immediately called in the first medical assistance that could be had: Dr. Hayes, Sir John Eliot, and Dr. Turton attended. These gentlemen found her labouring under the effects of the opium, and after several hours efforts, succeeded so far as to procure an intermission of her stupor. Her health suffered extremely from this rash step, and the distraction of her mind, and at the end of six weeks she was scarce able to walk. Her recovery was slow, indeed it was never perfectly obtained, as through the remainder of her life she was affected with a bilious complaint, that often disordered her and made many of her days unhappy.

The usual dose prescribed to treat a patient, according to a Victorian medical source, *The Dictionary of Daily Wants* (1858)—one of those useful compendia of popular medical and household knowledge—was no more than nineteen drops (twenty-one drops in Scotland). Sophia took all three hundred drops; small wonder she never fully recovered from the effects. Laudanum was used chiefly as a stimulant or tonic in small amounts, as a sedative in larger amounts, and as a powerful narcotic in mega-amounts. It was prepared by dissolving the opium powder in alcohol (wine) or water. The word comes from the Latin *laudare*, "to praise."

Laudanum was indeed praiseworthy for the elimination of pain, but its abuse was deadly. Another of Dr. Eliot's patients, Mary Robinson, was said to have abused laudanum occasionally; her death at only forty-two echoed Sophia Baddeley's early demise.

The stereotypically frugal Scotsman, Eliot never passed up an opportunity to make a penny, day or night. As a result of his great diligence in following the money wheresoever it led and from whomsoever it came, he became a wealthy man. The obituary writer in the *World & Fashionable Advertizer* remarked:

> *The love of bullion, was not at all wanting; but it was not unbecoming. If he did not spare the wealthy; his practice was gratuitous to the poor. And what he got assiduously, he spent sumptuously.*

Grace Dalrymple probably did not have to be convinced that Dr. Eliot's offer was a good one, as monetary advantages were always the most important element in marriage settlements. The good doctor could provide her with a house, a carriage, servants, charge accounts at shops all over town, including those of fashionable milliners and modistes—just about anything her girlish heart desired. Plus, he moved in a milieu inhabited by the wealthiest people in England. The man was really not a bad catch . . . on paper, if not in the flesh.

According to the obituary in the *World & Fashionable Advertizer,* John Eliot was born into modest surroundings in 1736 in Peebles—a Scottish border town directly south of the capital, Edinburgh. It was noted that his family was "humble [and] ill-provided." His father, Thomas Eliot, who died at the age of thirty-eight when John was a small child, was possibly a poor provider, but he came from a solid middle-class family that numbered doctors, professors, and ministers among them. Eliot was the only child of four born to Thomas and Mary Eliot to survive childhood. Mary Eliot, née Davidson, was middle-class also (her father was Thomas Davidson, a minister born in 1676), but her brother, William Davidson, was a wealthy man who owned a substantial manor house.

Mary Eliot's second husband was a minister, Thomas Randall, whom she married on September 12, 1742, in Perth, when John was six years old. She went on to have four other children with Randall, three boys (David, Thomas, and William) and one girl (Mary). (A direct descendant of this second marriage, Randall Thomas Davidson, was to become archbishop of Canterbury in 1903.)

Thomas Randall took an interest in his stepson, and "scholastic aids were so well given on one side, and so well taken on the other, that when but 13 years old, Eliott had much Latin, and no little Greek!" Or, one up on Shakespeare, according to this self-styled witty obit writer, for the Bard of Avon was said to have had "small Latin and less Greek."

*P*rivateers and Prize Money

Eliot's ease with languages is further noted (though with a sly caveat):

> *A knack at languages, was one of his happy peculiarities.—When more advanced in life, he got, with much speed and little pains, into French, Italian and Spanish.—French, like Latin, he spoke very glibly, but with little finesse, either in idiom or accent. Of Spanish, he had sufficient for all ordinary communications.*

After schooling, Eliot "served a [local] practitioner in medicine" and made his way to London while still a raw youth—as so many ambitious boys did—becoming an assistant to an apothecary in the Haymarket district. The knowledge of medicines he gained propelled him to his next step up fortune's ladder, when he signed on to a privateer as a surgeon's mate. The obituary states that the ambitious Eliot was

> *Not long satisfied with a situation, certainly so much below what befitted him, [and so] he went to sea. The death of his principal soon raised him from a mate to the surgeoncy of the ship. The day after this advance, a rich prize was taken!*

What luck for the ambitious young man from Peebles! From surgeon's assistant to surgeon, not an infrequent occurrence at sea, when men engaged in fierce battle and many lives were lost among these noncombatant medical personnel. At any rate, the outcome was the same: Eliot amassed a tidy fortune in prize money.

John Eliot now had to be at least in his twenties: twenty-six, if 1736 is the correct date of his birth, twenty-eight or older if it is not. (The pedigree Eliot had drawn up by the College of Heralds in 1784 gave this rather ambiguous birthdate: 15 April 17———. Other printed sources for his birth range from the mid-1730s to late in the decade.) His interest in medicine apparently still strong—remember that there were several doctors, professors of anatomy, and surgeons in his family—he was graduated with an MD from St. Andrews University in Scotland in 1759 and then admitted a licentiate at the Royal College of Physicians in London on September 30, 1761 (or 1762).

The Royal College of Physicians was the oldest medical institution in England, created by charter of Henry VIII in 1518. "The main functions of the College . . . were to grant licenses to those qualified to practice and to punish unqualified practitioners and those engaging in malpractice [with the] overall aim of upholding and improving standards of medical practice." Apothecaries as well as physicians were included in this body. The president of the Royal College of Physicians in 1762 was Thomas Reeve; William Battie succeeded him in 1764.

Eliot spent some time traveling in Holland and France, either before or after this medical training, but he pursued his career in London. As previously mentioned, there was a strong network of Scottish doctors there, many of them attached to the English court, and one of the most prominent was Sir William Duncan. Duncan attended King George III and was of immense help to Dr. Eliot in the setting up of his practice and in his subsequent

This is the building on Warwick Lane that John Eliot would have attended. It was the third home of the Royal College of Physicians, which is now located on St. Andrew's Place in Regent's Park; where this building once stood is now the Cutlers' Hall. (The Bridgeman Art Library)

introduction to the ton. Within a short time, Eliot, too, was also attending the royal personages, including the Prince of Wales, his wife-to-be's future lover.

Eliot's obituary writer again noted his luck, this time in securing the patronage of Dr. Duncan:

> *Here again time and chance immediately befriended him. Sir William Duncan took him up; and with something more than national predilection. He gave him introductions. He got him favour. And not long after, when in conjunction with George Grenville, Duncan, plunging into a a mad project of planting Greek wine in America, left England, he every where pushed Eliott as his successor, and to him transferred all the business that was thus transferable.*

How lucky could John Eliot get? In August 1784 *The Rambler's Magazine* had reported:

> *The celebrated Doctor . . . was the particular friend of Mr. Dal———. . . . To this friend Mr. Dal———produced his daughter, communicated his difficulties, and besought his advice—but all difficulties soon vanished—for the Doctor was instantly smitten, and immediately offered to take charge of that lady's reputation and fortune, and provide for both by making her the wife of his bosom.*

The Matrimonial Magazine, or Monthly Anecdotes of Love and Marriage, for The Court, the City and the Country, in its February 1775 issue, almost ten years prior to the *Rambler's Magazine* article, had stated that

> *[Hew Dalrymple was] a native of the West Indies, who by profusion and wasteful expence, like many other children of the sun, had dissipated his wealth in the vortex of the metropolis. [This is patently untrue, a fancy of the writer; Dalrymple was born in Scotland.] Being about to depart to the land of his inheritance, in order to retrieve his affairs, he was visited by Dr. E———, who finding him on the point of departing, begged leave to detain his youthful and engaging daughter. A match was presently proposed, and as readily consented to by the father. The proposition was no sooner made, than the bargain was struck, and the pair united. From such a rapid connection, and with a belle celebrated at once for wit and beauty, no very felicity could be expected, and perhaps the indulgence of the Doctor might, in many respects, add to her undoing; for he was pleased with the beauty of his pretty wife, and gave a loose rein to all her wishes and desires.*

All the contemporary journalists remarked upon the disparities between the couple. Age was not so much the issue, for women tended to marry much older men, men who were settled in their professions or had already inherited their money. The greater disparities here were of character, personality, and general outlook. These, coupled with the age discrepancy—Eliot was twice Grace Dalrymple's age—spelled a disaster in the making.

The *Rambler's Magazine* article described the doctor in exactly the same words used by the obituary writer in the *World & Fashionable Advertizer* three years later. (Exactly, exactly, the same words!) Grace, on the other hand, received a paean from that magazine, a veritable love ode to her beauty and style:

> The lady . . . was now on the verge of *17*, tall, and very elegantly shaped; her features beautiful, and not in the least marked by any degree of that provinciality which distinguishes the females from the north; her complexion was clear as the clouds of a May morning, and tinged with the roseate blush of Aurora; her disposition lively, her temper mild and engaging.

Grace was young, she was beautiful, and she also towered over her older, much less attractive husband, which never makes a pretty picture. The marriage license, one of those expensive "Special Licences" that were used frequently by members of the ton but were out of the reach of ordinary mortals, was issued on the morning that they married. Someone was in a big hurry, and the odds are that it was Hew Dalrymple who could not wait to get his daughter off his hands, followed by another man in a hurry, his purported friend the doctor, eager to get his hands on this beautiful creature's body. (For the text of the actual license, see the sidebar.)

Dr. Eliot was so keen to please Grace that he'd sold his house in the parish of St. Clement Danes and bought the home of the spinster Ann Pitt—the clever and adored sister and confidante of William Pitt the Elder—situated in the up-and-coming, posher neighborhood of Knightsbridge. He also bought his young bride a carriage and surrounded her with a multitude of servants. (The servants, it was to turn out, were a mixed blessing for Grace, as they later served up incriminating evidence in support of her husband's divorce petition.)

Dr. Eliot must have spent a great deal to please Grace and to impress others, for he moved in important circles, mixing with a variety of people—other

The Special Licence

Guildhall Ms 10.091/125   1771 (A-L)

London Diocese, 19th October 1771

Appeared personally John Eliot Doctor of Physick and made Oath, that he is of the Parish of Saint Clement Danes in the County of Middlesex aged upwards of Thirty two years a Batchelor and intendeth to marry with Grace Dalrymple of the Parish of Saint Pancras in the same County aged upwards of seventeen years but under the age of Twenty one years Spinster a Minor by and with the consent of Hugh Dalrymple Esquire the natural and lawful Father of the said Minor and that he knoweth of no lawful impediment, by Reason of any Precontract, Consanguinity, Affinity, or any other lawful means whatsoever, to hinder the said intended Marriage and prayed a Licence to Solemnise the same in the Parish Church of Saint Pancras aforesaid and further made Oath that the usual Place of Abode of the said Grace Dalrymple hath been the said Parish of Saint Pancras for the space of four Weeks last past.

There appeared personally the said Hugh Dalrymple of the said Parish of St. Pancras Esquire and made Oath that he is the natural and lawful Father of the above Minor and is consenting to the above intended Marriage. Sworn before me,

J. C. Simpson,

Surrogate   John Eliot

                            Hugh Dalrymple

physicians, peers, prelates, actors. (His associates included Horace Walpole, with whom he shared a daunting experience of highway robbery.) Remember that the writer of Eliot's obituary commented that "he spent sumptuously," which no doubt increased his popularity. That writer continued:

> *If he had no great superfluity of taste, he yielded sufficiently to those who had. For in all visible efforts of expence, equipage, table, books and pictures, there was choice, as well costliness apparent!*

Eliot was apparently a gracious host, too:

He was proud of his hospitality; of hospitality, as much at large, as in "the days of good neighbours." He delighted in doing the honours of his table!— Every man is too apt to delight in what he does well.

The church of choice for the wedding was St. Pancras (now called St. Pancras Old Church), which still stands, albeit in an altered and less impressive state, in a shabby neighborhood yards from the Kings Cross British Railway Station and behind the new British Library.

The building is situated across from a charmless council housing complex. It was once an eye-catching, pretty sight, isolated on a rise overlooking the mighty River Fleet (now one of London's "lost" rivers, it flows underground) on a broad expanse of greensward. The area was more country than town, and the old church hadn't been "improved" yet by Victorian additions such as the clock tower.

The sign at the entrance gate reads:

Saint Pancras Old Church is the most ancient building in the borough. Parts of the present building belong to the XIth century and contain Roman tiles. When the Church was enlarged in 1947–8 the Altar Stone was discovered and restored to use in the present Altar. It dates from the early VIIth century and was probably used by St. Augustine. The Fleet River flows past the Church and immediately south along its course are the St. Pancras Wells.

Grace wore her best dress—there were no dresses specifically for weddings at the time—and it probably wasn't white, either. (Almost any color save black was fine.) No description exists, but it's a safe bet that with her stature and beauty she looked gorgeous. She must have had to duck her head to enter the church—the door of St. Pancras Old Church is small and low and she, as we know, was uncommonly tall—but the eager and diminutive bridegroom, Dr. Eliot, should have had no trouble getting in.

The couple may actually have recited their vows over that ancient altar stone, but it sure didn't help; this marriage was doomed from the get-go. Grace's convent school education could not have prepared her adequately for what she'd face as a pretty girl set loose in the midst of an unfamiliar society—the bon ton—where she was out of her element and temptations of every sort abounded. Young unmarried girls had chaperones, but married women were generally unsupervised and left to their own devices. Who'd be surprised it wasn't long before she misstepped?

The fast-moving, dissolute society inhabited by the newlywed couple had to be heady stuff for Grace; this tender bride, barely out of the schoolroom, was ripe for the attention of rakes and gallants. Dr. Eliot, on his day-and-night quest for more business, more patients to attend, and more money to make, may have had little time to escort his lady to the events she was of a mind to attend.

Eliot was what we'd call a workaholic, and was probably too tired from his professional exertions to party on as much as a young bride would have liked. Though he was convivial, he might have preferred taking off his shoes at night and drinking some of his good Scotch whisky in a comfortable padded armchair rather than standing up on his poor tired feet in the crushing midst of the latest rout. Even Doctor Pleas'em needed his rest.

Moreover, Grace was probably extremely bored hearing him retell yet another one of his "rich . . . historical anecdotes" when she'd much rather dance the night away under a sparkling chandelier with the handsomest young men in London. Young men are energetic dancers, whereas tired old physicians . . .

As *The Rambler's Magazine* noted:

Indeed the lady's vivacity, and the Doctor's solemnity, were eternally at variance, and the improvement she made in fashionable dissipation, created many an alarm. No little pains were taken by the Doctor's friends to introduce his wife's beauty to public attention, nor were those friendly offices ever repulsed on her part, and she soon became the idol at whose shrine gallantry equally offered its incense.

The writer argued that the good doctor tried to save his marriage, but failed to stem the virile onslaught of gallantry upon his naïve—or perhaps too-willing?—spouse:

From her well-known, though perhaps unavoidable acquaintance with some characters notoriously distinguished for amorous pursuits, suspicions of the most alarming kind took possession of the unfortunate husband; a separation of beds took place by mutual consent; and upwards of a year was spent in various attempts of the Doctor to defend the fortress of his lady's virtue, against the attacks of several vigorous assailants, who were repeatedly repulsed by the vigilance and valour of the Commander, both which were more than once exercised in this toilsome and dangerous service.

The reality of the overbearing Dr. Eliot as a husband—her lord and master—must have sunk in rapidly for Grace. She had no mother to give her advice on marriage and tell her how to cope when money would not substitute for the other things a pretty, sociable young woman might crave from a relationship. (Her late mother had been savvy enough to leave a bad relationship, and she might have had the foresight, if she had lived, to advise against Grace's marrying Eliot in the first place.)

That "prudent kinswoman" who was her "faithful monitress" in choosing the best suitor for her hand made a terrible mistake. It's possible she was the "Mary Dalrymple" who signed the marriage register along with Grace's father at St. Pancras Church. What relationship she had to either the father or the daughter is not known, but she could have been a cousin or an aunt.

Whatever older female relatives existed—including her elder sister, Jacintha, who had married well, if not happily, twice—either neglected to impart what Grace needed to know or purposely kept the salient facts of married life from her. Grace and Dr. Eliot were polar opposites in personality and temperament—he was a prosy old bore and she was a vivacious party animal—and the age difference turned out to be a major problem. An astute, worldly-wise older woman would have been cognizant of that.

The feminist scholar Lillian S. Robinson in 1978 wrote a provocative essay, "Why Marry Mr. Collins?" that's crucial to a modern reader's understanding of the reality of marriage—what it really was all about—for an eighteenth-century woman. Robinson uses the example of the fictional Charlotte Lucas, the spinster friend of Elizabeth Bennet, in Jane Austen's *Pride and Prejudice:*

> *It is a truth universally acknowledged that Miss Charlotte Lucas married for material gain. . . . Charlotte, eldest daughter of Sir William Lucas, is twenty-seven years old and has never been handsome. Although a woman of good sense, she has not quite the "elegance of mind" that characterizes the two elder Miss Bennets. No one has offered for Miss Lucas and her prospects are not very bright, so when Mr. Collins, the estranged cousin on whom Mr. Bennet's Longbourn estate is entailed, proposes to her on the rebound from*

Terms for Unmarried Women

Ape-Leader, Old Maid, On the Shelf, Spinster (still used on British marriage licenses), Tabby, Vestal Virgin.

In Jane Austen's *Emma,* the title character's lower-class friend Harriet Smith exclaims, "But still, you will be an old maid! and that's so dreadful!" Emma, who is wealthy, responds: "Never mind, Harriet, I shall not be a poor old maid; and it is poverty only which makes celibacy contemptible to a generous public! A single woman, with a very narrow income, must be a ridiculous, disagreeable old maid! the proper sport of boys and girls, but a single woman, of good fortune, is always respectable."

Elizabeth Bennet after an assiduous three-day courtship, she accepts. Since it is a truth no less universally acknowledged that Mr. Collins is a schmuck, the conclusion about Miss Lucas's motives inexorably follows.

But who would be so unkind as to blame poor, homely Charlotte Lucas for wanting to better her rather grim situation? As a spinster with no looks or fortune—and, at twenty-seven, getting on in age—Miss Lucas was already an old maid. All she could look forward to for the rest of her single life was sponging off her married brothers, playing the thankless role of a poor relation trying to be useful in someone else's household, perhaps by taking care of young children or organizing the housekeeping.

The unmarried woman was regarded as a sad and pathetic creature, subordinate and subservient to others. Mr. Collins, as repulsive as he is personally, would, at least, give Miss Lucas the desirable status of a married woman, someone with status, someone who was in charge of her own household. As a wife she would not be beholden to her family for scraps—as it were—from their tables. As Mary Abbott notes in *Family Ties: English Families, 1540–1920,* that was not a fun prospect for the rest of one's life:

Unmarried women were understudies, filling in for missing mothers, daughters, and wives. Even in desperate need few sought paid employment. Daughters' marriages were negotiated by parents and guardians.

Looking at the situation objectively, Grace's father and other relatives would have been delighted at her catch. They would not have been overly eager to take a poor relation—like her or the fictional Charlotte Lucas—under their roofs, and support that person for the rest of her natural life.

(Spinsters, one observed, tended on the whole to live longer.) But the relatives were in too much of a hurry, for Grace had beauty, charm, and wit, even if she lacked what was considered a good dowry in those times.

Grace might have made a love match, might have attracted a peer's son (perhaps not the heir but a third or fourth son) and achieved a more reasonable pairing in age, temperament, and personality than she did. She was only sixteen in this, her first season on the marriage mart. She could have had one or two seasons more if the first one did not take—if, that is, her relatives had been willing to support her and see that she got to the proper venues.

As to what came later, they were probably hopeless to deal with it. It could also have been that Grace was too headstrong to pay well-meaning female relatives bearing advice any heed when—if!—they cautioned her to be more discreet in public, as a married woman should be.

It's known from Lady Shelley's *Diary* that Grace's only sibling, Jacintha, cut off communication with Grace entirely because of the scandal that ensued. Throughout her life Grace exhibited stubbornness—some would call it strength and a virtue, this absolute, unshakable belief in her own convictions—that led her to do things her own way, but it could also be a failing. She showed this during the events before and during the Reign of Terror in France. "Bloody-mindedness" is what the English call this characteristic; Americans would call it being pigheaded.

Whether owing to naïveté or to recklessness, she made choices, to her great detriment. She made the fatal mistake of carrying on—and, perhaps even worse, falling in love—with a married man, a consummate rake, under the eyes of her husband's friends and clients, people who no doubt delighted, as people do, in bringing him tales, whether true or

"Very finely knitted beadwork and ball tassel. Design includes the words *'Souvenir d'Amitié*—a remembrance or memento of friendship.' 4″ x 2″." (From novelist Candice Hern's collection of period beaded and knitted purses, as seen on her Web site, www.candicehern.com)

not, of the flirtations of his errant young wife. Eliot was a proud man, inordinately proud, a husband who would not tolerate any infidelities from his young bride, even if (as turned out to be the case) he was guilty of such goings-on himself.

Arthur Annesley, Lord Valentia, was one of that tribe of so-called gallants who seduced women for the sheer fun of it. Today they'd be termed "love rats," à la James Hewitt, Princess Di's tell-all lover. These wealthy men didn't have to work and so had the leisure time for such things. It was a game, and no one who knew the rules got hurt, but one had to know these rules. Female aristocrats seemingly took in the rules with their pablum in the nursery. If they didn't, all they had to do was open their eyes to observe what was going on around them in their society.

{Rake. According to the 1811 *Dictionary of the Vulgar Tongue*, a Rake, Rakehell, or Rakeshame is "a lewd, debauched fellow." This was a dissolute, profligate male specimen who indulged in indiscriminate sexual conquest, often of naïve young virgins or equally naïve recently married women. "Rake" may be derived from the Anglo-Saxon *rakel* or *rackle,* meaning rough and hasty. A rake was a type still appealing to many young women.}

How puzzling that Lady Diana Spencer, who became Princess of Wales in our time, seemed to be so clueless as to why Prince Charles was marrying her. Surely she had her own family's history to guide and warn her. Few families were immune to sexual scandal, least of all the Spencers. Just look at two other Diana Spencers, Di's ancestors Diana, Duchess of Devonshire, and Lady Diana, or Di, Beauclerk. Had she never heard of them?

Lucy Russell, the actress who played Grace Elliott in Eric Rohmer's film *The Lady and the Duke,* commented that one has to feel sorry for Grace because she'd obviously had no one to school her in how to get on in ton society, where sexual scandal ran rampant. Granted, Dr. Eliot was more controlling than most husbands, but a smart, discreet, manipulative wife could have worked around that and had him in her pocket. (Pockets, by the way, were worn under dresses and attached to a petticoat, accessible by a slit in the dress. As dresses narrowed, these pockets became too bulky, so purses, or reticules, came to serve the same purpose.) At any rate, Grace was reckless, or in love, which in effect amounted to much the same thing.

Tragically for her, what Grace did not seem to be aware of or to understand was that although aristocratic women could be tramps—even before, as well as during, marriage—young women from a lower stratum of society than the ton could not afford to fool around. They had to be a good deal more careful in carrying on their love affairs and infidelities. If Grace had been an aristocrat—if she'd had the word "Lady" to protect her name and if she'd hobnobbed then with more sophisticated, worldly women who did this all the time—her life would have been far different. (The woman who was later to become her good friend, Lady Worsley, had successfully overcome scandal far greater than Grace's, but she was the daughter of aristocrats.)

To the outside world, things looked fine—for who really knows what goes on between married couples? But trouble was brewing:

*Miss D—— listened to this advice, and in a short time she became the wife of Dr. E——. As he was extremely enamoured with her, there was no request she could make but was complied with. An elegant equipage [town carriage, coachman, footmen], and a magnificent set of jewels, were the smallest part of his indulgence; he neither refused paying her play [gambling] debts, or allowing her to frequent all the routs and drums [both are terms for parties] she pleased. In a word, every one pronounced Mrs.—— one of the happiest women in the metropolis; she was envied by all the married women who knew her, and courted by all the men who saw her. (*The Town and Country Magazine, *August 1774)*

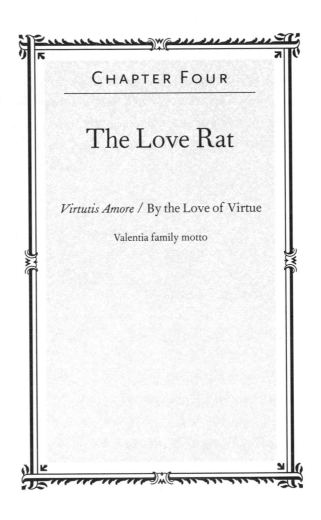

CHAPTER FOUR

The Love Rat

Virtutis Amore / By the Love of Virtue

Valentia family motto

MY LORD RAKE: GRACE ELLIOTT'S AFFAIR WITH ARTHUR ANNESLEY, LORD VALENTIA

By the love of virtue"—what a gross misnomer! Virtue appears to have been in very short supply in the Annesley family. Of all the men in the Georgian ton with whom to get involved, Grace Elliott had the singular misfortune to encounter Arthur Annesley, eighth Viscount Valentia, a rake of the first order.

Valentia was the scion of a dodgy Anglo-Irish family enmeshed in bigamy, kidnapping, attempted murder, usurpation of rightful titles, and all-around low behavior. A classic bad boy, he was the kind of man that women are instantly attracted to and just as instantly smitten with. According to the tabloids, Lord Valentia was of "athletic form and an agreeable countenance," and, born in 1744, he was only ten years older than Grace Elliott and no doubt taller and considerably more attractive to her than her dwarfish husband.

The scandal sheets started to take note of the developing relationship between Lord Valentia and Grace Elliott in 1774–1775, but the affair may have begun as early as the fall of 1773. Grace had married the good doctor in October 1771, and there had been a child who died. Within this time frame, with time out for pregnancy and birth and the long recovery time women of Grace's station were expected to take after these events, it is reasonable to speculate that between the fall or early winter of 1773 and the spring of 1774 she was ready to party on again.

The first article, in *The Town and Country Magazine*, appeared in August 1774, to be followed by a piece in the February 1775 issue of *The Matrimonial Magazine*. (Later articles would appear in the December 1777 issue of *The Town and Country Magazine* and in *The Rambler's Magazine* for August 1784, after Grace had taken up with Lord Cholmondeley and the Prince of Wales.)

As the writer in *The Rambler's Magazine* put it succinctly, "Troy stood ten years' siege but fell at last." Someone had at last stuck the horns on the head of the diminutive Scots doctor, that poor "cornuted" sucker. Or as the tabloid crowed (or perhaps more fittingly, cuckooed) someone had presented him with "hymeneal honours." The reference is to Hymen, the bisexual winged love god of marriage (and brother to that other important love god, Priapus) who personified the hymn sung to the happy couple outside the bridal chamber:

> *And at length an enterprising Hibernian, Lord Viscount Valentia—took the field, but assault not being his lordship's forte, he proceeded by stratagem, and very speedily completed the overthrow of the Doctor's doubts, by adorning his head with hymeneal honours.*

The Matrimonial Magazine (alas, it was to be a short-lived publication) had, in January 1775, opened with an interesting essay entitled "Thoughts on Marriage." A paean to the state of perfect wedlock, the essay must have caused more than a few guffaws in sophisticated circles, but it sheds light on what some in the eighteenth century grappled with concerning marriage and its ramifications for a good society. The writer (who is not identified and

{*The Oxford English Dictionary* defines the noun "cuckold" as "a derisive name for the husband of an unfaithful wife." The word is also a verb meaning "to dishonor a husband by committing adultery." This insulting term, derived from the Middle English *cukeweld* or *cokewold,* which came from the Old French *cucuault,* has been around for some eight hundred years. The word in modern French, *cocu,* is also the name of the European cuckoo, a bird that lays its eggs in the nests of other birds for them to raise, as men would raise children not their own, but rather (unbeknownst to them) the offspring of their wives' adulterous liaisons.

"Adultery" comes from the Latin root meaning "to corrupt," as in "adulterate." A cuckold is often depicted as wearing horns, a pagan image that may refer to the sign of the Horned God. Giving a man "the horns"—pointing at him with all the fingers of the hand turned in except for the little and index digits—is widely recognized in European cultures as referring to the sexual conquest of his wife and impugns his potency.

An incident at the opening of Parliament was attributed to King George III, that moral paragon, when he turned to Lord Grosvenor and the Duke of Grafton, who'd just divorced their wives for adultery, and said, "I am obliged to acquaint your Lordships that distemper has lately broken out among the horned cattle." A heavy-handed jest, to be sure, but the peers were said to have turned to one another and bowed in acknowledgment of their horned state. The times were rife with such adornments to the forehead.}

who may be either a man or a woman) first defines marriage as a man's "natural" condition and then states that it is under fire, assailed by the rampant "debauchery" of the times. (In the subsequent issue, the bad influence of French manners and morals was blamed for debauchery among the English ton.)

He or she then discusses three kinds of marriage—"insipid," "vexatious," and "happy"—and concludes that only the latter one, the "happy" marriage, is of permanent value, and that "personal perfections are the only foundation for conjugal happiness: the gifts of fortune are adventitious, and may be acquired; but intrinsic worth is permanent and incommunicable."

The writer goes on to say that as the usual kind of marriage among the well-to-do is the "insipid" marriage, that is,

when two people of no genius or taste for themselves meet together, upon

The Amazing Growth of English Newspapers in the Eighteenth Century

There were twelve daily newspapers and six weeklies in 1712, and six tri-weeklies and dailies in 1746. By 1770, there were five dailies, eight tri-weeklies, and four weeklies, and in 1783 there were nine dailies and ten bi- or tri-weeklies. There were thirteen morning, one evening, seven tri-weekly, and two bi-weekly papers in 1790. By 1792 there were sixteen dailies, and by 1811 the grand total from all categories was fifty-two. Newspapers were published every day but Sunday (owing to the prohibitive Sabbath laws). The first London Sunday newspaper was the *British Gazette & Sunday Monitor,* started in 1779.

such a settlement as has been thought reasonable by parents and conveyancers, from an exact valuation of the land and cash of both parties: in this case the young lady's person is no more regarded, than the house and the improvements in the purchase of an estate; but she goes with her fortune, rather than her fortune with her. These make up the crowd or vulgar of the rich, and fill up the lumber of human race, without beneficence towards those below them, or respect from those above them; and lead a despicable, independent, and useless life, without sense of the law of kindness, good nature, mutual offices, and the elegant satisfactions which flow from reason and virtue.

Now, note the "vexatious" marriage:

The vexatious married life arises from a conjunction of quick taste and resentment, put together for reasons well known to their friends, in which especial care is taken to avoid (what they think is the chief of evils) poverty, and ensure to them riches, with every evil besides. These good people live in a constant constraint before company, and too great familiarity alone; when they are within observation they fret at each other's carriage and behavior; when alone they revile each other's person and conduct: in company they are in a purgatory, when by themselves in an hell.

This is strong commentary on this "vexatious" marriage, a situation that combines the evils of marrying solely for money coupled with the forced union of incompatible temperaments, bringing together individuals incapable of coexisting, or even of showing the most basic good manners toward each other. It's a marriage of mutual contempt that grates on those around them, whereas the merely "insipid" marriage is neither here nor there, with no strong emotion getting in the way. Those entering this state strive not to get in each other's way, and to go their own way as much as possible after obligations to the title (chiefly the "heir and a spare") are met.

And how does the writer describe the sought-for ideal, the "happy" marriage? Note that he or she uses the L-word in averring:

> *The happy marriage is, where two persons meet, and voluntarily make choice of each other, without principally regarding or neglecting the circumstance of fortune or beauty. These may still* love *in spite of adversity or sickness: the former we may in some measure defend ourselves from, the other is the common lot of humanity. When esteem and love unite hearts, ostentation and pomp of living will not be coveted; solitude and mediocrity with the person beloved yield pleasures beyond what can be derived from shew and splendor.*

This is actually quite lovely, if ridiculously romantic for the time period, and can be used to analyze the Eliot/Elliott marriage. (The differing spelling of their common surname speaks for itself in this unhappy relationship.) Dr. Eliot brought money—much more than Grace's father had—and rank a bit above hers, but not much of the latter, for the Dalrymples were from a good family. They claimed a relationship to Scottish aristocracy—through the earls of Stair—that perhaps had more foundation in fact than the doctor's claim, in the peerage he had drawn up by the College of Arms, that he was descended from Scottish royalty. (Yes, from the legendary King Robert the Bruce, the greatest soldier king in Scottish history! Eliot may have been short, but he aimed high.) It was not an unusual exchange, but rather a timeless story, that of youth and beauty, on the one hand, and money, on the other.

This would not have been too bad—and, as noted, it was the usual way things went then—but it was doomed to fall into that second class of marriages, the "vexatious." The union of the doctor and Grace apparently grew to be extremely contentious. According to the writer of the August 1774 *Town and Country Magazine* piece, once Eliot got the proof of Grace's affair with Valentia, relations between them deteriorated so badly that after their separation of bed and board, the doctor "received from his wife . . . an extraordinarily laconic billet," in which the lady reputedly said:

I should be the happiest woman in the world, if you and Lord V—— were both dead.

One can appreciate the sentiment. The falling-out between this husband and wife was rancorous, and it bore terrible consequences for the teenage bride. The two had grown to despise each other, combining the worst aspects of the "insipid" marriage with those of the "vexatious." Ultimately, not only the marriage but their good names and reputation in society were destroyed.

WHO WAS THIS ARTHUR ANNESLEY?

The Complete Peerage gives the detailed ancestry of the Annesleys, but it is dizzying to trace this family's checkered past. It's perhaps easier to follow the account in *The Dictionary of National Biography*, which has less detail but considerably more flavor. We begin with an eccentric named Arthur Annesley, born in 1689, fourth Baron Altham, who set the (very low) standard for all who came after him. Material from the *DNB* and *The Complete Peerage* fills in the gaps within the Annesley family saga. (Online genealogical sources are not to be wholly relied upon.)

Annesley married a cousin, the daughter of Sir John Thompson, first Baron Haversham, in 1703. Her name may have been Phillips Thompson, and what happened to her is unclear. He married his second wife, Mary Sheffield, the illegitimate daughter of Lord John Sheffield, the poet and first Duke of Buckingham and Normanby, in 1706 (or 1707) at St. Margaret's Church, Westminster. (Buckingham Palace was built as this first Duke's country house.) Annesley had a son, James, in 1715, by this second wife, and here is where things begin to get murky. Was his first wife still alive when he married his second? Was the second marriage legal? Was James illegitimate?

Annesley had had at least two long periods of separation from this second wife, a period possibly before James's birth and another one afterward. One source says Annesley and Mary separated in 1717, another that they were separated not long after their marriage, but that they reconciled in 1713 and separated again in 1716. Both sources agree that the two were together during the crucial period when James Annesley would have been conceived. He was born in 1715 in County Wexford, Ireland.

Now enters the woman with the colorful name of Joan or Juggy Landy, whom the fourth Baron took under his protection sometime after his last separation from his second wife. He declared this woman to be Lady Altham, though he had not been divorced from Mary Sheffield, and Joan Landy may have been someone else's wife at the time. Bigamy was a crime not to be taken lightly, but apparently none of these players had any qualms about engaging in it. Mary Sheffield, the actual (or was she?) Lady Altham, "returned to England in 1723, having for some time suffered from paralysis, and lingered in London until her death in 1729," according to the *DNB*. Her husband had predeceased her by two years, having died in 1727.

The child James was said to have been recognized by his father the fourth Baron as his legitimate heir, but sources suggest that the Baron's mistress—a woman variously alluded to as a Miss Gregory or a Miss Kennedy—alienated the father's affections from the son and drove them apart. Then James apparently disappeared from the scene. One account had him removed to an obscure school where his death was subsequently announced, another had him wandering half naked through the English countryside, and yet another had him working for a time with a butcher. When James's father died in 1727, the title of fifth Baron Altham went to Arthur Annesley's brother Richard, five years his junior, who'd been born in 1694.

Is everyone still following this?

All right, here goes: In 1727 Richard Annesley took his brother Arthur's seat in the Irish House of Lords as Baron Altham. This Annesley had married three wives, the second bigamously; his first wife did not die until 1741. (Bigamy obviously ran in this family.) He had three daughters with his second wife. A third wife—Juliana Donovan—was validated by the Irish courts as his legal spouse. In 1737 he took his seat in the English House of Lords as an earl and in the Irish House of Lords as a viscount. His son Arthur was born in 1744, apparently legitimately.

Despite reports that James Annesley, Richard's elder brother's son—whom some considered the legitimate heir—may still have been alive somewhere in England, the title had passed to Richard. Now it becomes really nasty. Apparently, about four months after Arthur Annesley's death, Richard found his nephew James and had him kidnapped, then sold him into slavery. This was indentured servitude, a kind of slavery that is set under contract for a specified number of years, but not for life. James was indentured to an American plantation owner in the West Indies. (Another version of this has him being sold as a slave to an American planter in America, from whence he fled to Jamaica.) James's uncle evidently felt that James had a serious, legitimate claim to the barony. Otherwise, why go to so much trouble to get rid of this nephew?

How could an Englishman who'd been raised in relative comfort tolerate hard labor in a hostile environment? Such a man was unused to the harsh conditions of toil under the unremittingly hot tropical sun—or the equally brutal sun of the American Deep South's cotton plantations. To be sent to work long hours in the fields was tantamount to a death sentence. Richard no doubt felt secure in assuming that his nephew would never return to England to make a claim on his inheritance, that the unfortunate James Annesley would die forgotten and unmourned in the New World.

But thirteen years later, in 1740, the amazingly resilient kidnapped heir returned to England alive. He'd worked out his indenture and signed on in Jamaica to a ship in the fleet of an Admiral Vernon. He told his story to the ship's officers and was believed by them, and upon arrival in England he set about trying to redress the grievous wrong he'd suffered. He was supported in his legal actions by a Mr. Mackercher.

There was no easy redress in this convoluted case. James Annesley filed an action for ejectment against his uncle in 1743. He was awarded the family estates but not the titles, as he did not have the funds to see his case through the courts. There was also still some lingering doubt about his legitimacy. Some eyewitnesses swore he was Joan Landy's son, not Mary Sheffield's, and some questioned the legitimacy of the fourth Baron's second marriage to Mary Sheffield.

There was little doubt, however, that his conniving uncle had sold him into indentured servitude. Richard Annesley—along with two accomplices—was convicted and fined for assault for James's kidnapping. A fine seems an absurdly minor punishment for what he did his nephew. And it apparently did not deter this vicious individual, as there were several occasions when Richard Annesley attempted to have James disposed of in any way he could.

A hunting accident occurred in the spring of 1742 when James Annesley, out shooting with a gamekeeper at Staines, happened upon a poacher. His fowling piece (a kind of double-barreled shotgun) discharged without warning and the poacher was shot dead. Richard Annesley took the opportunity to press for the prosecution of his nephew for murder, and James was brought to trial in the summer. As it was clearly an accident, and there was an eyewitness, James Annesley was acquitted, but the word had gone out that Richard might pay anything to have his troublesome nephew done away with.

On another occasion that same year, James and some companions were attacked at a horse race and beaten severely. James barely escaped with his life by hurriedly mounting a horse and fleeing the violent assault. There were many times when he found himself in situations where he had to deal with his uncle's onslaughts via hired villains who would appear without warning. James's life was in danger at all times and the stress must have been terrible; surely it took a toll, along with all those years of hard labor, on his life expectancy.

James Annesley married twice. He had a son and two daughters by his first wife, a woman identified only by the surname of Chester. He had a son and daughter by his second wife, Margaret l'Anson, the daughter of Sir Thomas l'Anson, fourth Baronet l'Anson; they'd been married in 1751 in Bidborough, Kent. James died in Kent in 1760, at the age of forty-five; his two sons died in 1763 and 1764, leaving no "tail male" heir. The barony of Annesley and the barldom of Anglesey had expired in 1761.

James's curious life story inspired fiction. Sir Walter Scott's *Guy Mannering*, Tobias Smollett's *Peregrine Pickle*, and Charles Reade's *The Wandering Heir* were all based on poor James Annesley's dramatic experiences.

The way was now clear for the man who was to become Grace's seducer, Arthur Annesley (1744–1816), to inherit. Arthur Annesley was James's cousin, the son of his murderous uncle. As the closest "tail male" in the line, with no male issue from his cousin to contest his claim, Arthur Annesley was the heir apparent. He inherited the Irish title of Valentia in 1771, and tried to regain the two English titles lost by his family by pursuing his rights through the legal system.

Although Lord Valentia had the support of his powerful father-in-law, Sir Thomas Lyttelton, sixth Baronet Cobham and last Baron Lyttelton of

Frankley, he did not succeed in regaining the lost titles. He was, however, created first Earl of Mountnorris in 1793. Though the Mountnorris earldom died out with his son—this family seemed to have problems holding on to its titles—the Valentia title is still alive. The current—and fifteenth—Viscount Valentia is one Richard John Dighton Annesley (born 1929), a farmer said to be resident somewhere in Zimbabwe within the last decade.

Lord Valentia's much-put-upon wife—by all accounts a plain and virtuous woman—endured all his many infidelities and the scandals attached to same, not the least of which was to be his affair with Dr. Eliot's comely teenage bride. The wife's name was Lucy; she was the daughter of the above-mentioned Sir Thomas Lyttelton.

Lucy gave her husband two sons. Their first son, Arthur, born in 1769, died before his second birthday. George Annesley, their second son, born in 1770, succeeded his father as ninth Viscount Valentia and second and last Earl of Mountnorris. (Some sources say there were four children from this union, two boys and two girls, but this may reflect confusion with the children of his second marriage.)

George Annesley, in contrast to his father with the dicey reputation, was a distinguished author and world traveler. He wrote a four-volume travel history, *Voyages and Travels to India, Ceylon, the Red Sea, Abyssinia, and Egypt* (1809).

Lucy, Viscountess Annesley, died in 1783 after sixteen years of marriage; she was only thirty-six years old. Viscount Valentia remarried exactly seven months later, less than what some might consider the acceptable mourning period for one's spouse. (Mourning usually lasted a year.) His second wife was Sarah, the daughter of Sir Henry Cavendish, a baronet. Lord Valentia was thirty-nine and Sarah Cavendish was twenty, nineteen years younger than he was. Sarah gave him four more children, a son and three daughters. Only the daughters had issue. Sarah died in 1849, having outlived her husband by thirty-three years.

What concerns this story is the love affair between Lord Valentia and Grace Dalrymple Elliott. Was it merely lust on one or both sides? If it was Grace's introduction to sexual passion, to intense physical intimacy with a knowing and attractive man, it must have been overwhelming; her emotions had to have become engaged. For Valentia, however, it was probably the

Viscount Valentia's Lovely Daughters with Sarah Cavendish

The three girls (Catherine, Frances, and Juliana) were blond and beautiful. The prettiest, Frances Caroline (1793–1837), described by one source as a spoiled child, had married Lord Byron's good friend, the amusing but buffoonish and weak Sir James Wedderburn Webster. She may have had an affair with Byron in September 1813 when she was twenty and married only three years. The affair was supposedly suggested to Byron by his friend Lady Melbourne and took place when he visited the Wedderburn Websters at their home, Aston Hall, in Rotherham. He made a conquest of the young woman, but sources differ as to whether the attraction was consummated. He was, however, named godfather of a boy (who, some say,

The handsome and much-admired Lord Byron. (National Portrait Gallery, London)

Lady Frances Caroline Wedderburn Webster, stipple engraving, 1812, Robert Cooper after Arthur William Devis. (National Portrait Gallery, London)

may have been his) and Frances may or may not have inspired one of Byron's poems, "When We Two Parted." The poem was allegedly based on an affair Lady Frances was said to have had in 1815 with the Duke of Wellington. Lady Frances may also be the Ginevra of Byron's sonnets and the Medora of *The Corsair.* James and Frances Wedderburn Webster were a couple in whose personal affairs Byron was involved from time to time, and he was a generous friend. He lent them £500 on October 15, 1813, and the same amount on October 21, just a month after his visit to Aston Hall. This £1,000—as was the case with many of Byron's loans to friends—was never repaid.

same old game of the beast with two backs. In light of accounts published at the time, it's hard to believe he was emotionally involved:

> Lord V—— had hitherto proved the most tender and affectionate of husbands, and was pointed out for being most uncommonly uxorious. . . . However, his affections began to cool, and he diverted his thoughts by associating more with the world and less with his wife: as this indifference gradually increased, his lordship was now talked of for having formed some connections in the female world of a very intimate nature, and some women of rank were pointed at as the objects of his attention. These intrigues were . . . if not the effect of mere invention, carried on with such caution and address, that they for a long time produced no further proof than suspicion and calumny. ("Histories of the Tête-à-Têtes annexed, or Memoirs of L—— V—— and Mrs. E——t," The Town and Country Magazine, numbers 22 and 23, August 1774)

The gossipy series called the "Tête-à-Têtes" was the most popular feature of the eighteenth century's *Town and Country Magazine*, which was published by Archibald Hamilton Jr., to whom their concept was attributed. Archibald Hamilton Sr., his father, was the editor of the influential periodical the *Middlesex Journal and Evening Advertiser*. The "tête-à-têtes" were said to have been edited by a man named Beaufort, who held court at a coffee house near to where *The Town and Country Magazine* was printed, at St. John's Gate. Beaufort was said to have been aided and abetted by a mysterious Italian count named Caricoli or Carraccioli. (Cindy McCreery's essay "Keeping Up with the Bon Ton: The Tête-à-Têtes Series in *The Town and Country Magazine*" gives a good history of this tabloid phenomenon.)

Mrs. Elliott, from the tête-à-tête in *The Town and Country Magazine*, number 25. (British Library)

The features—there were to be 312 "tête-à-têtes" in total and they ceased publication after the August 1795 issue—were compiled from information sent in by what today would be called "stringers" and who were then termed "correspondents," and were of doubtful accuracy at best, not unlike what surfaces in today's gossip sheets. Some were probably revenge pieces, such as the one that purported to detail a love affair between Horace Walpole and the actress Kitty Clive, but was instead full of innuendo about Walpole's possible homosexuality.

Servants were also a likely source of information about their employees and may have been bribed by the correspondents. McCreery suggests in her essay that a number of the correspondents could have been women, who were protected by the anonymity of the series. As with today's scandal and gossip, these juicy articles were read avidly and discussed widely, not only in London but in the provinces.

The scandalous doings of the ton supplied more than enough fodder for the series. It was an editor's and printer's dream. The editors boasted that monthly sales exceeded eleven thousand copies and that—through shared copies—the readership was at least thirty thousand. (McCreery thinks a more reasonable estimate would be two to three thousand copies and a readership of almost five thousand, but all this is hard to prove.) Vis-à-vis engravings of a gentleman and his mistress normally illustrated the article, and these engravings were actually collected by readers, who cut them out and pasted them into albums, much as we would collect pictures into photo albums. (A vis-à-vis was also a kind of carriage in which the passengers faced each other.)

More aware readers noted the subtle body language between those depicted in the engravings. Were they smiling at each other and gazing fondly, eye to eye, or was one of them looking away, distracted, or, worse, frowning? There were all kinds of attitudes displayed that could be interpreted as clues to the relationship. In the engraving illustrating the piece on Grace and Lord Valentia, Grace is shown in profile looking at the Viscount, who is in full face, but ignoring her. Yes, that does say something!

In the *Matrimonial Magazine* article, there are no miniatures but there is a full-page engraving of Dr. Eliot coming upon the two lovers that's captioned, "The indiscretions of noble blood cured medicinally." (The later "tête-à-tête" of Grace and her next important lover, Lord Cholmondeley, has them both in three-quarter view, but while she is turned toward him, he is looking away from her. Again, clues to the relationship are given by the lack of communication implied.)

Political and personal satires often went hand in hand, as the line between politics and personal lives in the eighteenth

Lord Valentia, from the tête-à-tête in *The Town and Country Magazine*, number 26. (British Library)

century was at all times thinly drawn. Not so very different from today, when politicians' private lives are also fodder for the masses. McCreery asserts in her article:

> These three aspects of the tête-à-tête—its topicality, its appeal to both fashionable and middle-class elements of society, and its place within an ongoing commentary on gender roles and relations between the sexes—explain its remarkable success in the highly changeable world of gossip columns, and reflect eighteenth-century society's preoccupation with comparing individuals' private lives with their public characters.

The dearth of primary sources concerning these individuals forces one by default to rely more than one should on the gossip sheets and their dubious reporting. The 1774 "tête-à-tête" fills in the elusive character and physical appearance of Arthur Annesley, Lord Valentia, but "Caveat emptor" is not an empty caution to the reader. Lord Valentia was noted as having been born "with a lively fancy, and disposed to gaiety" and as "a young fellow of spirit" who was fond of "boyish pranks." These pranks were hardly admirable, for he was said to have "constantly fleeced his companions," though "his natural generosity induced him to let them partake of their spoils."

The Rambler's Magazine for August 1784 said of him, "No man tied a nosegay with more elegance. . . . No man made presents with more grace." He was said to grow into "a polite, elegant, well-bred man . . . favoured by

Grace Elliott (Miss Dalrymple) and Lord Cholmondeley, from the tête-à-tête in *The Town and Country Magazine*, numbers 34 and 35. (British Library)

Scandal 'Zines and Contemporary Plays

In *School for Scandal* (1777), the Irish playwright Richard Brinsley Sheridan has his character Snake rightly say of Mrs. Clackit, "Nay, I have more than once traced her causing a Tête-à-Tête in the *Town and Country Magazine,* when the Parties, perhaps, had never seen each other's Faces before in the course of their Lives" (act 1, scene 1). Sheridan, who was part of the Prince Regent's inner circle, knew whereof he spoke. In Oliver Goldsmith's *She Stoops to Conquer* (1773), the character Mrs. Hardcastle, who lives in the country, avows, "All I can do is enjoy London at second-hand. I take care to know every tête-à-tête from the *Scandalous Magazine*" (act 1, scene 2). In Hannah Cowley's comedy *The Belle's Stratagem* (1782), a character named Crowquil is introduced as a writer of tête-à-têtes in the magazines. A servant exclaims, "Oh, oh, what! you are the fellow that has folks nose to nose in your sixpenny cuts, that never met anywhere else" (act 1, scene 2).

the Graces" in looks, while his "athletic form and an agreeable countenance" made him "greatly admired by the ladies." He evolved into a typical gallant of the period. (Observe how many times the word "grace" is slyly and artfully employed by these writers.) The 1774 "tête-à-tête" piece notes, however:

> *We do not . . . find at this time any celebrated toasts upon the list of his gallantries. Some demi-reps of an inferior class, and a few kept mistresses of impotent noblemen, fill up the chasm at this period. His ambition, probably, led him to aim at an elevated alliance in the connubial state. Had his amours been too notorious, they might have been an obstacle to the execution of this part of his plan.*

Valentia had set his sights on Lord Lyttelton's plain but well-dowered daughter Lucy. Lyttelton could help him try to get the titles that had eluded his branch of the family, and Lucy was an heiress whose dowry could go a long way toward enriching his coffers. (There was a reference in the August 1784 *Rambler's Magazine* that said he'd broken an engagement to Lord Cholmondeley's sister Hester—who married William Clapcote Lisle in 1773—a comment that is nowhere else substantiated and that is of doubtful veracity.) Valentia didn't succeed in getting the title, perhaps because his powerful father-in-law was blocked by other powerful men who were his adversaries in the House of Lords, but he did get the faithful, dowered Lucy. Boredom, however, soon set in.

At this time the beautiful Grace Elliott was also becoming extremely bored with her dull husband. From a young woman who'd made an advantageous match and was widely—and enviously—thought to be "one of the happiest women in the metropolis," she'd suddenly become "peevish and fretful whenever in his [Dr. Eliot's] company [though] at other times she was the soul of mirth and gaiety."

Grace and Valentia may have met through Dr. Eliot. The 1784 piece claimed that the acquaintanceship came about through "the little writer of prescription" having paid house calls on Lord Valentia's family (was there no one in London who was *not* a patient of this workaholic Scotsman, this "son of Esculapius"?):

> *Dr. E——t having been consulted as a physician by some relations of Lord V——'s lady, and intimacy subsisting between their relations and the Doctor, the noble Viscount became acquainted with Mrs. E——t, in his visits to that family.*

The doctor soon became suspicious of his young wife's behavior and set servants and other paid minions to spy on her movements, among them the woman who made her dresses, her mantua maker, and the one who made her hats, her milliner.

According to the writer of this "tête-à-tête":

> *Dr. E——t's suspicions were not groundless: she had made a very particular acquaintance, and our*

The sedan chair first appeared for hire in 1634 London. The chairs were much cheaper than hackney coaches and also had the advantage of being carried directly into a dwelling. Like today's taxicab drivers, sedan chairmen were licensed by the city and had to display an identifying number. This lady, after a busy night out, is much the worse for it. (Print titled *Return from the Masquerade*, circa 1800, from Museum of London)

hero was this happy man. It is well known that a *Bagnio . . . is certainly the most secret place to carry on an intrigue. . . . [Lord Valentia] resolved that different bagnios should be places of their rendezvous, taking them successively round in turns. . . . Mrs. E——t always took a coach from her manua-maker's or milliner's, from thence to the playhouse, where she passed through the pit avenue, and then took a chair [sedan chair] to the place of destination. By this means all pursuit was evaded, and the same kind of caution was used upon her return.*

Irony of ironies, according to this imaginative writer, but who did the lovers run into but the good doctor himself, at the very same bagnio, or bawdy house, on an assignation with "his favourite milliner," a "Mrs. G——"! And here— even if it is not true, it is delicious—we have a scene worthy of a Feydeau farce, with people in the wrong rooms encountering those they never expected to meet:

The "Oracular Demonstration." Lord Valentia and Grace discovered by Dr. Eliot at the bagnio. (*The Matrimonial Magazine*, February 1775) (British Library)

[Dr.]Eliot was by accident shewn into the apartment where his wife was waiting for our hero. What was his astonishment and rage, may be better conceived than expressed. Lord V—— was almost at the same instant introduced to Mrs. G——. This lady's prudence taught her not to expose herself, and whilst the doctor was conducting his wife home in a coach, and upbraiding her all the way with the keenest and bitterest reproaches, our hero, like a man of true gallantry, supplied the doctor's place, as he had done often before, and was not displeased with the agreeable variety the mistake afforded him.

The writer—for who knows if this scenario ever actually took place, as the divorce papers painted another picture altogether of how the adulterous pair was discovered—describes the sprouting of poor Eliot's horns shortly before the truth was revealed:

Amongst a myriad of admirers was the Lord V——, for she [Grace] was the meteor of the Park, the Play-house, and Pantheon; and though the generosity of the Doctor might not suffer him to be suspicious, yet all saw plainly, what he perhaps did not wish to discover. The intrigue was palpable, and the friends of the easy Doctor shewed him the very disgrace of his forehead, which at length, from believing he saw them, he confessed he felt them. And now that perturbation of mind, which harrows up the foul, raged violently. . . . He was frantick with her ungenerous conduct and mad to be revenged.

And now, the "ocular demonstration" as he comes upon them in the flesh:

A little while soon gave him every ocular demonstration of his misfortune; it was but watching a favourite moment (and of them there were many) to detect this runaway wanton; and, to his unspeakable mortification, he surprised them on a couch, in those lullaby attitudes into which violent desires plunge violent lovers. The amorous lord supported the detection with ease and pleasantry, made a fashionable bow, wished the Doctor a good morning, and withdrew.

The Matrimonial Magazine for February 1775 was published while Grace and Dr. Eliot were separated, as he was pursuing his divorce action through the several courts involved. The engraving of Lord Valentia caught "in delicto," if not altogether "in flagrante delicto," down on one knee ardently kissing the hand of a rather primly depicted mobcapped Grace sitting on a couch, as the cuckolded Dr. Eliot, a shocked look on his face, burst through the door, added fuel and public sympathy to the good doctor's case, while reinforcing his impotency and humiliation. Truly a double-edged sword, this tabloid publicity.

And one has to admire—albeit grudgingly—Lord Valentia's aplomb. He is one cool customer. Obviously this hardened gallant has done this before. "Lullaby attitudes"! Could one just die from descriptions like this? The journalist continues with his supposed eyewitness report of the event:

The fallen fair one, with tears streaming down her rosy cheeks, was handed to her carriage and remitted to the country, where she continued about nine months; and now she hath once more broke her teather, [sic] and is galloping like a fine brood-mare, the wonder of the turf and the wanton world.

This is priceless stuff. The image of Grace as a spirited mare racing down the turf to continue her wanton activities is colorful indeed. Note, too, the reference to residing in the country for nine months—the length of an average pregnancy—and the description of her as a "brood-mare." The divorce papers stated that there was one child—who died—of the marriage of Dr.

The Harleian Miscellany

The Harleian MSS was a collection of rare, curious, and entertaining pamphlets, broadsides, and tracts, in manuscript and print, interspersed with critical and historical notes, that were found in the library of Edward Harley (1689–1741), the second Earl of Oxford, at his death and placed in the British Museum. A selection of the materials, edited by Harley's secretary, William Oldys, and Samuel Johnson, was published under the title *The Harleian Miscellany* in 1744–1746. A little bit of this, a little bit of that—one can see how the Georgian wits seized on this miscellaneous grouping of materials to describe the multi-sired children of Lady Harley.

Eliot and Grace Dalrymple, but this was very early on. Was there another, a possible love child of the Valentia indiscretion?

Grace's biographer Bleackley alluded to her as "Dally the Prolific" but produced no documentation for the allegation, so we shall never know. (There was also an allegation later on—in the early days of Grace's liaison with her lover Lord Cholmondeley—that she was expecting a child, but that story seemed to drop through one of the many cracks that yawned wide in Grace's life. And, too, it could have been idle gossip.)

It took several years for Dr. Eliot to rid himself of his troublesome young bride. His great fear was that she would produce an heir who could lay claim to his growing fortune. Although there was a stated separation of bedrooms, any child born to a married couple was the husband's child, no matter what the truth of its conception might have been. Lady Harley, the Countess of Oxford, had dallied with so many lovers that her numerous offspring were referred to as "the Harleian Miscellany." Lord Harley, the Earl of Oxford, accepted them all. He had to. So, one can clearly appreciate Dr. Eliot's fear; it had serious legal ramifications.

It took three courts and as many years and an unspecified (but be assured it was large) amount of money before the divorce was granted by the last court to weigh in, the House of Lords. The marriage had lasted—on paper—for less than five years. The separation was longer than the actual marriage.

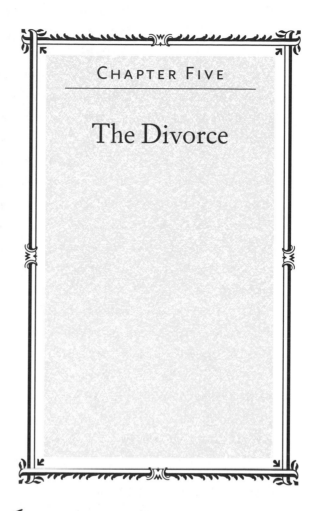

CHAPTER FIVE

The Divorce

After the initial papers were filed in 1774 and the case had gone through courts ecclesiastical (Consistory Court of the Bishop of London), for legal separation, and civil (King's Bench, Westminster), for "crim. con." damages, the final papers seeking a divorce by Dr. John Eliot from his wife Grace were presented to Parliament in 1776 in the form of a private bill.

The entire procedure from beginning to end took almost two years. This is the full and remarkable document of the divorce action that was filed with the House of Lords:

Humbly Sheweth and Complaineth to your most Excellent Majesty Your

True and faithful Subject John Eliot of the parish of Saint Clement Danes in the County of Middlesex Doctor in Physic,———

That on or about the Nineteenth day of October in the Year of our Lord One thousand seven hundred and Seventy one Your said Subject did Intermarry with Grace Dalrymple Spinster one of the Daughters of Hugh Dalrymple late of the parish of Saint Pancras in the said County of Middlesex Esquire Deceased,———

That the said Grace the Wife of your said Subject did in the Year One thousand seven hundred and Seventy four enter into and Carry on an unlawful Familiarity and Adulterous Conversation with Sir Arthur Annesley Baronet Lord Viscount Valentia in the Kingdom of Ireland and your said Subject hath not since the Discovery thereof which was in or about the Month of April in the same Year Cohabited nor had any intercourse or Communication with her the said Grace,———

That your said Subject did in or about Trinity Term [one of the four terms of the courts; refers to late spring/early summer term] in the said Year One thousand seven hundred and Seventy four bring his action in your Majestys Court of Kings Bench at Westminister against the said Sir Arthur Annesley Lord Viscount Valentia for such Criminal Conversation with the said Grace your Subjects said Wife and in Michaelmas Term [Michaelmas Term is in the autumn.] *following obtained Judgment against him therein.*

That your said Subject Exhibited a Libel in the Consistory Court of the Bishop

of London against the said Grace and did on or about the Twenty Third day of February One thousand seven hundred and Seventy Six obtain a Definitive Sentence of Divorce from Bed Board and Mutual Cohabitation against the said Grace for Adultery committed by her with the said Sir Arthur Annesley Lord Viscount Valentia.

King's Bench Walk, its name taken from the original 1621 site of the King's Bench Court at the Inner Temple, London. (Photo by Simon Tibbs)

"Criminal Conversation," the So-Very-English Civil Tort Familiarly Referred to as "Crim. Con."

"Criminal conversation" was the name of a civil action dating from late seventeenth-century England that a husband could take against a man who had seduced his wife. It was basically an accusation of adultery—the sexual intercourse of a married person with someone other than his or her spouse—though "crim. con." could be interpreted so as to embrace a range of interactions up to, but not including, the physical act.

Lawrence Stone's seminal work on the subject of judicial separation and divorce, *Broken Lives: Separation and Divorce in England, 1660–1857,* states that this action was basically "a writ of trespass, the theory being that, by using the body of the wife, the seducer had damaged the property of her husband, for which he could sue for damages. . . . The common law was empowered to award financial damages not merely for economic losses but also for emotional pain and suffering."

Was it "criminal" in the sense we know an action to be criminal today? Not really, as it was a civil action. Could it be termed an actual "conversation"? Conversation between two persons no doubt initiated the interaction or adultery, but it had to escalate swiftly into something else to cause a husband to sue for judicial separation or divorce. As mentioned above, it did not always get as far as actual sexual intercourse. (This was probably so in the case involving the Countess of Elgin and Robert Ferguson, which turned primarily on indiscreet correspondence,

specifically a very warm letter she sent to him. In that case, the circumstances were closer to alienation of affection than to actual adultery.)

The terms are odd, as legal terms often are to the layperson. Giving the injured party the option of suing for monetary damages did away with the resort to dueling, an illegal but common way to settle and avenge matters of honor between men. Thus it was a step up to more civilized social behavior than shooting at someone or slashing away at him with a sword, but it does have the ugly stench to modern observers of the treatment of a wife as chattel, mere property, upon whose person monetary damages can be assessed. It's unpleasant, but the inescapable fact in those times was that a wife's body did belong to her husband, not to her. A wife had no separate identity—legally—apart from her husband, and unless independently wealthy herself and buttressed by trust funds from her family, she had no funds or property of her own.

Two-thirds of all divorce actions before 1750 and one-third before 1780 make no reference at all to crim. con., but after 1780 it is rare for any divorce action not to make reference to it. Under this new kind of tort, a wronged husband could sue his wife's seducer for substantial sums in damages in one of the major civil common-law courts, such as Westminster Hall, King's Bench, or Common Pleas.

Three separate legal actions had to be undertaken to secure a divorce. The ecclesiastical court handled the separation from the adulterous wife; the common-law court decided the damages for crim. con.; but only Parliament could legally grant a full divorce.

Lawyers from the London Diocesan Consistory Court, popularly known as Doctors' Commons, were advocates who specialized in civil and canon law. (England, remember, had a state religion and an established church.) These lawyers were scrupulous in demanding detailed evidence that included the questioning of witnesses ("interrogatories") and the taking of depositions (by "Examiners" or court officials) from them. "Proctors" (lawyers) acted for each side.

The husband could then choose to secure either a legal separation or a full divorce; it was his prerogative, but proving crim. con. was often the precondition for a divorce by petition to Parliament, in the form of a "private bill" that was introduced in the House of Lords. Witnesses had to appear before a committee of the House and further depositions had to be taken; the bill then went through the House of Commons—there were at least two readings of the bill—before royal assent could be obtained and the marriage ended.

Not only were these proceedings time-consuming, expensive, messy, and unpleasant for the principals, but the matter did not end there. The sensational goings-on went public as London printers scrambled to publish them for sale throughout the kingdom.

The best-selling transcript of the trial of the notorious Lady Worsley, in the crim. con. action brought by her husband against her seducer, went through seven printings in its first year of issue.

Although divorces rose sharply in England during the latter part of the eighteenth century, only the wealthy, which for the most part meant the aristocracy, could afford to pursue them. As Stone remarks in *Broken Lives:*

> The cost of prosecuting a crim. con. suit, especially a contested one, were such as to put it out of reach of any but the landed elite and the upper levels of the middling sort. In conse-

Work for Doctors'-Commons, an etching after the design by Thomas Rowlandson (1792). (Lewis Walpole Library, Yale University)

quence the plaintiffs in these suits were all rich men, though the defendants might range from duke to stable boy. The number of cases and the amount of damages both rose sharply in the 1790s . . . [juries awarded] damages not merely in reparation to the husband for mental suffering and loss of companionship, but also of sufficient size to set an example to the nation, and act as a deterrent to future adulterers. He thus transformed a civil suit into a semi-criminal one in a manner which was quite illegal. As a result . . . damages [ran] to thousands of pounds. Some awards were for £10,000, £20,000, and occasionally £25,000. Damages so far beyond the capacity of the defendant to pay meant, in practice, the condemnation of the latter to a life in prison for debt unless the plaintiff chose to free him.

Could these incredibly large sums ever be collected? Robert Ferguson, assessed £20,000 for his dalliance with the Countess of Elgin, had no money of his own. The charge was reduced by half, and his wealthy father was thought to have paid it for him. Viscount Bolingbroke asked for the relatively paltry sum of £500 plus court costs from Topham Beauclerk, his wife Lady Diana's seducer. Arthur Annesley, Lord Valentia, Grace Elliott's seducer, was fined damages of £12,000. But something interesting evolved, a tricky little subterfuge indeed. According to Stone, the damages were paid, then returned, a collusion of parties that made it easier "to win an uncontested crim. con. suit, and to use the victory to obtain an uncontested Parliamentary divorce, thus [leaving] all three parties free to remarry."

It was a conspiracy as well as a way to save a bit of aristocratic face. Owning up to the public fact that one had been cuckolded was not pleasant for the husband—Dr. John Eliot may never have gotten over the humiliation—but the bad publicity was not good for any of the parties involved. The wife lost her reputation and perhaps her ability to remarry: sometimes she was specifically forbidden to marry her seducer, but in any case to remarry was unlawful unless the offending spouse was granted the privilege of remarrying and that privilege was written into the divorce action. (This restriction was often ignored by the parties concerned.) The seducer was acknowledged as a gazetted rake and brought dishonor upon his own family, and his wife and children, if he had them.

The English Law Commission Working Paper No. 9, completed for publication on December 8, 1978, noted that the "common law action for criminal conversation was abolished in England in 1857. In its place a husband was given the right to claim damages against a person who committed adultery with his wife." The law in England was thus more in line with what had always been the situation in Scotland. In *Alienated Affections: The Scottish Experience of Divorce and Separation, 1684–1830,* author Leah Leneman comments, "Although there was no such thing as 'criminal conversation' in Scottish law, a husband could nevertheless sue a 'seducer' for damages." The peculiar concept of criminal conversation was unique, in a class by itself, and a subject of ridicule on the Continent. The worldly, sophisticated French called such actions *le dessous de la pudibonderie anglaise* (the underside of English prudishness).

That your said Subject hath not any Issue living by the said Grace his now Wife.

That as your said Subjects said Wife hath by her Adulterous behaviour dissolved the Bond of Marriage on her part and your said Subject stands deprived of the Comforts of Matrimony and is liable to have a Spurious Issue imposed upon him to Succeed to his Estate an Fortune unless the said Marriage be declared Void and Annulled by Authority of Parliament,——

May it therefore Please your most Excellent Majesty (out of your Princely Goodness and in Compassion to your said Subjects Misfortune and Calamity) That it may be Enacted and be it Enacted by the Kings most Excellent Majesty by and with the Advice and Consent of the Lords Spiritual and Temporal and [words illegible in original] Commons in this present Parliament assembled and by the Authority of the same That the said Bond of Matrimony between the said John Eliot and the said Grace his Wife being Violated and broken by the Manifest and open Adultery of the said Grace be and is hereby from henceforth wholly dissolved annulled Vacated and made void to all Intents Constructions and Purposes whatsoever and that it shall and may be lawful to and for the said John Eliot at any time or times hereafter to Contract Matrimony and to Marry (as well in the life time of the said Grace as if she was actually Dead) with any other woman or women he might lawfully Marry in Case the said Grace was not living and that such Matrimony when duly had and Celebrated shall be a good just and lawful Marriage and Marriages and so shall be adjudged Deemed and taken in all Courts and to all Intents Construction and Purposes whatsoever and that all an every Child and Children born in such Matrimony shall be deemed Adjudged and taken to be born in lawful Wedlock and shall be legitimate and inheritable to and shall Inherit all the Lands Tenements and Hereditaments of the said John Eliot and all other Lands Tenements and Hereditaments from and by their Fathers Mothers and other Ancestors and Relations in like manner and form as any other Child or Children born in lawful Matrimony should could or might Inherit or be Inheritable unto according to the Course of Inheritance used in this Realm or in any of his Majestys Do-

{Tort. Damage, injury, or a wrongful act done willfully, negligently, or in circumstances involving strict liability, but not involving breach of contract, for which a civil suit and action for damages can be brought. From M.L. *tortum*, from L. *tortus*, twisted.}

{Alienation of Affection. A tort based on willful and malicious interference with the marriage relation by a third party without justification or excuse.}

minions thereunto belonging and to have and Enjoy all Priviledges, Preem-
inces, Benefits, Advantages Claims and Demands in as full ample and benefi-
cial manner as any other Child or Children born in lawful Wedlock may have,
or claim by the Laws Usages and Customs of this Realm or any of his
Majestys Dominions thereunto belonging,——

And be it further Enacted that the said John Eliot shall be entitled to be
Tenant by the Curtesy of the Lands Hereditaments and Inheritance of said
Wife or Wives as he shall so hereafter Marry and that such Wife or Wives
shall unless barred by a Jointure or otherwise be entitled to Dower and Thirds
of the Common Law or by Custom of and in the Lands Tenements and Hereditaments whereof the said John Eliot shall be Seized of such Estate whereof
she or they shall be Dowable as any other Husband or Wife respectively may
or might Claim have or enjoy and that the Child or Children born in such Marriage and Marriages shall and may derive and make Title by Descent or otherwise to and from any of their Ancestors as any other Child or Children born in
lawful Wedlock may do, any Law Statute Restraint Prohibition Ordinance
Canon Constitution Prescription Usage or Custom had made Executed or used
to the Contrary in any wise notwithstanding,——

And be it further Enacted and Declared by the Authority aforesaid That all
an every Child and Children as well Male as Female (if any there be) which
at any time since the first day of May One thousand seven hundred and seventy five have or hath been born or that may or shall at any time hereafter be
born of the Body of the said Grace are and shall be Deemed a Bastard or Bastards and a Spurious Issue and not be the lawful Issue of the said John Eliot on
the Body of the said Grace begotten and that no Child or Children which hereafter shall be born of the Body of the said Grace [words illegible in original]
shall be deemed taken or Reputed to be the lawful Issue of the said John Eliot
on the Body of the said Grace begotten or Inheritable to any Messuages Lands
Tenements or Hereditaments of the said John Eliot or any of his Ancestors or
Relations by Virtue of the said Marriage of the said John Eliot with the said
Grace.

And be it further Enacted by the Authority aforesaid That the said Grace
shall be and is hereby barred and excluded of and from all Dower [widow's
rights] and Thirds and of and from all Right and Title of Dower and Thirds
at the Common Law by Custom or otherwise and all other claim and demand

in to or out of the Lands Tenements or Hereditaments whereof or wherein the said John Eliot now is or at any time hereafter shall be Seized of or for any Estate of Inheritance and that all such Dower Right and Title of Dower shall from henceforth cease determine and be utterly void and of no Effect and shall be and be taken and construed to be as if the said Grace was actually Dead without Issue of her Body.

Provided always that nothing in this Act contained shall Extend or be Construed to Extend to Vacate or Destroy provision made for the Maintenance Suport and benefit of the said Grace since the obtaining the said Definitive Sentence of Divorce.

Note the very great concern expressed that the divorced wife and/or any "Spurious Issue" of her body would have a claim on lands, inheritances, or other properties of the husband or of his family. It is firmly stated that cohabitation between Grace and Dr. Eliot ceased in April 1774. The document goes on ad infinitum about this "Issue of her Body"; it's clear this is a major fear of the good doctor of physic, that a child of Grace and Lord Valentia's could inherit Eliot's fortune, future inheritances (such as a title), and properties. Eliot must have been relieved that Grace bore no child in 1774, but he was still married to her. Church courts could grant a legal separation, but until the divorce was finalized, any children born to Grace Elliott were Dr. Eliot's. That must have driven him insane!

Again he must have been relieved that no bastards were born in 1775, or in 1776, but time was a-wasting. The divorce had to be approved by Parliament and signed off on by King George III. The other big concern expressed in the divorce papers was that John Eliot be allowed to remarry. The Church courts could make no provision for the possibility of remarriage; as Mary Abbott explains in *Family Ties,* only Parliament could do so:

Church courts had the power to grant legal separations but, unlike most churches which broke with Rome, the Church of England made no provision for divorce with the possibility of remarriage. Until the nineteenth century a private Act of Parliament was the only proper method of dissolving a consummated marriage. . . . Parliamentary divorce was disgraceful, difficult and expensive. . . . Although it became commoner in the eighteenth century, divorce was normally undertaken to prevent an inheritance passing to a child conceived in adultery. When inheritance was not in question, a civil action for damages [that odd English legality called "criminal conversation," or "crim. con.," for which see the sidebar on pages 83–85] could be brought to salve the pride of the outraged husband. In some circles, discreet infidelity, which did not threaten the legitimate succession [i.e., there were already "an heir and a spare"] was condoned.

The divorce bill could be so worded that the wife would be prohibited from marrying her seducer, or from remarrying at all. That was not the case in this action of Dr. Eliot's, but he made sure—or his lawyers did—that *he* would be allowed to marry as if his wife was actually dead and he was a widower. There is much repetition of these points: that he be allowed to remarry (with the provision spelled out more than once!); that his holdings, properties, and fortune be kept out of Grace's hands and those of any "Spurious Issue"; and that she not be allowed to claim a dower—the common, or widow's, portion of a third of his estate—after his death.

An amendment to the divorce bill ensured that Grace would get her due—an annuity that would support her—from Eliot. This is the full text of that amendment:

> *Amendment to Dr. Eliot's Divorce Bill. . . . Leave out from the Word (to) to the End of the Bill and instead thereof invert (annual vacate or destroy) a certain Bond or Obligation bearing date the 18th day of March 1776 whereby the said John Eliot became bound to the Right Honourable Charles Earl of Peterborough and Monmouth and Stephen Lushington of Henrietta Street in the Parish of Saint Paul Covent Garden in the County of Middlesex Esquire (Trustees Nominated by and on behalf of the said Grace) in the Penal Sum of Five thousand Pounds of lawful Money of Great Britain Conditioned for the Payment of One Annuity or Yearly Sum of Two hundred Pounds of like lawful Money for and during the natural Life of the said Grace by Quarterly Payments clear of all deductions for the Support and Maintenance of the said Grace in manner therein mentioned.)*

It's stated that Grace Elliott nominated two men to act as her trustees: the Earl of Peterborough and Monmouth (this was Charles Mordaunt, fifth Earl of Peterborough and third Earl of Monmouth [1758–1814]) and Stephen Lushington [1744–1807]. Lushington was to become Sir Stephen Lushington upon being made a baronet in 1791; he'd had a long and distinguished mercantile career in London as director and then chairman of the East India Company from 1782 through 1805.

One wonders how this transpired, but no more information is forthcoming, though it's interesting to note that Peterborough was said by Frances, Lady Shelley, in her *Diary*, to have been a "first cousin" of her mother, Grace's sister Jacintha. That doesn't seem possible, but the important thing is that they asked for that £200 yearly allowance, which Grace needed for her support.

The irony here is that Dr. Eliot, so aggressive in pushing his right to remarry, never did remarry—he was to live for ten more years after the divorce bill passed, dying in 1786—and that he never sired any legitimate children. Four children, however, surfaced by name in his will, one son and three daughters by four different women (only the son's mother was not identified, so possibly she was deceased). And those titles he so very much desired to pass on to his heirs—he received two titles, one of which was inheritable—died with him.

There had apparently been a glitch when Dr. Eliot applied to Doctors' Commons, the ecclesiastical court, for legal separation, and there was some holdup of the proceedings. According to the February 1775 article in *The Matrimonial Magazine:*

> [Dr. Eliot] applied to the profound sages of Doctors' Commons, and the affair was a few days since brought to a hearing; when alas! the judge was of the opinion that the evidence produced was not sufficient to procure a divorce, so that the son of Esculapius, like many other worthy gentlemen, is obliged, against his will, to retain his spouse.

The account of the action (dated February 26, 1776) in the *Journals of the House of Lords* for the year 1776, page 566, is presented in a much less sensational manner. The record shows:

> Upon reading the Petition of John Eliot Doctor in Physick; setting forth, "That the Petitioner intended to have presented a Petition to their Lordships for Leave to bring in a Bill to dissolve his Marriage, and to enable him to marry again, within the Time limited by their Lordships Order for receiving Petitions for Private Bills; but the Petitioner was not able to procure a Sentence

of Divorce in the Ecclesiastical Court till Friday last"; and therefore praying
their Lordships, "That he may be at Liberty to present a Petition for the Pur-
pose aforesaid, notwithstanding the Time limited for receiving Petitions is ex-
pired."

It is ORDERED, That the Petitioner be at Liberty to present his said Peti-
tion, as desired.

Accordingly, Upon reading the Petition of John Eliot Doctor in Physick;
praying Leave to bring in a Bill to dissolve his Marriage with Grace his now
Wife, and to enable him to marry again; and for other Purposes therein men-
tioned:

It is ORDERED, That Leave be given to bring in a Bill, according to the
Prayer of the said Petition.

One can be sure that Eliot's influential friends at court—whose wives and
mistresses he counted among the many patients in his flourishing medical
practice—gave their attention to this matter and took every opportunity to
push it along, for it did soon proceed to Parliament, where witnesses would
by examined in the House of Lords. The papers would have at least two or
three readings, would be sent to committee, and, if all was well, would come
unchanged and approved out of committee and then go straight to the
King—as ruler of England and head of the Anglican Church—for the royal
approval and signature. Note that the initial steps were taken in the spring of
1774, the procedure went through all of 1775, and the papers were approved
by the civil and ecclesiastical courts by late February 1776.

On page 570 of the *Journals*, the matter is again taken up:

The Lord Cathcart presented to the House (pursuant to an Order of Leave
of the 26th of this instant February) a Bill, intituled, "An Act to dissolve the
Marriage of John Eliot Doctor in Physick with Grace Dalrymple his now
Wife; and to enable him to marry again; and for other Purposes therein men-
tioned."

The said Bill was read the First Time.

ORDERED, That the said Bill be read a Second Time on Friday the 15th
Day of March next; and that Notice thereof be affixed on the Doors of this
House, and the Lords summoned; and that the said John Eliot may be heard,
by his Counsel, at the said Second Reading, to make out the Truth of the Alle-

gations of the Bill; and that the said Grace Dalrymple may have a Copy of the Bill; and that Notice be given her of the said Second Recording; and that she be at Liberty to be heard, by her Counsel, what she may have to offer against the said Bill at the same Time.

On this occasion it's noted that Grace has a lawyer and that she is entitled to a copy of the bill for the divorce action, but she evidently does not have leave to appear before the House to give her testimony; her counsel is apparently the intermediary. And now comes the nitty-gritty, the appearance of witnesses for Dr. Eliot and against Grace. From page 576 of the *Journals:*

ORDERED, That William Constable, Sarah Constable, Charles Ryder, Thomas Sneed, Jane Price, Sarah Race, Richard Cosway, John Crawford, John Hayward, and John Bolton, do attend this House on Friday the 15th Day of this instant March, in order to their being examined as Witnesses upon the Second Reading of the Bill, intituled, "An Act to dissolve the Marriage of John Eliot Doctor in Physick, with Grace Dalrymple his now Wife, and to enable him to marry again; and for other Purposes therein mentioned."

On page 587 of the *Journals*, cutting closer to the chase:

ORDERED, That the Counsel be called in at One o'Clock on Friday next, upon the Second Reading of the Bill, intituled, "An Act to dissolve the Marriage of John Eliot Doctor in Physick, with Grace Dalrymple his now Wife, and to enable him to marry again; and for other Purposes mentioned."

It's now *"Dies Veneris, 15 Martii 1776"* (Latin for Friday, the time is 1 P.M., March 15, 1776) in the House of Lords, as per the *Journals,* pages 594–596. Present are the Duke of Manchester; the Duke of Chandos; the Lords Suffolk, Denbigh, Sandwich, Abercorn, Galloway, Dalhousie, Marchmont, Aylesford, Fauconberg, and Northington; and Viscounts Townshend, Falmouth, Dudley, and Ward, among other notables. Prayers are said. It begins (Drumroll, please!):

The Order of the Day being read for the Second Reading of the Bill, intituled, "An Act to dissolve the Marriage of John Eliot Doctor in Physick, with Grace Dalrymple his now Wife, and to enable him to marry again; and for other Purposes therein mentioned"; and for hearing Counsel for and against the same; and for the Lords to be summoned.

Counsel were accordingly called in; and Mr. Macdonald [a good Scots name!] appearing as Counsel for the Bill; but no Counsel appearing against it

[Poor Grace! What happened to her lawyer? Is she going to pull a noli contendere, i.e., not contest it? Can she contest it?] . . .

The first witness, a John Acton, who appears to have been a process server or Eliot's attorney's factotum, is brought in:

[Acton] being sworn, acquainted the House, "That he served Mrs. Eliot, on the 7th of March last, personally . . . [and] delivered to her a true Copy of the Bill."

He was directed to withdraw.

Then the said Bill was read the Second Time.

And Mr. Macdonald was heard in Support of the Bill, and to make out the Allegations thereof; and, in order to prove the Marriage, called Richard Minshull; who, being sworn, produced an Extract from the Register of Marriages of the Parish Church of Saint Pancras, in the County of Middlesex; and declaring "that the same was a true Copy, he having examined it with Original." The same was read; whereby it appeared that Doctor Eliot and Grace Dalrymple were married at the said Parish Church, on the 19th of October 1771.

He was directed to withdraw.

Then John Acton was again called in; and produced an Office Copy of the Judgement obtained in the Court of King's Bench against the Right Honourable Lord Viscount Valentia, in the Kingdom of Ireland, for Criminal Conversation with the said Mrs. Eliot.

He was directed to withdraw.

Then John Grene Principal Register of the Consistory Court of the Bishop of London, was called in; and, being sworn, produced the original Definitive Sentence of Divorce in the said Court, against the said Mrs. Eliot, for Adultery.

We're getting there.

The servants are finally brought in, and their testimony is devastating.

Servant eyewitness reports are always problematic. Reading eyewitness testimony from servants who were paid to spy on their employer's errant wife in divorce cases is unsavory as well as repetitious. Moreover, they are testifying for their employer, the person who pays their wages. Good jobs were hard to come by in the eighteenth century, and servants needed references to get these jobs. Guess who it is they are going to want to please.

The descriptions of secret rendezvous locations, disordered and discarded clothing, rumpled sheets, sounds of lovemaking, and meaningful glances between the purported lovers suggest the pornographic prints of Rowlandson working on overstimulated imaginations. It is easy to read between the lines as dismissed or resentful servants get even with their employers, while loyal retainers, faithful to the end, swear that they saw nothing. How could anyone believe that what these people professed—so often in total contradiction with one another—was the truth?

Meanwhile, Grace's actions are laid bare for the House of Lords, several members of which she's had to have met socially. It's embarrassing, and it could not be more of a public spectacle. (Crim. con. was not abolished in England until the early reign of Queen Victoria, with the passing of the Matrimonial Causes Act of 1857.)

William Constable is the first servant called in to give testimony. He describes Grace calling a carriage—not using her own—to "pay a Visit . . . to a Lady in Spring Gardens." He kept an eye on the vehicle, "which drove down the Strand, opposite to Craven Street, and then went up Saint Martin's Lane. . . . Mrs. Eliot got out of the Coach opposite to Maiden Lane, walked down Bulleyn Court, into the Strand, where she got into another Coach."

In that other coach was none other than Lord Valentia, "whom he, the Witness, personally knows . . . This Second Coach drove a very round-about Way to Berkeley Row [the street is given in the witnesses' testimony both as Berkeley Row and Berkeley Street], and stopped at the Door of a Mrs. Price, in that Street." The couple got out of the carriage and went into Mrs. Price's; Constable tore back in a hurry "to acquaint Doctor Eliot with what he had seen, having left another Person [another servant] there to watch them."

From the tactics used by Grace and Lord Valentia, instructing the coachman to drive "a very round-about Way," it appears that they might have been concerned that they were being followed, or that this was Valentia's modus operandi when seducing other men's wives.

The person set to watch at Mrs. Price's door is identified as the servant Charles Ryder, who states:

> That they got there about Nine o'Clock in the Evening: That he waited till they came out . . . which was about Half an Hour past Eleven o'Clock: That they went into a Coach, and drove to Charing Cross, where the Coachman

stopped; and, having received Directions, returned, by a very round-about Way, to Mrs. Price's, where he left them, being very tired with following the Coach, never having lost Sight of it."

Well, it's established that Lord Valentia is not a slam-bam-thank-you-ma'am kind of guy; he apparently took his time. An assignation lasting from nine to eleven is going at a nice, leisurely, satisfying pace. The notorious Mrs. Price was a procuress, or madam, and her home a bagnio; the area described was a well-known one near the St. James's district of ill-repute where this sort of traffic had existed for a long time. For a fee, the operator of the bagnio let rooms to married women meeting their lovers. For a fee, this procuress could testify against Grace for her husband Dr. Eliot. It was the least she could do, and no doubt one of the many things the woman was capable of doing with little prompting. (Waving a few quid around in a bawdy house gets a lot of attention.)

In the testimony given that afternoon in the House of Lords, a servant of Dr. Eliot's named John Bolton is asked "what sort of a House Mrs. Price's was," and he states that "it was looked upon by the Neighbours as an House for the Reception of Ladies and Gentlemen for Gallantry." Bolton is followed by another servant, named Richard Cosway, who confirms the information Bolton gave.

Dr. Eliot is nothing if not thorough. The next witness called is that same procuress, Mrs. Price, full name Jane Price, who testifies:

[That] she lived in Berkeley Street in April 1774; That she knows Lord Valentia; That she saw him at her House in the Beginning of April 1774; That he had been at her House Twice with a Female; That the First Time they supped together in the Parlour; That the Second Time they supped in a Bed Room opposite the Dining Room; That they were together for Two Hours the last Time, and went away between Eleven and Twelve o'clock in an Hackney Coach; That the Lady returned, and said, "she was much frightened, having been watched"; That Lord Valentia returned in Five Minutes after the Lady, who then went away in a Chair.

William Constable, that spying servant, continues the narrative, testifying:

That Mrs. Eliot returned home that Night in a Chair; That the Chairman said, "they were paid," which was not usual for Mrs. Eliot to do, as the Chair

Hire was always before charged to Doctor Eliot; That Mrs. Eliot's Cloaths, when she came home, were much tumbled, and her Hair loose.

Did we say Dr. Eliot was thorough? Mrs. Price's own servant, Sarah Race, is now called, and she testifies:

That she lived as a Servant with Mrs. Price, in Berkeley Street, in 1774; That she does not know Mr. Acton, but that a Gentleman applied to her about this Bill a Month after Lord Valentia was at Mrs. Price's in Spring 1774; That she believes Lord Valentia was there Twice with a Lady; That the First Time they were together in the Parlour; that the Second Time they were together in a Bed Room opposite the Dining Room; That they were together the last Time an Hour, and went away between Eleven and Twelve o'clock; That she was ordered to get a Coach for them, and was desired to go down Stairs; That she thinks they supped together each time in the Parlour; that she carried Supper in; That the last Time they were there the Lady returned (after having gone away with Lord Valentia in an Hackney Coach), and that Lord Valentia returned in about Five Minutes after her, and that the Lady then went away in a Chair; That she could not see the Lady's Face.

A bawd's servant: more of the same reliable, objective testimony. Additional eyewitness testimony is given to corroborate the ongoing relationship of Mrs. Elliott and Viscount Valentia, this time by a servant of Dr. Eliot's of five years' standing named Thomas Sneed. He testifies:

[That] he walked out with Mrs. Eliot [gentlewomen as a rule did not walk the streets unless accompanied by a manservant—usually a footman—or a maid] one Evening in Spring; That she was joined by a Gentleman at Spring Gardens [this was the old name of the pleasure gardens that later became known as Vauxhall Gardens], who walked with her; That he followed them, and in Cockspur Street the Gentleman with his Mistress was met by another, who called him My Lord, and that he heard the Gentleman who walked with her say, "he would take Care of her"; That they conversed together chiefly in French.

So far, this has been eyewitness testimony of Mrs. Elliott and Lord Valentia in situations ranging from a stroll on the streets to verified accounts of gross crim. con. at Mrs. Price's house of ill-repute. Now, under the orders of Dr. Eliot, Grace's privacy is aggressively invaded at her home by that same sneaky, relentless servant William Constable. Some minions do love their work:

Constable was again called in, and proved Three Letters to be the Hand Writing of Mrs. Eliot, One of which he, the Witness found in Mrs. Eliot's Bed Chamber directed to Lord Valentia. . . . The same was read at the Bar, as was also another Letter to Lord Valentia, taken out of Mrs. Eliot's Pocket by Doctor Eliot. Then another Letter from Mrs. Eliot to Doctor Eliot was likewise read at the Bar.

Poor Grace! Not only is a bold male servant out of bounds in making free with her bedroom—the province of female servants only—but Eliot, that creep, is accosting her person and grabbing letters out of her pocket. These pockets, remember, were bags attached to petticoats and accessible by a slit in one's dress.

How horrible it must have been to be followed by these awful men and to have one's most intimate contacts spied upon; how unutterably sordid all this had to be for the unhappy Grace, all of nineteen years old.

Eliot's toady servant Constable, on being asked about the couple's "Cohabitation," adds:

[That] they never had cohabited together since the Beginning of May 1774; That they had but One Child, which is dead; and that he never heard that Mrs. Eliot has had any Children since she and the Doctor parted.

It is ordered that the bill be committed to a committee of the whole House "on Tuesday next."

The committee having met,

the Earl of Abercorn reported from the Committee, "That they had gone through the Bill, and made One Amendment thereto, which he was ready to report when the House will please to receive the same."

Therefore it is

ORDERED, That the said Report be received Tomorrow.

Shortly thereafter, the *Journals* (pages 604–605) note that the matter has been resolved:

Hodie 3rd vice lecta est Billa [Latin for "Today's third reading of the Bill"], intituled, "An Act to dissolve the Marriage of John Eliot Doctor in Physick, with Grace Dalrymple his now Wife, and to enable him to marry again; and for other Purposes therein mentioned."

The Question was put, "Whether this Bill shall pass?"

It was resolved in the Affirmative.

It was March 21, 1776.

Other divorce bills had been acted upon on that day, and both Grace Dalrymple Elliott and a woman whom she probably did not know and would never meet, Sarah Keppel Horneck, became divorcées at the same time; theirs were among the 318 divorces passed by Parliament in that Year of our Lord 1776.

It took Charles Horneck, Sarah's husband, three years to secure his divorce. Charles and Sarah (who was the natural daughter of the third Earl of Albemarle) were married in the spring of 1773. It was a disastrous marriage; before three months had elapsed Sarah had eloped with one John Scawen, Horneck's friend and fellow officer. Horneck evidently did not have as many allies in the House of Lords as Dr. Eliot had. He remarried—one of the items he, like Eliot, petitioned for in his divorce—but the second marriage flopped, too. It takes two to make a marriage, and perhaps neither Grace nor Sarah was entirely in the wrong. Perhaps both had been married to losers.

It is instructive to compare what we have learned so far with what Horace Bleackley has to say about this episode in particular and the amorous adventures of Grace Elliott in general. Bleackley makes unbelievable pronouncements about Grace's character, the most outrageous being that "she was a courtesan at heart from her birth—not wholly through wantonness and sensuality, but because she loved adventure and aspired to dominate mankind."

If one wanted to define the term "specious argument," that is, something that seems to have the ring of truth or plausibility but is actually fallacious, one would need go no farther than this ridiculous, though authoritative-sounding, statement. How on earth is anyone "a courtesan at heart from her birth"? Absurd!

Bleackley went on to say that Dr. Eliot was "well known . . . [to have] wallowed deeply in the mire," stating that when Eliot's wife became aware of his practice of treating "disreputable sirens, such as Sophia Baddeley" she grew suspicious of his constancy to his marriage vows. But Eliot treated courtesans because he looked for money anywhere he could find it, and courtesans kept by wealthy protectors (such as Baddeley's Lord Melbourne) had money to burn. This practice also kept him in good favor with the ton.

Bleackley's characterization of Lord Valentia is consistent with what others had to say about the not very well admired young Irish peer:

[Lord Valentia] for a long time had been known as one of Mrs. Eliot's warmest admirers . . . a common-place nobleman of handsome person and licentious habits. . . . Since his marriage with Lucy Lyttelton, the daughter of the good Lord Lyttelton, young Valentia had managed to check his amorous tendencies until he became infatuated with Mrs. Eliot, who, meeting him more than half way, extinguished all his affection for his own plain wife.

Bleackley also mentions that "ugly stories reached the ears of Dr. Eliot about the date of Hugh Dalrymple's death . . . that every one of the cavaliers whom the complacent physician permitted to attend her to rout and masquerade could boast of her favors." However, Dr. Eliot, that obsessive little man, mentioned none of these so-called cavaliers by name in his divorce action, and it is interesting to note that he set the action in motion only after the death of his father-in-law was confirmed. (Dalrymple's death in the Caribbean had been reported in the newspapers in early March 1774.)

Though Hew was no great shakes as a father to Grace, the timing of Eliot's action now becomes suspicious. Could it be that Eliot had feared he'd have to face Hew Dalrymple's wrath if Dalrymple heard his daughter was being treated badly? Was Eliot so much the coward? It's possible. Dalrymple was self-assured enough to tackle powerful politicians in satirical verse to which he actually signed his name, and perhaps he was in decent physical shape. There's a good chance he was also younger than his son-in-law.

Would he have gotten angry at the disagreeable news, come back from the West Indies, and beaten Dr. Eliot to a bloody pulp? One can enjoy the speculation—and the image of the good doctor battered and bloodied—but there's no way of knowing what might have happened between the two Scotsmen. (Perhaps they would have drawn bagpipes at twenty paces; now, that could be nasty, if only to the ears of those unfortunate enough to be nearby.)

On page 633 of the 1776 *Journals of the House of Lords*, a note is made that the amendment to the bill was not passed—odd, because Grace Elliott did receive her annuity payment of £200 yearly—and on page 717 it is noted that King George III had signed off on the divorce, Act No. 52 in volume 34 for 1776.

It was all over. What was Grace to do?

The Aftermath

According to Bleackley, Grace was kicked out of her Knightsbridge villa by Dr. Eliot a month after the indiscretion at Mrs. Price's, that is, sometime in May 1774. (He still, however, would have had to support her.) Bleackley says that Valentia was not prepared to leave his heiress wife or seek a divorce (he would have had no grounds to divorce Lucy Annesley), and so "before the end of May, when her amorous adventures were the topic of the moment, it was commonly reported that the guilty pair had quarreled already."

Remember that comment in *The Town and Country Magazine* that Grace had supposedly written to Dr. Eliot saying that she'd be "the happiest woman in the world" if he and Valentia "were both dead"? Another version of that infamous letter surfaces in Bleackley's *Ladies Fair and Frail*, taking as its source a report in one of the newspapers that Grace had advised Eliot to shoot his rival, suggesting that they go to "a little spot on Oxford Road"—i.e., a known dueling spot—and that she hoped she'd be "rid of two rogues."

Dueling, though illegal, was a common enough way to settle differences, usually when honor was at stake. The options were swords or pistols, but the pistol soon became the weapon of choice. According to an online source, Kronos: A Chronological History of the Martial Arts and Combative Sports, there were ninety-one fatalities resulting from duels in England from 1760 to 1820. Based on an accepted fatality rate of 20 percent, the number of duels fought during this period is estimated to have been about 450, but this figure could easily have been higher. Duels were secretive events, and there were penalties for those caught in the act.

Feisty though he appeared to be from all reports, Dr. Eliot was also cautious. One cannot imagine that he would have taken the risk of dueling with a younger man with faster reflexes. Valentia, though, may not have been a good shot, either; he may have been more of a lover than a fighter. That Grace hoped to be "rid of two rogues" seems like a fair hypothesis. The two men might well have killed each other if they didn't know how to handle pistols. (And the pistols of the time tended to misfire, causing significant injury to the shooters.)

Newspaper articles of the period have to be taken with several grains of salt, but one can see where Grace was coming from. She'd been used—

screwed, actually and figuratively—by both that rake Valentia and by her scheming old husband. Grace was a smart girl and she'd figured it out. To Valentia, Grace was an indiscretion—probably indulged in only twice—that had ended badly and expensively; there was that £12,000 crim. con. charge hanging over him (or his rich father-in-law). As for Dr. Eliot, there was the welcome ridding of a wife who'd proved to be too troublesome, despite the delights of her youth and beauty. Grace was the one with the most to lose, and lose it she did.

What else did she lose? Bleakley notes that Grace had been sent to rusticate, that for "some months she appears to have lived in the country." This fascinates because this was code. Women were sent into the country then to conceal pregnancies and give birth in secret. They would return either with an "adopted" child or without any. (Children were often given away outright to farm families.)

Had Grace been pregnant? By Valentia or Eliot? Was there a child? Or was this the child—noted in the divorce action—that had died? Or had there been two children who'd died? Though the manservant Constable went out of his way in March 1776 to testify he had heard of no other child born to Mrs. Elliott from when she was parted from Eliot in the spring of 1774 until that time, two years later, his assertion now becomes suspect. Eliot, his employer, may have wanted to cover something up.

Bleackley goes on to say that Grace returned "towards the end of the year"—this is still 1774—and "resumed her liaison with Lord Valentia while her husband was taking steps to apply to the Ecclesiastical Courts for a divorce." The affair, he adds, ended "early in 1775 [when] "there came a final rupture with her lover, whom she could never forgive for being a married man."

CHAPTER SIX

Bed-Hopping and Social Status

What was to become of poor, cuckolded Dr. Eliot?

After this dip in luck, the Scots physician got back on his nimble little feet and scrambled onto the next upward rung on fortune's ladder. King George III and Queen Charlotte—paragons of good moral behavior—were known to have been sympathetic throughout his long, drawn-out ordeal, and so was one of the Queen's ladies, her keeper of the robes, Madame Schwellenberg. (The newspapers, which had a history of mocking and attacking the poor German lady, persisted in styling her "Madame Schwellenbergen," with two added letters at the end of her name.) She may have interceded on Eliot's behalf with the royal couple; she'd had a long intimacy with the Queen and been somewhat responsible for helping to procure Eliot his first title.

Why was Madame Schwellenberg so exceedingly kind to the diminutive doctor of physic? He was her doctor at court and treated her chronic asthmatic condition, so she may have been grateful for that, but there could be another reason as well. It's possible that the about-to-be-free Dr. Eliot may have dangled an offer of marriage before that unloved, unattractive, very large and lonely lady who had few friends at court. It was not beyond his conniving to do so. This piece in the *Morning Post* of March 13, 1776, substantiates that there was some sort of intimate relationship a-budding—or already blossomed—between the two:

> *We are credibly informed, that a treaty of marriage is on foot, between Dr. E——t and Madam Schw——n of Buckingham house, and that it will certainly take place as soon as the Doctor's bill of divorce has passed the royal assent.*

By June 1, the newspaper was stating:

> *It is confidently reported at the west end of the town, that Dr. E——t, and Madam Sw——n, are immediately to be married; that a certain royal pair have interested themselves much in the arrangement of this union, and that the Dr. received the honour of his knighthood the other day, at St. James's, as a preparatory honour enabling him to gift his wife, on her marriage, with the title of Lady.*

In 1776, at the age of forty, plain Dr. Eliot became Sir John Eliot, Knight; two years later he was created a baronet and officially became one of the personal physicians to the Prince of Wales. Now more than ever inordinately proud of his bloodline and accomplishments, in 1784 he had the College of Arms in London draw up his family pedigree. He always thought himself a little better than most, but his obituary does state that although the recommendations of others (invariably his fellow Scots) played a large role in his success, he was thought to have been deserving of these elevations in status:

> *Thro' Madame Schwellenbergen and Lord Sackville, he became a Baronet. And by that interest, yet more aided by Lady Melbourne and the Duke of Queensbury, he got the employment of the Prince. The confidence of the Prince, it is but fair to say, he got by his own powers.*

Some caution needs to be exercised on the validity of the pedigree Sir John had drawn up for himself in 1784. Research had been done by the Lord Lyon's office in Scotland, beginning in 1779, according to Patric Dickinson, Richmond Herald at the College of Arms, and Henry Gray of St. Etheldreda's Church. As Gray states,

> *more recent research has shown this pedigree to be not wholly reliable. While the generations back to Sir John's father and grandfather are probably accurate enough, the kinship with Baronets of Stobs (or Stobbs) seems to have been somewhat more distant than was supposed by Sir John. William Eliot of Peebles appears to have been not the younger brother of Sir Gilbert the first Baronet of Stobs, as shown in the pedigree, but a first cousin of Sir Gilbert's father (i.e., son of Gavin Eliot, a younger brother of Sir Gilbert's grandfather). You will note Sir John was also anxious to show his claim to be descended, through the Ker family, from King Robert II of Scotland (grandson of Robert the Bruce).*

What Sir John omits in the elaborate pedigree is his marriage—his sole and only marriage—to Grace Dalrymple, and, of course, his illegitimate children. Illegitimate children never make it to these documents; it's as if they never existed. That Sir John would go to such lengths—including much expense—to make more of himself than there actually was reinforces his main character trait of self-importance. He, poor man, seems to have had a good deal that he had to prove. Perhaps, though, it was insecurity rather than self-importance that was the major impetus here.

And what of poor old Madame Schwellenberg, who had the Queen's ear and who may well have been the prime mover in getting Sir John both his titles? What was her earthly reward? Alas, that poor lady was doomed to remain not merely a lady-in-waiting to the Queen, but a bride-in-waiting forever to Dr. Eliot.

We know that it was a licentious age. Those with the money, the inclination, and the time to pursue hedonistic gratification—especially in the sexual arena—never hesitated to do so. That the ultrarepressive Victorian age followed swiftly on the round heels of the Georgian era was a natural consequence of the scientific law governing actions and equal and opposite reactions. It was a given that someone had to apply the brakes. But sex simply went underground. While there were aspects of Georgian sexual morality that smacked of hypocrisy, the pious and upright Victorians made such hypocrisy an art.

The irony was that King George III was a more rather than less faithful husband to his steadfast, unattractive wife Queen Charlotte, with whom he had fifteen children. The Victorians would have hailed him as a role model for all men. And the Queen fulfilled the desires of many a chauvinistic male for a pregnant and barefoot spouse. (Well, maybe not the barefoot part.) A major maternity hospital in London is named after George's prolific mate.

Contemporary accounts of the King judged him a dead bore. While there were occasional rumors of other women, no serious charges of marital misconduct marred his sixty-year reign, a reign remarkably free of personal scandal. George III left the scandal to his brothers and, later, his sons. There's an old rumor of his marriage to a Quaker woman, Hannah Lightfoot, and of a son from that union, but there's nothing much that backs this up. He wasn't an unattractive man, but he was not considered to be particularly bright. He had an unfortunate stammer—he tended to repeat words—but this might have been nervousness.

Charlotte (who, from her portraits and contemporary descriptions, was a real bow-wow) was not his first choice; he would have rather probably been married to one of his cousins, Sarah Lennox (one of the four beautiful Lennox sisters), with whom he'd fallen in love when she was sixteen. His handlers, however, insisted on the German match, and George, ever mindful of his duty, acceded to their wishes.

Years later, when George III was impossibly mad, he was said to have imagined that Sarah Lennox (later Napier), and not Queen Charlotte, was his wife. In that series of interlocking circles upon interlocking circles that made up the families of the ton, Lady Sarah became the aunt of the Whig statesman Charles James Fox, her sister Caroline's boy, a chum of the Prince of Wales.

Stella Tillyard's excellent book about the fabulous Lennox sisters, *Aristocrats* (1994), was the basis of a BBC television series. All the sisters—Caroline, Emily, Louisa, and Sarah—were amazing women, Sarah perhaps the most interesting for her love life. Caroline, the eldest, eloped at nineteen; Emily married for love at sixteen and had nineteen children; Louisa, like Sarah, had an arranged marriage, but did not leave her husband for her

Madame Schwellenberg, a Keeper of the Queen's Robes

Madame Juliana Elizabeth Schwellenberg was mercilessly attacked by the English press beginning about 1772. They mocked her corpulence, her broken English, her pernicious influence on Queen Charlotte (whom she'd known since that lady's infancy), and her general demeanor. They even accused her of using her position to sell favors, a charge that turned out to be patently untrue. Whatever else Madame S. may have done, she did not get rich from her service to Queen Charlotte as a joint keeper of the robes, a position she shared with Madame Johanna Louisa Haggerdorn, another German-born woman. In *Ladies in Waiting: From the Tudors to the Present Day* (New York: Alfred A. Knopf, 1984) Anne Somerset remarks that when the Queen wanted to raise the annual income of her keepers of the robes to £200 from £127, Madame S. refused.

The fullest picture to be had of the lady comes from the young novelist Fanny Burney (she had written *Evelina* and *Cecilia*, books that had found favor with the Queen), who replaced Madame Haggerdorn as the other keeper of the robes in 1786. Burney was under the misapprehension that she could help her brother in his naval career and improve her musician father's chances at court if she took on this service. Neither turned out to be true, and she was miserable throughout her five-year tenure. Madame Schwellenberg was the major cause of Burney's misery. Though the Prince of Wales referred to her as his "dearest Swelly," Burney paints her as a veritable dragon, a vulgar, illiterate, rude, violent-tempered creature

An Angel Gliding on a Sun-Beam into Paradise, the death of Juliana Elizabeth Schwellenberg, by James Gillray, a hand-colored etching published by Hannah Humphrey, October 11, 1791. Will those small wings hold up this chubby lady? (National Portrait Gallery, London)

who was obsequious toward the royals and her betters—a toad-eater to the max—but a petty tyrant and bully who was vicious to those she deemed to be beneath her.

The satiric poet known as Peter Pindar, a physician, great good friend of Mary Robinson, and nonpracticing priest named John Wolcot (1738–1819) who'd taken his pseudonym from the great lyric poet Pindar of ancient Greece, once said that it was better to be damned than not to be mentioned at all. Of Madame S., he wrote:

> *Whose palate loves a dainty dish*
> *Whose teeth in combat shine with flesh and fish,*
> *Whose Strelitz stomach holds a butt of beer,*
> *Who soon shall keep a saleshop for good places*
> *For which so oft the people squabble,*
> *And thus provide for great and little rabble.*

Dr. John Eliot did not remarry, though, as noted earlier, his divorce did not prohibit his doing so. Were the newspaper articles mere fiction, or did he use, and then jilt, his patient, Madame Schwellenberg? Nowadays, there are rules governing ethical behavior between doctor and patient, but not then. It is unlikely that Eliot would have courted her seriously. Though he was no beauty himself, he had an eye for beauty in others, and the hefty, unattractive Madame S. would have fallen far short of his standard. And, if he was looking for heirs, she would not have done, as she was probably older than he was. Madame S. died—still unmarried—in 1791. She had served Queen Charlotte faithfully for thirty-six years.

lover. (How differently English history might have turned out if George III, too, had been able to marry for love.)

Boring old George was dubbed "Farmer George" by the wags, partly for his zeal (which was genuine) for agricultural reform, but also for his skill in planting seed into the willing body of his wife. Jethro Tull's revolutionary seed drill had nothing on George's baby-making skill. (Below is a diagram for one of the machines that helped transform eighteenth-century English agriculture.)

So did his naughty offspring plant a lot of royal seed, but, alas, their activities were confined to the wrong side of the blanket. By 1817, according to Christopher Hibbert's *Queen Victoria: A Personal History* (2000), it was calculated that King George III "had no fewer than fifty-six grandchildren . . . not one of them legitimate."

His sons' profligate behavior had multiple origins. George III's court was considered the dullest in Europe (the French court was probably the liveliest), and the King and Queen were in turn overly possessive with their children and severe in their disapproval of them. Their poor-to-indifferent parenting skills were not untypical of European royals of the time: Archduchess Maria Theresa of Austria (Marie-Antoinette's mother) was another horrific royal parent.

King George III had an act passed, the Royal Marriage Act (1772), that stipulated only the reigning monarch could decide whom heirs to the throne could marry before they reached the age of twenty-five. (His two brothers provided the impetus for putting such an act in place, both of them having married commoners, and his sons' wild behavior reinforced its importance.) Once his sons reached that age, there were other stipulations in place to curb any desire they might have to marry hastily and unsuitably.

The Act of Settlement (1701), which forbade marriage with Nonconformists (like Quakers) or Roman Catholics, had to be adhered to, also, if England was to remain a Protestant nation. (Fears of papists were still strong, two centuries after Henry VIII's breakup of the Roman Catholic Church.) But the King went over the top where his children were concerned and became a total control freak. Tragically, he kept his daughters from marrying until they were too old to bear children. Controlling the succession is one thing, destroying any happiness one's children might hope to have by preventing them from leading normal lives that included marriage and families is another. His wife was equally to blame.

The attitude of the Hanoverian dynasty—who now call themselves the Windsors—has not changed significantly with regard to a monarch's control over marriage. Those two acts are still very much in place, but Prince Charles was permitted to marry a divorced woman, Camilla Parker Bowles. There's the rumor heard from time to time that Mrs. Parker Bowles converted to Catholicism when she married her first husband, Andrew Parker Bowles, who is a Roman Catholic, but this has not been substantiated.

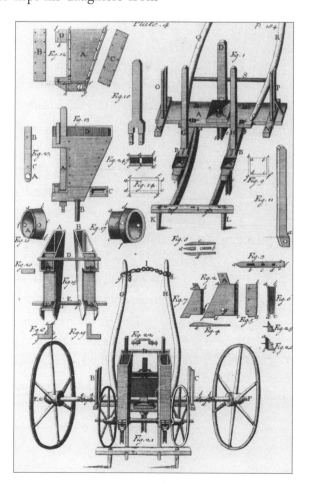

Jethro Tull's revolutionary seed drill from his *Horse Hoeing Husbandry*, London, 1733. (With the permission of the Museum of English Rural Life, Reading, UK)

Prince Charles gazes fondly upon his long-time companion—now wife—Camilla Parker Bowles at the Mey Highland Games, June 28, 2004. (EMPICS)

Like his grandfather George II before him, George III openly despised his firstborn son, George, Prince of Wales. (George III's father, Frederick Louis, died young, before he could succeed George II to the throne). Queen Charlotte, as well, had no use for her first male child, and, little surprise, the future King George IV managed to live up to every one of his mother's and father's negative expectations, and then some.

George, the Prince of Wales—familiarly called "Prinny"—was handsome in a stocky, Germanic way, with a pink-cheeked complexion and a sturdy build. He had a romantic disposition and was highly sensual and probably oversexed—or so bored with everything else that sex was the only thing that interested him. There was no end to females determined to catch his roving eye, and he came to exploit his privileged situation with a vengeance, as any such princeling with a healthy libido would, by indulging in unbridled sexual exploits. (Of the two current English princes, William and red-haired Harry, the younger—who so much resembles the ancestors of his mother, Lady Diana Spencer—appears from news coverage to be somewhat more in this mold than his more sedate brother.)

Prinny's first documented infatuation was with a girl named Mary Hamilton, who was an attendant to his princess sisters. He was sixteen. At seventeen, he fell madly in love with the pretty, older, married actress Mary Darby Robinson, who was appearing onstage to great acclaim as Perdita in *The Winter's Tale* by Shakespeare. This Mrs. Robinson—shades of Simon and Garfunkel!—was to retain that character's name as her nickname for the rest of her life.

Signing himself "Florizel," the name of Perdita's wooer in the play, the besotted young prince wrote a series of impassioned but ill-advised letters to Robinson, promising her a very large sum of money—£20,000, a fortune—if she would come to his bed. Perdita, who had a young daughter and an alcoholic and philandering husband to support, eventually gave in, but the whirlwind liaison lasted barely a year. The Prince was a fickle lad. (A political cartoonist later referred to him as "Perdito.")

Robinson was replaced immediately by Elizabeth Cane, aka Mrs. Armistead, a courtesan who'd been hand-trained in the most exclusive of the St. James's area brothels by a prominent madam. (Armistead was later to hook up with Grace's old flame Lord Cholmondeley.) Prinny went from Armistead's arms and charms to those of Grace Dalrymple Elliott, newly returned from a sojourn in France as a mistress of Louis-Philippe-Joseph, the Duc d'Orléans, and no doubt full of new and kinky French bedroom tricks with which to lure the Prince under the sheets.

The French court was anything but dull; the French thought they'd invented sex. Grace, alas, did not stay long with Prinny—one of the tabloids sneered it was barely an hour, but it was probably some weeks, or even months. Grace had been a paramour (one of many in his harem) of Philippe, whom she first knew as the Duc de Chartres, before he inherited the title of Duc d'Orléans and the immense fortune that came with it. Not only was he the wealthiest man in all of France (if not all of Europe), he had married the wealthiest young heiress in the country, and was, moreover, a "prince of the blood." He was related to his cousins King Louis XVI and Queen Marie-Antoinette by different royal bloodlines.

The Orléans men were so irrepressible when it came to libertinism and the art of love that they added the noun "roué" to the French language. Though Philippe kept that harem of lovelies, he was an avowed Anglophile who held Grace in special favor, and it seems they remained friends long after sex was no longer a factor in their relationship.

There was a definite *La Rondeish* quality to what was happening in the Prince of Wales's circle around the time of his twentieth birthday. Grace Elliott's claim that the child she bore on March 30, 1782, was that of King George III's son could have been legitimate, although the baby girl—later christened Georgiana Augusta Frederica Elliott—was not. (The Prince of Wales's full Christian name, in case one wonders how Grace selected the names of her daughter, was George Augustus Frederick.) The name of George, Prince of Wales, appeared four months later on the baptismal register at St. Marylebone Church, though the infant's surname was that of her mother, Elliott.

It would have been strange if no issue had sprung from the seed in Prinny's loins during this testosterone explosion; it was shooting through the roof. Look at the complete (more or less known) record of just one year in the Prince's love life, the year post-Perdita: Elizabeth Armistead, Grace Elliott, Lady Augusta Campbell, Lady Melbourne, Elizabeth Billington (a singer), and Maria Amelia, Countess of Sudbury. He was a young pig romping in clover, or whatever happy stuff young pigs love to romp in.

One also has to wonder and speculate on the instances and number of venereal diseases that accompanied this Georgian version of *La Ronde*. Prinny's companions in vice were legion; foremost among them were Lord Cholmondeley and Charles James Fox, but there were many others, and they went by the name of the Carlton House set.

The Carlton House set were a debauched lot, gambling, brawling, wenching, and drinking to excess. Though not all in the set had the same vices—for example, there were those who gambled, like Beau Brummell, but who did not spend any time wenching and were not, as they put it, "in the petticoat line"—but most were randy. They were the despair of many a cuckolded husband, whose only recourse was (a) to ignore the whole thing; (b) send his wife to "rusticate" in the country, or on an extended European sojourn; or (c) sue for divorce and charge the seducer with "criminal conversation."

This licentious lot were surely in need of birth control. What types of birth control were readily available to people of means in this period? More than one might imagine. In fact, according to John Riddle in his *Eve's Herbs: A History of Abortion and Contraception in the West* (1997), European men and women have had recourse to effective means of contraception and abortion since at least the time of the ancient Greeks. In eighteenth-century England, there was awareness among physicians, sexually astute men, educated women, and midwives that blocking sperm from entering the cervix would possibly prevent conception. Early diaphragms and cervical caps were available to women and were effective birth control methods.

A Perpetual La Ronde: *Sexual Hijinks in the Prince of Wales's Set*

The Prince of Wales beds the actress Mary Robinson—Perdita—who travels to France with the blackmail money paid by King George III for his son's indiscreet letters; she's replaced by Elizabeth Armistead. Robinson narrowly misses being seduced by Philippe, Duc de Chartres, the lover of Grace Dalrymple Elliott. Grace returns to London after running into her former lover, Lord Cholmondeley, who's traveling through Europe with an unnamed courtesan. Grace takes up again with Cholmondeley—and may have had a few nights with a young rake named Charles Wyndham—and shares Prinny's bed as well. Armistead winds up in Europe with Lord Cholmondeley and takes up with a number of other peers before going on to the man she'll eventually (secretly) wed, Charles James Fox (who himself has recently sampled the pleasures of Mrs. Robinson's bed). Meanwhile, back in Paris, this same Perdita, having fled the unwelcome amorous advances of Grace Elliott's former protector Philippe, takes up with a noted rake, a boastful aristocrat and French army officer named Lauzun; when she returns to London she meets Colonel Sir Banastre Tarleton, who'd fought for the British cause in the American Revolution, and begins a long relationship with him. Before taking up with Tarleton exclusively, however, she's to have brief flings with Charles James Fox, Lord Cholmondeley, and a Lord Malden. Grace has a couple of off-on years with Cholmondeley—her second go-around with him—then leaves him and goes back to France, taking up again with Philippe, who becomes the Duc d'Orléans. She shares him with Agnes de Buffon, but the ménage à trois (or more) remains cordial. Back in London, years later, after Tarleton dumps Perdita, he woos Susan Priscilla Bertie, Cholmondeley's ward and the daughter of his good friend the fourth Duke of Ancaster; she's been raised by the Cholmondeleys along with Georgiana, Grace Elliott's daughter, and a girl named Harriet, who's the daughter of another Cholmondeley inamorata, a Madame St. Alban. Cholmondeley marries Ancaster's sister, Lady Charlotte Bertie. Tarleton has a brief affair with a woman named Kolina—and has a bastard daughter, Banina—before fully settling down to wedded bliss with Susan Priscilla. The Prince of Wales meets and (secretly and illegally) marries the Roman Catholic widow Maria Fitzherbert before being forced into an official, dynastic marriage with Princess Caroline of Brunswick. Charles James Fox and Elizabeth Armistead live happily together in their secret marriage. Mrs. Fitzherbert is dumped by Prinny, who goes on to have numerous affairs with increasingly older women and tries—but fails—to divorce Princess Caroline for adultery. Who *is* he kidding?

About Carlton House, the House

The Prince of Wales was granted Carlton House as his exclusive residence on August 12, 1783, when he turned twenty-one. Parliament allowed £60,000 for its renovation. Sir William Chambers surveyed the property and made essential repairs, but Henry Holland was responsible for its remodeling. He was commissioned by the Prince—who'd been turned on to French neoclassical architecture and interior design by his friend the Duc d'Orléans—to build it in that style, with touches of chinoiserie and the Gothic. In a little over ten years, when Parliament's allowance had failed to cover debts of more than £250,000, Holland was nonetheless given another £60,000 to continue the work. Walsh Porter arrived in 1805 to decorate the interior. Others who worked on the Carlton House project were Thomas Hopper, James Wyatt, and John Nash, who completed the assignment.

After Carlton House was completed, the Prince turned his attention to Buckingham House. Alas, in 1826 John Nash reported that Carlton House had to be demolished because of structural problems, and it was taken down the next year. *Sic transit* architecture *mundi.* . . .

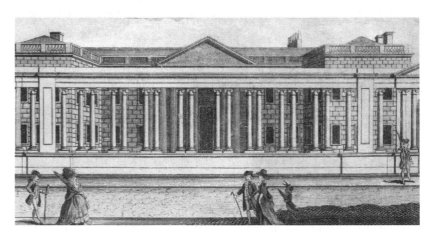

Carlton House in the eighteenth century. (With permission of The Royal Society)

In *The Floating Brothel* (2001), Sian Rees describes a kind of cervical cap made of half a squeezed lemon and melted, shaped beeswax. Casanova was an advocate of the half lemon (or lime) as well; the citric acid from the fruit served as spermicide. Beeswax, opium resin, and oiled paper could also be shaped into thimbles that fit over the cervix. Women knew that a vinegar-soaked sponge (pessary) inserted into the vagina could be an effective barrier to impregnation. Douching with acidic preparations immediately after intercourse and using a syringe and crouching over a pot of boiling water to catch the steam were other methods of birth control.

In his excellent and best-selling historical novel *The Crimson Petal and the White*, set in Victorian England, Michel Faber describes how his heroine, the prostitute Sugar, prevents conception after each sexual encounter:

> *She's so tired now that she can't even remember whether she has performed her prophylactic ritual or not. . . .*
>
> *The tureen of contraceptive is where she left it, and yes, she remembers now, she has used it. Thank God for that. Not that she can actually recall inserting the plunger, but there it lies (tipped not with cloth, like Caroline's, but with a real sea sponge), sopping wet beside the tureen.*
>
> *How many hundred times has she performed this ceremony? How many sponges and swabs has she worn away? How many times has she prepared this witches' brew, measuring the ingredients with mindless precision? Granted, in her Church Lane days the recipe was slightly different; nowadays, as well as the alum and the sulphate of zinc, she adds a dash of sal eratus, or bicarbonate of soda. But in essence it's the same potion she's squatted over almost nightly since she began to bleed at sixteen.*

Among ordinary folk, coitus interruptus (withdrawal before ejaculating into the vagina) was a cheap, handy, and widely used method of contraception, though one wholly dependent on male self-control. Using orifices other than the normal route of entry—such as the anal passage—was an option, too, and there was always abstinence. If all else failed, there was abortion. Though it was technically against the law to abort a "quickened" fetus (i.e., a fetus that had been felt to move in the womb, usually at about four months), bringing on late menses before this quickening was not considered abortion.

Condoms, or "cundums"—also called "machines," "armour," "engines," and "English overcoats"—were strictly urban contraceptives, but they had been around for a good while in the sophisticated world. Although prevention of venereal disease was by far condoms' primary function and the reason they were developed, the cognoscenti—as noted above—believed they could prevent conception, too. Gallants of the ton knew where to procure them and were well versed in their use. The British Museum owns a fascinating image of an early condom factory in London that dates from 1741. There were several such makeshift factories in the Covent Garden area; the workers were young females, shown in the etching seated at tables in the drawing room of a typical Georgian house. The museum also has prints of riots at brothels that show boxes of condoms being thrown out of windows.

Condoms could be purchased at various emporia (sex shops) in the sleazy area in and around Covent Garden. They came in three sizes and were sold in silk sachets, eight to the package. The purveyors of these specialist goods went by the name of "salvators." Among them were a Mother Douglas, an entrepreneurial young woman named Constantia Phillips who established her shop on Half-Moon Alley, a Mrs. Muilman in Salvator House on the Strand, and Mary Perkins and J. Jacobs of Oliver's Alley.

The person given credit for the invention of the condom was an Italian doctor named Gabriele Falloppio (he gave his name to the Fallopian tubes, too). He saw its dual use in protecting against both disease (particularly syphilis) and conception. The earliest condoms were imported from France, and France and Holland had a reputation for producing the best-quality condoms.

It was too bad the materials used then were not reliable. If they had been impermeable membranes, they would have worked fine, but their permeability meant that relying on them for disease prevention and contraception was iffy at best.

These "machines" were fabricated from the intestines of animals such as sheep, or even from fish guts. There were earlier condoms, from the time of the English Civil War and Restoration (mid-seventeenth century) that were

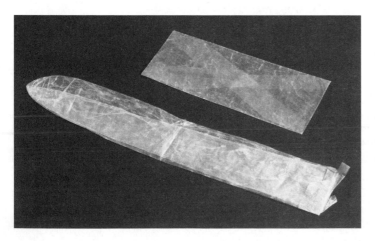

Contraceptive sheath made of animal gut and bound with a pink silk ribbon, circa 1800–1850, and its waxed paper envelope. In the last hundred years condoms have evolved from linen and animal intestine, via vulcanized rubber, to the multicolored, multiflavored latex varieties available today. (Science and Society Picture Library, London)

made of linen soaked in brine or a saline solution, an early (and ineffective) type of spermicide. Remnants of the former have been found in archaeological digs.

A 2003 exhibition at the British Museum—*London 1753*—included two of only a few surviving examples of condoms. One had not been used: the narrow scarlet silk ribbon at the open end of the condom, where it was to be tied tightly at the base of the penis, was bright and fresh, and the body of the condom was clean and unwrinkled. The other condom was crushed, dull, and faded from washing, showing signs of more than one use. Yes, these condoms were made to be used, washed (one hoped!), and reused. Yuck!

The condoms were donated to the British Museum by Eric J. Dingwall, nicknamed "Dirty Ding," who collected erotica and material on aberrant sexual customs; Dingwall was a librarian at Cambridge University and later at the British Museum. The description read:

Two prophylactic sheaths, c. 1790. . . . Animal membrane, one with a silk ribbon, length 208 mm. and 190 mm. . . . Presented by Eric J. Dingwall. . . . The condoms shown here are of the type—made from animal gut, reusable and secured with a ribbon—which James Boswell describes using with "dull satisfaction" in an encounter with a prostitute in January 1763 . . . and which can be seen flying from the window of a brothel [refers to a print by Charles Mosley (fl. 1737–1756), The Tar's Triumph, or Bawdy-House Battery, *1749]. These contexts illustrate the main purpose of the condom as prophylactic rather than contraceptive. Condoms were developed by the late sixteenth century, their name traditionally derived from that of Dr. Condom,*

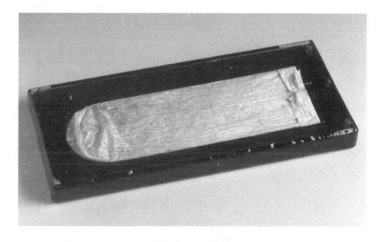

Condom made of animal gut, with a silk ribbon, is shown (below) in its original case. It was part of the exhibit The Tyranny of Treatment: Samuel Johnson, His Friends, and Georgian Medicine," held at Dr. Johnson's House, 17 Gough Square, London, September 2003 through January 2004. It's dated from 1790. (Science and Society Picture Library, London)

physician to Charles II. By the eighteenth century they were readily available in London.

A third condom from this period is owned by the Royal College of Surgeons in London. All three came from a cache discovered in an unnamed English country house in the 1950s. In an article titled "Early Contraceptive Sheaths" in the *British Medical Journal* (January 3, 1953), Dingwall wrote that they were found in "a muniment room [a room where important household documents are stored] in a large English country mansion . . . [in] a locked box. . . . They were in packets of eight, of three different sizes, and the inner (white) and outer (blue) wrappers were apparently those in which they had been delivered." He dated them from the very end of the eighteenth century to the beginning of the nineteenth century.

Dingwall did a thorough examination of these specimens and concluded that they were "made from some animal membrane, and . . . [that they were] seamless, the edge of the open end being turned over and roughly stitched with cotton to form a hem through which is threaded a strip of silk."

They were not impermeable; both water and a solution of salt and water passed through them. Dingwall quotes a 1744 source that warns, "for the sake of safety, two are advised to be worn," and a 1770 source that noted they were "subject to tears." Caveat emptor!

The randy aristocrat John Wilmot (1647–1680), second Earl of Rochester, described by Samuel Johnson as having a life of "drunken gaiety and gross sensuality . . . with an avowed contempt of decency and order," was an advocate and popularizer of condom use and wrote some startling, graphic poetry on sexual devices, among them dildoes—"Signior Dildo" (1673).

The rakish earl succumbed to syphilis at the age of thirty-three, bearing stark witness to the flaws of early prophylactics. The poem "A Panegyrick upon Cundums," extolling the virtues of the condom, was said to have been written by him in 1674, but though it bears the earmarks of a poem by Wilmot, it should be noted that some literary scholars date this poem from 1741—some sixty years after his demise—and attribute it to someone else entirely.

It is, however, period poetry—whoever its author—and the sentiments are genuine, among them the reference to "Unknown big Belly, and squawling Brat," which more than implies pregnancy might be prevented if condoms were used. It is wickedly graphic. The most quoted lines from this long "panegyrick" are these:

> Happy the Man, who in his Pocket keeps
> Whether with green or scarlet Ribband bound
> A well-made cundum——He, nor dread the Ills
> Of Shankers or Cordee, or Bubos dire!

Eighteenth-century gallants had access to Wilmot's verse and much other poetry and prose dealing with sexual matters. There was a vast literature on the subject available to educated men, from the poetry of Ovid studied in university Latin classes and the naughtiness of John Cleland's contemporary novel *Fanny Hill,* to *Aristotle's Masterpiece* and the herbals of Nicholas Culpeper. Works like Ovid's and Cleland's titillated and got one into the mood; *Aristotle's Masterpiece,* meant for the average person, attempted to explain the workings of the body and went into great detail on pregnancy and birth; the herbals provided information on plants that would bring on menstrual periods, i.e., abortifacients.

Wealthy men also had the means to collect pornography, and there was a goodly amount of it in circulation for those in the know. The illustrator Thomas Rowlandson, always in debt, poor man, owing to his heavy gambling, became the private pornographer of the Prince of Wales. (Prinny's collection of Rowlandson's pornographic prints is rumored to be under lock and key at Windsor Castle, but inquiries there met with official denial of their existence.) Among the titles of these prints, all published circa 1810, are *Cunnyseurs;*

One of Rowlandson's most notorious and enduring pornographic prints, *Cunnyseurs,* a play on the slang word for the vagina ("cunny") and the French verb *connaître,* "to know." (The British Museum)

Another crude, bold, and amazing print by the audacious James Gillray: Mrs. Maria Fitzherbert, as "Dido Forsaken," on a heaped-high funeral pyre of phalluses and testicles—yes, phalluses and testicles!—as her lover and secret husband the Prince of Wales sails away from her toward Windsor Castle. The allusion is to the desertion of Queen Dido of Carthage by the Trojan Aeneas in the *Aeneid*. Hand-colored etching published May 21, 1787, by Samuel William Fores. (National Portrait Gallery, London)

Meditations among the Tombs, with its rather blasphemous phallus-decorated tombstones; *The Jugglers,* which has to be seen to be believed; *Preludes; The Dairy Maid's Delight; A Music Master Tuning His Instrument;* and *The Willing Fair.*

Continental pornography included illustrations in the following marriage manuals and dirty books that were part of the sexually knowledgeable English gentleman's library included these: *Conjugal Love Reveal'd,* originally published in 1687, and a reprint circa 1750 entitled *Conjugal Love, or The Pleasures of the Marriage Bed; The Fruit Shop* (1765); and *The Pleasures and Felicity of Marriage* (1745), all by Nicholas Venette; a work called *Geneanthropeia* in the 1642 Italian edition and *Rare Verities, The Cabinet of Venus Unlocked and Her Secrets Laid Open* in the 1657 version in English; *The Ladies Physical Directory* (1716); and editions of Pietro Aretino, such as *L'Aretin français,* which included *Les Epices de Venus.* Tommaso Piroli's illustrations for Aretino included *La Carriola* (The Wheelbarrow), a remarkable depiction of sexual agility and athleticism.

Snuffboxes and waistcoat buttons of the most dissolute men sported lewd drawings along the lines of Rowlandson's pornographic prints. Grace Elliott's lover the Duc de Chartres—later called "Vile Égalité" by Lady Sarah Napier—was scolded in letters to Horace Walpole from his female friends for the remarkably flagrantly painted buttons he wore at mixed gatherings. Painted sporting scenes on waistcoat buttons were popular with fashionable men, but *these* sporting scenes went beyond what was considered polite, especially in company that included women. England was not France. The *Morning Herald* of May 22, 1783, noted the minor contretemps:

> *The set of coat-buttons lately worn by the Duc de Chartres, and which gave offence to several ladies on account of the subjects exhibited on them, are now laid aside. Some of the maids of honour who have examined them very minutely have declared that the most exceptionable button in the set consisted alone of a little frolicksome device from the antique, and that they would have no scruples to have an apron worked after the pattern.*

The wives of these men (not to mention their mothers, aunts, sisters, daughters, and mistresses) also could have had access to these libraries and the opportunity to educate themselves. And women knew enough to consult midwives, who had recourse to the old remedies, even though these medical practitioners were slowly being forced out by male doctors, like John Eliot and the brothers William and John Hunter, who treated the upper classes.

Aristotle's Masterpiece is a book of unknown authorship first published in 1684 that has nothing to do with the Greek philosopher Aristotle. It is a strange little work (it's roughly the same size as a mass market paperback) about the human body, covering biology, mythology, and points in between. It was hugely successful and went into numerous printings. It offered anatomical illustrations—engravings of female bodies, cutaway views of babies in the womb—sexual advice, and discussion and depiction of medical aberrations such as Siamese twins. From this little tome comes the old wives' tale that what a mother sees or is frightened by can imprint itself upon a fetus. (In some cultures, people believe this bit of lore even today.)

One illustration showed a hairy woman whose mother, while pregnant, supposedly gazed upon a picture of Saint John the Baptist dressed in animal skins. Another showed a white couple who had a black baby because the woman had looked at a picture of a black man at the moment of conception. The latter, especially, is a likely tale indeed, but these stories were apparently widely believed.

In some editions there was a special section addressed to midwives. It was a mishmash of information, much of it—we know today—wrong. It was not difficult at all to secure for oneself a copy of *Aristotle's Masterpiece*. It was a

From *Aristotle's Masterpiece,* here are
Siamese twins. (Collection of the author)

best seller, both in Europe and in America. (Yes, even in America! The Puritan Cotton Mather, minister at Second Church, Boston, condemned it as unsuitable for female reading.)

There is a large amount of material on how to arouse the female sexually, and this included—how modern!—a discussion of clitoral stimulation. It's clear that the twenty-first century did not invent sex; this knowledge has been around for a long time. It should be noted, however, that there was a moralistic Christian emphasis to the work: procreation outside of marriage was a definite no-no and there was a good deal of advice on overcoming the problem of barrenness (infertility) in women.

Nicholas (or Nicolas) Culpeper (1616–1654) was a London apothecary who put together three of the most important compendia on herbal medicine of the mid-seventeenth century. (Before antibiotics and synthetic drugs, this was the only kind of medicine there was.) His classic work on herbs, known as *Culpeper's Complete Herbal,* is still used as a reference book and remains in print in various editions. Culpeper was also an advocate of astrology and its use in treating illness. In *The English Physitian, or An Astrologo-Physical Discourse of the Vulgar Herbs of This Nation* (1652), he described himself as "Nich. Culpeper, Gent. Student in Physick and Astrologie."

His first book was an important reference source. Published in 1649 as *A Physical Directory,* it was retitled *Pharmacopoeia Londinensis, or The London Dispensatory* in 1653. This work, aimed at practitioners of the medical arts, contained lists and descriptions of herbs together with instructions on their medicinal uses. It was Culpeper's own

The hairy child. (Collection of the author)

unauthorized translation from the Latin of the College of Physicians' *Phamacopoeia*, and it made him extremely unpopular among his learned colleagues because he made this information—formerly the purview only of doctors and apothecaries—available to the common man.

There were other herbal compendia, such as the anonymous *Tractatus de virtutibus herbarum*, first published in Mainz in 1484 and known to physicians, that gave the names of herbs (and preparations using herbs), that brought on a woman's "courses"—as menstruation was called—with the hidden subtext of causing miscarriage. The plants listed included a number of "vulgar" (common) herbs ranging from the familiar parsley, sage, rosemary, and thyme to rue and wild mint. There were other plants deemed useful in expelling fetuses and bringing on the menstrual period: celery, asarum (a fern), calamint, artemsia, birthwort, licorice, marjoram, pennyroyal, peony, dittany, juniper, savin (a type of juniper), willow, poplar, Queen Anne's lace, asafetida, geranium, chaste plant, death carrot, sage, garlic, and more. Pessaries—cervical caps—made of birthwort combined with oil of myrrh and pepper and ones made of century plant and sage were said to be especially effective in expelling the contents of the uterus. Birthwort in all its varieties could be taken in a drink, as could a decoction of poplar bark or asarum.

The German botanist Valerius Cordus submitted a number of recipes to the apothecary guild in Nuremberg in 1542 that were combined into a work called the *Dispensatorium*. One of his recipes, reprinted in *Eve's Herbs*, "was entirely for women: a powder molded into a cake (pill) called 'Trochisca de myrrha D. Rais.' . . . It was compounded

Most gallants of the Georgian period had a copy of *Aristotle's Masterpiece* in their private libraries; doctors most definitely had the book. This is one with the special section for midwives. (Collection of the author)

of the following ingredients (note that 1 scruple = 20 grains = 1.2 grains): 3 scruple myrrh, 5 scruple lupine, 2 scruple opopanax, 1 scruple each rue, wild mint, pennyroyal, cumin, blackberries, asafetida, sagapeni . . . and artemisia." This concoction supposedly "provoked menstruation."

Plant and herbal lore was the province of wisewomen and midwives, who kept up an oral tradition that chronicled the various uses. Midwives not only assisted in delivering babies, they had the means of preventing pregnancies as well. Every village in England had its midwife, and London was full of them. Their power waned as male gynecologists and obstetricians—known as men-midwives—began to take over what was once wholly the province of women practitioners. What these women knew went underground; it was still available, but not so readily.

Meanwhile, aristocratic women could call on physicians like Dr. William Hunter, a man-midwife to the stars. In Carola Hicks's *Improper Pursuits*, a biography of Lady Diana Beauclerk, the methods used by ladies of the ton and their doctors to prevent and—if that failed—to abort pregnancies are gone into at length. Lady Di became pregnant by her lover, Topham Beauclerk, while separated from her husband "Bully," Viscount Bolingbroke. For birth control, she drank once or twice a day a concoction made from willow bark that was supplied by her apothecary; she apparently also consumed a good deal of rye bread after she became pregnant, as the ergot fungus that grew on rye was considered a particularly effective abortifacient. At about this time there began to be pills advertised in the newspapers and sold in the open marketplace that were aimed at female complaints. Hicks writes:

> There were a range of drugs and potions, based on plants and herbs, including pennyroyal, hellebore, savin, and ergot of rye, which were believed to be effective abortifacients. These domestic or kitchen-garden remedies were being increasingly supplemented in the expanding consumerism of the day by "female pills" which were widely advertised as claiming to be able to regulate various women's disorders, by controlling or rather bringing on menstruation.

Where there was a will to control conception and the means to do so, there were those who aided and abetted women in need. (Alas, Lady Di's methods did not work: she gave birth to a daughter, Mary.) It is interesting, too, that to this twenty-first-century day, women still know about this obscure little herb called rue.

Rue was thought to be especially effective in bringing on miscarriages, and it remains one of the hardest plants to keep growing in a community garden plot, according to horticulturists. This isn't because it's a difficult plant to grow. Rather, it's the victim of its own popularity, as visitors who apparently know something of its reputed special properties keep plucking it whole. Here is the entry on the Uses of Rue from *The English Physitian:*

GARDEN RUE.

This is so well known, both by this name, and the Name Herb of Grace, that I shall not need to write you any further Description of it: But shall only shew you the Vertues of it as followeth.

Vertues and Use.

It provoketh Urine and Womens Courses, being taken either in Meat or Drink. The Seed thereof taken in Wine, is an Antidote against all dangerous Medicines or deadly Poysons. The Leavs taken either by themselves, or with Figs and Walnuts is called Methridates his Counter poyson, against the Plague and causeth all Venemous things to become harmless: Being often taken in Meat or Drink it abateth Venery, and destroyeth the ability to beget Children.

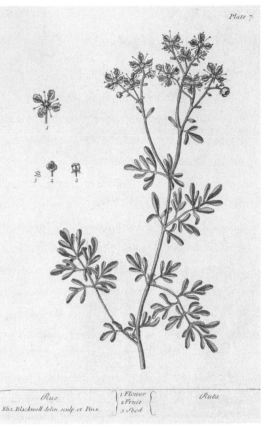

Garden rue, *Ruta graveolens.* (Bridgeman Art Library)

It goes on—and on, and on—but one should get the idea. This is a good deal of information, and it's apparent that there was knowledge of birth control—from older female relatives, from midwives and doctors, from herbals such as this, and from other medical texts—in Grace Elliott's era. Grace, with her intimate connection to medical professionals, among them her own husband, her extramarital affairs and friendships with worldly men, and her own personal experience with pregnancy and delivery, could not have been unaware of the facts of life. Whatever else could be said of Grace Elliott— and much was—she was not a stupid woman.

Grace Elliott might well have wanted to become pregnant by the Prince of Wales. Or, having found herself pregnant by Lord Cholmondeley, she

The Peerage: Dukes

The peerage has five descending degrees: duke, marquess, earl, viscount, and baron. (Baronets and knights are not considered peers, but while the title of Baronet can be inherited, the title of Knight cannot.) All peers have a family name as well as a title, but there are exceptions. (Diana, née Spencer, the late Princess of Wales, was the sister of Charles Spencer, who is also Earl Spencer, not the Earl *of* Spencer. The family name is the same as the earldom.) Titles of peers are usually—but not always—territorial, referring to a place, but all dukedoms are territorial. There were no dukes in England until 1337, when King Edward III made his eldest son the Duke of Cornwall. The young man was still a prince; this was an added distinction. Peers as a rule have more than one title; they are known, however, by their highest title. Sons and heirs of peers take the highest courtesy titles from their fathers; the eldest son of a duke, for example, would probably have the title of marquess until he inherited the dukedom from his father. The English system is based on primogeniture—the eldest son is the heir and he gets all; younger children of peers are commoners.

It's duke/duchess, marquess (or marquis)/marchioness, earl/countess, viscount/viscountess, baron/baroness. There are rare examples of women inheriting titles in their own right; these usually are baronesses. Anne Boleyn was created a marchioness in her own right by King Henry VIII; however, only her male heirs—of which she had none—would have been able to inherit this title. Dukes and duchesses are addressed as "Your Grace" and all other titleholders are addressed as "Lord" or "Lady." Widows of peers are called dowagers, as in "Dowager Duchess."

The title of marquess was created in 1385. That of earl originated in Anglo-Saxon times, when earls were local rulers; Arundel, the oldest earldom in England, dates back to 1433. The title of viscount was awarded to recognize service to the Crown over and above a barony. Baron is the oldest of the peerage titles, having been around since 1264.

Why are individuals given titles? And what does one have to do or be to deserve a dukedom, the highest rank? E. S. Turner, in *Amazing Grace: The Great Days of Dukes,* says that the "reasons for making men dukes were many and not always creditable," and he includes the following:

- winning great victories in the field
- public and political services
- fascinating a male sovereign
- fascinating a female sovereign
- betraying a sovereign (i.e., for services to Protestantism)
- being a bastard of the sovereign
- having ancestors who served the State well
- having an ancestor who was unfairly executed
- defeating, subduing, or otherwise taming the Scots or Irish
- supporting, or not opposing, parliamentary reform

- marrying a duchess
- amassing, or inheriting, or marrying into, enormous landed wealth

Turner adds that sometimes dukes were created for a combination of these reasons, but that at times it was impossible to discern why a man received the distinction. He writes that "the first Duke of Ancaster seems to have been honoured because he had a clever brother" and remarks that none of the members of this otherwise undistinguished family rates inclusion in *The Dictionary of National Biography*. Military commanders like Marlborough and Wellington were given huge rewards of land as well as titles, for, "in general, a dukedom went only to those with large estates." But, Turner opines, "often the highest rank was won by those families with the greatest talent for bedding heiresses. . . . There is hardly a ducal family which has not benefited at some stage by the rich spoils of marriage." Harold Brooks-Baker, the late publishing director of Burke's Peerage Partnership, put it even more succinctly: "There are only three ways titles can be acquired, fighting a war, sex or buying" (quoted in his obituary in *The New York Times*, March 8, 2005).

Lacking male heirs in the correct bloodline, titles become extinct. The dukedom of Portland, for example, became extinct in 1990 when no "tail-male" heir could be found.

The monarch has it in his or her power to create new titles at will.

Lordly Elevation, James Gillray, 1802. In this hand-colored etching, the dandy Lord Kirkcudbright has just succeeded to his father's grand old estate. His self-image as a sexy and handsome young peer is clearly at odds with the facts of his long, big-browed face, hunched back, and diminutive body, all possibly indications of dangerous inbreeding. (Bridgeman Art Library)

might have conspired with him (and possibly the Prince) to pass the child off as a royal bastard. If she'd not wanted the child, she certainly had the knowledge of where to go, whom to see, and what to do to facilitate an abortion. That Grace did not do so, and never made any secret of her pregnancy, indicates that something else was afoot, namely, securing royal favor and patronage.

Bed-hopping, it appears, was just another way to climb socially—perhaps more enjoyable than most—and having a royal bastard gave a woman a certain cachet. Though there were many doors that would be closed, others would certainly open as a result. Peers and monarchs could shower such offspring with favors, if they were so inclined. King George IV, unfortunately, was no King Charles II, who gave his bastards titles, land, and wealth—descendants of his sons with Nell Gwyn are among the most toplofty aristocrats in England—but Grace's daughter Georgiana did not do so badly with George as a putative father.

The Prince of Wales regularly cuckolded the men in his Carlton House set, who turned a complacent eye toward his activities. (Among these women were Isabella, Marchioness of Hertford, and Frances, Lady Jersey.) Having one's wife a favorite of the monarch or monarch-to-be gave these men cachet as well. They climbed the social ladder every time one of their ladies was bedded by their leader. It was an honor to be singled out in this manner, and this attitude persists in the upper rungs of the British peerage even to the present day.

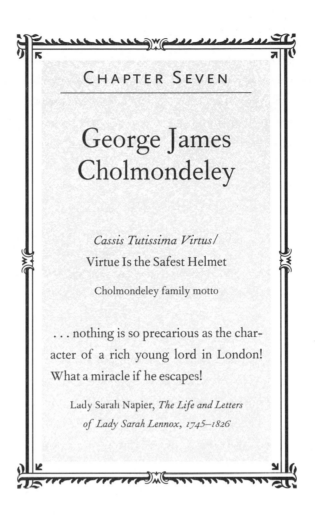

CHAPTER SEVEN

George James Cholmondeley

Cassis Tutissima Virtus/
Virtue Is the Safest Helmet

Cholmondeley family motto

... nothing is so precarious as the character of a rich young lord in London! What a miracle if he escapes!

Lady Sarah Napier, *The Life and Letters of Lady Sarah Lennox, 1745–1826*

SOULMATE? "THE ATHLETIC PEER": GEORGE JAMES, LORD CHOLMONDELEY

George James, Lord Cholmondeley, a Georgian gallant par excellence, had many sobriquets. He was described as a "bouncy" lad and athletic, too—"the Athletic Peer" was a gibe at his sexual athleticism—and was said to have had "little in his handsome head beyond pleasure and fashion," not unlike others in his fast-moving set. "Lord Tallboy" conjures up an image of a towering, solid piece of bedroom furniture (it *would* be bedroom furniture, wouldn't it?); "the Whimsical Lover" came from a "tête-à-tête" that alluded to his well-documented tomcatting (he went, one supposes, where his whimsy led him). Lastly, he was "the Torpedo"—a reference to the satirical and scurrilous poem that dwelt at long length (!) on his private parts.

It was a perpetual spring break, the carryings-on of rich young lords in London, far from their country estates and parental supervision. "Drunk as a lord" was a truism and dissipation was a common fate.

Young gentlemen were hurried through Eton and Oxford, where they learned to drink and swear and to call a man as well as to play tennis and billiards and to write Latin, and were thrust into Brooks's before they knew the difference in value between a farthing and a banknote: at nineteen they were hardened rakes or accomplished men of the world, or both. (Winston Churchill, Richard Carvel, *volume 5, chapter 31)*

{What's a Gallant? A gallant is variously defined as someone showy in dress or appearance, chivalrous, who plays court to ladies, who engages in amorous pursuit. This life of pleasure was termed "gallantry"; it was used to refer to playboys whose primary occupation was running after women.}

The times were fraught with peril for these scions of wealthy English noble houses bent on sampling each of the aristocratic vices in turn or simultaneously. They were young—some of them, who'd seen little of the world, were naïve—and London was a large and dangerous city. They'd probably been safer on their grand tours of the Continent than they were in London, where they were prey to any number of temptations. The value systems their parents and tutors had attempted to instill in them, as well as their innate characters, would soon be put to the test.

Lord Cholmondeley was an earl before he was a marquess, and he remained one afterward; peers can acquire a number of titles but are known by their highest one. The present Marquess of Cholmondeley—the seventh holder of the marquisate—is also Earl Rocksavage, Earl of Cholmondeley, Viscount Malpas, Baron Cholmondeley of Namptwich, Baron Newburgh, Viscount Cholmondeley, and Baron Newborough. The last two are Irish titles and all the others are UK peerage. The title of marquess, in the order of precedence, comes before that of earl. The Cholmondeleys also share the office of Lord Great Chamberlain with another family of peers. (By 1820, of 291 peers in the kingdom, 17 were marquesses.)

He has the duty of issuing the tickets of admission on state occasions, but

London's Population Explosion

In 1801, when the first national census was taken, London's population was 958,863, about a tenth of all the people in England and Wales and almost double what it was in 1700. In 1750, the total population of the nation was only 6,140,000, so the growth in the fifty years from 1750 to 1801 was phenomenal. Cosmopolitan London had people of every nationality and religion, from Sephardic Jews to French Huguenots. Some 20,000 were blacks.

his major role is the part he plays in royal coronations, having the right to dress the monarch on Coronation Day—claiming his archaic right to bring the monarch his "shirt, stockings, and drawers" and to serve the monarch water before and after the coronation banquet. He invests the monarch with the insignia of rule. He also attends peers and bishops upon their creation. At the time of the Regency, one applied to the Lord Great Chamberlain's office for a card of admittance to be presented to the Queen at one of her drawing rooms.

George James Cholmondeley, first Marquess of Cholmondeley and the husband of Charlotte Bertie, fulfilled these functions at the coronation of his good friend King George IV in 1820. The office is now held by David George Philip Cholmondeley, seventh Marquess of Cholmondeley, who has had it since 1990. Should he die without issue, his three sisters would be co-heiresses to his branch's portion of the office of Lord Great Chamberlain. The radical House of Lords Act of 1999 granted only two permanent seats to hereditary peers in the House of Lords, one to the Duke of Norfolk, who serves as the Earl Marshall, and the other seat to the Lord Great Chamberlain.

Enter notorious divorcée Grace Dalrymple Elliott into the life of the young Lord Cholmondeley. (Note that then all divorcées were notorious, not just our Grace.) She and Lord Cholmondeley were roughly the same age; he was five years older than she was, but she was probably a bit more mature. Her wit, too, may have been quicker than his, but he had charm and affability. They were both tall and good-looking. Grace and Lord Chol-

The Office of Lord Great Chamberlain

The Lord Great Chamberlain of England is a hereditary ceremonial office that ranks sixth among the Great Officers of State, beneath the Lord Privy Seal and above the Lord High Constable. Dating back to the days of William the Conqueror, it was held by the de Vere earls of Oxford until 1626, when it passed to Lord Willoughby de Eresby. In 1779, upon the death of Robert Bertie, the fourth Duke of Ancaster and Kesteven, who'd held the office less than a year, the House of Lords debated the question of splitting the position between his two surviving sisters, the Ladies Priscilla Bertie and Charlotte Bertie.

It was decided in 1781 that the office could be held jointly. The arrangement was questioned in 1902 in the House of Lords, upon a petition by Lord Ancaster that he had sole right to the office. The decision made in 1781 was reaffirmed, however, and the office continues to be shared. The families alternate their service and they can appoint deputies to take their places.

The Lord Great Chamberlain should not be confused with the Lord Chamberlain, who is the salaried chief officer of the royal household. (In 2002, the then-holder, Lord Luce, received a salary of £57,326.) The Lord Great Chamberlain's role is unpaid and primarily ceremonial. He has charge of the palace of Westminster and also oversees the furnishing of Westminster Hall and the Houses of Parliament—with emphasis on the House of Lords—on state occasions. When the sovereign opens Parliament in person, the Lord Great Chamberlain is responsible for the domestic arrangements. Though the controversial House of Lords Act of 1999 removed the automatic right of hereditary peers to sit in the House of Lords, the Lord Great Chamberlain was exempted so that he might continue to carry out his ceremonial functions.

At the opening and closing of each session of Parliament, the Lord Great Chamberlain has the duty of issuing the tickets of admission. He disposes of the sword of state—to be carried by any peer he may select—and walks in the procession on the right of the sword, a little before it and next to the sovereign. He carries a white stave—a six-foot-plus wooden pole—and on the back of his red cloth costume is embroidered the emblem of his appointment, an ornate golden key. He enters before the sovereign as she comes into Parliament, walking backward and carrying the stave. (Upon the death of the monarch his duty is to break his stave of office over the grave.)

mondeley were a handsome couple, a good match, certainly far better than the physically mismatched Grace and Dr. Eliot and considerably better than Grace and that scoundrel Lord Valentia.

Given Cholmondeley's sexual reputation and what had to be Grace's awakened sexual desire after the affair with Valentia, one assumes that theirs was a passionate and satisfying physical relationship. They were a striking pair, and were major celebrities as well. The newspapers, magazines, and cartoonists splashed their faces and exploits all over the metropolis. Recall the media frenzy over the former couple known as "Bennifer"—Ben Affleck and Jennifer Lopez—and one begins to get an idea of this pair's allure.

The Earl was a generous protector to all of his mistresses, and Grace Elliott was perhaps his most doted-upon acquisition. He lavished expensive gifts upon her and eagerly showed her off to his fellow gallants. To quote Grace's biographer Horace Bleackley:

> It was manifest that he was as deeply infatuated as ever, in spite of the rumours that he was growing tired of her, for during the whole summer [this was 1776] he never left her side, accompanying her to Margate, and entertaining her at his residence in Roehampton and at his house in Piccadilly. His generosity knew no bounds, and Grace's splendid carriage and pair [the horses were a pair of matched greys, the most desirable to own] and her blue and silver liveries were the envy of all the frail sisterhood.

Her sisters in the trade also envied her grand box at the Opera. Her fiercest rival, Mary Robinson, lost no time in competing with her. The number of Grace's box doesn't come down to us, but according to a recent biographer of Mrs. Robinson, that lady's box number was—believe it or not—69, and she was said to have decorated it in an elaborate, attention-drawing manner so typical of her.

There must have been an open-ended charge account at the modiste's as well, as Grace's rich costumes were evidently the talk of the town. All of these accoutrements showed the gallants in his set that the Earl knew how to treat a girl and raised the ton's estimate of him. Grace favored a "vivid" shade of blue, according to Bleackley, a shade he said matched her eyes. (Her eyes don't appear blue in either of the portraits Gainsborough painted of her, but they could have been a changeable hazel.) Bleackley crowed: "Not even the Duchess of Devonshire or the Countess of Derby excelled her in the magnificence of their costumes." She was what the times dubbed "a fashion plate."

Bleackley asserts that Lord Cholmondeley was eager "to gratify her vanity and encourage her extravagance." Money was no object. (And as the peerage rarely paid their bills from tradesmen on time, if ever, it really wasn't.) Grace had her portrait painted by Gainsborough, a striking full-length work that was exhibited as No. 114 at the Royal Academy in April 1778. It was reproduced in mezzotint for commercial distribution (as was commonly done with popular portraits) by the engraver John Dean, who exhibited widely in London between 1777 and 1791. Thomas Gainsborough was the top portrait painter in London, next to Sir Joshua Reynolds; both charged the maximum rates for their work. Nothing but the best would do for His Lordship's beautiful *chère-amie*.

Grace came to Cholmondeley with more baggage than simply her divorce, which was baggage enough. Bleackley alleges that Grace's amours had been many and frequent since her parting with her seducer Valentia, saying that she "had become more flagrantly immoral," but he can name no man other than "a rich young coxcomb named William Bird." A "tête-à-tête" published in *The Town and Country Magazine* in 1778, however, named two other men, Lambe and Archer. She was labeled a "velvet wanton" and said to have a voracious sexual appetite; such stuff sold magazines.

Katie Hickman, in *Courtesans,* mentions that Grace participated in "wild and debauched parties" with her friend Gertrude Mahon and another woman, a sometimes actress and prostitute named Margaret Cuyler, who operated out of Mrs. Matthews's King's Place "nunnery." Hickman doesn't, however, provide any further information on these parties, and Grace was

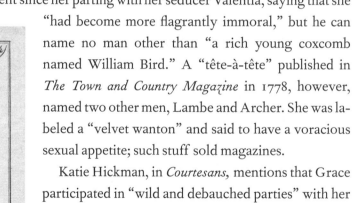

an 8. *Costume Parisien* *(184)*

Costume de Bal.

From the *Journal des dames et des modes,* printed in Year VIII of the French Revolution (1799/1800). Parisian fashion 'zines were highly prized. (Courtesy of novelist Candice Hern, www.candice hern.com)

Scandal: The Newspapers' and Print Shops' Stock-in-Trade

It was a scandalous age; no one disputed that. People behaved in flamboyant ways and other people eagerly observed, read, and gossiped about it all. The juicy *on-dits* made the rounds of the fashionable world and trickled down to hoi polloi in no time. Even the illiterate and poor—those who couldn't afford newspapers—could view the graphic cartoons posted for sale in the print-shop windows that illus-

Hannah Humphrey's Print Shop. James Gillray drew this picture in 1808; Humphrey's shop was arguably the best known of those selling caricatures. Humphrey and the popular cartoonist Gillray had a relationship that was more than just business; they lived together. (Bridgeman Art Library)

trated the outrageous antics of the bon ton. It was a public and dirty trough, filled to the brim daily by the gossip columnists and caricaturists, the Georgian paparazzi.

Women are tarred with the gossip brush, but London gossip had its start in the men's coffeehouses. Talk originating there migrated to the tabloids for publication, according to Roger Wilkes in *Scandal: A Scurrilous History of Gossip* (2003). Most newspaper gossip columnists masked their identities with pen names lest they face being attacked in the streets, as was Dr. James Hill, a newspaper personality almost on a par with Henry Bate, the controversial editor of several gossip-filled London newspapers. Under the nom de plume "The Inspector," Hill wrote a gossip column for the *London Advertiser, and Literary Gazette.* He was described as "a rakish figure in his early thirties [who] criss-crossed fashionable London in a magnificent chariot, picking up paragraphs and sowing mischief in his daily column. . . . He made many enemies along the way, and his column was . . . littered with retractions and apologies." Captain Philip Thicknesse became another notable gossip columnist, but unlike Bate and Hill—whom people could identify—he was well hidden behind the pseudonyms "A Wanderer" in the *St. James's Chronicle* and "Polyxena" in *The Gentleman's Magazine.* Thicknesse not only wrote truly scurrilous material but was a blackmailer; he was paid handsomely to keep gossip from his columns. Even the unscrupulous Henry Bate thought him no gentleman but a "hoary offender [who] has menaced public men [and] held numerous families in apprehension and horror."

James Boswell, Dr. Samuel Johnson's biographer, wrote gossip under the pseudonym "The Hypochondriack" for *The London Magazine* between 1777 and 1783. Wilkes describes Boswell's columns as akin to modern gossip writing, as they were "brief and chatty . . . often dashed off at great speed, against a deadline, or thrown together from scraps of things he had read. He was interested in ideas and oddities alike [and his] columns read like information being delivered . . . as though Boswell himself, glass in hand, had met the reader at a party packed with his acquaintances."

Gossip columnists were—and are—fun to read, but their profession still isn't considered respectable journalism. Today's gossip sheets—and the paparazzi they encourage—are at the lowest end of this profession's scale. Like prostitution, the most outrageous tabloids wouldn't survive without a clientele; if there was no one to buy these scandal sheets, they'd soon fold. Gossip, though, has a way of enduring and is taken up with gusto the world over; purveyors of gossip supplied a great deal of entertainment in the late Georgian period.

never associated with any of the brothels. (Note that the "Mrs. Elliott" described in one of Jack Harris's notorious published lists of prostitutes in 1793 is not our Grace.)

Grace had been kicked out of her home by her husband in 1774 (though he had to provide some basic support); she was not to receive an annuity until their divorce was finalized. Her family shunned her. That she found interim protectors after Valentia should come as no surprise. The remarkable thing is that she didn't sink to the level of a common prostitute, but rather wound up with a man like Cholmondeley, a high-ranking peer. She went up, not down, and did very well for herself. How many men there were along the way, and how many "debauched parties" she indulged in, is irrelevant.

What more is known of George James Cholmondeley?

Although Lord Cholmondeley was no thundering intellectual—George Selwyn, the noted wit and friend of his granduncle Horace, called him an "idiot"—he was savvy enough to take what he had been given by heredity and inheritance and make more of it. His was not a sizable legacy. His father, who'd died young, had been a dissolute rake and the family fortune was not at all what it once had been, but Cholmondeley had the fortunate attribute of affability. He became a favorite of his granduncle Horace Walpole, and

How Much Did They Get for a Painting?

George Romney charged about half of what Gainsborough and Reynolds (the two most eminent portrait painters of the time) did. In 1795 he painted a portrait of Lord Westmorland for £147, according to Marcia Pointon's study *Hanging the Head: Portraiture and Social Formation in Eighteenth-Century England* (1993). In today's money, that's £8,820—$17,640 in U.S. dollars—but one has to bear in mind this is a large painting, not a miniature, and it took the artist more than five whole months to paint. (Romney regularly undercut the other two; it was thought to be the prime reason he was never asked to join the Royal Academy, of which Reynolds was president.) In the 1750s and 1760s, Pompeo Batoni, the Roman painter so popular with Englishmen on their grand tour, who painted Lord Cholmondeley, charged only £25 for a full-length portrait. That's £1,500/$3,000 today. Before the Bath-based Gainsborough saw the better action in London and the chance to raise his fees considerably, he was charging 60 guineas (just over £3,650/$7,250) for his work. Reynolds, in London, was charging £150 (£9,000/$18,000); the noted portraitist Allan Ramsey, in Edinburgh, was asking £84 (£5,040/$10,080); and Joseph Wright of Derby was low man at £52 (£3,120/$6,240).

By the 1780s, Batoni had doubled his rate to £50 (£3,000/$6,000), still paltry by London standards: the distinguished society painter Joshua Reynolds had raised his to £200 (£12,000/$24,000) for a full-length portrait. His full-length of Philippe, Duc d'Orléans, in April 1785, cost the Frenchman 250 guineas, "considered dear by Philippe's friends in England,"

according to the Evarts Seelye Scudder biography *Prince of the Blood*. In today's currency, that's about £20,000/$40,000. Reynolds's prices were definitely

Thomas Gainsborough, Self-Portrait, 1758/1759. Gainsborough, who was said to have embodied the classic "artistic temperament," had only one serious rival in London: Sir Joshua Reynolds. (National Portrait Gallery, London)

going up, but as Orléans was the richest man in France—if not in the whole of Europe—perhaps the artist did some padding of the final bill. That extra bit was apparently taken note of by his English patrons.

James Northcote, a student of Reynolds's (and his future biographer) was another portraitist at the low end of the pay scale; he was getting only 16 guineas

(£1,000/$2,000) in 1784. And, in 1760s America, writes Pointon, "John Singleton Copley estimated that his income was three hundred guineas a year . . . equal to nine hundred in London." That's just over £18,000/$36,000.

George Engleheart's fee book verifies that this miniaturist painted 4,853 "pictures in little" during the course of his thirty-nine-year career. Engleheart, while not nearly as well regarded as Richard Cosway, produced beautiful work. His income was eminently respectable, exceeding £1,200 (£72,000/$144,000) a year.

An extraordinarily successful young female artist was Anne Mee, who in 1804 was receiving 40 guineas for a single miniature painting (about $5,000 at today's exchange rate). This obscure young woman's fee was comparable to what the most distinguished portraitists of the day were charging for their work. The Prince of Wales became her patron.

Of course, there were some drawbacks to the excellent prices the very best—or most popular and trendy—portrait painters in London were receiving for their work. The ton was slow to pay (royals were impossible) and so painters began to ask for half their fees before a painting commenced, if they were to get anything at all. (Marcia Pointon cites a humiliating incident with the commission of a painting for the Marquess of Townshend in which George Romney had to swallow the consequences of dealing with this imperious aristocrat.) It was not an easy life. These very busy painters sometimes overbooked themselves, and as a consequence often took a very long time to complete their commissions. Horace Walpole complained in a letter that his friends, the Misses Berry—who, against the grain of the times and society, had actually been so naïve as to pay up front in full for a portrait—waited months to receive the final product.

when Walpole died a stately manor, Houghton Hall, was left to Cholmondeley over others in the family who might have had a better claim. Over the years, he received other bequests. He was, as well, successful in the legal arena; he liked to sue, and he always won.

Cholmondeley can be easily dismissed as just another period gallant dedicated to the single-minded pursuit of pleasure, but he was a bit more complex than the stereotype he represented. A little-known aspect of his life is that he started a faro bank at his men's club, Brooks's. The canny earl was clever enough to have made a fortune out of other men's addiction to gambling by serving as the banker. The house/banker rarely loses in most games of chance; although the odds are not so tilted in favor of the house in faro as in other card games, they are tilted enough to be profitable.

His Lordship was no fool, George Selwyn's assessment of him notwithstanding. He made an immense fortune, earning the enmity of many along the way, by running that faro bank. In truth, everything he touched seemed to turn to gold. It could be said that George James Cholmondeley had the Midas touch. According to the *Journal of Thomas Raikes:*

> *He [Cholmondeley] was one of the four who set up that celebrated Faro bank at Brookes's which ruined half the town. They would not trust the waiters to be croupiers, but themselves dealt the cards alternately, being paid three guineas an hour out of the joint fund, and at this rate, Lord———, and other noblemen of the highest rank, were seen slaving like menials till a late hour in the morning. Their gains were enormous, as Mr. Thompson of Grosvenor Square, and Lord Cholmondeley, realized each between 300,000£ and 400,000£. Tom Stepney had a share, but would always punt against his own partners, and lost on one side what he gained on the other. A Mr. Paul, who brought home a large fortune from India, lost 90,000£ in one night, was ruined, and went back to the East to make another.*

{Faro. From Pharaoh, a French game played with a pack of fifty-two cards. (The name came from the illustration on the back of a deck of cards that showed an Egyptian pharaoh.) Players bet against the house, with the banker or dealer drawing two cards, a winning one and a losing one, from a deck or box, to complete a turn. Bets on which card will win or lose are placed on each turn; the game was a favorite of professional cardsharps.}

Cholmondeley was perhaps as successful in his litigation as he was in his gambling enterprise; he appeared in the newspapers from time to time as the claimant in various property suits. What enemies he had and what bad feelings he engendered grew in no small part out of his success in the courts as well as his success with gambling. As Thomas Raikes comments in his *Journal:*

> *Lord Cholmondeley had in his life been peculiarly fortunate in discovering old claims to property which had been either dormant or unknown to his family. An instance of this sort gave rise to a lawsuit, which at one time was very much talked of. The late Lord Clinton, then quite a young man, became a member of Watier's Club, and unfortunately lost a considerable sum at whist: wishing to raise some money for this purpose on mortgage, he sent the title-deeds of his family estate to be investigated by a lawyer; this man, on looking over the deeds, found that an old claim existed on the whole property in favour of the*

The Men's Clubs of London

Why join a club? They were—and many of them still are—bastions of male society to which only the right people belonged. They were rarefied environments, places to eat, drink, be convivial, gamble for high stakes, make the right connections, and know one was safe among one's own kind. A man could sit in the bow window at White's (the oldest gentleman's club still in existence in London), read one of the many freshly ironed newspapers (ironed to keep the ink from getting on one's hands or gloves), and—a snifter of brandy at his side, waiters at his beck and call—trade bon mots with the good fellows and wits of his set whilst observing and commenting on all those less fortunate who passed by outside. His coach would drop him off and pick him up. This kind of man preferred the company of men to the prattle of women, and as no women could be members then, it was idyllic. Note the following fictional musing from Beau Brummell—a fixture at White's—as written by Rosemary Stevens. This snippet captures beautifully the men who frequented these clubs:

I turned onto St. James's Street where I was less likely to be waylaid by any female. Ladies simply do not parade up and down the street where gentlemen's clubs are prevalent. Should a lady walk or drive her carriage past these male sanctuaries, she would be inviting comment on her person. Very fast behavior indeed . . . Arriving at my destination, I slowed my pace and ambled into that exclusive terrain of four hundred and fifty privileged gentlemen, White's Club. We gather here not just for convivial conversation, but also to discuss topics of a broader scale: politics, literature, science, drama. White's is, of course, still a good place to read one of the myriad of newspapers kept there or to place a wager in White's famous Betting Book as to, say, which opera dancer might bestow her favors on which peer of the realm first. Important matters, you understand. (Rosemary Stevens, *Death on a Silver Tray,* Berkeley, 2000)

The following are some of the more famous and interesting period clubs:

- The Alfred Club, 23 Albemarle Street (founded 1808). The Earl of Dudley called it the "dullest place in existence," but it attracted the literary set; Lord Byron was a member. Merged with another club, the Oriental, in 1855.

- The Beefsteak, 24 King William Street, the Strand (founded 1735). Primarily a dinner club with no particular qualifications for members— but very exclusive nonetheless. No gambling; no visitors; all waiters are called "Charles."

- Boodles, 28 St. James's Street (founded 1762). First known as the Savoir Faire, it was where county society and the lesser peerage could easily mingle and was favored by Charles James Fox and the Duke of Devonshire. The name comes from its original headwaiter.

- Brooks's, 60 St. James's Street (founded 1778). Whig club, hence politically liberal; popular with gamblers. Extremely exclusive, the Prince of Wales is a member. It had a set membership in 1799 of 450 men.

- The Cocoa-Tree, 64 St. James's Street (1700). Founded in the reign of Queen Anne and originally called Will's Cocoa House, after its first owner, it was associated with the Jacobite cause and later with the Tories. Notorious for gambling and duels. There was an encounter there between Henry Bate, the pugnacious editor of the *Morning Post,* and the notorious "Fighting Fitzgerald," a lover of Mary Robinson's; another duel was fought at the Cocoa-Tree over the actress Mrs. Hartley.
- The Traveller's Club, 106 Pall Mall (1819). This was for individuals who'd traveled or resided abroad. Members had to have traveled at least five hundred miles from London. Foreigners meeting the qualification and having proper recommendations were welcomed. No conversation—or guests—allowed. The neoclassical clubhouse resembles an Italian palazzo.
- Watier's, 81 Piccadilly (1807). Named after the Prince of Wales's chef, it had excellent food. Deep gambling play also took place; Beau Brummell was its president and enforced strict rules. The club dissolved in 1819, owing, it's said, to overwhelming gambling losses suffered by members and a change for the worse in the composition of its membership.
- White's, 37–38 St. James's Street (1693). The oldest club in London. It began life as a chocolate shop and moved to its present location circa 1755. It was known as a Tory stronghold and was right across the street from its great rival, Brooks's. (In reality, many gentlemen belonged to both clubs.) Hazard and faro were the most popular games played. Beau Brummell and his set—as well as Lords Alvanley, Foley, Sefton, and Worcester and the Duke of Argyll—hung out at the bow window. Excellent food and wine cellars and highly restricted membership. Brian Wheeler, writing for the BBC News online magazine, recently investigated Prince William's preference for plain old White's over nightclubs such as the Ministry of Sound, Annabel's, and China White's and noted that "the gentleman's club, that much lampooned bastion of privilege and tradition, is enjoying something of a renaissance" and that "young aristocrats who would have once spurned the crusty portals of White's, Boodles and Brooks's, the trio of clubs that form the backbone of London's clubland, in favour of more egalitarian pleasures are now queuing up to join."

What does it cost to be a member of White's? If one passes the screening—a proposer and two seconders are needed—a mere £650 ($1,300) per annum. If one is blackballed, eight years must pass before one reapplies. And what does a young aristo get for this quite reasonable sum, which works out to about £50 ($100) a month? In his article, " 'If Anybody Wants Me, I'll Be at My Club,'" Brian Wheeler quotes a member of forty years' standing, Tom Stacey, who says, "You can be completely unselfconscious. You are among people you have grown up with, people you went to school with. You speak the same instinctive language. It is not snobbish. It just allows you to relax. You can break wind and nobody minds."

Women are still barred from membership at White's. The excuse given is that there is not enough space. With all that breaking of wind, it's perhaps a mercy.

 hose Pesky British Upper-Class Names!

According to novelist and native Britisher Jean Ross Ewing, "Names connected with the upper classes are particularly likely to have odd pronunciations. Witness: Beauchamp, Coke, Cholmondeley, Featherstonehaugh, Home, Leveson-Gower, Mainwaring, Ruthven, Menzies. Respectively: Beech'm, Cook, Chumley, Fanshaw, Hyume, Loos-n-gor, Mannering, Riv'n, Mingies (or Minjies)—except for the London stationers who have given up and call themselves Menzies, as spelt." H. L. Mencken, in his 1918 book *The American Language,* noted: "Hools for Howells, Sillinger for St. Leger, Sinjin for St. John, Weems for Wemyss, Stubbs for St. Aubyn, Vane for Veheyne, Kerduggen for Cadogen, Moboro or Mobrer for Marlborough, Key for Cais, March-banks for Marjoribanks, Trosley for Trottercliffe, Darby for Derby." Eccentricity in the rendering of a family name can confer cachet; an oddly-pronounced name, once heard, is never forgotten. Who hasn't heard of the Chumleys, even if one has no idea who they are?

Cholmondeley family, and forthwith informed his Lordship of the circumstance, who lost no time in commencing his action for the recovery. It made a great noise at the time; and as appearances at first were very much in favour of the suit, it was considered not only a very hard case upon Lord Clinton, who would thus be totally ruined, but an act of rapacity on the part of the other, who was in such very affluent circumstances. The claim, however, was never clearly made out, and a compromise took place.

It does seem extremely rapacious for an already very rich man to take advantage of a poorer one, but this particular individual was one made poorer by his own shortcoming, his penchant for gambling. And did Lord Cholmondeley really have a choice? It was his family's fortunes that were at stake, and family, with him, was always all. Whether it was a nice thing to do, or a right thing to do, his actions were ever to be governed by this consideration. According to Raikes, he told one critic that he felt he was justified in pursuing any avenue that contributed to his family's "future interests."

Lord Cholmondeley knew—and was related to—everyone there was to know and to be related in the kingdom; he was extremely well connected, light-years from the social-climbing postures of old Dr. Eliot, who could only dream of being intimately a part of His Lordship's company. The Cholmondeleys were the real thing; they had been around forever. Their titles consisted of no mere knighthoods or nouveau-baronetcies like those eventually given to the good doctor of physic.

The Cholmondeleys were an old Cheshire family who'd come to England with William the Conqueror. From the male side they were descended from the Norman Marcher barons of Malpas (Border lords who guarded the Welsh frontier) and on the female side from William's half sister. It doesn't get any better than this in England, bloodlines that go back to King William I.

One Hugh Cholmondeley was named to the peerage with the title of Baron of Namptwich in 1689 and given the earldom of Cholmondeley in 1706. The family seat in Chester was Cholmondeley Castle and in Norfolk, Houghton Hall. At the time Grace and George James began their affair he hadn't yet acceded to the title of marquis of Cholmondeley and was not in possession of Houghton Hall.

John Eliot, Grace's soon-to-be-ex-husband, was basically a trumped-up "Cit" who'd moved up a level by becoming a doctor, a member of one of the professional classes, but he would never be the equal of Lord Cholmondeley, no matter how many pedigrees he paid the College of Arms to draw up for him claiming (dubious) descent from Scottish kings.

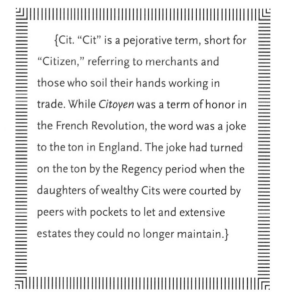

{Cit. "Cit" is a pejorative term, short for "Citizen," referring to merchants and those who soil their hands working in trade. While *Citoyen* was a term of honor in the French Revolution, the word was a joke to the ton in England. The joke had turned on the ton by the Regency period when the daughters of wealthy Cits were courted by peers with pockets to let and extensive estates they could no longer maintain.}

It must have irked Eliot terribly to see his errant wife with someone like Lord Cholmondeley; one imagines Grace's revenge on her husband must have been sweet. Horace Bleackley, however, insists that she was humiliated and despondent when her ex-husband was awarded his titles. Perhaps there was some of that, but she was surely harboring strong hopes she'd become Lord Cholmondeley's countess, a rank two

Dilettanti-theatricals, or a peep at the Green Room, James Gillray, published by Hannah Humphrey, June 18, 1804. Lord Cholmondeley and a squad of other gallants—among them Richard Edgcumbe, second Earl of Mount Edgcumbe; Frederick Howard, fifth Earl of Carlisle; and Edward Smith Stanley, twelfth Earl of Derby—are shown doing one of the things they did best, hanging out at the theater's greenrooms to meet actresses. Lord Cholmondeley is depicted as a very large man in yellow (not a good color for a large person), seated on a throne and wearing a laurel wreath. About his ample middle he has a sash spoofing his family motto. It says *Amor Vincit Omnia* ("Love conquers all"), a not very subtle reference to his well-documented amorous adventures. The actual Cholmondeley motto is *Cassis tutissima virtus* ("Virtue is the safest helmet"). (National Portrait Gallery, London)

rungs above mere baroness. With that to look forward to, why would she have cared about Eliot's titles?

Before Grace, Cholmondeley had been a regular stage-door Johnnie—a habitué of the theater's greenrooms. He'd been notorious for his many love affairs with actresses, opera dancers, courtesans, married women—the list goes on. Few women—the actress-courtesan Sophia Baddeley being a notable exception—had spurned his ardent advances.

Cholmondeley had also been a fixture at the masked balls at the Pantheon and other venues where fashionable courtesans came to meet prospective patrons, and he frequented the high-end brothels not far from clubland on St. James's. The scurrilous poem *The Torpedo* came out in 1777, when he'd been with Grace a year. Dedicated to his generously endowed private parts, it was perhaps the worst of all the satires that were to appear in his lifetime.

In 1774 or 1775—a couple of years before *The Torpedo* made its appearance—an incident had occurred that was to be satirized years later, in 1794. Though Cholmondeley was the subject of the piece, he was not the butt of the joke. The butt was Gertrude, the widow of Lord John Russell, fourth Duke of Bedford. She evidently had conceived a passion for the young Cholmondeley and was avid, public, and ridiculous in her pursuit of him.

It was the work of Charles Pigott, author of the satire *The Jockey Club, or A Sketch of the Manners of the Age* (1772). It was called *The Female Jockey Club,* and it was a nasty piece of work:

> *Amongst other highly distinguished Personages, Male and Female, celebrated in this Work, are the following . . . Lord Ch——Im——de——ly . . . G——t——de D——ch——ss of B——f——d.*
>
> *"The wrinkled G——t——de carries on her face,*
> *Memento mori to each public place."*
>
> *. . . Remembrance of what thou hast been, is a poor miserable substitute for what thou art. Age when thus disfigured, loses all claim to that respect, which otherwise it would command, and satire is justly and honourably employed, when it holds forth its deformity, as an example of pity and contempt to the world . . . nor can there be a more instructive lesson against the melancholy disgusting follies and vices of old age, than is afforded by the character now under review.*
>
> *. . . the violence of her tender passions . . . [was] not long since most pointedly illustrated in the delicate proposal made by her to a certain gigantic nobleman*[*E——l C——m——dley], whose secret perfections have been long the theme of female enthusiasm. His fame had reached the ears of Gertrude, who could not resist the temptation, and a carte blanche was offered to the much envied and courted lord; but Oh! Ungrateful man! The matron's suit was rejected, and at the age of seventy, she was left to pine under all the anguish of disappointed love. Well might she exclaim in the words of the furious distracted Dido:*
>
> *"Nec lumina flexit,*
> *Nec lachrymas victus dedit, aut miseratus Amantem est." Virgil.*
>
> *This tale created a fund of ridicule at the expence of the love-sick D——ss, and in truth we must allow that the ridicule was well applied, for it is difficult to conceive a more ludicrous being in nature, than an old woman in love.*

Regardez moi.

    . . . It appears in general that age is more disgusting in woman than in man. . . .

    . . . Let us however be candid where we can, nor refuse to Gertrude the justice she deserves. From her, the indigent prodigal sometimes finds relief, and her house is a kind receptacle to cavaliers and noble damsels in distress; but here, a reflection obtrudes itself. We know not which is most to be pitied, the old woman who feels the want of a young beautiful cavalier, or the unfortunate cavalier, who by the hardest services only, can obtain from her the recompence he needs.

In 1794, George James was still an earl—hence the reference to E——l C——m——dley, rather than the Marquess of Cholmondeley. "Gigantic" refers both to his height—he was much taller than the norm—and to his reputed attributes, those "secret perfections" that inspired "female enthusiasm." (And note the charming bit about these young men providing their "hardest services.") It was this special endowment after which the sex-mad septuagenarian Gertrude, Duchess of Bedford, was supposed to have hankered.

The implication was that the dirty old duchess was looking for a boy-toy and had found an admirable candidate in Lord Cholmondeley, thirty years her junior, whom she propositioned. True? False? It makes for a good bit of titillation. While the woman comes off as a foolish old hag, the much younger gallant becomes celebrated for his sexual prowess, thereby adding to his social desirability.

The Duchess, born in 1719, died in 1794, the year this anonymous twaddle was printed. She may have been going senile for some time before her death. Edward Gibbon, the historian, had commented in a letter to his stepmother on July 3, 1775, that it was bruited about that the Duchess had "made regular proposals of marriage to the young Earl Cholmondeley and was regularly refused. Poor as he was . . . he was not quite poor enough to accept them."

The ton was always fair game for these shadowy scribblers. Why such old gossip was published so late, long after Lord Cholmondeley had disappeared from the gossip sheets and become a respectable, married family man no longer so poor, is puzzling.

Talk about Lord Cholmondeley's special endowments and his skill as a lover had been in the air since 1777, when the scurrilous pamphlet *The Torpedo, A Poem to the Electrical Eel* was published anonymously in London. Neither author nor printer was named—to avoid possible legal action by Lord Cholmondeley—and the copyright notation reads only, "London . . . Printed: and sold by all the Booksellers in London and Westminster." The title page further states that the poem is "Addressed to Mr. John Hunter, Surgeon: and Dedicated to The Right Honourable Lord Cholmondeley." The pamphlet was readily available and it found a wide audience, as its cost was only a shilling and sixpence. Beginning with a four-page dedication, the forty-eight-stanza poem, in an AABCCB rhyme scheme, runs seventeen pages, for a total of twenty-one pages.

There is a bizarre drawing on the title page, an elongated oval, stippled, with a slit in the middle. At the top the words "The Torpedo" are written in

FACING PAGE: *"Regardez-moi"* ("Watch me"), by James Gillray, 1781(?), depicts the accomplished and popular Italian dancing master Gaetano Apoline Balthazar Vestris showing the latest steps to a gigantic goose with a human head and long pigtail queue. Vestris stands with his legs together, chest thrown out, arms curved. *"Regardez-moi"* was his characteristic instruction. On a stool behind the goose is an open book inscribed *"Electrical E.E.L.";* on the ground at its feet is another inscribed *"The Torpedo, 'Dedicated to Ld——C——, My Lord, I take the Liberty——The greatness of whose Parts are known . . . '"* This indicates that the goose is Lord Cholmondeley. *The Torpedo,* circa 1777, was the scurrilous poem satirizing the Earl. On the wall behind Vestris and the goose there's a framed picture of Charles James Fox, the Whig leader, depicted with a fox's head, seated opposite Cholmondeley and throwing dice. This is a reference to the faro bank held by Cholmondeley at Brooks's. Fox appears satisfied, while Cholmondeley clenches his fist and exclaims in anger. A devil climbing on the top of the frame holds out a claw to grab the head of Fox, who was a gambling addict. Vestris was a popular teacher of dance to the ton and also gave ladies lessons in movement, such as the proper way to enter one's box at the theater. (National Portrait Gallery, London)

script, and at the bottom are what appears to be an *M* in a circle and a quotation attributed to Shakespeare, "I am not what I seem . . ." Emanating from this figure are what appear to be stippled rays, perhaps of light. The eel's mouth? Something prurient? It's anyone's guess.

John Hunter was the esteemed Scots anatomist and surgeon who left his collection of objects (including the remains of very small and very large human beings, such as the Irish Giant and the Sicilian dwarf) to the British nation. (The collection is now housed in the Hunterian Museum of the Royal College of Surgeons.) He was a scientific experimenter with wideranging interests, and he had a lifelong curiosity concerning the propagation of eels (he was never to figure it out) and in diseases of the penis. He also fashioned a hypothesis that two diseases could not exist simultaneously in the same organ and thus believed that syphilis and gonorrhea—what we now know to be two different diseases—were symptoms of the same disease. At the time, many believed his hypothesis had validity.

According to medical lore, Hunter used himself as a guinea pig in 1767 to further his knowledge of venereal disease and to strengthen his theory. Not unlike what his pupil Edward Jenner did with his experiments in smallpox, Hunter was said to have cut into the flesh of his own glans and prepuce with a scalpel that had been dipped in a prostitute's suppurating lesion. The woman had been suffering from both gonorrhea and syphilis, and the diseases were supposedly passed on to Hunter. Medical historians are not at all certain that this transpired; it may be an apocryphal story. They believe it more likely that he inoculated someone other than himself with the pus from the prostitute's lesion to study gonorrhea, not realizing that the prostitute also had syphilis.

Ironically, Hunter himself may have suffered from this deadlier of the two venereal diseases, having gotten it in the usual way. He died in 1793, purportedly from its complications. He gave his name to the Hunterian chancre (or true chancre), the hard sore at the site of entry of syphilitic infection.

So it's significant that this anonymous versifier chose a physician associated with the male organ, venereal disease, and the study of eel propagation to whom to "address" this work "dedicated" to a gentleman who probably had intimate knowledge of things venereal and whose sex organ—in length and motility—could be likened to an eel. As he states in his dedication:

My Lord,

I take the liberty of addressing the following Poem to you, as I know no one to whom it can be dedicated with so much propriety, or who possesses qualities so essential for the Patron of this piece. I speak with some degree of confidence, having the honour of remembering your Lordship from a very early period, when you discovered the greatness of those parts which have since made so respectable a figure in Society.

The implication is that this is someone who is, or was, an intimate of Lord Cholmondeley's. He continues:

It has been your peculiar happiness to proceed uniformly . . . and the enlargement of your powers has been in proportion to your manhood. . . . Give me leave to add, that you have never suffered those parts, when you could help it, to lie dormant; nor lost the opportunity of seeking out new objects to employ them upon. . . . With such parts, my Lord, you seem formed by Nature for great attempts, and the tenor of your life has shewn, that nothing could resist your progress.

He is basically calling him a male slut, indiscriminate in the exercise of his "parts."

He continues in this sarcastic vein, drawing some labored metaphors while mocking the elaborate, over-the-top style that poets and writers use to flatter their subjects:

In the Sciences, what is it that your Lordship has not accomplished? In Architecture, have you not erected a column which strikes every beholder with admiration at its beauty as well as novelty? Beautiful from its superior size, and novel from the frieze being at the bottom. Madame ———, that celebrated antiquary in Paris, has often, I have been informed, handled this Pillar, but never could determine its Order. In the Mechanics, few people are ignorant of your improvements, particularly in those which relate to the Motion of Bodies, the doctrine of Elasticity, and the great pains you have undergone in making experiments upon the Wedge.

Erecting tall columns, motions of bodies, elasticity, handling of pillars, and so on are not-so-very-subtle descriptions of the various stages of the sex act. (The "frieze" could refer to the testes or to pubic hair.)

Not satisfied with these innuendoes on Cholmondeley's great contributions to the "Sciences," the author waxes eloquent on the peer's nonpareil importance to the "Arts":

> In the Arts, my Lord, you seem to have been equally successful, as far as your disposition may have led you. In Painting, who has excelled you in drawing at full length; in your fondness for the Nude; and, what is still more uncommon, if we may credit some Female Connoisseurs, in taking a strong likeness of yourself!

At this time—1777, when Lord Cholmondeley was twenty-eight years old—there were already rumors of illegitimate children, hence the "strong likeness[es]" of himself. Cholmondeley had had many other liaisons besides his current one with "Dally the Tall." The satirist goes on:

> Though master of this extensive knowledge, you descend to every thing. You have the goodness to make the Female World your particular care, and to take the Ladies under you, to whom you have an uncommon method of conveying instruction; uniting Pleasure with Improvement, the only way of making your lessons sink deep into the heart. But this, my Lord, is but a small part of your praise: it is your moral character that demands my attention. Have you not been remarked for your laudable enquiries after Innocence? Have you ever refused the purchase of any virtue that was to be had? Nay, have you not employed others in the same amiable pursuit?

It gets nastier, casting Lord Cholmondeley not only as a male slut, but also as a whoremonger, a chaser of virginal girls, and an employer of pimps ("have you not employed others in the same amiable pursuit?").

> And by various little presents which you have bestowed on the deserving, have you not convinced us, that in the language of Scripture, you considered modesty "as a treasure far above rubies." I do not exaggerate, my Lord, when I say, that all the great Virtues are yours,—Patience, Fortitude, Justice, Charity. In the pursuit of many a favourite object, have you not patiently endured what would have provoked the most gentle? And tho' the ill-natured part of mankind is too apt to denominate a laudable ambition, Impudence; have you not, in spite of detraction, persevered in attempting every thing? As to Justice—it is said you are a Justice of the Peace;—and I shall say of your Charity, that you are a perpetual Contributor to the Magdalen.

Note the enlistment of the Bible, Proverbs 31:10–11—"Who can find a virtuous woman? for her price is far above rubies. The heart of her husband doth safely trust in her."—to suggest that this rake seduces wives, too, cajoling them with gifts as well as attempting "every thing" to induce women to submit to his advances. Adultery, or "crim. con.," is no laughing matter, nor is the ruin of a married woman's reputation.

The point of the reference to "Justice of the Peace" is that Cholmondeley, as a large landowner and nobleman, would have been the magistrate for the area surrounding his country estate in Cheshire. The implication is that His Lordship is not morally fit for such a job, but is rather a "perpetual Contributor to the Magdalen" who has single-handedly created legions of prostitutes. (Magdalen is a term for a prostitute.)

And then there's the penultimate cut—one that suggests the writer has been an injured party or a good friend of someone injured by Lord Cholmondeley, or is simply someone acutely envious of the young lord's station in life and his success with women—a bleak prediction of the diminution of Lord Cholmondeley's sexual prowess. Without it, Cholmondeley is worthless and has no reason whatsoever to live, for this prowess, the ability to produce a strong erection—for what it is—is all that he can show as his contribution to the greater good of society:

> *My Lord, having all the veneration for you which such qualities deserve, I look forward with sorrow to that period, when age shall render your parts of no further service. Those being lost, you can have no occasion for life; and we shall with less regret spare your departure from Society, where you have long stood so valuable a member.*
>
> *I have the honour to be*
>
> > *Your Lordship's most devoted*
> > *And humble Servant,*
> > *The Author*

The first footnote to the poem further mocks Cholmondeley's value to society:

> *This Gentleman's extreme leanness is attributed to the great fatigue he undergoes at the Council Office, he being obliged to sit with a pen in his hand for above an hour at a time.*

It must be mentioned here that the meaning of "torpedo" has nothing to do with naval usage. Those cigar-shaped projectiles used in submarine war-

Who Wrote "The Torpedo"? And Why?

The Bakken Museum in Minneapolis, Minnesota, collects archival materials—rare books and scientific instruments—relating to the history of electricity and magnetism. It was founded in 1975 by Earl E. Bakken, inventor of the cardiac pacemaker. Among its eleven thousand books are two copies of this poem. One is titled *The Electrical eel, or Gymnotus electricus: and The torpedo, a poem."* It was printed in London in 1777, and reprinted in London. The second is titled *The electrical eel, or Gymnotus electricus; Inscribed to the honourable members of the Royal Society, by Adam Strong, naturalist. Described as the third edition, with considerable additions,"* it was printed in London in 1777, for J. Bew. "Adam Strong" is a pseudonym. The Bakken Library's librarian, Elizabeth Ihrig, noted in an e-mail that there are two possible attributions. Samuel Halkett and John Laing's *Dictionary of Anonymous and Pseudoanonymous English Literature* attributes the poem to one James Perry (1756–1821), a Scotsman who was editor of the London newspaper the *Morning Chronicle,* whereas the *Wrenn Catalogue* attributes it to William Whitehead (1715–1785), a poet and playwright who was the poet laureate of England from 1757 to 1785.

Two interesting candidates, but it would be less of a stretch to imagine a newspaper editor like Perry, who was clever with words, had penned the merciless satire. Lord Cholmondeley was a figure of fun to men more learned and less wealthy than he was, men like Perry. His name and exploits were constantly in the tabloids. Perry was a writer of many anonymous pamphlets, political and otherwise, and he dabbled in poetry. The literary style of "The Torpedo," however, is not that of a polished poet, as Whitehead presumably was, and Whitehead's connection with Lord Cholmondeley remains obscure. While Cholmondeley and Whitehead may have known each other, James Perry is by far the stronger candidate for the pseudonymous "Adam Strong, naturalist." Attacking a powerful peer anonymously was a safer route to take than hazarding the charge of libel. The editor Perry was intimate with libel, having once been found guilty of libeling the House of Lords, for which he was sen-

The Morning Chronicle (showing James Perry), etching by Richard Dighton, reissued by Thomas McLean, 1824. (National Portrait Gallery, London)

tenced to three months in Newgate Prison. Two other charges, one of seditious libel in 1793 and another in 1818 for his critical remarks against King George III, did not stick. Whitehead's most popular bit of verse was the tongue-in-cheek love poem "The Je Ne Scai Quoi" (The I Know Not What). (Modern French would be written *"Je ne sais quoi."*) An answer—of sorts—to "The Torpedo" was "The Old Serpent's Reply to the Electrical Eel," printed in 1777 by M. Smith "and sold by the Booksellers near Temple-Bar, and in Paternoster-Row." It is also anonymous, but its author is thought to be a woman. There is a reference on page 21 to Priapus, the Greek god of fertility known for his huge member, always displayed erect, "Like Chom in Piccadilly." Lord Cholmondeley's town house was at 94 Piccadilly.

William Whitehead, oil painting by Benjamin Wilson, 1758. (National Portrait Gallery, London)

fare postdate the period in which this poem was written. The word actually refers to the electric ray, family Torpedinidae, a fish that possesses an organ that stuns its prey with an electric shock. Thus Lord Cholmondeley's sex organ stuns its prey with—one is given to presume—its great size and shocking movement. (The shock of the electrical eel was thought to be, in moderation, therapeutic.)

The older definition of "torpedo," from the Latin *torpeo,* "to be stiff," is also intended. Eels, the state of being stiff, electric rays, and electrical charges—the satirist plays with these meanings and images throughout.

Note among Cholmondeley's numerous paramours and fellow gallants the reference to Grace Dalrymple Elliott, "Ell——t's wanton Wife":

> What tho' Lord Ch——lm——d——ly may conceal
> A most enormous length of Eel,
> Admir'd for size and bone;
> This mighty thing when lank, depress'd,

A mere noun adjective at best,
Is useless when alone.
But warm'd by Ell——t's wanton Wife,
The ponderous body feels new life,
Prepar'd to give the stroke,
Erect in all the pride of Nature,
E'en then to please this beauteous Creature,
It stoops to wear my yoke.

There are many references to the greatness of Cholmondeley's extended length, along with the satirist's complaints that his own abilities are overlooked, as in this stanza:

Tho' his Conductor may be large
As the tall mast of Lord Mayor's barge,
Erect and fixt in air;
Yet I emit as full a stream,
Pregnant with warm Electric Flame,
And mine's a larger Sphere.

The Torpedo is an astonishing and daring poem. It illustrates how easily character could be assassinated by anonymous scribblers and how the lowest kind of fun could be had in impugning an individual. There was no serious legal recourse for those so zealously satirized—unless they were members of the royal family—and besides, the damage was done. Did Lord Cholmondeley laugh it off? What did John Hunter make of it? Nothing, alas, is recorded for posterity, but none of this seems to have diminished the young peer's marriageability. Cholmondeley had no trouble finding a wealthy heiress from a noble family when the time came to marry and sire legitimate offspring, or, as common parlance had it, to "set up his nursery."

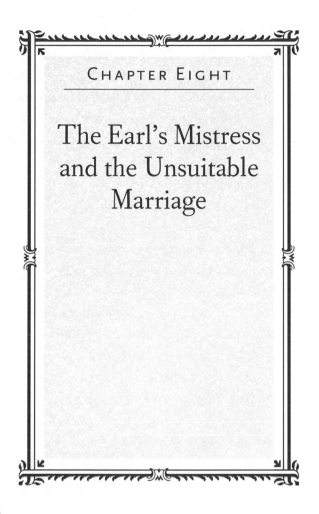

CHAPTER EIGHT

The Earl's Mistress and the Unsuitable Marriage

$\mathcal{G}$race Elliott and Lord Cholmondeley had been public lovers since the Pantheon masquerade ball on January 24, 1776. She was legally separated from her husband, Dr. John Eliot, and only months away from the finalization of their divorce. She had probably never been so happy as she was in those first heady months of her passionate physical relationship with Cholmondeley. It had to be a new experience for her.

The Earl was a sexual athlete, young, handsome, charming, well built, and probably a good deal of fun, a delightful companion to Grace as they made their nightly rounds of balls, parties, *ridottos*, and routs. There could not have been more of a contrast between him and John Eliot, who'd left it

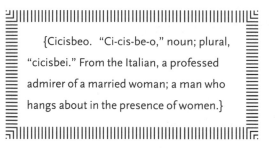

{Cicisbeo. "Ci-cis-be-o," noun; plural, "cicisbei." From the Italian, a professed admirer of a married woman; a man who hangs about in the presence of women.}

to cicisbei to escort his child bride, that lovely trophy wife, to social events, preferring to treat patients and to chase the mighty pound instead of paying Grace the attention she deserved. That one of the cicisbei put the horns on the good doctor's forehead was perhaps only to be expected.

Grace and Cholmondeley's liaison appeared to be a strong one; there was at least one rumor of an impending marriage between them. On March 11, 1776, just ten days before her divorce was finalized, the *Morning Post and Daily Advertiser* was reporting with excitement:

The buz of yesterday, amongst the ton was, that Lord C———y had actually engaged to marry Mrs. E———t, as soon as her husband's divorce bill had received the Royal assent.

The rumor surfaced again two years later, in 1778, according to an entry in an unpublished journal of Lady Mary Coke (1727–1811), a Scotswoman like Grace (Lady Coke was born a Campbell) who was married to Edward, Viscount Coke. Lady Coke related the gossip that

Lady [wrong—Grace never got the title; Eliot divorced her before his knighthood and baronetcy were awarded] Elliott . . . now lives with Lord Cholmondeley. She is with child and he intends to marry her.

This snippet is from a set of papers called the MS Journals of Lady Mary Coke, which are unpublished and held in a private collection in Scotland. (Lady Coke wrote her journals between 1756 and 1791, but the published parts only go up to 1771.)

Horace Bleackley also reported that "it was generally believed that a child was born three months after her [Grace's] picture was exhibited at Somerset House," but he may have gotten the painting of 1778 confused with the second portrait Gainsborough painted of Grace in 1782. That was the year she gave birth to Georgiana at the end of March.

No marriage occurred and nothing more is known about the rumored child. It may have been pure gossip, another one of those phantom children who keep popping up in Grace Elliott's life. There might have been a child who'd died or was sent away, but there's no follow-up anywhere to Lady Coke's comment, and the lady is unfortunately not always a reliable source.

Such loose talk, however, may have put a strain on the relationship and alarmed Lord Cholmondeley's family.

Grace's notoriety increased during the years she was with Cholmondeley. In 1777, the hack writer and poet William Combe, later known as the verse writer for Rowlandson's *Dr. Syntax* series, published a follow-up to his poem "The Diaboliad" (1776) called "The Diabo-Lady, or A Match in Hell." The latter poem was dedicated to "the worst woman" in the kingdom, as the first poem had been dedicated to "the worst man" (the dubious honor for the ladies went to the bigamist Elizabeth Chudleigh; the gentleman may have been Simon, Lord Irnham). It showcased various courtesans, prostitutes, and notorious ladies of rank, possibly including Grace as the "E——" among the "jovial group of female libertines":

> The Court was now disturbed. A jovial troop
> Of female libertines appeared en groupe:
> O——, B——, E——, B——,
> H——, T——, and a Hundred more;
> Which noisy Amazons made such a riot,
> That Satan though't had been a Polish Diet.

The connection between Grace and Lord Cholmondeley survived the reports (false or not) of imminent wedlock and was to endure for some months more. Their initial relationship was to last three and a half years before the first rupture would take place.

Did Grace want to remarry?

Though some chroniclers of the age have remarked that a mistress's lot was far preferable to a wife's in many respects—personal independence, for one—chances are that she did want to marry Lord Cholmondeley. He was very well connected, and rich (eventually he became much richer); they were physically compatible; and he could give her everything she desired. But when an offer of marriage was not forthcoming, Grace may have given up in the face of insurmountable odds, not the least of which could have been pressure from her paramour's family.

Bleackley reports a strong reaction from the latter, which he admits might be "a fable," but he relates it nonetheless. He says that Grace " 'sported a coronet' on the panels of her coach," causing outrage in Cholmondeley's family. He goes on to say that "it was alleged that his lordship, at the instigation of indignant relatives, forbade her to use his cipher [his earldom's crest] or his liveries [the uniforms of his drivers and footmen], and exchanged her gorgeous chariot [her carriage] with a pair of dashing greys for one of 'plain Melbourne brown.'"

Maybe so, maybe not. Whether the affable Lord Cholmondeley had made and then reneged on an offer of marriage, perhaps bowing to the pressure of family and friends, causing her to fly into "a paroxysm of rage"—as another anonymous tattler asserted—the truth might have been that she'd looked squarely and honestly at her situation as a kept woman. If she'd not snared Cholmondeley in "the parson's mousetrap" in the three-plus years they'd been together, then perhaps she'd never succeed in doing so, and the realization had hit her hard. The relationship might have gotten overripe, as relationships do, or she indeed might have made the mistake of insisting too strongly and too vociferously—that "paroxysm of rage," alas—on legal commitment. The C-word was every bit as scary to men then as it is to them now.

What relative would have had the most influence on the young earl, influence enough to put the kibosh on his plans to marry Grace Elliott?

Granduncle Horry, Man of Letters, Letter Writer, Closeted Homosexual

Now enters the likely villain of the piece, Cholmondeley's granduncle Horace Walpole, and the plot thickens considerably. Granduncle Horace was a man obsessed with many things, not the least of them finding suitable and wealthy heirs and heiresses for his numerous nieces and nephews. One imagines that the thought of a notorious courtesan like Grace Elliott coming to tea at Strawberry Hill and calling him "Uncle Horry" might have turned him a most alarming shade of puce.

Walpole was the brother of Cholmondeley's grandmother, Mary, and served in loco parentis for his grandnephew, as Cholmondeley's own father had died young. "Villain," however, may be too strong a word to describe someone of Walpole's character and temperament. Perhaps a more apt description would be interfering busybody.

While there are a great many good things that can be said about Lord Cholmondeley's granduncle Horace, the part he probably played in destroying the romance of Grace Elliott and George James Cholmondeley is not to his credit, though the obvious reason his for doing so—the preservation of the family name, wealth, property, and land, at all costs—is understandable in light of what made the eighteenth century tick. There were rules one had to follow to ensure perpetuity of all these elements.

"Dr. Eliot's pretty wife," as Horace Walpole referred to Grace in one of his letters, could not even remotely have been on the list of possible brides for Lord Cholmondeley. It was obvious to all the clan that this marriage was unsuitable and should be prevented by all means possible. The only one who could have driven this mandate home to Cholmondeley was Walpole; his influence, in the absence of a strong father figure, was key.

Lord Cholmondeley's father George, Viscount Malpas, had died in 1764 when only thirty-nine, at the culmination of a dissolute life. (A good role model for his son he was not.) Viscount Malpas had been deceased twelve years when Lord Cholmondeley took up with the notorious courtesan who'd been the wife of Granduncle Horry's physician and friend Dr. John Eliot. Yes, it was a tight circle. That very same physician, the ubiquitous Dr. John Eliot, physician to the world, was not only Walpole's doctor but his friend. How could that have boded well for Grace?

Dr. Eliot's name figures from time to time in the voluminous Walpole correspondence, as in this to George Selwyn on January 27, 1785:

> I have been very seriously ill indeed. . . . The attack on my breast was so violent, and the least talking gave me much fits of coughing, that till today Sir John Elliot has allowed me to see nobody but one or two of my family, and those only for a moment.

Apparently the problem was not so easily alleviated, not to mention contagious. A week later (February 5, 1785) he wrote to Sir Horace Mann:

> This time indeed my recovery was a little artificial, and not entirely owing to my own management and to my own Herculean weakness. Sir John Eliot had happened to attend my housemaid, and would not take a fee; to prevail, I pretended to talk on my own gout, and he was so tractable, and suffered me to prescribe to him what he should prescribe to me, without giving me powder of volcanoes and other hot drugs, that I continued to see him, and I do believe,

that at the crisis I should not have conducted myself quite so judiciously as he did.

One can only imagine the bedside stories the good doctor of physic told his patient and friend, as he was recovering from his bouts of illness, concerning his slutty wife. The inside information, plus the scurrilous tales in the scandal sheets, had to play a part in the sealing of Grace Elliott's doom. In a letter to his friend Lord Hamilton on June 19, 1774, Walpole commented with no little sarcasm that Dr. Eliot, in deciding to cite Lord Valentia for criminal conversation with his wife, "has selected Lord Valentia from several other lords and gentlemen who have been equally kind to the fair one."

If Grace had been an aristocrat, and—more important—a wealthy heiress, much would have been forgiven. There was precedent for scandalous behavior and illegitimacy in the Walpole family, as—frankly—there was in most ton families. Grace could have had a shot at becoming the countess of Cholmondeley if she'd been rich enough and titled enough. Otherwise, not on Horace Walpole's watch, in his lifetime, would it ever happen.

Here, on June 8, 1774, he recounts his teasing of Ann Pitt, William Pitt's sister, who'd sold Dr. Eliot her house in Knightsbridge upon his marriage to Grace Dalrymple. The receiver of this gleefully related bit of gossip is again his friend Horace Mann:

> *I am sorry to tell Mrs. [Ann] Pitt [despite the title of Mrs. he gives her, Ann Pitt never married] that her house at Knightsbridge has been led astray, the moment she turned her back: see what it is to live in a bad neighborhood? Pittsburgh, the Temple of Vesta, is as naughty as Villa Kingstoniana [Elizabeth Chudleigh's home]; not that Dr. Elliot's pretty wife has married another husband in his lifetime [Chudleigh was a bigamist]; but she has eloped with my Lord Valentia, who has another wife and some half-dozen children. The sages of Doctors' Commons are soon to be applied to.*

Walpole is having fun with the vestal virgin allusion vis-à-vis Ann Pitt, who never married and was presumably a virgin, and also with the reference to Elizabeth Chudleigh. How many children Lord Valentia had with his "own plain [wife]" as Walpole described Lucy Annesley, is unclear. Genealogical sources variously give them two boys; three boys and a girl; and three boys and three girls.

Consulting "with the sages of Doctors' Commons" was the first step toward securing a legal separation and/or divorce. Their official name was "The College of Doctors of Law exercent in the Ecclesiastical and Admiralty Courts," but "Doctors' Commons" was what they were ordinarily called.

On December 28, 1781, Walpole remarked to Mann:

After Doctors' Commons had lain fallow for a year or two, it is again likely to bear a handsome crop of divorces. Gallantry in this country scorns a mask. Maids only intrigue; wives elope. C'est l'étiquette.

He mentions the notorious Lady Worsley (who was to become a good friend of Grace Elliott's) and her connection to his own gallant grandnephew Lord Cholmondeley. Cholmondeley had been one of the lady's lovers (there were said to be thirty or more) and had testified at her trial. Walpole goes on:

I am a little angry for my nephew Lord Cholmondeley, who has been most talked of for her, and who is thought to have the largest *pretensions to her remembrance.*

"Largest" is italicized in the original letter and is a sly reference by Walpole to Cholmondeley's much-lauded physical endowments.

This talk appears to have amused Walpole; he does not censure his grandnephew for his liaisons and love affairs. It's as if boys will be boys, they have to strew those wild oats, and be "a bit of a lad," in today's British slang. In another letter, to Lady Ossory, on June 22, 1782, he says:

My nephew Lord Cholmondeley, you know, Madam, is going to Berlin— he refused Russia, which I should have thought he would have preferred, as he is more formed to succeed with a gallant Empress [Catherine the Great, notorious for her many love affairs, who was rumored to like hugely endowed men] than with a peevish old politician, and could carry better credentials.

Can one just hear the snickering and the elbow-jabbing here?

Poor lazy, virile Lord Cholmondeley of the larger-than-life private parts didn't last long in his post as "envoy extraordinary and minister plenipotentiary to the Court of Berlin," according to the *London Gazette*. He was appointed on June 14 and was replaced on September 21 by Sir John Stepney, a baronet.

Lord Cholmondeley, alas, didn't take very seriously the opportunities offered to him on a silver platter to serve in the British diplomatic corps. Though Walpole used his influence to get him appointed ambassador, he lasted in the position only three months. Making matters worse, he'd taken the courtesan Elizabeth Armistead with him, and, according to her biographer, I. M. Davis, the London newspapers had much sport with the idea of "the athletic lord" Cholmondeley and "his fair amanuensis" in Berlin, making "merry with the picture of an embassy led by this rattle and accompanied by 'the Armstead.'"

Things like this give nepotism a bad name. But even this diplomatic failure did not impact negatively on Cholmondeley's relationship with Granduncle Horry, who was able to forgive much where his favorite was concerned. The boy could do no wrong.

It was too bad for Grace that Walpole lived to a ripe old age for those days. He died in 1797 at eighty, having led a far less dissolute life than his nephew Viscount Malpas. Walpole suffered terribly from gout, that scourge of those who live and eat well, but he hadn't fallen prey to gonorrhea or syphilis, ills that brought down many a gallant.

Who really was this man who had such an impact on the story of Grace and Lord Cholmondeley? So much is known about him, but what's hinted at is even more fascinating. It's fitting that the best portrait of him extant (in this author's opinion) has now been retitled *Unknown Man, Formerly Known as Horatio ("Horace") Walpole* by the curators at the National Portrait Gallery in London. "Unknown Man," indeed. There was so much more going on with Horace Walpole than met the eye.

Horatio Walpole was the youngest son of the eminent Whig politician and statesman Sir Robert

This oil painting at the National Portrait Gallery in London attributed to Nathaniel Hone, circa 1765, is now called *Unknown Man, Formerly Known as Horatio ("Horace") Walpole, 4th Earl of Orford*. Horace Walpole was painted many times, by many artists, and this probably looks as much like him as those other images do, but another portrait by Sir Joshua Reynolds is the one most used to represent him. Whatever the image, Horatio/Horace would win no prizes for beauty. (National Portrait Gallery, London)

Walpole, first Earl of Orford, and his wife, Catherine (née Shorter), though some say he was the result of an adulterous liaison between his mother and another man, possibly Carr Hervey, who later became the second Earl of Bristol. Robert Walpole was an outstanding statesman who served King George I and King George II as prime minister (though that title was not in use then) as well as in other important positions. Sir Robert was a brilliant man, a consummate player of the game of power politics, and an adulterous husband with a longtime mistress and several illegitimate children. (Who could blame his wife if she'd cheated on him the once?)

Although Horace never showed an interest in politics, he did share his father's love of art and delight in collecting it. Horace Walpole is well known for his connoisseurship—his exceptional taste in art and architecture—and for his collection of art treasures. He was a writer of some merit and even installed his own printing press at his home. Among his several books are *Anecdotes of Painting in England* (1762) and the popular gothic novel *The Castle of Otranto* (1764).

The major part of his life, however, was taken up by two things, his extensive correspondence and the renovation of his beloved home, Strawberry Hill. He was a nonpareil correspondent, writing thousands of letters to friends and acquaintances commenting on the events and personages of the day; these letters are a primary source for anyone intent on doing research in the mid-to-late Georgian period.

Walpole's delightful Georgian Gothic castle at Twickenham, Strawberry Hill, which he bought in 1747, is considered one of the best examples of this funky style of architecture and interior decoration. Walpole transformed the modest house, doubled its size, and bought surrounding property around the original five-acre plot that increased his holdings to forty-six acres. He added towers and battlements and put stained glass into the arched cathedral-like windows. Strawberry Hill soon housed his fast-growing collections of art treasures, prints, and books.

In 1791, his eccentric and rakish grandnephew George (1730–1791), the third Earl of Orford, died unmarried and heirless, and so Horace Walpole succeeded to the title of fourth Earl, surprising himself more than anyone else and increasing his wealth and status considerably. He also acquired Houghton Hall, the magnificent Palladian mansion set in parkland in Norfolk, which was to figure prominently in Lord Cholmondeley's story later on. Walpole enjoyed his elevation to the peerage for six years.

One of Walpole's most outspoken biographers, Lewis Melville, in *Horace Walpole (1717–1797): A Biographical Study* (1930), summarily dismisses his subject's life, jeering that Walpole was a *"splendid example of the man of inaction."* It was a life in every way atypical of the Georgian gallant. The biographer states that Horace Walpole:

- never ran away to fight another day, as he neither fought nor ran;
- did not ride, or hunt, or shoot;
- was not a gamester—cards and dice held no attraction for him;
- belonged to clubs, as a man of fashion did, but did not frequent any;
- had a place at court, but appointed a deputy to do his work;
- sat in Parliament for twenty-six years, but had no real interest in politics;
- may have admired a certain few women but never became attached to any.

Melville comments caustically: "The only 'event' in his life occurred in his thirty-third year, when he was robbed, and nearly shot, by footpads in Hyde Park." Walpole had this scary experience in common not only with the King, George III, but with his friend and physician Dr. John Eliot, who'd been shot at by highwaymen when traversing the heath on a dark and gloomy night during the period when he was bringing his divorce action against Grace. (Mysteriously, no attempt was made to rob him, and one has to wonder if a frustrated Grace Elliott took the initiative and hired hit-highwaymen to rid herself of her husband.)

Melville admits that Walpole did one thing "superlatively well," and that was to write, over a time span of fifty-six years, those splendid letters of "scarcely a dull page" to more than 150 of his friends and acquaintances. Over three thousand missives so far have been collected in print, but possibly twice that number were written, a fantastic accomplishment, if only for the stupendous outlay of goose quills and ink.

Walpole was to the eighteenth-century world of letters what Samuel Pepys was to the seventeenth-century world of diaries and journals; both chronicled their worlds with wit, intelligence, high-quality narrative, and detail, detail, detail. And Walpole had opinions on everything, even lovers' jewelry.

*L*over's Eyes

[Richard] Cosway painted four eyes: one each of Mrs. Fitzherbert, the Prince of Wales, Emma, Lady Hamilton, and "a lad." . . . The Dowager Countess Spencer wrote to the Duchess of Devonshire 6 Feb. 1786 about the Prince of Wales's carrying Mrs. Fitzherbert's "picture (or her eye, which is the same thing) about and showing it to people." . . . On 6 Dec. 1787 Lady Eleanor Butler was shown "An eye, done at Paris and set in a ring. A true French idea, and a delightful idea, which I admire more than I confess for its singular beauty and originality." Walpole disdained it as another example of "French folly" or "silliness." (Notes to Letter from HW to Lady Ossory, October 27, 1785, in *Horace Walpole's Correspondence*, the Yale edition)

A lover's eye, set as a ring. Photo by Ray Wadia. (Collection of the author)

What does his voluminous correspondence contribute to one's understanding of Walpole's character? The online version of *The Cambridge History of English and American Literature*, volume 10, chapter 11, "Letter-Writers," contributes the following astute comments:

Walpole's character may be easily understood by anyone who studies his correspondence. In early life, he was not very different from a large number of the highbred men of the eighteenth century who took pride in their social position, for it is necessary to remember that there were two classes of men in the English society of this age—the jovial and coarse, and the reserved and refined. Sir Robert Walpole belonged to the former, and his son Horace to the latter. Horace was never very young, and his father said of himself that he was the younger of the two. . . . The son began life with a character for frankness and enthusiasm; but, as he grew into the cynical man of the world, he became colder in manner to mere acquaintances, reserving his true self only for his bosom friends. He cultivated an extreme fastidiousness and severe refinement, which caused him to exhibit a distaste for a robust humour that he considered vulgar.

In other words, he appears to have become somewhat of an old maid. There's a tendency to become more conservative as time passes, but Walpole endears himself to contemporary readers by one other telling characteristic, what Lewis Melville terms "that nice spice of malice that makes the whole world kin." He had a sharp, cutting edge, a trait he shared with one of his best friends, the wit George Selwyn, and neither of them hesitated to let that rapier slice away and bring everyone down to size. He could be catty; he could be spiteful.

Walpole apparently never forgave a slight or a personal affront, and he was capable of carrying resentments forward for years. In 1737, Thomas Fermor, first Earl of Pomfret, was appointed ranger of parks. He was the father of the deceased Lady Sophia Fermor, a lady Walpole had admired greatly. But Walpole remembered how much he'd detested Lady Sophia's mother, the Countess of Pomfret, who'd been cutting and dismissive of him as a young man with no title and no wealth. He got in a sly dig by offhandedly referring to Lady Fermor as the "Queen of Duck Island," after Duck Island Cottage, the bird keeper's lodge at St. James's Park used by the ranger of parks. This bit of malice was six years after his Lady Sophia had died in childbirth, and, really, was it necessary?

Horry was attracted to women, but in the platonic and idealistic/romantic sense more than the physical, and he was a great admirer of physical beauty when it was allied with cleverness and wit. One of the beauties he admired openly and effusively was this reigning society beauty Lady Sophia Fermor, an acknowledged "Toast" who broke the heart of his great friend Henry Fiennes-Clinton, the young ninth Earl of Lincoln.

Did she make inroads into Horry's heart, too? He may have had a crush on her, but it would never have come to anything. Walpole's relations with women bear scrutiny. The modern consensus is that he was a closeted homosexual. Several of his close friends who were also bachelors—like George Augustus Selwyn—were probably gay also. Sodomy was a hanging offense in the eighteenth century and it wasn't wise to own up to what society considered aberrant proclivities. Things of a sexual nature went on between men and men—and between women and women—but one kept those things secret if one was wise.

Walpole christened Lady Sophia "Juno," after the queen of the gods, and

Agnes and Mary Berry (and their dog), a line engraving by Henry Adlard after Johan Zoffany, published by Thomas Longman circa 1830–1860. (National Portrait Gallery, London)

thought her "shape . . . charming." An interesting sidelight to the adoration of Lady Sophia by both Lord Lincoln and his pal Horry Walpole is that it's now believed by some biographers that Lincoln and Walpole had been involved romantically and sexually themselves—together. But though Walpole never married, Henry Fiennes-Clinton did; he was married to his cousin Catherine Pelham, daughter of the first Duke of Newcastle, in 1744.

Walpole is thought to have had an earlier homosexual relationship with the poet Thomas Gray, who accompanied him on his grand tour. The two quarreled and had a famous falling-out, but made up in about 1745. Walpole's cousin and close friend Henry Seymour Conway, who made a career in the army, is another man who may have been Walpole's lover during their youth.

Horace Walpole was included in A. L. Rowse's compendium *Homosexuals in History: A Study of Ambivalence in Society, Literature, and the Arts* (1977), standing alongside the likes of the Duke of Buckingham (George Villiers), Lord Byron, Thomas Gray, James I, Queen Isabella, Edward II, Frederick the Great, Cardinal Richelieu, et al.

Toward the end of his life Horace Walpole became extremely fond of the two Berry Sisters, Agnes and Mary. This relationship began in about 1787, before Walpole inherited the title of fourth Earl of Orford and ten years before his death. The sisters were in their early twenties and he was about seventy years old. In a letter to one of his favorite correspondents, Lady Ossory, he called them "the best-informed and most perfect creatures I ever saw at their age . . . entirely natural and unaffected, frank, and, being quali-

A marble bust of Elizabeth Farren, 1788, by Anne Seymour Damer, showing the actress as Thalia, the muse of comedy and idyllic poetry. There were rumors that the two had a lesbian relationship prior to the beautiful Farren's marriage to the twelfth Earl of Derby. (National Portrait Gallery, London)

fied to talk on any subject, nothing is so easy and agreeable as their conversation."

In 1791, the sisters moved to a house on the Strawberry Hill property called Little Strawberry Hill. It had once been occupied by another dear female friend of Walpole's, the actress Kitty Clive, whom he'd much admired. Walpole's fondness for Mary Berry was boundless; there was talk that the septuagenarian had gone so far as to consider marrying the young woman, but it was said he feared ridicule because of the great age difference and had decided regretfully against it. The cottage was willed to the Berry sisters for their lifetime and Mary was appointed Walpole's literary executrix.

The Berry sisters and Walpole had an intense, affectionate friendship that never wavered. His favorite, Mary, later entered into another intense friendship—said to be a lesbian relationship—with Walpole's goddaughter, the child of his close friend and cousin Field Marshall Henry Seymour Conway. This was the widowed sculptress Anne Seymour Damer, who had inherited Strawberry Hill from Walpole.

Horace Walpole became involved in the marriage plans for his other grandnephew, also named George James Cholmondeley (1742–1830), the son of the Reverend Robert Cholmondeley, his nephew and Lord

Anne Seymour Damer, a miniature of Horace Walpole's goddaughter and Henry Conway's daughter, by Richard Cosway, 1785. (National Portrait Gallery, London)

Cholmondeley's uncle (his late father's brother). He was functioning as a self-appointed matchmaker, in his usual busybody persona, indicating his concern in letters back and forth to his friends that this George James—who had no title and was therefore a commoner—should marry well.

He wrote to Mary Berry on July 3, 1790:

> *It has rained all day and I have not been out of the house: in the morning I had 3 or 4 visitors, particularly my nephew George Cholmondeley with an account of his marriage settlements and the toothache.*

George James Cholmondeley held various government offices and had a long public career, unlike his cousin of the same Christian names, George James, Lord Cholmondeley. In a letter to Horace Mann on July 3, 1783, Walpole played on words, describing him as "a young man of sense and honorable principles, and among the best of my nepotism . . . he has some humour, and some voice, and is musical: but he has not good health, nor always good spirits."

This other George James—who was probably perfectly nice but a bit on the dull side—was to receive a bequest of only £500 in his granduncle's will, whereas the clear favorite, Lord Cholmondeley, was to acquire the magnificent property Houghton Hall. Yet Walpole went out of his way to involve himself deeply in finding suitable young women for his less interesting nephew, suggesting and cajoling. This was in the nature of insurance. If Lord Cholmondeley died without issue, the title would go to his uncle, the Reverend Robert; the other George James would then be next in line to inherit.

It does not take much imagination to realize what Walpole was capable of doing where his favorite Lord Cholmondeley was concerned. Anyone might easily wager that it would be a great deal more than Walpole did for Reverend Robert's son. Walpole had a special interest and stake in the marriage of Lord Cholmondeley, for, to this old bachelor, the young man held the immediate future of the family and its properties in his hands.

George James Cholmondeley the untitled actually married three times. His first marriage was the one his granduncle was so concerned about. Horace passed away, unfortunately, and missed out on giving his input for the next two. The first wife was Marcia Pitt (1759–1808) of Dorset, daughter of John Pitt and sister of William Morton Pitt, MP. George and Marcia were married at William Pitt's home, Kingston House, in 1790.

Their first child was stillborn and they were to have no others. As Horace Walpole wrote to Mary Berry on May 26, 1791, a year after the marriage, "George Cholmondeley's wife after a dreadful labor is delivered of a dead child." It was a son, as reported in the "Births" column of the *Oracle* on June 2, 1791: "A few days ago, the lady of George James Cholmondeley, Esquire, of a son . . ."

The second wife was Catherine Francis, the daughter of Sir Philip Francis (1740–1818), reputed author of the infamous *Letters of Junius;* they married in 1814. Sarah, Catherine's sister, gave another impression of George Cholmondeley, describing him as "absurd and . . . delightful." Catherine Francis Cholmondeley died in 1823; the couple had no children.

George's third wife, whom he married in 1825, was Mary Elizabeth Sydney, daughter of John Thomas "Turnip" Townshend, second Viscount Sydney, the noted agricultural reformer. The Townshends were related by marriage to the Walpoles through "Turnip" Townshend's second wife, who was the sister of Sir Robert Walpole.

The only child of these three marriages was Frances Sophia Cholmondeley, George's daughter with Mary Elizabeth. This third wife must have been much younger than her husband, who died in 1830 at the age of seventy-eight, as she gave birth to another child in 1834, after she remarried.

Whatever he felt about this other grandnephew's marriage to Marcia Pitt, the only one he was ever to know, Walpole was extremely pleased with his favorite grandnephew's marriage. Lord Cholmondeley had picked off a very great heiress, Charlotte Bertie, sister of his late friend Robert Bertie, fourth Duke of Ancaster. Lady Charlotte brought an old and distinguished title into the Cholmondeley family, along with extensive land holdings, a huge dowry, and the hereditary title of lord great chamberlain (see the sidebar on page 132 for more on this exalted office) that resided in the Bertie family.

Here is Walpole's description of that wedding, written to his favorite Mary Berry on April 23, 1791, a Saturday. The wedding had taken place at the Ancaster home in Berkeley Square earlier in the day:

> *At night. Well, our wedding is over, very properly, though with little ceremony, for the men were in frocks and white waistcoats, most of the women in white, and no diamonds but on the Duke's wife [Mary Anne Layard, the wife*

of Brownlow Bertie, fifth Duke of Ancaster and Charlotte Bertie's uncle]; and nothing of ancient fashion, but two bride-maids: the endowing purse I believe has been left off, ever since broad pieces were called in and melted down. We were but eighteen persons in all, chiefly near relations on each side, and of each side a friend or two; of the first sort, the Greatheds [Bertie Grethed was Charlotte's first cousin]. Sir Peter Burrel [Charlotte Bertie's brother-in-law, who married Charlotte's only sister, Lady Susan Priscilla Bertie, and to whose seat at Beckenham, Kent, the newlyweds went after the ceremony] gave away the bride: the poor Duchess-mother wept excessively; she is now left quite alone, her two daughters married, and her other children dead—she herself I fear in a very dangerous way. She goes directly to Spa [in Belgium, a popular watering hole for the ton], where the new-married are to meet her. We all separated in an hour and half. The Elliot girl [Grace Elliott's daughter Georgiana] was there, and is pretty—she rolls in the numerous list of my nephews and nieces . . . [The Reverend Robert Cholmondeley and his wife, Lord Cholmondeley's uncle and aunt] to my surprise were not invited.

Grace was in France, and had been there for several years, when her former lover married . . . suitably. How did she feel? With no letters from her to consult, one cannot know, but how could Hew Dalrymple's daughter Grace have competed in the same arena as these aristocratic heavy-hitters? Lord Cholmondeley's fortunes, and the future of his family, would have sunk into a quagmire if he had made the mistake of following his heart (or his loins). This George James was far too pragmatic for that. He and Granduncle Horry, as it turned out, had that characteristic of hardheaded pragmatism in common all along.

Lord Cholmondeley's looks, charm, and immense sexual appeal, along with his excellent marriage, were apparently key factors in Walpole's decision to cast the family's lot with him. He'd married very well, and his wife's fortune and bloodlines would go far in shoring up the Cholmondeley name, land, and properties. Walpole could go peacefully to his eternal rest trusting that all would be taken care of, and that no usurpers—among them a certain notorious divorcée—would visit ruin upon the family.

As to poor Grace Elliott, the lovely and treasured mistress who might have been the great love of Lord Cholmondeley's life, she was history. Her dodgy father was dead and her respectable middle-class family had disowned her. She had neither dowry nor lands nor property. She was a flamboyant divorcée celebrated in the gossip sheets whose only friends—if they could truly be called friends—were gallants and courtesans. Her survival after the breakup with Cholmondeley would continue to depend on the kindness of wealthy strangers and on whether she retained her good looks, wit, and sparkling personality. After the fiasco with Cholmondeley, remarriage was never to be an option for Grace Elliott.

The record leads one to believe that Lord Cholmondeley must have had a good heart. He looked out for Grace and her child and grandchild through the rest of her life and theirs, but it's understandable that, under the influence of his granduncle, he balked at marriage. Some aristocrats did marry their mistresses—witness Eliza Farren and the Earl of Derby, to name one instance—but those few peers who did so tended to be far wealthier and far less concerned with family repercussions than the Walpoles and the Cholmondeleys. These latter families were, to use a Georgian term, "very high in the instep," that is, very conscious of who they were and what they thought was their family's exalted place in society.

Horace Walpole had written finis to Grace's chapter as the Earl's mistress, though she was to surface again from time to time in Cholmondeley's life. It should be made clear that Walpole probably bore no ill will toward Grace personally, nor toward her daughter Georgiana, whom he'd described as being—like her mother—"pretty." (In fact, he believed Georgiana was actually Lord Cholmondeley's child, and thus his great-grandniece.)

It was all about money, and an alliance with Grace Elliott was a losing proposition for the Walpole and Cholmondeley families from any perspective one cared to take. Lord Cholmondeley's friendship with the Prince of Wales—and the accommodations he provided to the heir to the throne in private and personal affairs—led to the granting of his marquisate in 1815, long after his relationship with Grace had ended. He was with her again circa 1781–1784, but it was not the exclusive relationship it had been the first time around.

Still, their passionate relationship, however it had waxed and waned, managed to last in one way or another up until Grace's death and even beyond. How much the two saw of each other in the last years of her life, or if they saw each other at all, is not known, but the contact—and perhaps a remnant of feelings for each other—was never completely lost. In the end, however, family ties among aristocrats were to prevail and prove more formidable than any of the loose gossamer bonds forged by love . . . or lust.

LORD CHOLMONDELEY'S LATER YEARS

Lord Cholmondeley had a mellow old age. In reading what people had to say about him as a senior citizen it's hard to recollect the young gallant who'd set the ton ablaze. Was he admired in his dotage? Was he loathed?

There were no scandals after the marriage to Lady Charlotte Bertie, not one breath of impropriety, and most of his contemporaries appeared to look upon him kindly (though one imagines that those whom he'd made paupers of via litigation and faro had a different opinion of Lord C.). The diarist Thomas Raikes was an unabashed admirer. He noted in his *Journal* that Lord Cholmondeley was considered "a very agreeable man, full of anecdote." Cholmondeley was gently made fun of by those, like Frances, Lady Shelley, who noted that he served "atrocious wines" but that the good company at his congenial home more than made up for the bad liquid refreshment:

> *He had always an excellent French cook, but was very sparing of his wine, though no other expense was grudged. I have often seen him keep a bottle of Sillery champagne in the ice-pail, close to him, and dole it out by thimblefuls to the company, as if it gave him pain to part with it. He kept up to the last the old custom at large dinners of having the upper servants in full dress; his, I remember, were in dark brown coats with a broad gold lace.*

At Houghton Hall there is a listing of Lord Cholmondeley's life accomplishments, including the building of Cholmondeley Castle in Cheshire, 1801–1804, and the following posts, mostly ceremonial or of short duration:

> *Lord Lieutenant of Cheshire, 1770–83; Chamberlain of Cheshire, 1770 till his death; Colonel in the Army, during service, 1779; Envoy to Berlin, June to September, 1782; Captain of the Yeomen of the Guard, April to December 1783; Chamberlain to the Prince of Wales, 1795–1800; Lord Steward of the Household, 1815–21 . . .*

Lord Cholmondeley sat for several formal portraits, as befit a man of his

Houghton Hall

The earlier house on the property dated from the Restoration and was demolished by Sir Robert Walpole, who set about building a new home. Sir Robert was a distinguished statesman, serving as first lord of the treasury and chancellor of the exchequer from 1721 to 1742. The Walpole family were lords of the manor of Houghton by the early fourteenth century; it passed to the Cholmondeleys in 1797, willed to the fourth Earl of Cholmondeley by his granduncle Horace Walpole, the fourth and last Earl of Orford. Sir Robert, the first Earl of Orford and Horace Walpole's father, had amassed a fabulous art collection that was sold by his grandson, the rakish and unstable third Earl, to Catherine the Great of Russia in 1778. The collection of 204 works by outstanding artists was touted as the most celebrated in England and was looked to as the perfect foundation for a proposed national gallery of art. Walpole's taste ranged from Italian baroque to contemporary art and included fine examples of sporting paintings. Its sale was consid-

ered an outrage. (A display, Painting, Passion, and Politics, held at Somerset House from September 2002 to March 2003, brought some of these paintings back to London temporarily.)

The present house was begun in 1722 and com-

ABOVE: *Lady with a Squirrel and a Starling*, c. 1526–28 (oil on panel) by Hans the Younger Holbein (1497/8–1543). (Bridgeman Art Library)

LEFT: Houghton Hall. (Photo by Kristina F. Hickey)

pleted by 1735; Colen Campbell was the architect, Thomas Ripley the construction supervisor, and William Kent designed the interiors and the furniture. The Palladian-style house—one of the earliest in England and arguably the finest example of this style—had 134 rooms when finished. Sir Robert Walpole was said to have boasted to his neighbor, Lord Leicester, that Houghton had cost him £200,000 before he began to burn all the bills.

The upkeep of such magnificent properties is significant. Sybil, Lady Cholmondeley, who married the fifth Marquess in 1913 and lived at Houghton for seventy years, was born Sybil Sassoon, heir with her brother Philip to the Sassoon fortune. (Their mother was a Rothschild heiress.) It was she who brought about the renaissance of Houghton Hall. The gardens are magnificent. A recent article in British *Vogue*, "Minding the Manor," by Hamish Bowles, detailed the work of the seventh Marquess of Cholmondeley in refurbishing the gardens and house. There was a major sale at Christie's in 1994 of art treasures from Houghton Hall that brought in £21 million; an earlier sale of the Holbein painting *Lady with a Squirrel and a Starling* to the National Gallery added some £10 million to the family coffers.

Running a magnificent estate the size and quality of Houghton Hall, with the constant upkeep of historic buildings and the employment of a considerable staff, necessitates that a good deal of revenue is brought in, and taxes can be very high. (The real killer is inheritance tax.) Houghton Hall is open to the public in season. The Web site is www.houghtonhall.com.

station; they remain at Houghton Hall, the grand and beautiful Palladian mansion that's now the primary seat of the Cholmondeley family. (The other seat is Cholmondeley Castle in Chester, near Malpas.) The earliest portrait at Houghton Hall, by Pompeo Girolamo Batoni (1708–1787), pictures him in uniform, a young man on his grand tour.

Batoni seemed to have painted all the young gentlemen on their grand tours; in fact, a painting by this Lucca-born artist resident in Rome was almost a must-have souvenir of one's stay in Italy. He was the leading portrait painter of young and wealthy men, particularly Englishmen. By 1750 he was devoting all his time to painting such portraits. The visitors were getting a bargain; Batoni charged far less than comparable painters in England.

Cholmondeley was also painted by John Simpson, John Hoppner, Sir Joshua Reynolds, and possibly Karl Anton Hickel, at various stages in his life. One portrait shows him in peer's robes and another wearing the Star of the Order of the Garter. Simpson's portrait bust presents a long-faced, gray-

haired middle-aged man facing right, full white cravat up to his chin. His features are strong: a long, large nose; a sensual mouth; arched and thick dark eyebrows; hooded eyes. He looks out from the painting with a rather languid air. This is a man used to sitting for artists; he takes to it easily and naturally, with aristocratic aplomb.

George James Cholmondeley, first Marquis of Cholmondeley, died exactly one month before his seventy-eighth birthday at his London home, 94 Piccadilly. A Gillray etching made twenty-six years before had already shown a man sadly much diminished in looks.

He'd predeceased his wife Lady Charlotte by eleven years and outlived his former mistress Grace Dalrymple Elliott by four years. Sadly, he also outlived Georgiana Seymour, the child he may have fathered, by fourteen years. Georgiana's daughter, Georgina—who may have been his granddaughter—was sixteen years old when he died. On Wednesday, April 11, 1827, the *Times* reported:

> *The Marquis of Cholmondeley was seized, at one o'clock yesterday morning, with an apoplectic fit, which terminated his life at nine.*

The newspaper went on to report that the weather had broken somewhat and that agricultural prospects were good:

FACING PAGE: (*Left*) Lord Cholmondeley as a young man on his Grand Tour, painted by Pompeo Batoni. (*Right*) The Marquis of Cholmondeley in his old age, by John Simpson. Both paintings are at Houghton Hall, Norfolk. (Bridgeman Art Library)

Corporeal Stamina, an unflattering etching by James Gillray (published by Hannah Humphrey, April 13, 1801), depicting a rather schlumpy, potbellied, fifty-two-year-old Lord Cholmondeley, a far cry from his former gallant self. (National Portrait Gallery, London)

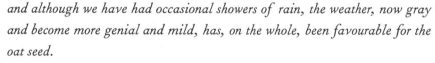

For this last fortnight we have been nearly free from the wintry blasts which had prevailed for so unusually long a period, and although we have had occasional showers of rain, the weather, now gray and become more genial and mild, has, on the whole, been favourable for the oat seed.

Time, weather, and crops wait for no man. Sic transit . . .

An "apoplectic fit" is what we nowadays would call a stroke. It must have been a massive stroke, as Lord Cholmondeley lasted only eight hours from its onset to his death. He left a widow and three legitimate children and who knows how many bastards. He was succeeded by his son George Horatio (1792–1870), who became the second Marquess of Cholmondeley.

That the Cholmondeleys are still among the wealthiest families in England is a testament to Lord Cholmondeley's business acumen, the family philosophy of keeping their fortune within the family circle, and their continuing skill in marrying well. The present Marquess is number 666 out of 1,000 on the *Sunday Times* "Rich List for 2004," tied, at £60 million, with actor Comedian Rowan Atkinson, music publisher Bryan Morrison, and financier Christopher Ondaatje; and it's noted that his money is in "Land."

Another Natural Daughter? The Strange Case of Madame St. Alban and Harriet Cholmondeley

In 1785, after Grace Dalrymple left London and the arms and protection of Lord Cholmondeley—for the second time, and for the same man, Philippe, Duc de Chartres (later Duc d'Orléans)—another *fille de joie* appeared on the scene. The mysterious lady was known as Madame St. Alban (sometimes spelled St. Albans or St. Aubin) and she seemed to have come out of nowhere. An item in the *Morning Herald* on April 4, 1785, described her as "a Gallic [French] belle of no inconsiderable attractions" and noted that she and Lord Cholmondeley were living together. For a while, biographers confused her with Grace Elliott, saying they were one and the same, but this doesn't wash. Horace Bleackley, Grace's biographer, tried to clear the matter up in *Notes and Queries* (March 18, 1916), but while he effectively separated the two women from each other, he added no new information on this new paramour of Cholmondeley's. William T. Whitley, a biographer of Gainsborough, had stated that this lady sat for the painter in 1785 and was Grace Elliott herself. (As mentioned earlier, Mrs. Elliott had sat for two other portraits by Gainsborough and there was possibly a third, which was either lost or unfinished; a copy may be at the Lady Lever Art Gallery in Port Sunlight, near Liverpool.) Unfortunately, that portrait Gainsborough supposedly painted of Lord Cholmondeley's new *chère-amie* has never been identified among Gainsborough's oeuvre. Mrs. Paget Toynbee, editor of a collection of Horace Walpole's letters, had previously stated in her work

Harriet Cholmondeley as a Child. Engraving by C. Turner after John Hoppner. (Collection of the author)

that they were the same woman. Bleackley comments he'd persuaded Mrs. Toynbee at the time of the publication of the Walpole correspondence "that the two ladies were distinct and separate personages," the confusion having arisen only because the two were intimate friends of Lord Cholmondeley at approximately the same time. The first tidbit in the *Morning Post* (April 5, 1785), made the naughty suggestion that "Lord Ch——ndl——y . . . now resides entirely in St. Albans." (St. Albans is also an English place-name.) On June 29, the rival newspaper the

Morning Herald noted that Madame St. Albans was "sitting to Gainsborough." The pair evidently visited France together in early 1786, but he returned without her; she was not far behind, however, the *Morning Herald* noted, assuring its readers that "she is on her way hither" (January 10, 1786). During 1786, the *Morning Post* reported that the generous nobleman bought her a new coach (May 23), and took her on holiday to Margate (August 23), where they stayed at Kingsgate House (September 15). Not to be outdone, the *Morning Herald* reported on her new jewels (March 13) and new wardrobe (March 28). An online genealogy source, Leo van de Pas's Genealogics, lists her as "Madame NN [no name] St. Alban," giving no date of birth or death, either, but linking her with Lord Cholmondeley and indicating they had a child, a daughter named Harriet (d. July 11, 1815), who married John George Lambton, first Earl of Durham. Frances, Lady Shelley, mentions this Harriet Cholmondeley in her *Diary:*

Georgiana Seymour and Harriet Cholmondeley were the bright stars in that firmament [Houghton Hall]. The latter was the daughter of Lord Cholmondeley, and afterwards married the great parti [highly eligible bachelor] of the day, Mr. Lambton. She and Priscilla [Susan Priscilla Bertie], afterwards Lady Tarleton, were adopted daughters of the Cholmondeleys and were brought up with Lady Cholmondeley's own children.

There is a portrait of Harriet Cholmondeley, a breathtakingly beautiful blond child in a gauzy white dress against a country background, at the Tate Gallery in London. She appears to be gathering wildflowers and putting them in her skirt. It's an oil painting by John Hoppner, a court painter of German descent whose best work is deemed to be of women and children. The painting was exhibited in 1804; C. Turner made an engraving of it in about 1801 (Harriet looks about four years old in this work.) The affair of Lord Cholmondeley and the mysterious Frenchwoman began in 1785. Harriet eloped with and married John George Lambton—a politician and statesman known as "Radical Jack" for his controversial and liberal politics—at Gretna Green in Scotland on January 1, 1812, so she was probably in her mid-twenties; he was nineteen. Harriet died on July 11, 1815; she and Lambton had one child together, Lady Frances Charlotte Lambton (1812–1835), born ten months after their marriage. She married John George Brabazon Ponsonby, fifth Earl of Bessborough, in 1835 and died less than four months later at the age of twenty-three.

This information brings the total of "adopted" children at Houghton Hall to three: Georgiana Elliott/Seymour, Harriet Cholmondeley, and Susan Priscilla Bertie. Harriet, who bore Cholmondeley's name, was obviously acknowledged by that surname as his by-blow, or natural/illegitimate child. Susan Priscilla had been acknowledged by her father, Robert Bertie, fourth Duke of Ancaster, in his will as his natural child. Georgiana was up for grabs.

Lady Cholmondeley was a saint.

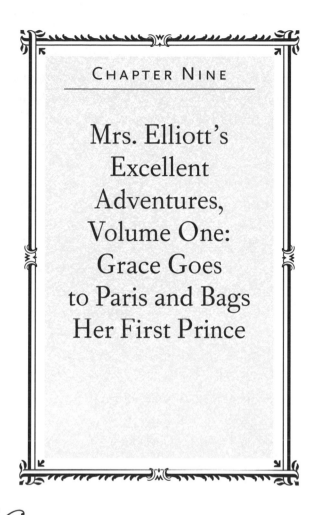

CHAPTER NINE

Mrs. Elliott's Excellent Adventures, Volume One: Grace Goes to Paris and Bags Her First Prince

With marriage no longer a viable option for Grace, it was time to look elsewhere for a new patron with bigger pockets who could support her in even grander style than the magnanimous Lord Cholmondeley had done. The plain facts were that she was now twenty-five years old—no longer young and marriageable by the day's standards—and she was simply too notorious. Her name was bandied about to an excessive degree in the media. Though it surely pays for courtesans to advertise—and newspaper gossip was free publicity—the exposure was becoming over the top.

The first news that Grace had left England broke in late May of 1779:

Miss Dal——ple has lately embarked for France, and it is said parted with her noble gallant in a manner that did not imply an inviolable attachment on either side. (Morning Post and Daily Advertiser, May 27, 1779)

Two days later, the press reported that Lord Cholmondeley had given a successful "petite déjeune[r]," or breakfast, for eight hundred guests, giving no outward indication of his distress—or at least none was noted—at the departure of his longtime love. Callous indifference? Covering up a broken heart? Or was it simply a matter of having already paid for all that food in advance?

> *Lord Cholmondeley's petit déjeune on Thursday morning last, is spoken of by every one with the warmest panegyric. . . . About 3 o'clock, the company retired highly delighted with their morning's entertainment. (Morning Post and Daily Advertiser, May 29, 1779)*

Lord Cholmondeley appears to have been in a major party mode in the late spring of his mistress's departure, as, on the heels of that breakfast in May he "organized at the Pantheon an unusually expensive fete—the subscription fee was three guineas—designed to be as magnificent as it was costly." Yes, he could still have been desolate and crying on the inside, but packets to Calais— ships that plied regular routes and carried passengers, freight, and mail— were plentiful, and he could have brought Grace back easily if he'd been willing to do so. It's obvious he wasn't willing. What she'd done, apparently, was give him the standard ultimatum in these situations: marriage, or it's all off. It didn't work.

The *Morning Chronicle* noted that "the only avowed Impure who found admittance" to Cholmondeley's Pantheon gala was "Mrs. A——d," i.e., Elizabeth Armistead, one of the less showy of the top tier courtesans. This was a sly dig at the "impure" aristocratic wives in the company, to be sure, but it was also an interesting departure from the norm of having the entire Cyprian Corps in attendance at such a stupendous party. Remember that Cholmondeley had had it on with Mrs. A. before Grace. Now Armistead saw the vacuum left by her frail sister and quickly took her place.

And then—ka-boom!—came the capper:

> *The fatal separation between Lord C——y and his beloved Miss D——le was occasioned, it seems, by the warmth with which the latter urged the promise of marriage, said to have been made to her by her noble inamorato;—his Lordship hesitating to recognize the sacred vow, she flew from him in a paroxysm of*

*rage, ordered posthorses, drove instantly for Dover, and crossed the water to seek an asylum from the insults of man within the walls of a cloyster; but how long the flesh will be sacrificed for female Spirit, probably a few Calais packets will determine. (*Morning Post and Daily Advertiser, *June 1, 1779)*

It's hardly credible that Grace Dalrymple Elliott hied herself off to a "cloyster" after the breakup of her relationship with Lord Cholmondeley. She'd been there, done that, years before when she was a mere prepubescent schoolgirl at a French convent; a repeat episode would have had little appeal to this worldly woman. The story may have originated with the misinformation Richard Bentley disseminated in the prologue to his 1859 publication of Grace Elliott's memoir, *Journal of My Life During the French Revolution;* it's Bentley who relates the story of the phantom brother whose questionable appearance is taken up and stated as fact by J. G. Alger in the *Dictionary of National Biography* article on Grace that appeared years later.

Bentley has the poor woman locked up in this cloister from 1776—when the Eliot divorce is finalized—until Lord Cholmondeley rescues her in the early summer of 1781:

Her husband, after some indecent treatment, resorted to a court of law at once to procure a divorce. . . . In the mean time her brother [that mysterious

94 Piccadilly, once the home of Lord Cholmondeley and other distinguished men. Because of the "In" and "Out" on the entryway pillars, it was known as the "In and Out" when it housed the Naval and Military Club. The current owner has gotten planning permission for a luxury hotel; in the meantime it is an exclusive venue for parties. (Photo by Kristina F. Hickey)

brother!] removed her to a convent in France, assigning as a reason for the course which had been adopted, that the lady was about to contract an unsuitable marriage. (Journal, Richard Bentley, prologue, 1859)

Poppycock! But the mention of the "unsuitable marriage" is interesting. There's a nugget of truth if this foiled-marriage reference was to Lord Cholmondeley. It seems possible, as the story's most probable origin was Georgina Cavendish-Bentinck, Grace's granddaughter. Georgina may have heard something within the family circle that confirmed the Cholmondeley family's outright opposition to a marriage between the two.

More apocryphal anecdote ensues with the story of Cholmondeley then introducing Grace to his friend the Prince of Wales:

*She was subsequently introduced to the Prince of Wales, who had been struck with the exquisite beauty of her portrait, which he had accidentally seen at Houghton. (*Journal, *Bentley, prologue)*

This is simply not true. Lord Cholmondeley was not yet in possession of Houghton Hall in 1781 (he was to acquire it only upon the death of Horace Walpole in 1797), and it seems unlikely that the Gainsborough portrait of Grace (for which she sat in 1778, when according to Bentley she was locked up in that French convent) was hanging at the estate which then belonged to the previous Earl of Orford. If the Prince had seen it anywhere, it was probably in town at the artist's atelier, at a Royal Academy show, at Cholmondeley Castle in Cheshire (dubious), or, best guess, at 94 Piccadilly. The information in Bentley's prologue and postscript frequently tends to be muddled and not to hold up upon closer examination. (When Grace's *Journal* is criticized for inaccuracies, one should bear in mind that these often occur in the sections written by Bentley, rather than in the memoir itself.)

Getting back to the actual chronology of events, as reported by the newspapers and other sources, it's more likely that Grace pulled herself together and went to stalk bigger game on the Continent. No one took her anywhere; she was an adult and presumably had some money of her own at this juncture. She went abroad herself, and in her sights were the fabulously rich noblemen of the ancien régime. She'd lived in France and she spoke French fluently, unlike other English courtesans. She knew the French court was a good deal more sophisticated—and less condemning of women like her—than its English counterpart.

Her name had been linked with several wealthy and titled sons of France even before she made her abrupt departure from London. Among others, there were Armand-Louis de Gontaut Biron, the Duc de Lauzun; the Duc de Fitzjames; the Duc de Chartres; and King Louis XVI's younger brother, the handsome Charles, Comte d'Artois (later to reign as King Charles X of France, 1824–1830). These were all noted womanizers, men who'd made regular visits across the Channel to hobnob with the English court and engage the beguiling courtesans on its fringes.

Bleackley dismisses Lauzun as "a base fellow who boasted and lied about his conquests," referring to his indiscreet and provocative *Mémoires secrets du Beau Lauzun* and confirming the opinion that most had about him. But Lauzun had gone to fight for a few years in America, taking a courtesan with him, and he does not seem to have been involved with Grace at all. (He later became involved briefly with Mary Robinson.) In *Marie Antoinette: The Journey* (2001), Antonia Fraser refers to Lauzun as another "sexual athlete" and relates anecdotes of the man's attempts—they all failed—to seduce the Queen. Lauzun was a member of the Duc d'Orléans's circle.

The Duc de Fitzjames, or FitzJames, was a direct descendant of England's James II's illegitimate son with his mistress Arabella Churchill; the prefix "Fitz" often denotes bastardy. Bleackley says that "although he soon became one of Mrs. Eliot's patrons," Fitzjames was otherwise engaged "pursuing the wanton widow of the late Lord Barrymore."

Bleackley reports that nothing of substance occurred between Grace and Fitzjames, for, after the widow Barrymore, he "began to show an evident preference for Mrs. [Elizabeth Sarah] Gooch . . . another Englishwoman . . . living in Paris . . . who had broken her marriage vows." Mrs. Gooch was the sole heiress of the wealthy William Villa Real, of Nottinghamshire. She'd married William Thomas Gooch (1749–1833), son of Thomas Gooch, third Baronet, in 1775 and was divorced by him in 1781. Grace had supposedly made a friend of her when she'd arrived in Paris. According to Bleackley, Fitzjames's interest soured Mrs. Elliott on Mrs. Gooch and the English ladies' budding friendship came to an abrupt end.

There was a difference of opinion as to which of the other two contenders for Grace's favors, the handsome Artois or not-so-handsome Philippe, Duc de Chartres, "was the first to offer Grace a home in Paris." According to Bleackley, Artois seems to have had the first dalliance with Dally:

Day after day she drove down the Allée de Longchamp, in the Bois de Boulougne, before the eyes of the whole nobility, in an open carriage with the Comte d'Artois, and when the affection of that fickle prince had cooled, the Duc de Chartres was eager to take his place.

Artois was witty, affable, and athletic, a skilled conversationalist, and, according to Antonia Fraser, he possessed "irrepressible spirits." He was also married. His reputation as a devout womanizer was so great a rumor had circulated that he'd seduced his sister-in-law, the Queen. It was untrue; they were actually good friends. (The devout womanizer was also a devout Roman Catholic who abdicated the throne of France in 1830, after six years as king, because he did not believe in constitutional monarchies.)

Having taken up with Philippe, then still the Duc de Chartres, Grace Elliott did very well for herself. He was to become the richest man in France, if not all Europe. She was set up in grand style with a large house in town in an exclusive neighborhood and was principal sultana of Philippe's harem for a while.

LOUIS PHILIPPE, DUC D'ORLÉANS, AKA CITOYEN ÉGALITÉ, PRINCE OF THE BLOOD AND TRAITOR TO HIS CLASS

No man ever was more blamed than Orléans during the Revolution, but the faults of ambition and intrigue were his friends', not his own; it was his friends who wished him to be on the throne. Personally he possessed the charming manners of a polished grand seigneur: debauched and cynical, but never rude or cruel, full of gentle consideration for all about him but selfish in his pursuit of pleasure, he has had to bear a heavy load of blame, but it is ridiculous to describe the idle and courteous voluptuary as being a dark and designing scoundrel, capable of murder if it would serve his ambition. (Encyclopedia Britannica, *1911 edition*)

The then Duc de Chartres, Louis-Philippe-Joseph (who will be referred to in these pages as Philippe, Orléans, or Égalité), had married young Adelaide de

Louis-Philippe-Joseph, Duc de Chartres (1747–1793), mezzotint by Samuel William Reynolds after Sir Joshua Reynolds. He succeeded his father as Duc d'Orléans in 1785. (National Portrait Gallery, London)

Bourbon, Mademoiselle de Penthievre, at Versailles in 1769. His new wife's dowry and the wealth and landholdings of his own long-established and distinguished family were to make him the richest man in France. In addition, his lineage was impeccable: he was a direct descendant of King Louis XIII and a cousin to both King Louis XVI and Queen Marie-Antoinette via two separate bloodlines. As the Orléans heir, he would have been next in line for the throne if the Bourbon line had failed to produce any males.

His wife's father, the Duc de Penthievre, was the renowned grand admiral of France and a royal bastard of Louis XIV's. Though her father was illegitimate, this mattered less in more worldly, sophisticated France than in England. Blue blood was blue blood, from whichever side of the blanket, and Adelaide's lineage was almost as impressive as Philippe's. The title of duc d'Orléans was the creation of King Philip VI in the fourteenth century, but it had twice become extinct owing to lack of heirs.

Monarchs have the power to reinvoke titles, and so in 1661 King Louis XIV had resurrected the Orléans title and bestowed it on his brother, Philippe, who had married the third sister of King Charles II of England, Henrietta Anne. Her mother, Queen Henrietta Maria of England, wife of King Charles I, had been a French princess and sister to King Louis XIII.

Bear with this next part; everyone in the Orléans family had the same Christian names. Philippe's great-grandfather was Philippe, second Duc d'Orléans, who'd been regent of France during the minority of King Louis

{Ancien Régime. From the French, ancien = old, and régime = regime, that impossible medley of brilliance, genius, squalor, poverty, great luxury, rigid ceremony, and lively carnival atmosphere that characterized the political and social system in France before the Revolution of 1789; or, any sociopolitical or other system that no longer exists.}

{Roué. Noun. A libertine; a dissolute man in fashionable society. "The profligate Duke of Orléans, Regent of France, first used this word in its modern sense. It was his ambition to collect round him companions as worthless as himself, and he used facetiously to boast that there was not one of them who did not deserve to be broken on the wheel—that being the most ordinary punishment for malefactors at the time; hence these profligates went by the name of Orléans roués, or wheels. The most notorious roués were the Dukes of Richelieu, Biron, and Brancas, together with Canillac and Noce; in England, the Dukes of Rochester and Buckingham." www.bibliomania.com. Or, roué (French term) = "gallant" (English term).}

XV. This Orléans duke reigned supreme in France from 1715 to 1723, or until the boy reached his majority. Appointed prime minister, he died within the year of apoplexy, almost as if the fall from very great power had been too traumatic a loss. There could not have been a more powerful family of the ancien régime than the Orléans dukes, nor any greater libertines. (The Regent was one of the nobles loathed by Voltaire, who wrote biting satiric pieces about him that landed the playwright in the Bastille for a year.) Of this powerful figure, Philip the Regent, the biographer Evarts Seelye Scudder writes:

> [His] character was said to combine the traits of "a braggard and a coxcomb." His habits were corrupt, his mind was intelligent and sometimes brilliant and his tastes were luxurious. . . . He had been responsible for the policy which favored an alliance with England.

A motif surfaces here that will hold true for all the Orléans men—save one—in the next several generations. There was a love of luxury, a leaning toward corrupt behavior and indolent living, and more than a touch of gluttony that may have played a part in the creation of those heavyset figures. There was also a soft spot in these Gallic hearts for England. Philippe's fervent Anglophilia—probably one of the things that eventually led to his fall from grace with the revolutionaries—was come by naturally.

Philippe's grandfather, the Regent's son, was a total contrast to his flamboyant father—a father-son dynamic that often occurs. Biographer Scudder writes that the grandfather held the twin reputations of madman and saint—depending on whom one asked—and was said to have set a curse upon his grandson when the child was five years old. Enemies of Philippe used this old tale to assert that the sainted grandfather (or the extremely mad grandfather: take your pick) had seen troubling, even evil, signs in the young boy's makeup. Absurd, but interesting.

Philippe's father, Louis-Philippe, was known as Philippe the Fat. He'd had some success in the military arena when young but had then turned with a vengeance to a life of utter indolence. Scudder characterizes him as having an "indecisive and incurious nature and . . . [a] love of good living," traits that were to mark his son. This was a case of the branch not falling far from the tree. Philippe's mother was the noted beauty Louise-Henriette de Bourbon-Conti, who died of consumption when she was only thirty-three. Her demise was said to have been hurried along by debauchery.

Philippe's biographer sums up these colorful immediate ancestors, remarking:

> There was a striking family resemblance in all the Orléans line only interrupted by Philippe's saintly and cursing grandfather. Father to son, the same heavy figure, the same temperament, the same love of war and love of pleasure, and as often happened when they were prevented by the King from taking part in a world of action, the same debauchery, gout and apoplexy.

Philippe was a controversial and contradictory character. It was accepted by most that he tended toward indecisiveness and indolence. Although critics claimed he was manipulative and worked behind the scenes, the record shows he was more of a follower than a leader and extremely suggestible to the whims of others. Was there a more sinister side to his character? Was he capable of lying, deviousness, plotting, even murder? Was he as ambitious as some said? His enemies—and there were many—believed that he used the revolutionary movement in France to further his own agenda, that is, to have the King and Queen—whom he despised—overthrown so that he could grab the throne of France for himself.

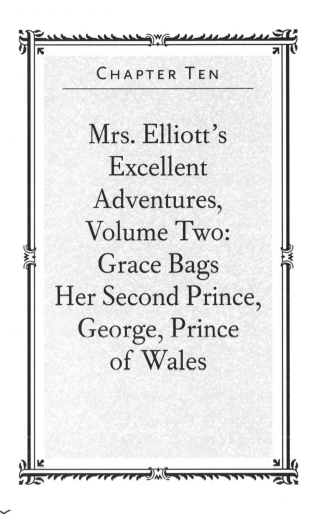

CHAPTER TEN

Mrs. Elliott's Excellent Adventures, Volume Two: Grace Bags Her Second Prince, George, Prince of Wales

*P*hilippe, like most rich men who use their wealth to seduce women, was, though generous like Lord Cholmondeley, notoriously fickle and inconstant like the Prince of Wales. Two things appear to have happened, in the spring and early summer of 1781, that persuaded Grace to leave Philippe's protection after three years and return home to England.

The first was the arrival in Paris of her ex-lover, Lord Cholmondeley, who was visiting the Continent with a traveling companion. The reappearance of Cholmondeley at what may have been a low point in Grace's personal life could have triggered warm memories she'd cast aside when she'd left him so impetuously in May 1779. Who was accompanying him on this journey? Mary Robinson? Elizabeth Armistead? It's not clear to whom Horace Bleackley is referring when he mentions that "another lady bore him company" on a European trip in April 1781.

It's true that he did pay frequent trips to the Continent and he was often accompanied by a woman, but it's hard to confirm it was either of those two "impures." Mary Robinson was to go to France that year, the payoff from King George III for the return of Prinny's indiscreet letters, but that was in the fall; the busy Mrs. Armistead was busily warming Prinny's bed—still hot from Perdita's lovely body—in April. There were so many compliant ladies, and so many possible companions for Cholmondeley. He was to go to Europe with Armistead at one point, but it was not until mid-1782, when he went to take up that abortive diplomatic post in Berlin.

Grace may have indeed departed from Paris in a pique in June 1781. She'd been described as departing from London in a similar pique three years before when she and Cholmondeley had broken up their relationship. This time, perhaps, it could have been because her patron the Duc de Chartres was no longer paying close and personal attention to her, and the catalyst for leaving could well have been glimpsing her old lover.

One English visitor to Paris at the time had reported to the English gossip sheets the tidbit that the once-celebrated courtesan Grace Dalrymple Elliott had seemed only "an occasional solace" of the notoriously fickle Philippe, and that she no longer reigned supreme as the principal sultana in his harem of lovelies. It may have been past time—once again—to cut her losses and return home. She was twenty-seven and youth was fleeting, if not entirely fled.

The Prince of Wales had dumped Perdita, his first real love, rather callously in the winter of 1780–1781 and jumped with enthusiasm into an affair with the ever-available Mrs. Armistead. The newspapers made the most of it, envisaging a drawn-out battle between the two "impures" for the heart of this fickle Prince. During this period of engagement, Mrs. Armistead was also linked with the returned hero of the war with America, Colonel Sir Banastre Tarleton (who was later to take up with Mrs. Robinson). At some point here, Charles James Fox was carrying on with Mrs. Robinson, too. The meanderings, exchanges, and assignations showed that *La Ronde* was alive and well.

The Career of Elizabeth Bridget Cane, aka Mrs. Armistead

Armistead, who went by many names and various spellings of said names over the course of her career—Armisted, Armitstead, Armstead, Elizabeth Bridget Cane, et al.—is an elusive girl. There's no record of her birth or antecedents. She'd been trained in the courtesan's arts (some said by the "abbess" Mrs. Goadby) at one of the high-end King's Place brothels in the St. James's area. With her height, fashionable looks, and considerable charm, she'd soon become one of the most sought after Cyprians of the day. Unlike Mary Darby Robinson (Perdita) and Grace Elliott (Dally the Tall)—and Jackie O, Princess Di, J. Lo, and others beloved by the scandal sheets in centuries to come—she was neither a fixture of the tabloids nor bestowed with a sobriquet that eliminated the need to utilize those pesky dashes. She was always plain Mrs. Armistead. She numbered among her protectors the Lords Bolingbroke, George Cavendish (brother of the Duke of Devonshire), Richard Fitzpatrick, and Cholmondeley; a nabob (someone who'd made his fortune in India), General Richard Smith; the Duke of Ancaster and the Duke of Dorset; the Prince of Wales; the politician Charles James Fox; and others. These were not necessarily exclusive liaisons. Armistead was with the Prince in the early 1780s as well as with his friend Cholmondeley. An article in *The Town and Country Magazine* quoted by I. M. Davis in Davis's dual biography of Armistead and Fox crowed that "Mrs. A——st——d . . . [could] claim the conquest of two ducal coronets, a marquis, four earls and a viscount."

Fox actually married Elizabeth Armistead in 1795,

and they shared an idyllic domestic life in St. Anne's Hill, Surrey. The marriage was one of those odd secret Georgian marriages like Prinny's to Mrs. Fitzherbert and the Earl of Peterborough's to the opera singer Anastasia Robinson. Mrs. Fitzherbert was one of many ex-girlfriends of Prinny's who received annual allowances—called annuities—from the Privy Purse. Hers, awarded in 1823, was £500, more than double what most received. (Grace received £200 less from the Privy Purse, and she supposedly bore the Prince a child!)

Elizabeth Bridget Fox (née Cane), mezzotint, 1825, by Samuel William Reynolds, after Sir Joshua Reynolds. (National Portrait Gallery, London)

The upshot was that Grace left France in early June. She arrived just as the Prince of Wales had begun to tire of Mrs. Armistead and was looking for new conquests. He was arriving at the realization that he could summon a legion of beautiful, available women with the crook of his little finger. He crooked; Grace came running.

And what of Lord Cholmondeley, ostensibly Grace Elliott's prime reason for returning to England? In early June, a few days after her arrival on her native shores, George Selwyn remarked in a letter to his friend Lord Carlisle that he had seen Grace " 'in a vis-à-vis [a carriage] with that idiot Lord Cholmondeley,' who had deserted his recent inamorata, Mrs. Robinson, for his old love."

But according to Bleackley, the Prince, not her former lover, was now the major recipient of Grace Elliott's favors:

This new amour was conducted with great secrecy. Although many curious idlers [including the Georgian paparazzi] were on the watch, the royal equipage was never seen to drive up to the door of Mrs. Eliot's house at Tyburn Turnpike, while some of the newspapers even alleged that she had failed in her endeavours to captivate the Prince, and was about to return in disgust to her friends in Paris.

Grace was the flavor of a very short time, perhaps a few months, but

likely only a few weeks. *The Rambler's Magazine*, a magazine for gentlemen that could be described as a Georgian equivalent of *Playboy* with just articles and no centerfold but plenty of gossip, gave this snide recap of the affair:

> *Miss Dal——— soon returned to her native isle, and spoke very coolly of French gratitude and French generosity. Her return operated with the force of novelty on many of her former admirers, and, among the new ones, she is said to have confined her conquests not solely to coronets, but to have soared higher; and that even the second star in our hemisphere has felt the effects of her charms; and that she was introduced to him by her old lover Lord C———; the result, however of ONE shortlived hour, was soon visible in Dally's enlarged state. . . .* (The Rambler's Magazine, *August 1784)*

Beyond the physical, the initial fascination seems to have dissipated and the two may have had nothing to say to each other. Grace was now one of what would be an endless string of ex-girlfriends of the Prince of Wales. Though a romantic, he was notorious for his inconstancy. His only female biographer, Cynthia Campbell, in *The Most Polished Gentleman: George IV and the Women in His Life* (1995), states that while the Prince was "sensual, like most of the Hanoverians, he was not a cynical exploiter of innocent maidens; he tended to fall in love, passionately, devotedly, romantically, and regularly."

"Regularly" is the key. Regardless, however, of his character and personality and the ease with which he fell in love, whatever transpired in the summer of 1781 between the Prince and Grace Elliott had ended. And, as the Prince seldom paid for services rendered (Mrs. Robinson and Mrs. Armistead had both discovered this), Grace, with only her annuity from her ex-husband— now Sir John Eliot, Baronet—to sustain her, along with the no doubt dwindling supply of money she might have brought from France, must have been getting desperate.

But as luck would have it, she found herself pregnant in the autumn of 1781, as the affair was ending, which changed the scenario significantly. Was this child, though, really the child of the Prince of Wales? Grace insisted it was the Prince's, but it appeared—as gossip had it—that there were other candidates for

FACING PAGE: Grace was said to have lived in this area of north London on her return to England in 1781. The Tyburn Turnpike Gate, at what's now the junction of Oxford Street and Bayswater Road, was the busy tollgate on the Great North Road that opened into north London south of Islington. The tolls were 10 pence for a carriage drawn by one or two horses, 4 pence for a sole horseman; drovers paid 5 pence for twenty oxen, 2 pence for twenty pigs. (City of Westminster Archives Centre)

the honor of fathering this baby, among them the Duc de Chartres, Lord Cholmondeley, and at least two other gentlemen.

On Christmas Eve in 1781, Henry Bate, the scandal-mongering editor of the *Morning Herald & Daily Advertiser*, announced that "Dally the Tall" was carrying a royal bastard:

The Dalrymple has declared herself pregnant, and taken care to have it well understood that Lord C——y cannot possibly lay claim to a single feature of the amourous produce, be what it may; solemnly averring on her honour, that his Lordship was totally effaced from her memory before she had the faintest conception of the bliss that now awaits her! However difficult it may be to ascertain its real sire, one is already named for it, who is said to be extremely flattered by the novelty of the title, and has already given orders that the ceremonies of the straw be supported with the utmost magnificence and éclat.

{The Ceremonies of the Straw. This was the custom of laying down straw in the streets around the house of an invalid, someone on his deathbed, or a woman in labor. The straw acts as a cushion, or as insulation, softening traffic and street noises.}

By the beginning of 1782, a number of tabloids, chief among them this same *Morning Herald & Daily Advertiser*, were noting that

Miss Dal———le looks to be the most exalted of illegitimate mothers about the beginning of April:—a fickle and inconstant season, by the bye, for such an event!

The "fickle and inconstant" can rightly be interpreted as a dig at the royal person of the Prince of Wales. But although the Prince was inconstant to many women, this was not to be wholly the case with regard to Grace Elliott and her love child. Though he never publicly acknowledged the child as his, he never publicly disavowed her, either, and he was said to have taken an interest in Georgiana for as long as she lived.

And no one—no emissary from King George III—tore out the page of the baptismal register at St. Marylebone Church that stated in bold handwriting that Georgiana Augusta Frederica Elliott was the "Daughter of His Royal Highness George Prince of Wales & Grace Elliott." Even though the King's underlings saw to it that the marriage register with the Prince of Wales's marriage to Maria Fitzherbert disappeared from all sight forever, this particular baptismal register remains intact.

The baby girl, christened Georgiana Augusta Frederica Elliott on July 30, 1782, had been born four months earlier, on March 30. She was a pretty baby, dark of hair and eye.

Georgiana's portrait, painted by Sir Joshua Reynolds in 1784, shows a brown-haired, brown-eyed toddler almost two years old. She's a sweet little girl with a serious expression on her face. Her prettiness is probably to be expected, with such a beautiful mother. Her putative father, the Prince of Wales, was at that time a handsome young man with the distinctive light blue eyes (or were they hazel?) and blond hair of his Hanoverian German forbears. (Later, his hair shows up much darker in portraits, having turned a medium-to-dark brown.)

Careful examination of the Gainsborough portrait bust of Grace that was painted in 1782, the year of Georgiana's birth, shows dark blond or possibly brown hair under all that white powder, not light blond, verifying the actual lock of hair in a miniature in a private collection. The style of the day was to powder one's hair. (That odd term "powder room," for a women's restroom, comes from the name of the room in which one powdered one's hair.) Grace's eyes—also from close observation of that portrait—could be a light-to-medium brown or possibly hazel, despite what one contemporary magazine asserted were a stunning azure.

Amorous and Bon Ton Intelligence, & c. . . .

Miss Dalrymple is so azurized, that nothing under the blue sky can exceed her; she wears a blue hat; her eyes are blue; her breastbones and ribbons are of the same colour; her carriage is also blue; her veins are blue, her garters are blue;

Georgiana Augusta Frederica Elliott, by Sir Joshua Reynolds, 1784. (The Metropolitan Museum of Art. Photo by Herbert von Sonnenburg.)

and she is called by way of distinction, 'The blue belle of Scotland.' (The Rambler's Magazine, *May 1784*)

Portrait painters have the option of exercising artistic license and painting what is seen in the palette of their mind's eye, not necessarily what a color photograph would reveal. Grace could have had eyes more hazel than blue that changed color dramatically according to what color clothing she wore. Even if Grace actually had blue eyes, however, in light of current knowledge of how eye color genes operate it would not necessarily have put the Prince of Wales out of the running as her daughter's father.

What of the other paternal suspects? What can one deduce from the circumstantial evidence? There were at least four other possible fathers, and two men who don't make the final cut.

George James, Lord Cholmondeley, appears from close observation of his portraits to have been a dark-haired gentleman, possibly with hazel or brown eyes. He was widely rumored to have been the father of Grace's daughter. Indeed, his granduncle Horace Walpole referred to Georgiana as his "niece" in the letter dated April 23, 1791, to his confidante Mary Berry describing a family wedding:

> *The Elliot girl was there, and is pretty—she rolls in the numerous list of my nephews and nieces. . . .*

Lord Cholmondeley was in company with Grace in early June; she followed him to London after encountering him in Paris when she was under the protection of the Duc de Chartres. The possibility that Grace and Cholmondeley had a passionate reunion is not beyond consideration. Absence may indeed have made these hearts—or loins—grow fonder. The resumed affair could have gone well into July, the most likely time that Georgiana was conceived.

Louis Philippe, Duc de Chartres, became upon the death of his father the Duc d'Orléans. A prince of the blood, he was closely related both to King Louis XVI and Queen Marie-Antoinette. He set Grace up in lavish style and deeded her a beautiful home, an elegant *hôtel particulier* in Paris near the fashionable faubourg St.-Honoré.

As her lover and official patron, he could emerge as the strongest candidate for the paternity of Grace's child—if, that is, they were engaging in

# Rosacea

This is a mysterious condition that still has no cure and whose symptoms can be more pronounced in male sufferers than female; the males have typically ruddy complexions and red, unattractively swollen noses. A predisposition to rosacea, or acne rosacea, may be genetic. The condition may be exacerbated by "triggers" such as the regular consumption of too much rich food and liquor; another trigger posited by researchers is the demodex mite, which lives in significantly higher numbers on the skins of people with rosacea than on the skins of those without the condition. An English wit, seeing Philippe on one of his many visits to London, proclaimed him "very rubified" and noted that he might better have been titled "the Duke of Burgundy."

The face of the Duc de Chartres is so completely overspread with a rosy tinge that the lilies of his ancestry may be said to receive not the least countenance from him.
(Morning Herald, *May 12, 1783*)

sexual relations at the time. But there are indications that the sexual relationship may have cooled by mid-1781, and she was already gone from Paris at the beginning of June. It's not likely that he was the father. The end of March is a full nine months from the end of June, and the last possible time they could have had intercourse was the first week of that month.

Plus, the child was pretty, and Philippe was remarkably ill favored by Nature; no one had ever called him handsome. He was large and heavy and had a wide, flat nose and a bumpy, flushed complexion, a countenance that many found repulsive. Thomas Carlyle said, "Carbuncles stud his face, dark studs on a ground of burnished copper." It was possible he was suffering from acne rosacea.

As to beauty, it is rather more than in the eyes of the beholder, and people who marry well, live well, dress well, and have the means to take care of themselves are more likely in the group known as the Beautiful People (the BPs)—a term popularized in the twentieth century by the fashion magazine *W*—than those in the poor, malnourished peasantry and underclasses, or even the up-and-coming middle classes. But was the English aristocracy made up entirely of BPs?

Returning again to the most likely suspects, those friends and boon com-

Beautiful People?

The English aristocracy, if one is to believe the evidence of thousands of paintings of sleek, well-groomed men and beautifully costumed women with perfect English rose or ivory complexions (but remember that smart artists flatter their subjects), or to trust gushing anecdotes passed on by contemporary travelers to Britain, were a handsome lot. They were the Beautiful People of their day.

"I have been struck everywhere in England with the beauty of the higher classes," the American writer Nathaniel Parker Willis commented in his *Pencillings by the Way* (1835). The remark was occasioned by a visit to Gordon Castle, where Willis mingled with the aristocracy, luxuriating in elaborate dinners and participating in a variety of leisure-time activities. Willis asserted that peers and gentry differed from the lower classes "as the racer differs from the dray-horse or the greyhound from the cur." Hard to believe an American not so far removed from the Revolutionary War wrote this; he sounds quite elitist.

The fawning Willis observed that the ton was peopled by individuals more pleasing to the eye than the general run of hoi polloi. Malnourishment and disease exacerbated by poverty stunt growth and negatively affect one's looks as well as one's life span. The ravages of smallpox, cholera, typhoid, rickets, and scarlet fever—only a few of the time's prevalent scourges—could mark and maim for life. Smallpox pitted the face and left scars; scarlet fever resulted in loss of hair; rickets bowed legs; cholera and typhoid killed.

The aristocracy had been living and eating extremely well off the fat of their land for a very long time; they could retreat to the countryside when epidemics raged in the dirty, crowded cities—and they, of all people, had access to the best medical attention available. They could take better care of themselves than the average person.

As to their gene pools, breeding for centuries with the most beautiful women of each successive generation would tend to produce attractive human beings. Wealthy heiresses, yes, were quickly snapped up, but beautiful, wealthy heiresses were snapped up even faster when it came time to marry and breed. Beauties have always had an edge.

Then there were the beautiful lower-class and middle-class women, among them courtesans, actresses, and prostitutes, who caught the roving eyes of aristocratic men. Lord Cholmondeley may have caved in to family pressure in not making an honest woman of his paramour, beautiful Grace Elliott, but others did marry beauties far beneath them in rank and class. They also fathered beautiful bastards with beautiful women.

For every breathtakingly beautiful Elizabeth Linley Sheridan, Elizabeth Farren, Sophia Baddeley, and Grace Dalrymple, there were funny-looking old geezers like the Duke of Derby, the Marquess of Queensberry, John Eliot, and Gillray's caricatured duke, Lord Kirkcudbright. Genes, however, are tricky: marrying a beautiful woman does not guarantee that one's offspring will be as attractive. The English aristocracy had no corner on beauty; their sycophants, however, like the American writer Willis, encouraged them to think they did.

panions of the Prince of Wales, that coterie of bon vivants making up his Carlton House set, as well as other notable society figures, who else could possibly have fathered Georgiana?

One who did not disallow the possibility of being the child's father was Charles Wyndham, playboy brother of the wealthy Lord Egremont, George O'Brien Wyndham, third Earl of Egremont. Charles Wyndham was a dark-haired man who'd been a lover of Grace's at one time and was seen with her when she returned to London in the summer of 1781. But though he boasted about being the father, not many, it seems, took his claim that seriously. He appears, according to Bleackley, to have been involved with Grace after the birth of Georgiana, as well as before.

One of the few to support Wyndham's claim was Thomas Raikes, whose *Journal,* covering 1831 to 1847 and published in 1857, was unequivocal about it. However, Raikes confused Georgiana with Harriet Cholmondeley, the other young girl Lord Cholmondeley raised, and managed to muddle her story as well. Raikes thus comes off as unreliable, at best.

The too-eager Charles Wyndham may have been futilely attempting to emulate his elder brother, in a strange case of sibling rivalry. According to James Munson, the immensely wealthy Lord Egrement "was credited with having left seventy-two illegitimate children at his death. It was rumoured that 'the Egremont nose could be traced all over Sussex.'" (From *Fitzherbert: Maria Fitzherbert, the Secret Wife of George IV,* 2002.) In childhood, Georgiana's charming nose was not one of those large, celebrated Egremont honkers, though it must be noted that it became significantly larger in adulthood.

Then there was the bizarre and laughable tale of George Augustus Selwyn and Maria-Emily, or "Mie-Mie," Fagniani, his supposed daughter, which has some bearing on the paternity of Georgiana

George O'Brien Wyndham he of the "Egremont nose," in profile and full face, from a pencil drawing by Sir Francis Leggatt Chantry, 1829. (National Portrait Gallery, London)

Elliott. Selwyn (1719–1791) was "frivolous, undependable, [and] cynical"; he was dubbed "George Bon-mot" by the press for his frequently quoted witticisms and was a close childhood friend of Horace Walpole, Lord Cholmondeley's granduncle.

Selwyn was on the short list of possible candidates for the honor of siring Grace Elliott's daughter, but a careful examination shows how patently absurd this allegation is. Selwyn would have been sixty-three at the time of Georgiana's birth, not an impossible time of life for a man to become a father, but he'd once said that he'd last had sexual relations with a woman—a maidservant in a coaching inn—when he was twenty-nine years old.

Like his friend Walpole, Selwyn never married. He was described by Walpole as someone "whose passion it is to see coffins and corpses, and executions." Stories of Selwyn's necrophilia abound in the letters and diaries of the time, and there was also an interesting aside suggesting that he went to the executions of criminals dressed as a woman. (George Selwyn in drag is not such a far-fetched image.)

Apart from his reputation for great wit, his supposed fondness for witnessing executions, and rumors of his cross-dressing, it was said of Selwyn that he enjoyed playing with children and to be especially "partial to little girls." He allowed himself to be manipulated by his friend "Old Q," the lecherous fourth Duke of Queensberry, into entering into an agreement to acknowledge the paternity of a child who was actually old Queensberry's natural daughter with the Marchesa Maria Fagniani.

This deflected undesirable public attention from Queensberry, who was an odd, solitary, rather misanthropic character, while Selwyn was delighted to assume the role of father. Men who did not carry on with women—whether married women, single women, courtesans, or whores—were suspect. Selwyn was probably gay, though tightly closeted like his friend Horace Walpole.

Selwyn—unexplainably for such a cynic—wholeheartedly adored this child who was not his biologically, going so far as to fight for her custody with her own mother. Old Q left the girl £150,000 in his will and Selwyn bequeathed her £33,000. Walpole, not at all amused by his friend's obsession, expressed little patience with his behavior and once sourly referred to the girl as "that brat."

Let us also quickly dismiss two other wildly remote possibilities, Grace's

A Bon Mot and Famous Anecdote from the Mouth of George Selwyn

Selwyn once mockingly asserted that women were constitutionally incapable of writing a letter without adding a postscript. One lady, determined to disprove his absurd hypothesis, sent him a letter the following day. To Selwyn's delight, however, there was a curious note after his correspondent's signature: "P.S. Who is right now, you or I?"

Perhaps the most oft-quoted anecdote about Selwyn is the one attributed to the politician Henry Fox, first Baron Holland. On his deathbed, Lord Holland told his servant, "If Mr. Selwyn calls again, show him up: if I am alive, I shall be delighted to see him, and if I am dead he would like to see me."

---

seducer Lord Valentia and her ex-husband Dr. John Eliot, from this short list. Grace and the abhorrent rake Valentia parted ways before 1776, and there is no evidence they ever saw each other again. Dr. Eliot's divorce papers stated that conjugal relations between him and Grace ceased in 1774. It's ludicrous to think that they might have shared a bed after that acrimonious and nasty divorce; they loathed each other.

The most likely of this mixed lot of possible sperm donors, then, were George James, fourth Earl of Cholmondeley, or his good friend George Augustus Frederick, Prince of Wales. (It's a safe bet that Georgiana Elliott's biological father was named George.)

Probably both men were intimate with Grace at the approximate time of Georgiana's conception. Lord Cholmondeley took Grace under his protection before, during, and after this pregnancy. She returned to England either with him or shortly after he left Paris in 1781. Further, theirs had been a long and complicated relationship with more than its share of drama, closely chronicled in the newspapers and in the *on-dits* that made up the daily gossip quotient of the ton. They were a well-recognized couple who never seemed far from each other when in the same geographical area.

Lord Cholmondeley, whatever occurred between him and Grace, whatever disagreements, estrangements, or physical separations they may have had, always seemed to show a concern for her welfare. He paid Grace Elliott's bills to the very end.

The Prince of Wales, too, is a serious contender. Even if he and Grace en-

# Who's Your Daddy?

There were no blood, DNA, or other scientific tests to determine paternity in the eighteenth century, and offspring, then as now, did not necessarily resemble their parents. Blue-eyed parents could have brown-eyed children, something our ancestors observed and no doubt occasionally questioned, but only today is there valid scientific assurance that this is neither an anomaly nor all that rare. It happens, and the milkman and postman can be absolved, finally, of blame.

The time-honored concept taught in biology classes that there were only two genes for eye color, and that blue eyes were always passed on to offspring as recessive genes and brown eyes as dominant genes, has not been considered accurate for many years. Inheritance is rather more complicated than the Mendelian two-gene model where eye color is concerned. Contemporary genetic understanding has confirmed that eye-color inheritance is polygenic, with many genes at work. One gene for green eye color has already been discovered; there may be a second green gene, and other colors as well. In other words, blue-eyed parents can have brown-eyed children, hazel-eyed children, or green-eyed children as well as children with blue eyes like theirs, depending on their own genes and the gene configuration of those with whom they mate, and on conditions—such as the layering of color causing variance in pigmentation of the iris—not yet fully understood.

gaged in sexual intercourse on only a few occasions, the Prince was said to have managed to get his wife, Caroline of Brunswick—that unfortunate creature so odious to him—pregnant after only one drunken night together in the conjugal bed. (Others claimed he spent three drunken nights with her, not just the one.) But it only takes one time. Given the lack of hard evidence based on blood type or DNA, one has to concede that the jury is still out, and will never be brought in for a final verdict.

THE POST-PRINNY BLUES

Horace Bleackley summarizes Grace's life for the next several years, after the birth of her daughter, by saying that she "lived alternatively in London and Paris, shining as a star of the first magnitude in both capitals, one of the most brilliant and popular among the fashionable 'impures.'" He tracks her cohabiting with "her devoted Wyndham" and then going back to Lord Cholmondeley before leaving again for Paris and the allure of life in that city, the most sophisticated of Continental capitals, under the protection of Philippe. Her attempts to get together with Prinny—according to the newspapers—were evidently fruitless; he wasn't interested. The newspapers ate it up.

The lines in the *Morning Post* of November 11, 1780, that had mocked Mary Robinson might equally have served, at this juncture, for the jilted Grace:

> Now, Lady—where's your honour now?
> Can no man fit your palate but a Prince?

And what of little Georgiana, that darling toddler? In 1784 she is two years old, and Sir Joshua Reynolds is commissioned to paint her portrait. As the painting stays in the extended Cholmondeley–Cavendish-Bentinck family, it's a sure bet that Lord Cholmondeley has commissioned it, as he probably commissioned the 1782 painting of Grace by Thomas Gainsborough that also remained in the family.

All three of the exquisite portraits of Grace and her daughter were sold to Americans in the World War I era and were then given to museums; the Reynolds and the Gainsborough full-length went to the Metropolitan Museum of Art and the Gainsborough portrait bust to the Frick Collection.

There is another portrait of Grace, a strange one in its provenance, at the Lady Lever Art Gallery in Port Sunlight. At first thought to be the work of Thomas Gainsborough's nephew, his sister's son Gainsborough Dupont, it is now attributed to Gainsborough himself; at first thought to be a portrait of Grace Elliott's daughter, it is now called *Mrs. Elliott*. The painting is a portrait bust and shows an attractive woman with big, powdered hair, long neck, sloping shoulders, a fine hand, and a deep décolletage. As in the portrait bust by Gainsborough at the Frick, the dress shown has a bow at the bosom. The face of the sitter is long, like Grace Elliott's, but narrower; the nose is long and also narrower. The mouth is much smaller, and the eyes appear blue, not brown. There's a sharpness to this lady's features totally unlike Grace's face in the other Gainsborough portrait bust, but not unlike her face in the full-length Gainsborough. It could be Grace. She was probably pregnant with Georgiana when the portrait at the Frick was painted; pregnancy can fill out the contours of a woman's face. Unfortunately, the gallery is not sure who the

(National Museums and Galleries on Merseyside)

sitter is or who painted the portrait, though it is now attributed to Gainsborough and not his nephew. It is possible that it's a copy—not a very good one—of that third painting by Gainsborough Grace was supposed to have sat for, but that seems to have been lost.

Depending on which version of the story one wants to believe, Lord Cholmondeley supposedly asked Grace if he could raise Georgiana, or the Prince of Wales asked Cholmondeley to raise her in lieu of doing so himself. Apparently there was no objection from Grace—who was to have intermittent visits from Georgiana in France through the mid-to-late-1780s—and, indeed, mothers living apart from their young children were not considered odd in these circles. If this was a favor to the Prince, it was a smart move for the young earl to make; it would give him a certain cachet to bring up a royal bastard. He would be well rewarded by the future king.

For all her notoriety and hobnobbing with princes and important members of the ton, it is surprising that only one political cartoon of Grace surfaces during this time. (There appear to be none dealing with her scandalous divorce or her pregnancy.) On September 23, 1783, William Wells, a printer operating out of 132 Fleet Street, distributed a drawing by Hannibal Scratch (the pseudonym of a John Nicholson), *The Aerostatick Stage Balloon*, number 6284 in the British Museum's multivolume *Catalogue of Political and Personal Satires* edited by Frederic George Stephens and Mary Dorothy George.

Grace Elliott, holding a fan, is in the top tier of the three-tiered hot-air balloon; she's flanked on her right by Mary Robinson (Perdita), shown clasping her hands ecstatically, and on her left by her friend Seymour Dorothy, Lady Worsley. Grace is the tallest of the three women. It's seven years after Grace's divorce from Dr. John Eliot but only a year since Lady Worsley's lurid crim. con. trial. All three women, in April 1783, when this drawing was probably being circulated, were on a list published in *The Rambler's Magazine*. The ranking was of the most fashionable "Votaries of Venus," and it established Mrs. Robinson as number 2, Lady Worsley as number 3, and Mrs. Elliott as number 6. (A Lady Corbyne was number 1, Lady Grosvenor number 4, Mrs. Armstead number 5, and a Mrs. Wilton number 7.)

In the center gallery sit two portly ex-prime ministers, Lord North and Charles James Fox. North's arm is on Fox's right shoulder and Fox turns to him with a smile on his face. Each man rests his hand on the railing in front of him, and the two hold a slim thread that is attached to the nose of the Duke of Portland, who is at left in profile, facing them. On the right, his back turned to these three, is the orator Edmund Burke, dressed like a Jesuit priest, looking at the Pope—in furred robe and triple crown—who peers out over the right side of the balloon. On the extreme left-hand side of the balloon is a winged Devil, a net in his hands, looking at the men seated on the second tier as if he could eat them up.

The lowest railed tier is occupied by a number of celebrated quacks, charlatans, and other familiar London characters, including "Vestina," the so-called goddess of health, who advertised the virtues of Dr. Graham's Celestial Bed (touted as a fertility device); she holds a scepter wreathed with flowers and looks at the quack Dr. Graham, who's seated next to her. The knock-kneed gentleman is a dwarf named Jeffery Dunstan, a traveling salesman of old wigs (a reference to the Whig Party?) who was mock-elected the mayor of Garrat; he carries a sack filled with his wares. (Dunstan figured in a number of other cartoons, such as Rowlandson's 1784 *The Discovery*.) The pub owner Sam House of Wardour

Hand-colored etching by "Hannibal Scratch" (John Nicholson) shows the ton seated in boxes behind railings around the outside of a hot-air balloon, along with politicians, notorious courtesans, and mountebanks, as if they were spectators at a theater. The balloon, filled with their vanity, is about to be punctured or set aloft by a mock Frenchman who, sounding like a stock German, says, "Oh Begar dis be von fine Cargo." (British Museum)

Ballooning—the New Craze—and "Ballooniana"

The first successful manned free-flight ascent of a hot-air balloon was made in Paris by a French science teacher, François Pilatre de Rozier, accompanied by François Laurent, the Marquis d'Arlandes, an officer in the French army, on November 21, 1783. The balloon was made by the premier personages associated with early ballooning, the Montgolfier brothers Joseph-Michel and Jacques-Etienne. It was seventy-five feet high and forty-nine feet wide, and it had a capacity of seventy-nine thousand cubic feet. It took off from the Bois de Boulogne and landed five and a half miles away at Butte-aux-Cailles.

A longer airborne flight—in a hydrogen-gas-powered balloon this time—took place on December 1 of that same year when Jacques Charles, a physicist, and Nicolas Robert set off from the Tuileries in front of a crowd of four hundred thousand people and landed two hours later at Nesle-la-Vallee, twenty-seven miles away. It reached an altitude of over nine thousand feet. Philippe, Duc de Chartres, also took part in a (failed) balloon try in Paris at around that time.

After these first successful balloon trips in Paris, public balloon ascents began to be held in the plea-

LEFT: *Mrs. Sage and Mr. Biggin, English Aerial Travelers, 1785.* (*New London Magazine,* November 1, 1785) (Science and Society Picture Library, London)

BELOW: A stickpin commemorating a Montgolfier flight. (Photo by Ray Wadia) (Collection of the author)

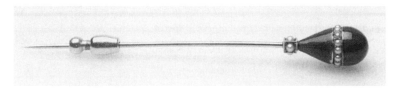

sure gardens, both in Paris and London. There was an explosion of balloon art—"ballooniana"—and depictions of balloons began to show up on decorated ceramics such as plates, vases, and snuffboxes, in jewelry (stickpins, brooches), and on ladies' painted fans, as well as in prints and paintings. Collectors snapped them up.

Late eighteenth-century decorated snuffbox from the Penn-Gaskell collection of ballooniana. (Science and Society Picture Library, London)

Street, an avid supporter of Fox, is shown holding a frothy pint of ale and looking at Dunstan; his pub, the Intrepid Fox, was named after the politician Charles James Fox.

Also in that lowest tier is the popular conjurer and quack doctor (he claimed to cure the influenza), Gustavus Katerfelto. (He is gazing up at the moon while one of his black cats (he had two, called "the Doctor's Devils") gazes back at him. The cat is asking if there are mice on the moon. Katerfelto (or Katterfelto) came to London in about 1782. His advertisements in the newspapers—headed "Wonders! Wonders! Wonders!"—are shown in the broadside he holds in his right hand. Katerfelto's usual costume (not depicted here) was a long black gown and a square cap; his wife and daughter, who were present at all his shows, dressed in like manner. His public entertainments consisted of card and magic tricks, demonstrations with a "solar microscope," and experiments in electricity and chemistry. He died in Bristol, having fallen upon hard times, in 1799.

The huge balloon is encircled from top to bottom by ropes that are knotted beneath it; from these, ropes lead to a wooden platform. On the platform sits a washtub, the word "Vanity" inscribed on its side; it's filled to overflowing with soap bubbles. On top of the foaming suds is written the word "Froth."

Dancing on one leg to the side is a mock figure of a Frenchman ("Monsieur") brandishing a knife that seems poised to cut through the ropes and send the balloon aloft, or, possibly, to prick the balloon itself, let all the hot air out, and tumble these assorted quacks, politicians, and ladies of ill-repute down to the ground. In the far background are the undreaming roofs and spires of London, the most prominent of which is St. Paul's Cathedral. Beneath the title is written, "Setts out from Swan with two Necks Lad Lane every Monday Morng." The Swan with Two Necks, a coffeehouse and coaching inn on Ladd Lane, was the terminus for northbound coaches. Vanity flew weekly.

Tentanda via est qua me quoque possim tollere humo, etching/engraving/aquatint by James Gillray, published by Hannah Humphrey, August 18, 1810. Grace Elliott has been found to be in only one political cartoon, where she is shown about to ascend in a balloon. Here, Lord Cholmondeley is shown cheering on another balloon ascension. Unlike his former mistress, he was featured in a good number of cartoons. (National Portrait Gallery, London)

A long caption in the form of a poem explains:

Who choose a journey to the Moon
May take it in our Stage Balloon,
Where love sick Virgins past their prime
May Marry yet and laugh at time,
Perdita—W——sley Fillies free,
Each flash their Lunar Vis à Vis,
There N—— may realize his Dreams,
And F——x pursue his golden schemes
And Father B——ke may still absolve 'em
Howe'er the Devil may involve them;
The Pope may plan his Machinations
With Panders Quacks & Politicians.
Sam House enjoy his Tankard there
And Old Wigs still be Garats May'r
Great Katerdevil work his Wonders
Spruce Gr——ham launch Electric thunders
Vestina too————nor fear a fall
Sr Satan's Net shall catch ye all
So said Monsieur in broken Brogue
And up they mounted W——e and R——e.

Political cartoons like these were a means to satirize regimes in circumstances where the wrong step could lead to a fine, arrest, or imprisonment for libel. Often they were anonymous or pseudonymous. Instruments of serious criticism masquerading as flip or scurrilous commentary, they contained hard kernels of truth that poked fun at the powerful, wealthy, and celebrated, much like the jokes of the late-night talk show comedians do today.

Studying these eighteenth-century cartoons gives one a clearer and broader picture of society, personalities, and current events than merely reading history books. When one learns to "read" these prints, as well, their value is marked.

By appearing in a cartoon with some notable heavies of the London scene, Grace Elliott had been brought to the attention of a wider audience, and she was vulnerable to more serious criticism. It may not have been entirely to her liking; she takes up permanent residence in Paris a year after the print is published in 1783. It's a clever cartoon, taking advantage of the craze for ballooning to make some philosophical points. Courtesans, politicians, and promoters of celestial beds, quack cures, and abhorrent religions are sent to Hell. The message is clear: Get out of town! Grace took the hint.

In the *Catalogue of Political and Personal Satires,* M. Dorothy George, doyenne of the English political cartoon, calls *The Aerostatick Stage Balloon*

> *One of many satires on balloon ascents . . . here combined with a satire on the Coalition, or on politicians, who are associated with mountebanks and women of damaged reputation.*

Two London hot-air enthusiasts of the period were the couple George Biggin and Mrs. Laetitia Sage, who took a flight together on a Vincent Lunardi balloon on June 29, 1785. Mrs. Sage later published an account of her experience as England's first female aeronaut.

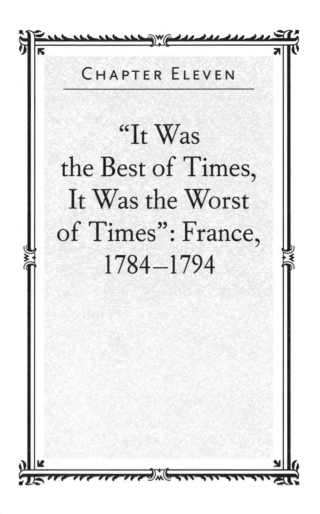

CHAPTER ELEVEN

"It Was the Best of Times, It Was the Worst of Times": France, 1784–1794

One could do very much worse here than cite the oft-quoted opening of Charles Dickens's phenomenal novel of the French Revolution, *A Tale of Two Cities*:

It was the best of times, it was the worst of times, it was the age of wisdom, it was the age of foolishness, it was the epoch of belief, it was the epoch of incredulity, it was the season of Light, it was the season of Darkness, it was the spring of hope, it was the winter of despair, we had everything before us, we had nothing before us, we were all going direct to Heaven, we were all going direct the other way. . . .

There were a king with a large jaw and a queen with a plain face, on the throne of England; there were a king with a large jaw and a queen with a fair face, on the throne of France. In both countries it was clearer than crystal to the lords of the State preserves of loaves and fishes, that things in general were settled for ever.

Grace leaves England for France with Philippe at the end of the summer of 1784. Bleackley states that she'd decided to cast her lot with her ex-protector, even though she knew she would have to share his affections with his new favorite, Agnes de Buffon (whom she detested). But life is, on the whole, very good. Grace is living well. She is healthy, still relatively young, and beautiful. Her daughter, too, is living well, and is loved and protected in the bosom of a good family. If not all that Grace has ever desired has come her way, one might never know it. To the outside world, she's a lucky woman, about to get luckier living under the protection of a wealthy man in a country where the very wealthy live very, very well. She will buy a new country house, a cottage at Meudon, not far from her protector's large home at the Parc Monceau.

Philippe has some shortcomings. His is not the strongest of characters, he doesn't appear to choose his friends wisely, and he's easily led by others. However, it's said he's kind, generous, even-tempered, and nonjudgmental with those he loves. He's been gifted with such great wealth, this prince of the blood, though not with good looks. No, Philippe would never qualify as one of the eighteenth century's most beautiful people. He is basically "a man of pleasure," as Bleackley puts it in *Ladies Fair and Frail:*

An hereditary taint, augmented by his own debaucheries, had covered his face with pimples, his eyes were dull and fish-like, and his features coarse and expressionless. In spite of his unwieldly bulk he could ride well and danced gracefully, but beyond these he had no accomplishments, being wholly uneducated and dull by nature. . . . The whole of his life had been spent in shameless immorality, and there was not a more idle and selfish voluptuary in all France.

Yet Grace Elliott found him amiable, never once mentioned his looks, and avowed that he had "the best temper in the world." Obviously, he was charming as well as generous. (Though there were some in the ton he never did charm.) She kept coming back to him, and it couldn't have been only for his money. One has to concede that there must have been positive aspects to the man, if one is to believe anything Grace goes on to say subsequently. He

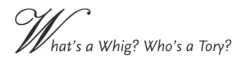

What's a Whig? Who's a Tory?

"Whig" is a shortening of the Scottish *"whiggamore"* (or *"whiggamor"*), referring to someone who drives cattle and horses. The name derives from an action called the Whiggamore Raid that took place in Scotland in 1648 against King James II. The term "Whig" in the following decades came to stand for proponents of the rights of the people over those of the monarchy or court. After the Glorious Revolution of 1688, the principles that governed the Whig party were, overall, an advocacy of personal freedom and the assertion that the king was empowered and ruled only by the consent of the people and Parliament, eschewing the notion of the divine right of kings. Though its leadership in the eighteenth century was largely aristocratic and was hardly drawn from common folk, the Whig party was also the party of the new mercantile and financial interests and of religious dissidents like Quakers, Methodists, and Roman Catholics. The mercantile and financial interests profited in wartime while the landed aristocracy and gentry bore the brunt of heavy taxes to support such wars. Those landed groups opposed—and feared—the growing power of the middle classes in principle as well as in their pockets.

The Tories believed in the divine right of kings to rule as they wished, and were staunch followers of the established state church, the Church of England. They abhorred Dissenters and Roman Catholics. The Whigs supported the American Revolution; the Tories supported the American Royalists. The term "Tory" was originally meant to be insulting, but in this case it was an Irish term of disrespect, not a Scottish one, and referred to outlaws.

The great Whig leader during the latter part of the eighteenth century and the early part of the nineteenth century was Charles James Fox. Other Whig leaders were the Duke of Newcastle; George Grenville; Charles Watson-Wentworth and the Marquess of Rockingham; the Earl of Chatham; the Duke of Grafton; the Earl of Shelburne; and the Duke of Portland. Many of them served a year or less as prime minister in this unstable period under King George III. The Whigs' support of French republicanism and Roman Catholic emancipation caused them to lose power from 1793 to 1830. The Tories were headed during this period by John Stuart, third Earl of Bute; Lord North; and William Pitt the Younger.

In today's Britain, the Tories are the Conservatives and the Whigs are the Liberal Democrats.

took care of her and he was kind, if not faithful. But then, he wasn't faithful to his wife, either. Bottom line: He was very, very rich.

From the good life under the wing of the Duc d'Orléans to the first bloody days of the French Revolution and the unimaginable horrors of the Reign of Terror, Grace Elliott experienced it and lived to write about it. Of her Parisian circle, she was one of the few survivors. That part of her story is told in her *Journal,* and that's where one has to go next, as, according to Bleackley, nothing much is heard of or from Grace Elliott from the end of 1786 to the fall of 1793, when this *on-dit* appeared in the newspaper *The World* on September 26, 1793:

> *Mrs. Elliott, the former favourite of Lord Cholmondeley, is in the most deplorable state of poverty in France. She has had FREEDOM to the full, and now feels the consequences.*

The newspaper is full of what is happening in France and how it will affect the English in all areas. The King has been executed, the Queen is about to be killed, the young dauphin is imprisoned, and the more moderate of the revolutionaries, the Girondists, will be arrested and guillotined within a few weeks. The Reign of Terror is in full swing and the French seem to have gone stark, raving mad. *The World* sums it up in a quip that is all the more chilling because it is offhand:

> *The JACOBIN CLUB have adopted a new mode of making themselves MONARCHS of FRANCE. All who differ from them in the CONVENTION are beheaded. No new Members are chosen, so that after a certain degree of MORTALITY has taken place—they must reign of course.*

THE DEMISE OF DOCTOR ELIOT

What was happening to other players in Grace's life in England while she was in France? One of them, Dr. John—now Sir John—Eliot, passed away in 1786, only ten years after their divorce. He had become a knight, then a baronet, but had little time, as fate would have it, to enjoy the honors of his exalted status.

His personal character has to come under closer scrutiny. Sir John was less—and more—than was apparent at first glance. The record, for what it is, substantiates his mistreatment at the hands of his comely wife and her seducer. But what of the good doctor's own behavior? Was he guiltless and blame-free? Did Grace have any reason to be unfaithful beyond her boredom with his lifestyle and manner? Perhaps she did, for the good doctor's life does not stand up to close examination. (And let's not even discuss how he led on that poor old "Swelly"!)

Eliot's last will and testament is an eye-opener. It stands as proof that

The will of Sir John Eliot, Knight and Baronet. (National Archives, Kew)

what was sauce for the gander in Georgian times was not necessarily sauce for the goose. Dr. Eliot could have it both ways, fidelity-wise, but Grace Elliott could not. The double standard was not only alive but functioning extremely well. Eliot was awash in mistresses and natural children.

The will of Sir John Eliot, Doctor of Physic of Peebles, Peebleshire, dated November 29, 1786, is seven pages long. It's written in accordance with the template for wills in those days, in a small, precise copyist's hand, but marred with blurred or undecipherable words and proper names. In it, Eliot lists many bequests, for he was a wealthy man with extensive properties. Among these bequests are amounts to a number of women and their—and his—offspring, Eliot's bastard children. What a hypocrite, divorcing his wife for her adulterous behavior! But, as noted, that was the way the game was played in Georgian England. Advantage: men.

Eliot begins his will, "I, Sir John Eliot, of Peebles, Knight and Baronet and Doctor of Physic," eschewing the usual religious preamble. It's telling. What it's telling the reader or listener is that John Eliot is an important man—two titles, and a medical doctor, to boot!—and that anyone reading or hearing this read out should be made cognizant of these facts. He is consistent to the end in his need to assert his superiority over other men. (Is it one of those short-man things? One wonders.)

He does pay lip service to the religious formalities. After stating that he finds himself "strong and vigorous in mind," he acknowledges that he is "yet weak in body" and says, "I die in the faith of my ancestors." This is not a man who goes willingly to his death. It's ironic that this strong-willed, ambitious doctor could not heal himself.

There are bequests to faithful retainers: to his housekeeper Elizabeth Poulallow he leaves "the Sum of twenty Guineas, together with a Suit of Mourning"; to his two coachmen, John and Thomas, he also leaves mourning clothes and, in addition, to John "one year's wages over and above what may be due him at the time of my death." There are specific bequests of valuable or sentimental objects to friends: a miniature portrait, a silver Standish (inkwell), miscellaneous pieces of silver plate, special books.

He also leaves booze from his cellars to some worthies: "Old Burton ale . . . which I know he likes" to his friend Thomas Wood, and to an important man who is the chairman of the East India Company, "a few dozens of Rum forty years old in my Cellar as I know he takes a little Tiff of punch."

He names as his executor his "dear uncle William Davidson . . . of Muir-House," near Edinburgh, his mother Mary Davidson Eliot Randall's brother. He leaves special bequests to Davidson, to his good friends Richard Davenport and James McPherson, and to his Scottish siblings and assorted relatives. To one he calls "my son John Eliot" he leaves a "very handsome fowling

ills Before 1858

Eve McLaughlin's *Wills Before 1858* tells all there is to know about last wills and testaments in the Georgian/Regency era. The proving of wills (the probate process) was a matter for the ecclesiastical courts. People usually did not make wills until they were somewhat on in age or suddenly became ill. (McLaughlin says most people didn't make wills until they were at least seventy.) What did such wills routinely contain, and in what order?

- Religious Preamble. Wills normally started with a phrase such as "In the Name of God Amen" or "In the Name of the Father Amen," but this did not mean that the person who made the will was particularly religious. It was standard ecclesiastical-court terminology.

- Charitable Bequests. These usually came next, and covered matters such as distribution of shillings to the poor on the day of the funeral, bequests to servants and retainers, and so on. How much from the estate to spend on the funeral was sometimes noted.

- Bequest to Widow. This would specify how the widow would be taken care of, whether she was to remain in the house for her lifetime, what the annuity—if any—paid to her would be, and how many times a year it would be disbursed (it was usually quarterly).

- Provision for Children. The eldest son would inherit the major part of his father's real estate—this was called primogeniture—and this was understood and was not always written down. Younger sons might be given secondary real estate—which had to be specified in the will—or otherwise given sums to set them up in business or in apprenticeships. Daughters were generally given a dowry in money. If there were a great deal of land, a daughter might get some. Eldest daughters might get more money than their younger sisters. Unmarried daughters were expected to live with their family, but provisions (e.g., annuities) might be set up for spinsters. A father who was wary of a son-in-law might make specific provision for his daughter and/or see that her monies passed on to her children, not to her spouse. There has been some controversy over children left only a shilling, as if this was a mark of disfavor or disinheritance. That is not the case. When it's stated a child is left only a shilling it means that the child has already received all the money he or she is likely to have gotten. If a child has been ungrateful, it will probably be spelled out very clearly in a will; the about-to-depart do not mince words.

- Dispersal of Real Property. At this point a wealthy and/or titled man could choose to "entail" his property, that is, try to keep it in the family and ensure that only each of his sons in turn—the "tail males," or heirs of his body—could inherit it, and say what to do if the male line should run out. This part of a will can be extremely complicated and full of legalese.

Muirhouse

The mansion was the home of the Davidson family for many years; it was purchased in 1776 by William Davidson, John Eliot's maternal uncle, who died in 1794 or 1795 and is buried in Cramond Kirk. Davidson left the house to his sister's son, John Eliot's half-brother, a minister named Thomas Randall, upon condition that Thomas assume the Davidson name. (A twentieth-century descendant, Randall Thomas Davidson, became archbishop of Canterbury.) Muirhouse is on Marine Drive, on the shore of the Firth of Forth, less than five miles west of Edinburgh. The present building is a Tudor-cum-Gothic-style mansion dating from 1830; all that remains of the previous dwelling (built circa 1670) are two round towers. The Davidsons gave their name to the nearby village of Davidson's Mains.

piece" (shotgun), two family Bibles, and all the silver plate not reserved for anyone else. This is the first word we have anywhere that Sir John Eliot had a son, and it's a stunner. Eliot goes on to name other children, three daughters, and their mothers—three different women—but he does not say who the mother of his namesake son is, a son who may have been born before or during his marriage to Grace.

What else is known about this son? His date of birth is unknown, but the chances are this John Eliot was not a child, as, at Eliot's death, he was in service as a writer with the East India Company at the Fort William establishment in Calcutta, Bengal Province. We know of him because on September 4, 1816, he made out a new will just before marrying Augusta Thackeray (1785–18??), the sister of his "worthy" friend, on October 5 at St. John's Cathedral in Calcutta. Augusta was the sister of Richmond Thackeray (1788–1815), and aunt to *Vanity Fair* novelist William Makepeace Thackeray (1811–1863). (The Thackerays were old India hands; William was born in Calcutta, sent to England for his education, and never returned to his birthplace.)

It was to be a brief union. On March 21, 1820, no more than six months after John Eliot's death, Augusta married for the second time at the Calcutta home of her brother-in-law Henry Shakespear. The bridegroom was a Dr. Alexander Halliday.

This John Eliot's will was probated in London on November 16, 1819, so he lived scarcely three years after marrying. If he was at least twenty-one in 1786, he could have been in his mid-fifties at the time of his death. A true son of his father, he left bequests to several natural children.

John had three half-sisters: Ann, Mary, and Marianne. Their ages are not given, but the assumption can be made that they are minors, under the age of twenty-one. Ann is living with a Mrs. Pillot on Edgware Road in London; Mary is living with her mother, Mrs. Martha Stringer, in Upper Marylebone Street; Marianne is with her mother, Mrs. Suky(?) Edwards, residing on Oxford Road. Whether his mother is one of these three women is not known. Why Ann is not living with her mother is also not known.

In his will, Sir John Eliot leaves annuities—as noted, these were usually payable quarterly—to these women and girls: to daughter Ann, £50; to Mrs. Ann Evans, identified as Ann's mother, £50; to daughter Mary, £80; to Mary's mother, Martha Stringer, £30; to daughter Marianne, £60. There is no annuity noted for Marianne's mother, but there are annuities for several other women, their relationship to Eliot unknown.

Eliot also leaves outright gifts of money as dowries for the girls: £2,500 for Ann, £1,500 for Mary, and £500 for Marianne. He names his uncle William and his friends MacPherson and Davenport as "guardians of my three daughters Ann, Mary, and Marianne in full confidence that they will be so kind to these children that they will not feel the want of a father" and

View of Fort William, Calcutta, with the church of St. Anne in the foreground. (English school, eighteenth century, Bridgeman Art Library)

adds, "it is my will that my said three daughters take my name and bear my ARMS."

Looking at these bequests, it would appear that Eliot's daughter Ann Evans was the most favored, or perhaps the eldest, as elder daughters tended to receive more. Uncle William is instructed at one point to give any of Eliot's "effects as may be proper for the education and support of my dear daughter Ann," which smacks of favoritism. But what's written in wills can be deceiving. If Mary and Marianne are older they may have already received cash disbursements from their father. So Ann is not necessarily the favorite or eldest, although she could be. She could be at a dame school—a circumstance that might explain why the lady she's living with isn't her mother: Mrs. Pillot might be a school mistress. Or perhaps Ann's mother was ill and unable to care for her. As for the lack of an annuity for Marianne's mother, money may have been given to her previously.

Four children, a son and three daughters—and who knows how many mistresses—show that Eliot was a busy man. He may have had one or more of these mistresses before and during his marriage to Grace Dalrymple. Wives were never supposed to know of such arrangements, and, if they did, were supposed to pretend that they didn't know. "Dally the Prolific"? More like "Little John the Prolific"!

It's to his credit that Sir John Eliot acknowledged his natural children in his last will and testament and gave them his name. He couldn't pass on his titles or arms to them, however, as all his offspring were illegitimate, and three of them were females. Marrying the mother of his son after the fact wouldn't have made the son legitimate and eligible to inherit a title.

Eliot reiterates in his will that his uncle William is to ensure that his ex-wife Grace's annuity is paid to her without fail. Note, too, that he has taken his name away from her and that she is Grace Dalrymple, not Elliott: "to Mrs. Grace Dalrymple an annuity of 200 pounds during all the days of her life."

Eliot goes into minute detail over the dispersal of his real estate. He seems to give his son the option of buying all his Scottish holdings (he does not elaborate on their number, size, or location) "within six years" of his death for £4,000. And he leaves him the odd sum of £1,786 outright. Again, there is no way of knowing what he had already given him over the years.

Whether or not his son exercised this option to buy the Scottish land and property is unknown. After the elapsed time, those holdings were most likely sold by the executors.

His books, pictures, drawings, furniture, and London house on Cecil Street, Eliot instructs his executor, are to be sold. He's not happy about the dispersal of these objects—which include, he says, "Hogarthes works"—but it has to be done for estate purposes. (A listing of his art sold at auction was once in the collection of the British Library but was found to be misplaced, lost, or stolen last year when an inquiry was made.)

In addition to his natural children by several different women, Sir John Eliot produced a number of works in medicine. These were not charitably received by critics; they were not particularly insightful and they broke no new ground in the causes, diagnoses, or treatment of illnesses. His books, all published in London, included the following: *Essays on Physiological Subjects* (1780); *An Account of the Principal Mineral Waters of Great Britain and Ireland* (1781); *The Medical Pocket-Book, containing a short but plain account of the Symptoms, Causes, and Methods of Cure of the Diseases incident to the Human Body* (1781); and *Elements of the Branches of Natural Philosophy connected with Medicine* (1782).

The Medical Pocket-Book consisted of Eliot's own alphabetically arranged notes for use in his medical practice; according to the author of his biographical entry in the *DNB,* they proved that he had "very limited medical knowledge." But is one being excessively hard on Dr. Eliot here? In those early days of medicine, few practitioners could have withstood picky investigations into their effectiveness as physicians, or their ideas, methods, or treatments. Dr. Eliot was a simple practitioner, not a scientific genius, and he did manage to have a number of books published. Those books were a testament, if nothing else, to the man's prodigious energy.

Sir John Eliot died at Brocket Hall, Hertfordshire, family seat of his friend Peniston Lamb, Lord Melbourne, the one-time protector of Eliot's patient Sophia Baddeley. Brocket Hall, a 543-acre estate, is now a corporate meeting venue with a trendy lakeside restaurant (a former hunting lodge), and it's the site of the Nick Faldo Golf Institute, with two eighteen-hole golf courses. There are luxurious suites decorated in period style, among them the Prince Regent, the Lady Melbourne, and the Queen Victoria suites.

James Paine was the architect who rebuilt the estate for Sir Matthew Lamb in 1760.

Of what did John Eliot die? According to his obituary:

He was naturally temperate. And tho' the pleasures of the table were very probably the efficient cause of his death, he sacrificed his strength, robust as it was, less to appetite than to sentiment.

Not terribly clear. Further muddying the waters, the writer goes on to say:

The concluding scenes of this life, yield little other product than the well known truth, that health prodigally wasted, cannot often be retrieved. Sir John Eliott, it may be thought, lost not a moment in the discovery of his illness; nor left untried any possible experiment for its removal. Bath, Bristol, Wales, and a sea voyage from Gravesend to Torbay, from Torbay to the Western Islands, all were tried—but tried in vain; for he died suddenly, after a short interval of apparent recovery. . . . [His death] was thought to proceed from a rupture in one of the larger vessels.

Cancer? Heart disease? Aneurysm? The comment about "a short interval of apparent recovery" might indicate remission from cancer. The remark that "health prodigally wasted, cannot often be retrieved," though, is puzzling. He apparently enjoyed the pleasures of the table and his wine, but he was only about fifty years old (the parish register states he was fifty-two, and there are still questions about his true age), and he was not one of the debauched and dissipated tribe that gathered around the Prince of Wales. The clues point to an illness that was probably environmental or hereditary, like the aforementioned cancer or heart disease. A "naturally temperate" man does not die as suddenly as this from overeating, and he was a doctor, so had to have some ideas about how to stay healthy, if only from observa-

Brocket Hall, Hertfordshire. Watercolor by Helen Allingham. (With permission of the Helen Allingham Society, www.helenallingham.com)

tion of patients over many years. No, something else was going on, something he could not control with the medicines and cures he had at hand.

NEAR THIS PLACE LIE INTERRED
THE REMAINS OF SIR JOHN ELIOT BAR^T
LATE AN EMINENT PHYSICIAN IN LONDON.
HE WAS BORN IN EDINBURGH, IN THE YEAR
  M,DCC,XXXVI.
WHERE HE HAD THE FIRST RUDIMENTS OF
  HIS EDUCATION,
WHICH HE FURTHER IMPROVED DURING HIS
  RESIDENCE
IN FRANCE AND HOLLAND.
HE DIED AT BROCKET-HALL, THE SEAT OF
  HIS FRIEND LORD MELBOURNE,
ON THE VIIITH OF NOVEMBER M,DCC,LXXXVII.
HAVING BEFORE HIS DEATH GIVEN DIRECTIONS
THAT HE SHOULD BE BURIED IN THE PARISH CHURCH-YARD OF
THE PLACE WHERE HE SHOULD HAPPEN TO DIE.

   THUS, WHEN THE POISON'D SHAFTS OF DEATH ARE SPED,
   THE PLANT OF GILEAD BOWS HER MOURNFUL HEAD:
   THE HOLY BALM THAT HEAL'D ANOTHER'S PAIN,
   ON HER OWN WOUND DISTIL'S ITS CHARM IN VAIN.
                                        JERNINGHAM.

HIS UNCLE W^M DAVIDSON OF MUIR-HOUSE NEAR EDINBURGH
CAUSED THIS MONUMENT TO BE ERECTED.

Sir John Eliot's memorial tablet at Saint Etheldreda's Church. (Photograph by Henry W. Gray, 2004)

Sir John died on November 7, 1786, according to the burial entry in the parish register, and he was buried on November 12 in St. Etheldreda's, the historic parish church of Bishop's Hatfield. A memorial tablet with lines by the poet-playwright Edward Jerningham (1737–1812), a good friend of Horace Walpole's, was put up by Eliot's uncle. (Note that the tablet states he died on November 8, 1787. Ah, the joys of historical research!)

Despite his love of the good life and the expenses he did not spare during his lifetime, John Eliot, though he died a wealthy man, went back to his frugal Scots roots and directed that the charges for his funeral should not exceed £25. (The obituary said it was £20, the will said £25.)

A final note about Sir John Eliot.

The man did indeed have excellent friends, friends with money, influence, and power. Nowhere in that long, rather odd, obituary is there the slightest whiff of the scandal attached to his divorce from his wife Grace Elliott. She is never even mentioned! Given the nature of journalism in those days, when scandal sold newspapers and all were vulnerable to gossip and innuendo, one can only surmise that a number of journalists, editors, and publishers were paid off—and no doubt paid off handsomely—to keep that old, sad story out of the tabloids. (The newspapers could be merciless. They dug up the old scandal attached to Banastre Tarleton and Mary Robinson when Tarleton was about to marry Susan Priscilla Bertie, the girl who was a ward of Lord Cholmondeley's.)

How good were his friends? Very good, indeed, to the point of sharing their eternal rest. One supposes that Sir John had treated Lord Melbourne's mistress Sophia Baddeley in a superior manner indeed when he was her physician, because a grateful Melbourne returns the favor in spades. No ordinary burial in St. Etheldreda's good—if damp—English soil for him! No, it's one step up from that good English earth for Sir John, burial in the Melbourne family crypt. According to *The Gentleman's Magazine* for November 1786:

> *His remains were deposited in the family vault belonging to Lord M. at Hatfield.*

Sharing the family vault for eternity . . . now, is that a friend, or what?

Trips to Spa and Brussels: Was Grace Elliott a Courier for the Royalists, a Spy for the English, or a Little Bit of Both?

Meanwhile, back in France, especially after the fall of the Bastille in 1789, things were heating up. As a Royalist to the core, Grace Elliott wasn't happy with the deterioration of the natural order of things. It's not unreasonable to speculate that she would have wanted to do something to help the King and

Queen of France. As someone with good contacts at the English court, she was well placed to be of use, and it seems that her talents indeed might have been utilized. The center of the action was the ancient town of Spa in what is now Belgium.

Prior to the eighteenth century, Belgium was part of the Spanish Netherlands—the Low Countries—and was afterward ceded to Austria in the Treaty of Utrecht in 1713. After the French Revolution, it was annexed by France. A revolt begun in 1830 created the nation of Belgium, whose first king was the man who'd been the widower of Princess Charlotte, daughter of the Prince of Wales. Brussels, in the Brabant area, is in the approximate middle of the country. Spa is south-southeast of Brussels, directly south of Liège and Verviers, not far from what is now the German border; in those days some referred to it as part of Germany.

Spa, in the Walloon-speaking region, was a resort for the wealthy of England and the Continent, who came there in the seventeenth and eighteenth centuries to combine the pursuit of health with the pursuit of pleasure. Though Spa was first and foremost a health resort, the beautiful people gathered there to gamble and play with one another, and it was known as a place where spies and couriers could exchange letters, packages, and valuable in-

The Pouhon Pierre le Grand, in Spa. A water source named after the Russian Czar Peter the Great (who visited Spa in 1717) is housed in this 1880 edifice. Grace Elliott would not have known the building, but would have been familiar with the *pouhon* (well) it housed. (Bridgeman Art Library)

formation. It was a European crossroads, and had been so since the Romans—always keen on hot springs—had discovered its thermal baths.

The pleasures of Spa included fine dining, gambling, and consorting with beautiful women as well as taking the waters. Most of these activities came with hefty price tags. (Spa was where Elizabeth Armistead took a repairing lease in 1781 after her liaison with the Prince of Wales came to an abrupt end. Finding herself short of funds, she hied herself over to recoup some cash. It was there that she ran into Lord Cholmondeley and his friend Lord Coleraine and thus did some excellent recouping.)

During 1790–1791, Grace Elliott made a number of trips—some short, some long—to Spa and to Brussels on behalf of Queen Marie-Antoinette and others, among them the Duc d'Orléans. She acted as a courier or go-between on these occasions. Grace made no secret of her high regard for the French royals and she was especially fond of Marie-Antoinette, "as amiable and good a princess as ever lived." Grace comments in her *Journal* that Orléans used to tease her about her fierce monarchism:

> He . . . laughed at me, saying that "I was a proud Scotchwoman, who loved nothing but kings and princes." (The passages in this section are all from Grace Elliott's Journal.)

The Duc d'Orléans knew whereof he teased. . . .

In the spring of 1790, Grace went to Brussels and "saw many of the Duke's agents," but she doesn't say for what purpose. She does, however, relate an incident in which she's told she needs a pass to get out of town and she protests to the English minister at Brussels, a Colonel Gardiner, who tells her that

> he was not surprised at anything . . . [they] did; that they had some days before stopped his own messenger going to England, and had broken open his despatches; that he had . . . [complained] but had no redress; that he did not mean to go to them any more till he heard from his Court what he was going to do; and that if I insisted on his going on my account he would, but he thought he had better not.

Gardiner's wishy-washy response to Grace is puzzling. He's not going to complain until he hears from England, but he would go see someone on her account if she were to insist, but he doesn't think he should. No, yes, no. Someone clearly does not have his marching orders from above. Undaunted,

Grace goes by herself to the person in charge, someone she names Vander-nott (probably H.C.N. Vandernoot—Grace is never good with names), and she's told that it was a mistake she was stopped and that she'll be issued a pass to come and go as she likes. The person adds, however, that he happens to know she is an associate of the Duc d'Orléans and sympathetic with his revolutionary cause, which she angrily disputes:

> I assured them that I was not; that though I saw much of those people, yet I never had liked their revolutionary conduct either in France or Brabant [an area of Belgium in which the name of Orléans had been bandied about as a possible ruler and that had its own revolt in the 1830s]; that I always was a royalist, and should ever be such.

Because she is so open about her respect and admiration for the French monarchy, Grace says in her *Journal,* writing in July 1790, "her Majesty charged me once with a *mission* to Brussels." Grace italicizes the word "mission" for emphasis. She is honored by the request, and by the Queen's visits to her cottage at Meudon. The mission is to act as a courier between Marie-Antoinette and the Austrians, no friends of the French. Remember that Marie-Antoinette had been an Austrian princess, that France was fighting Austria, and that several French generals and other army officers—among them Dumouriez, Bouillé, and Philippe's heir, Louis-Philippe—were defecting to the Austrian army. Grace was in Brussels at least once before in the spring of 1790 on an errand for the Duke:

> Her Majesty, hearing that I had thoughts of returning to Brussels, sent a great lady to my house with a small box and a letter for the Archduchess, which I was to deliver into her own hands. I did not intend going to Brussels, but I never made that known to her Majesty. I got a passport from Lord Gower, our ambassador, and felt myself happy in taking this journey to be of use to the Queen. When I got to Brussels, the Archduchess had just left it with the Duke Albert; and as the Queen had foreseen the possibility of this, she had desired me in that case to deliver it to General Boileau [François-Claude-Amour Bouillé, the French general who had defected to Austria], who was at Mons, commanding the Austrian army.

General Bouillé had let King Louis down when the royal family fled Paris on June 20, 1791. He was supposed to meet them along their escape route with a contingent of soldiers, but he failed to appear at the rendezvous and they were caught and arrested at Varennes. (Grace made the accusation in her *Journal* that the Marquis de Lafayette betrayed the monarchs out of fear for his own life.) She was there when they were brought back on June 25:

> *[They were] brought back to Paris in a most barbarous manner. I saw them in the Champs-Élysées as they came back, and witnessed such a scene as it is impossible to describe. The insolence of the mob and the wretches that surrounded the traveling coaches they were in was very terrible. The faithful Garde de Corps, who had followed the King, were tied hands and feet with ropes on the coach-box of their Majesties' carriage, which went at a foot-pace, that the monsters might follow. They were leaning on the coach, smoking, swearing, and talking the most indecent language. They prevented any air getting into the carriage, though the poor Queen was dying with heat and fatigue, for they had not been in bed since they left Paris, and it was one of the hottest days I ever felt. This was another dreadful event.*

Grace let drop that she knew, and had hosted at her home, Royalist conspirators who plotted to aid the King and his family. "But all their plans were ill-conceived and very ill-executed, turning out always to the unfortunate King's disadvantage." She added, "These nobles were what were called Les Chevaliers de la Poignard."

Grace meant *les chevaliers du poignard*, among whom were the young aristocrats who'd armed themselves on February 28, 1791—known as the Day of Daggers—at the Tuileries Palace in a counterrevolutionary plot a good four months before the flight to Varennes. They were arrested that day by Lafayette, commanding the National Guard. (A *chevalier* is a knight and a *poignard* is a dagger.)

It's not surprising that Grace Elliott would know these particular counterrevolutionaries and other groups like them, but she's beginning to be reckless in openly expressing her Royalist affections and is becoming known to others for having them. Philippe, too, knows she's consorting with people who could get her into trouble.

That night of the royal family's return to Paris from Varennes, Grace hightails it back to Spa, and then on to Brussels. This is the third such trip in two years that's noted in her *Journal,* but there may have been others she did not record. Remember that she wrote her memoir of the French Revolution in about 1800, some ten years after the events had taken place. She recalls:

I left Paris that evening for Spa, and found Monsieur, now Louis XVIII., at Brussels [Monsieur (1755–1824) was the Comte de Provence, the elder of Louis XVI's two surviving brothers]. He had succeeded in making his escape by Valenciennes. I wish that the King had taken that road and gone alone, but he never could be persuaded to leave the Queen, as he feared that the mob would murder her. I stayed at Spa till September. Would that I had never again returned to France! But at that moment we expected the Prussians, the Austrians, and Swedes to join and save France from any further faction; for though the King's arrest at Varennes had much damped the spirits of the royalists, the case was too interesting to be given up. Spa was full of emigrants, and they all expected soon to return to France.

What was Grace doing in Spa and Brussels? Seeing the émigrés, for one thing, and they included King Louis XVI's self-exiled brother (the French called the eldest of a king's brothers Monsieur); she was also meeting with others she does not name—for all her openness in the *Journal*—and she takes letters back to contacts in France. These letters may have been innocent, more personal than official, but we only have her word for that, and she is keenly aware that passing information from abroad to those in France could be dangerous for her:

I cannot recollect any other events of that year, except that on my return to Paris I found the Duc de Choiseul and the Comte Charles de Damas had been arrested for being colonels of the regiments which were to have favoured the King's escape. I had a letter given me at Spa by Comte Roger Damas for his brother, and I was determined to deliver it into his own hands, for fear it might contain anything about the passing events. He was imprisoned at the Mercy, a convent of Brothers in the Marais. I obtained admission there and saw both him and the Duc de Choiseul. They were in very low spirits. . . . After this, I remained always either at Issy [where she rented a cottage] or in Paris, till I bought my house at Meudon.

The unnamed person who reviewed the *Journal* for the *Times* (in two very long pieces that ran consecutively on January 26 and 27, 1859, together with a letter from the publisher Richard Bentley that ran on January 28) agreed that Mrs. Elliott was up to something in Spa:

As the Revolution proceeded, Mrs. Elliott made another visit to Spa and Brussels, apparently serving the Royalist party by her communications to and fro. She saw at Brussels Monsieur, subsequently Louis XVIII, and she speaks of the King of Sweden as if she had some communication also with him. On her return she charged herself with the delivery of a letter to one of the colonels who had been implicated in the escape to Varennes, and who was therefore in arrest.

It's clear that Grace was becoming known in ever-widening circles as someone sympathetic to the King and Queen and the Royalist cause who could be trusted to function as a courier or go-between. Whether or not she was officially a spy or courier on a payroll, i.e., under the control of a spymaster who issued orders, can't be nailed down; however, signs indicate she had a functioning relationship of some kind with the spy/courier network operating in and out of France during the Revolution. (It's very possible that she got her orders from Philippe, who some thought was working actively with the English.)

This can't be ignored, and it is a fact that Royalist sympathizers were actively courted and recruited by the British secret service. Later, as things turn from terrible to horrific for those sympathetic to the Royalists, Grace's penchant for taking letters—innocently or officially—will get her into trouble with the revolutionary authorities. Those authorities were absolutely correct; she *was* involved in something suspiciously counterrevolutionary.

Grace's first arrest occurs when revolutionary guards enter her house and begin a search of its premises and her effects. (She is more concerned about a Frenchwoman hiding in her closet as they search than about her own possible danger.) They find a letter:

I assisted them to search my papers; and those which were English they packed up. At last they found a sealed letter, directed to Charles Fox. Sir Godfrey Webster, who was then at Naples, had sent it to me by a French courier who had come to Paris from Admiral Latouche Freville [does she mean Latouche-Treville, the naval officer—and later rear admiral—who was elected to the States General in 1789?], who had been before Naples to make a manifesto in the name of the French nation. I knew very little of Sir Godfrey Webster; but he thought that I could get this letter sent to England. The people who made the visit to my house were ignorant men, who had heard of Mr. Pitt and Mr. Fox, but did not know anything of their politics [both men were initially sympathetic to the republican ideals of the French Revolution, as were many

La Ronde, Redux

The letter that got Grace into trouble was meant for the great Whig statesman and orator Charles James Fox. It was sent by Sir Godfrey Webster, fourth Baronet, who lived abroad with his young wife Elizabeth in Florence. Sir Godfrey was to be cuckolded in 1793 by Henry Richard Vassall-Fox, third Baron Holland, who was the nephew of this same Charles James Fox. The couple was able to marry in 1797 after Webster obtained a divorce. The old story: young wife, husband twice her age, young man. (In London, Grace was to live in a house in which this couple had once resided.) A convict ship that plied the Australian waters was named for Sir Godfrey Webster; later, Lord and Lady Holland's London salon was to become the *in* place in Regency England. Louis-René le Vassor de Latouche-Treville was a naval officer who saw most of his service in the New World and was a member of the National Assembly; he died of a heart attack in 1804 while commanding the blockaded French fleet at Toulon against Lord Nelson.

The Passport

The portmanteau word (combining two words to make a new word) gives it away as a French innovation: *passer + porte*, i.e., a document allowing travelers to pass through a port or door. Most international travel in the eighteenth century was done by sailing ship, leaving one port city, arriving at another. Visas, as well as passports, were required by some countries. Passports were numbered and where one could use them to travel was spelled out. Several signatures and seals were required. Great Britain did not require a passport for getting into and leaving the country, though France and Belgium did. These could be gotten from the Belgian or French consulate. A detailed description of the traveler was required. (On British passports, descriptions weren't a requirement until World War I.) A kind of passport for Grace Elliott—an "autograph letter" sent to the Comité de Surveillance, dated 10 Nivôse I (December 30, 1792)—is in the National Archives in Paris.

Whigs and liberal-leaning English]. They thought that I should be sent the next day to the guillotine; and they were enchanted at the discovery they had made. They told me that they had long suspected me, but that now they had found out that I was in correspondence with the enemies of the Republic, and that I should pay dearly for it.

Now she had done it. She'd put herself on the revolutionaries' radar and there she'd stay. Not even the Duc d'Orléans—who was having his

UNITÉ·INDIVISIBILITÉ
DE·LA·RÉPUBLIQUE
LIBERTÉ·EGALITÉ
FRATERNITÉ·OULA·MORT

The motto "Liberty, Equality, Fraternity" was but one of several in use during the French Revolution. In 1790, Robespierre had suggested that the words be printed on flags and on the uniforms of the national guard. (Bridgeman Art Library)

own problems—could help her out of this scrape.

Grace Elliott, perhaps the strongest supporter of the Duc d'Orléans, takes the oft-repeated line in her *Journal* that he was a weak man easily manipulated by others. She insists on his innate goodness, even after she has expressed horror that he was the one who'd cast the deciding vote to send his cousin King Louis XVI to his death. He'd promised her that he would absent himself from the vote, but he showed up and voted despite his promise. His cry, "I vote for death!" was thrown back in his face when he himself was sentenced to the guillotine. Tit for tat. Regicides are not beloved.

Though even Grace acknowledged that Philippe had an unfortunate tendency to be led by those with stronger wills and personalities—which in his case covered just about everyone—and that these pernicious influences led him to make this fateful decision, he's perhaps more to be pitied than cursed. His actions didn't save him from the guillotine, if that was his motive: the King was executed in January 1793 and Philippe in November.

Orléans, Grace says over and over in her *Journal,* was not so much a traitorous monster who turned against his king and his class as he was a man of very weak character too easily led by whoever had his ear—or his heart—at the time. Unfortunately, Orléans had a new favorite in his harem of ladies, Agnes de Buffon, daughter-in-law of the great naturalist, and her personal influence over him during this period was greater than any that Grace Elliott could exert. (It is unclear whether or not the physical relationship between Grace and Philippe was entirely over, but if not, it was greatly diminished. They were, however, good friends.) So despite Grace's reasoned arguments—set down as she says she remembered them several years after all

Why "Égalité"?

Philippe took his name, "Citoyen Égalité" (Citizen Equality), from the three ringing goals of the French Revolution, "Liberté, Égalité, Fraternité" (Liberty, Equality, Fraternity).

The story his biographer Scudder relates is that since the name of Orléans "signified the old regime—tyranny, aristocracy, privilege, everything, in fact, that was opposed to popular feeling at the moment," Philippe wanted a name untainted by any of the above. Did he necessarily want "Égalité"? According to Scudder, it was forced upon him and he feared he'd offend if he rejected the suggestion of Louis-Pierre Manuel, a writer and teacher who was the *procureur-syndic*—roughly the equivalent of mayor—of the Paris Commune. Manuel supposedly gestured to a statue of the nymph Equality that adorned the municipal office and said it would be "an admirable name to adopt." Philippe claimed afterward he'd had no choice but to agree.

In Antonia Fraser's *Marie Antoinette*, a slightly different story emerges:

Names underwent their own revolution. Titles were already abolished and the Duc d'Orléans found himself offered a choice of two politically correct names; he chose Philippe Égalité over Publicola, the Roman consul who helped oust Tarquin Superbus.

That ousting took place in 509 BC; Tarquinius Superbus was the last Etruscan king of Rome. An interesting sidelight: the *procureur-syndic* Manuel was himself a victim of the Reign of Terror. When the time came, he, unlike Philippe, refused to vote for the execution of King Louis XVI. Instead he resigned his post and returned to his country home in Montargis, from whence he was arrested; he was guillotined in Paris on November 17, 1793, less than two weeks after old Equality himself was executed on the same spot. In death, if not in life, all, truly, are equal. Égalité turns out to have been an appropriate name.

---

these dramatic events transpired—there was no way Philippe would heed her. Agnes had the upper hand.

Agnes was to be the last in a long string of women with whom Philippe had fallen in love since he was a teenager. Grace wrote in her *Journal* that Philippe "was very madly in love with Madame de Buffon, driving her about all day in a curricle, and at all the spectacles in the evening." Ever his loyal, stand-up friend, Grace adds that he was so obsessed with his new mistress that "he could not possibly be planning conspiracies." (As if plotting conspiracies and making love were mutually exclusive . . .)

Evarts Seelye Scudder echoes Grace's "madly in love" assessment of Philippe at this time of his life in *Prince of the Blood:*

The Buffon Family

Buffon, the naturalist and director of the French Royal Museum, is best known for his classic forty-four-volume work on natural history, *Histoire naturelle, générale, et particulière* (begun in 1749). He also translated the works of Isaac Newton into French and was in charge of the Jardin du Roi. This French scientific genius came from a middle-class family of lawyers who became wealthy owing to an inheritance; with it, they bought a town, Buffon. When he was created a count in 1773, George-Louis took the name of the town. His son, George-Louis Marie, called Buffonet (1764–1794), was a victim of the Reign of Terror, accused of participating in a conspiracy against the Revolution. His last words—which he exclaimed proudly to the blood-hungry crowd—were, "Citoyens, mon nom c'est Buffon" (Citizens, my name is Buffon). As a symbol of the old order, Buffon, if he'd lived into the 1790s, would surely have been guillotined alongside his son. They were both alive when his son's wife, Agnes, became publicly involved with the Duc d'Orléans.

George-Louis Leclerc, Comte de Buffon (1707–1788), engraving by C. Baron after Drouais, 1761. (Bridgeman Art Library)

> *Philippe was as madly in love with Madame de Buffon as a boy of sixteen, and the need to see her outweighed all others.*

At one point in their relationship, again according to Scudder, Agnes told a third party that Philippe had thought of leaving France and starting life all over again in America. This was when he was residing in London at 3 Chappel Street, Park Lane, from October 1789 to July 1790. Chappel Street (now Chapel Street) was one of the areas in London that attracted French émigrés. Scudder writes:

> *Mme de Buffon told Mirabeau's friend, La Marck, long afterwards that*

Philippe proposed to her at this time to go to America and live there together. She refused, she said, giving as a pretext that she would not be able to survive the regrets which the Duke of Orléans might have for having done so rash a thing.

The Duc d'Orléans fit in very well with the Prince of Wales's profligate set. He was thrilled with gambling and horse racing (he adored jockeys) and spent much of his time at the men's clubs and at the track. It was said that Orléans introduced the Prince to the finer things associated with French culture, including toilet water and fancy underwear. One of his good friends was George Parker, fourth Earl of Macclesfield, a Whig politician. (Letters from Parker to Philippe are preserved at the National Archives in Paris.)

Orléans shared some of the Prince's playmates, too. They'd both been involved with Mrs. Elliott, Philippe before 1781 and then after 1784, and the Prince in the fall of 1781. That fall was when Mary Robinson was visiting Paris and was said to have taken the French court by storm and to have been a special favorite of the Queen (or so Mrs. Robinson averred in her *Memoirs*); Philippe waged an imaginative and vigorous campaign to seduce her, but the lady simply wasn't interested. According to Robert D. Bass, in *The Green Dragoon*:

> *In the French capital Mary was welcomed as a heroine. Sir John Lambert, resident English banker, realized the value of a client just come into £5000 [£300,000/$600,000 today]. He secured her a commodious apartment and a box at the Opera. The venerable chevalier then introduced la belle Anglaise to Philippe, Duke of Chartres.*
>
> *Duke Philippe, possessor of the largest private fortune in Europe and a harem of concubines, immediately laid siege to Mary's affections. He had always taken what he wanted, and the Parisians eagerly watched the sparring between the actress and the rake whose profligate Orléans ancestors inspired the word roué. The* Morning Post *kept Mary's supporters alerted: "She was much admired at the French Opera, and never appeared there without drawing his Royal Highness, the Duke de Chartres, and several other leading men of fashion into her box."*
>
> *Philippe was swarthy and pimpled. His nose was flat, and he wore rings in his ears. He was haughty and his person contrasted garishly with that of the Prince of Wales. Mary disdained his advances.*

Philippe knew all about laying sieges. He persisted . . . and failed again. This is from *Perdita: The Memoirs of Mary Robinson,* edited by M. J. Levy (London: Peter Owen, 1994)

> *On the birthday of Mrs. Robinson, a new effort was made to subdue her aversion and to obtain her regard. A rural fete was appointed in the gardens of Mousseau [Monceau, the Duke's country home outside of Paris], when this beautiful Pandaemonium of splendid profligacy was, at an unusual expense, decorated with boundless luxury.*
>
> *In the evening, amidst a magnificent illumination, every tree displayed the initials of la belle Anglaise, composed of colored lamps, interwoven with wreaths of artificial flowers. Politeness compelled Mrs. Robinson to grace with her presence a fete instituted in her honour. She however took the precaution of selecting for her companion a German lady, then resident at Paris, while the venerable Chevalier Lambert attended them as a chaperon.*

Mrs. Robinson's passionate affair with the Prince of Wales had ended badly in December 1780, but, undaunted (and with the blackmail money from King George III warm and safe in her reticule), Perdita had had affairs with several other men before going on to make new conquests in France. Among Prinny's successors to the actress's favors in England was Grace Elliott's on-again, off-again longtime paramour Lord Cholmondeley. In the early spring of 1781 Lord Cholmondeley had succeeded where Orléans was to try and fail later that year. (Others who got to home plate with the promiscuous Mrs. Robinson that spring were Lord Malden—who had acted as Prinny's intermediary in his initial courtship of the actress—and the Duke of Dorset; in the fall she made a conquest of the French nobleman and army officer Lauzun.)

And what did the long-suffering, neglected Duchesse d'Orléans think about Madame Agnes de Buffon, this new flame of her always errant voluptuary of a husband? Scudder quotes from a letter (undated) in which the Duchesse writes to her husband with a candor an English peer's wife would not have dreamed of using in reference to her spouse's mistress. (The peer's wife would not have acknowledged the existence of a mistress.) Addressing Philippe as "my dear friend," she writes:

> *I confess that at the beginning of your liaison with her I was in despair. Accustomed as I was to your phantasies, I was frightened and profoundly affected*

when I saw you form a tie which could take away your confidence from me.
Mme de Buffon's behavior since you have formed the connection with her has
made me reconsider the prejudices which I had against her. I have recognized
that she has so true and so disinterested an attachment for you, and that her
feeling for me is so perfect, that I cannot help being interested in her. It is im-
possible that some one who really loves you should have no rights over me—so
she has some that are very real, and on this point you can be still quite at ease
with me. I repeat it, my dear friend—what I should wish for—what would re-
ally make me happy is that you should be completely at your ease with me and
then you should find in your wife a gentle companionship which would attract
you and contribute to your happiness.

At first reading, this is pathetic, even groveling, uncomfortable for a twenty-
first-century female to accept, but then, upon rereading, the eye catches the
phrase "someone who really loves you," and all one has to know about dynastic marriages in the eighteenth century is revealed. There was no love
lost between Philippe and his wife Adelaide; she really did not care about his
women. Or so it seems.

The last mention of Agnes de Buffon in Scudder's biography of the Duc
d'Orléans is her reaction to seeing the severed head of the Princesse de Lamballe (the sister-in-law of Philippe's wife and one of Queen Marie-
Antoinette's maids of honor as well as a close friend) paraded past the
Palais-Royal, as she and Philippe were dining with English friends. Philippe's
strange coldness as the severed head of a woman he'd known well—someone
to whom he was closely related by marriage—bobbed grotesquely above the
cobblestone street in front of his house was noted by several of the party.

Madame de Buffon, however, was overwhelmed by the sight. She "half
fainted, exclaiming: 'My God! My head will be paraded like that one
day!' . . . One of the Englishmen, overcome by horror, left the room." Earlier that day, Grace Elliott was to recall, as she herself was traveling in a carriage through the Paris streets, her carriage was stopped for the procession
and so she saw close up the bloody head of the Princesse—whom she'd also
known personally—as it was borne on that pike. She, too, was terribly
shaken, seeing portents of dire events to come.

The Princesse de Lamballe was a gentle soul. She'd been born Marie-
Thérèse-Louise de Savoie-Carignan in Turin and was half Italian and half

The sweet-faced, red-haired Princesse de Lamballe, an early victim of the French Revolution. (Bridgeman Art Library)

German; her mother was a German princess. The Princesse was the widow of the Duchesse d'Orléans's brother. All who knew her admired her greatly; her devotion to her father-in-law had earned her the sobriquet "the Good Angel." The savage manner of her death—the butchery upon so gentle and good a lady—touched everyone's heart. She was killed with over a thousand others taken from the Abbaye and other prisons during the first week of September 1792, in what later became known as the September Massacres; her death came because she refused to denounce the King and Queen. It's a nasty story.

The forty-two-year-old woman was taken forcibly from her cell, hit on the head with several blows of a hammer, decapitated, stripped naked, her heart torn out, and then disemboweled. There were also reports she'd been violated sexually and that her breasts had been hacked off. Her head was put on the end of a long stave—her innards and her naked body set on two other pikes—and she was paraded through the streets by a jovial mob high on bloodlust.

The head of the Princesse was thrust through the bars of the windows at the Temple, the prison where the King and Queen were being held; the couple had been playing backgammon with their children. The Queen swooned at the awful sight, fainting dead away. Then, according to the story, Princesse de Lamballe's head was taken to a young woman named Marie Grosholtz, who was herself in prison awaiting execution for the crime of consorting too closely with royalty. (She'd been teaching art at Versailles to the King's sister.) The girl, who'd learned the art of making wax figures from her physician uncle, was ordered to make a wax cast of the severed head.

Colonel Sir Banastre Tarleton, friend of Prinny's and future lover of

Madame Tussaud and the French Revolution

Everyone knows of Madame Tussaud's Wax Museum, but how many know the circumstances under which this woman, born Marie Grosholtz in Strasbourg in 1761, began this world-famous enterprise? Marie Grosholtz learned the art of making models from wax from her uncle, Dr. Philippe Curtius, a physician. The first wax figure she made, when she was seventeen, was of the philosopher Jean-Jacques Rousseau; she also did Voltaire and Benjamin Franklin. Her talent brought her to the attention of royalty and of the famous personages of the day, including the revolutionaries in France. In 1789, on the invitation of Louis XVI, she moved to Versailles to teach art to his sister. Two days before the fall of the Bastille, wax heads made by Dr. Curtius of two men popular with the people—but not the King—Jacques Necker, director-general of finances and minister of state, and Philippe, Duc d'Orléans, were carried in a protest march through the streets of Paris.

Marie was arrested by the revolutionaries for what were perceived to be her Royalist connections. Her experience was not unlike what happened to Grace Elliott. Like Grace, she was within hours of her execution when she got an unexpected reprieve. Her hair had already been cut, as Grace's was. In Marie's case, the stay came when she was recruited to make death masks of victims of the Terror. The first mask was made from the battered head of the Princesse de Lamballe, which the revolutionaries thrust into her lap; she was forced to work on it right under their eyes. She went on to make death masks of Queen

Wax figure of Madame Tussaud as a young woman. (Mary Evans Picture Library)

Marie-Antoinette, the revolutionaries Marat and Robespierre, and many other unfortunates.

Later she married François Tussaud, an engineer. Having inherited Dr. Curtius's collection of wax figures, Madame Tussaud toured the British Isles with the collection from 1802 to 1835. She opened her first permanent museum in 1835 on Baker Street in London. *Madame Tussaud's Memoirs and Reminiscences of France* was published in 1838. She died at the age of eighty-nine in London and is interred in the catacombs of St. Mary's Church, Cadogan Place, Chelsea.

Mary Robinson's, was strolling the Paris streets that first week of September 1792 when the September Massacres were taking place. According to Robert Bass:

> On September 2 as he walked along the Rue de la Paix he met the mob— still in a frenzy from slaughtering the Royalist prisoners. They began shouting "Á la lanterne!" Seizing his only chance to escape swinging from a lantern post, he ran to join them, shouting as loudly as any: "Á la lanterne!"

Ban Tarleton apparently was one of the English guests at Philippe's dinner party when the Princesse de Lamballe's head was paraded on a pike before the windows. That was September 3, the day after the massacres began. His biographer Bass continues:

> Next day Ban dined with the Duke of Orléans. "During the meal there was a great hubbub in the street and the guests got up from the table to look out at its cause. They beheld a head carried aloft on a pike. Philippe said coolly: "Ah! C'est la Lamballe; je la connais à ses cheveux." [Ah! It's the Lamballe; I recognize her by her hair.] For refusing to sign the oath against monarchy, red-headed Princess Lamballe had been torn to pieces by the mob. In her fate the noble dinner guests read their own. A year later Banastre Tarleton was the only one of the twelve who had not been guillotined.

Bass is not exactly right here, though the image is so dramatic one hates to challenge it. Agnes de Buffon was at that dinner party, if the earlier mention by Scudder in *Prince of the Blood* is accurate, and she escaped the guillotine. If there were other English guests there as well as Tarleton, they presumably were as smart as he was and left Paris immediately; unfortunately, none is named.

What was Tarleton up to in Paris? He may have been on a secret mission, possibly spying for England; his connections at court were as good as Grace Elliott's.

Grace Elliott's *Journal* persists in arguing that Philippe was innocent of all charges leveled against him by his enemies and was simply behaving foolishly when he decided to join the revolutionary cause. When his was the vote that brought about the execution of King Louis XVI, she was upset and angry with him and made no bones about expressing her feelings. Philippe was heading down a path of self-destruction from which no one could deter him. Like Grace, when it seemed that his life was in more and more danger

The Palais-Royal: The Eighteenth-Century Shopping Mall cum Principal Paris Residence of the Duc d'Orléans

The Palais-Royal arcade, revamped by Philippe in 1784, was a mix of grand shopping mall and theme park, with requisite coffee shops, bookstores, and retail outlets common to today's malls but with eighteenth-century features such as gambling dens and brothels. There was a carnival atmosphere akin to a twenty-first century theme park, a fantastic city-within-a-city of magic shows and street entertainment. It appealed to all classes, rich and poor. Its English counterparts were London's more refined pleasure gardens of Vauxhall and Ranelagh, except that the Palais-Royal charged no entrance fees, and, although prostitutes plied their wares in the English pleasure gardens as well, there weren't actual whore-houses on-site as at the Palais-Royal. (Scudder notes these brothels earned Philippe the name of "Grand Pimp of the Kingdom.")

Orléans added to the masses' high regard for him in throwing open the grounds of his home, causing some to believe his hidden agenda was to seek popular favor in an eventual bid for the French throne. Interestingly enough, the police had no authority over the grounds of the Palais-Royal and so couldn't step in to stem the increasingly vast number of pamphlets—prorevolutionary, antichurch, and antimonarchy—sold in the shops. The Palais-Royal provided a steady stream of welcome revenue for Philippe until he came into the largesse of the Orléans dukeship.

Le Palais Philippe Égalité, Le Palais-Royal. (Colored engraving, 1791, by Jean Lespinasse/Musée de la ville de Paris, Musée Carnavalet, Paris, France/Bridgeman Art Library)

from the radical revolutionary forces that were gaining the upper hand over the moderates, he chose to stay instead of to leave. And so he missed his last window of opportunity to flee the chaos.

Philippe may have been in acute denial that anything terrible could happen to him—after all, he might have reasoned, he was a deputy to the National Assembly! Deputies, however, were not exempt from arrest and execution, and their families and close friends were also at great risk.

It cannot be denied that he took care of his ex-mistress, and took care of her exceedingly well, treating her better—especially in the financial sense—than any of her former lovers had done. (Lord Cholmondeley is a close second.) And it's Grace Elliott's account of his last days that comes down to us. Loyal to the end, she is loyal to his memory, too. Perhaps she has painted a better picture of the man than he deserved, perhaps not, but her portrait endures.

The words she penned in her *Journal* describing Philippe as merely "a man of pleasure, who never could bear trouble or business of any kind; who never read or did anything but amuse himself" resonate in her assessment of the man she claimed to know so well. She never saw him as a plotter or manipulator, but rather as one manipulated by others. She wrote that "[his] misfortune was to have been surrounded by ambitious men" who led him to make terrible decisions. Is she right in her assessment, or misguided and wrong? It's a question that still stirs controversy.

Are there any other moments we might consider that would define Philippe? How he met his death, perhaps, may be another indication of the kind of man he was. Meeting one's death has always been looked upon as a moment of truth.

Philippe was arrested on April 7, 1793, and was moved with some members of his family—including two of his sons, Montpensier and Beaujolais—to Marseilles. On April 16 his properties were confiscated. On May 23 he was locked up in solitary confinement at the fort of Saint-Jean. On October 15 he was told that he was to be taken to Paris. Accompanied by a lifelong loyal servant named Gamasche, he departed Marseilles on October 23.

What would happen to Orléans now was a foregone conclusion. The King had been beheaded; the Queen had followed in October; the young heir to the throne, the Dauphin, was in prison, kept under miserable conditions. (The ten-year-old would die there.) Philippe was among the next in line to be king, so it was his turn to face execution. The usual trumped-up charges surfaced at the mockery of a trial; Philippe endured it all. At the age of forty-six, Louis-Philippe-Joseph Égalité, ci-devant the Duc d'Orléans, was led back to the Conciergerie prison, accepting his fate. He made his last confession to a priest and was escorted into a waiting tumbrel. It was the sixth of November in 1793, the year that began that ignominious period in the history of France that would be known forever as the Reign of Terror.

Along the Paris streets, the death-carts rumble, hollow and harsh. Six tumbrils carry the day's wine to La Guillotine. All the devouring and insatiate Monsters imagined since imagination could record itself, are fused in the one realisation, Guillotine. (Charles Dickens, A Tale of Two Cities, *book 3, chapter 15, "The Footsteps Die Out for Ever")*

Scudder says that Philippe's companions on this final journey were three men: a member of the National Convention named Coustard, a mender of chairs named Lesage, and a seventy-three-year-old soldier named Laroque. Jeers and insults followed the cart along the well-traveled route to the guillotine, and Laroque reviled Philippe. Those who viewed the scene and wrote about it later said that he'd held his head high and tried to encourage his fellow victims. The tumbrel stopped in front of the Palais-Royal and Philippe saw the sign indicating his home was now "national property." Scudder writes:

As the tumbrel crawled on towards the Place de la Révolution more and more people gathered along the route. Cries of "I vote for death!" and insults of every sort were hurled at him. He made no sign whatsoever that he even heard them. When the horrible form of the guillotine came into view his face, usually so red, turned deathly white, but he gave no other sign of emotion. The cart arrived at the foot of the scaffold. He called Lothringer [the priest] to him and once more received absolution. Then he mounted the platform with a firm step. Samson's assistant [Samson was the executioner] wanted to take off his boots.

"You can do that more easily to my dead body," he said. "Come—be quick."

The knife fell, and the head that was held up to the crowd had a mocking smile of indifference on its dead lips.

And his last lover, Agnes de Buffon, was she in the crowd watching the once-wealthiest man in France meet his demise? One wonders if she dared show her face that awful sixth of November, 1793.

Grace got the news of Philippe's execution from one of her servants, and she relates the same events in her customary clear, measured prose, prose considerably less purple than Scudder's. She is one day off on the date and she has a woman in the tumbrel along with the man Coustard. There is no mender of chairs in the cart, and no elderly soldier, but there is a blacksmith. Eyewitness accounts—as well as records of who was supposed to be at what prison and lists of persons killed—can be frustrating to the researcher. There are always contradictions, as witness the differences in the account given by Grace compared to that by Scudder (who may have gotten *his* information from an account by one Montjoie, an eyewitness). Note particularly that the eyewitness report from Grace's servant states that Orléans said nothing, but that Scudder's second- or third-hand information includes a conversation about Philippe's boots:

On the 5th of November [actually November 6] I heard of the fate of the unfortunate Duke of Orléans. It is needless to say what I felt on that occasion. I was not aware that he had been removed from Marseilles to Paris till I heard of his death. I know that he died with great courage. He was tried, condemned, and executed in the space of two hours! A man-servant of mine by accident met the cart in which he was, in the Rue du Roule, near the Pont Neuf. He knew that there were condemned people in it, but he was shocked to death when he saw the Duke of Orléans in it. My poor servant was nearly fainting, but was determined to follow the Duke to the scaffold. There was very little mob the whole way, though by the time they got to the Palais Royal, the Duke's own palace, people began to assemble. Till that moment no creature had even an idea of the Duke's having been tried. Under his own windows they stopped him for ten minutes. He looked, my servant since told me, very grave, and as he did in former days when he was going out on any occasion of ceremony. He was very much powdered, and looked very well. His hands were tied behind him, and his coat thrown over his shoulders. His coat was light grey, with a black collar. When the cart moved from the Palais Royal, the Duke looked at the mob with a sort of indignation. He did not alter in any way, but carried his head very high till the cart turned on the Place Louis

Quinze [Place de la Révolution]; then he saw the scaffold before him; and my man said that he turned very pale, but still held up his head. Three other prisoners were with him in the cart—a Madame de Kolly, a very beautiful woman, wife to a farmer-general, a man of the name of Coustard, a deputy of the Convention but of the Gironde party, and a blacksmith of the name of Brouce, for having made a key to save some papers. It was nearly four o'clock when the cart got to the scaffold, and it was almost dark. Therefore, in order that the mob might see the Duke's head, he was the first one who was executed. He leaped up the ladder with great haste, looked round at everybody, helped the executioner to undo his neckcloth, and did not speak one word or make the least resistance. They afterwards held up his head to the mob.

Thus ended the life of a man who will never be forgotten, and whose last crime will cause his name ever to be remembered with horror! I dare hardly say that he had many amiable qualities, and that his horrible fate was brought about by a set of ambitious men. As I have previously observed, they left him in the hands of men still worse than themselves. Unfortunately the Court never allowed him a chance of getting out of their hands. I could say much on this subject; but I should not be believed, and the subject always makes me unhappy.

The conversation about Philippe's boots—and they must have been gorgeous boots, because he, per the description of Grace Elliott's manservant, dressed very well for his execution—is repeated in Thomas Carlyle's book *The French Revolution.* Carlyle also contributes to the controversy about how many—and who—were the poor souls sharing his tumbrel:

Three poor blackguards were to ride and die with him: some say, they objected to such company, and had to be flung in, neck and heels . . . but it seems not true. . . . Philippe's dress is remarked for its elegance: greenfrock, waistcoat of white pique, yellow buckskins, boots clear as Warren; his air, as before, entirely composed, impassive, not to say easy and Brumellean-polite. . . . On the scaffold, Samson was for drawing of his boots: "tush," said Philippe, "they will come better off after; let us have done, dépêchons-nous!" . . . Probably no mortal ever had such things recorded of him: such facts, and also such lies. For he was a Jacobin Prince of the Blood; consider what a combination!

There was only one guillotine, that instrument of mass murder, in opera-tion in Paris, but it moved from place to place, dismantled and reerected as needed. The guillotine appeared at the place de la Révolution, where Philippe Égalité met his end, at the Bastille, at the place du Trône, and elsewhere. Charles Dickens, in his novel of the Reign of Terror, *A Tale of Two Cities,* published in serial form in 1859, got it exactly right: more commoners than nobles were killed at the guillotine, perhaps as many as two-thirds to one-half more. Remember Dickens's Sydney Carton and the little seamstress? Neither of them was an aristocrat. Grace Elliott narrowly missed becoming one of these commoner victims in 1794.

Philippe's body was dumped into a lime pit along with those of over three thousand other headless victims of the Revolution, in the same grave as his royal cousins. Later, Louis XVIII would direct that a memorial chapel, the Chapelle Expiatoire, be built on this site to mark the first burial place of the King and Queen. The place where the remains of Louis XVI and Marie-Antoinette lay buried had purportedly been pointed out to him by the grandson of one of the gravediggers.

The bodies were transferred to the cathedral of Saint-Denis, that final resting place of kings, and buried in its crypt. The Chapelle Expiatore is said to be the saddest spot in Paris, comparable to other places in the world where innocents lost their lives in scenes of incredible cruelty and lie buried and unknown.

Too bad Grace Elliott didn't put more in writing. Her reticence is unfortunate, because Philippe Égalité remains to this day an enigmatic and disturbing figure and she was in a unique position to shed light on his behavior. As to the manner in which he met his demise, however, sources agree it was with dignity. Whatever else one might say about the man's weakness, duplicity, or lack of character, he seems at the end to have met the ignominiousness of his death with the dignity befitting a true patrician.

La Chapelle Expiatoire, 29, rue Pasquier, Square Louis XVI, Paris. (Photo by Colette Pozzi-Barsot)

What Day/Week/Month/Year is it? The Weird French Revolutionary Calendar, "Le Calendrier Révolutionnaire"

In *Versailles* Kathryn Davis's evocative novel (Boston: Houghton Mifflin, 2002) of the last days of Marie-Antoinette, the imprisoned queen muses bitterly on the execution of her husband, King Louis XVI, trying to reconcile the calendar she knows with the one that the revolutionaries have imposed upon the French people. Marie-Antoinette was executed on October 16, 1793, a full month before the decree establishing the new calendar went into effect. Davis takes a bit of artistic license here:

It was January 21, 1793. Excuse me. I mean the second day of Pluviôse. Year One, because of course they had to change everything. Even epiphany cakes weren't to be called Cakes of the Kings anymore but Marat Cakes. Even the cakes.

On October 25, 1793, Philippe Fabre d'Eglantine, composer of the popular song "Il pleut, il pleut bergère" (It rains, it rains, shepherdess), proposed a new nomenclature for the Gregorian calendar in which the months would be replaced by a story of the year relating the earth's natural bounty of flowers, plants, fruit, grasses, and grains. Prior to this, in 1788, in one of many attempts to de-Christianize the Revolution, Pierre-Sylvain Maréchal had published *The Almanac of Honest People,* a type of calendar in which the names of saints associated with specific days of the year in the calendar of the Roman Catholic Church were replaced by those of famous people. On November 24, 1793, the National Convention passed the decree and went back to the middle of the previous

year to set the parameters of this new system. The year would now start in the autumn instead of on January 1, synchronizing Vendémiaire with the autumnal equinox.

Article 1 of the decree stated that counting would be computed from September 22, 1792, the equinox and the day after the French Republic was proclaimed. Article 7 set the division of the year into twelve equal months of thirty days each. Following this year were five days that completed it. Those free-floating five days were not connected to any month. Article 8 divided each of the twelve months into three equal periods of ten days each, called *décades.* Sunday, the Sabbath, disappeared entirely.

Article 9 named the individual days of the *décades:* Primdi (sometimes given as Primidi), Duodi, Tridi, Quartidi, Quintidi, Sextidi, Septidi, Octodi, Nodidi, Décadi, repeated three times. This last day, Décadi, was a day of rest. (So much for eliminating the Sabbath—but whereas the old calendar gave workers four days of rest in the month, this took away one of their days off.) The months were also named. Autumn consisted of Vendémiaire, the grape-harvesting month (September–October); Brumaire, the month of mist (October–November); and Frimaire, the month of frost (November–December). Winter was Nivôse, the month of snow (December–January); Pluviôse, the month of rain (January–February); and Ventôse, the month of winds (February–March). Spring was Germinal, the month of germination

(March–April); Floréal, the month of flowers (April–May); and Prairial, the month of meadows (May–June). Summer was Messidor, the month of harvest (June–July); Thermidor, the month of heat (July–August); and Fructidor, the month of fruit (August–September). The last five days of the year were called the *sans-culottides* and were named Jour de la vertu (Day of Virtue); Jour du génie (Day of Genius); Jour du travail (Labor Day); Jour de l'opinion (Day of Reason); and Jour des récompenses (Day of Rewards).

The *sans-culottes* (the trouserless) consisted mostly of skilled workers and shopkeepers from the middle classes. They preferred to wear the trousers of the working man rather than the fancy breeches of the upper classes and aristocracy. They were identified by the pike, the most common weapon used by the mob against the King's soldiers and other citizens.

A sixth day for the leap year that came every four years was added to the *sans-culottides* and named Jour de la révolution (Day of the Revolution). According to Article 16, republican games were to be celebrated to honor the Revolution on this day.

Calendar convention for indicating the year was to use Roman numerals, i.e., the first year was Year I; the second, Year II, and so on. The republican calendar remained in use for thirteen years, until 10 Nivôse Year XIV (or December 31, 1805).

The decree establishing the new French calendar. (Collection of the author)

CALENDRIER
POUR L'AN TROISIEME DE L'ERE RÉPUBLICAINE.

VENDÉMIAIRE, ou MOIS DES VENDANGES. — BRUMAIRE, ou MOIS DES BROUILLARDS. — FRIMAIRE, ou MOIS DES GELÉES. — NIVOSE, ou MOIS DES NEIGES. — PLUVIOSE, ou MOIS DES PLUIES. — VENTOSE, ou MOIS DES VENTS.

It was an extremely cumbersome system demanding a good memory. It was intended to be a simplified workers' calendar glorifying the seasons, but it served only to confuse. Each of those ten days had its own separate name and the names were different for each month! In Pluviôse, for example, Primdi was styled Laurier (Laurel), whereas in *Floréal* the corresponding name for Primdi was Rose (Rose).

The system confused Grace Elliott and led to charges by critics of her *Journal* that she was inaccurate and sloppy with dates. Grace herself freely admitted that she was confused by it. It would confuse anyone. There are sites on the Internet such as www.wundermoosen.com that convert the days of the Calendrier Révolutionnaire into those of the Gregorian calendar. It's nearby impossible for anyone to try to do it otherwise.

The British, of course, in their inimitable style— and strangely anticipating Disney's *Snow White and the Seven Dwarfs*—lost no time in satirizing the new French calendar, translating it thus: Vendémiaire, Wheezy; Brumaire, Sneezy; Frimaire, Freezy; Nivôse, Slippy; Pluviôse, Drippy; Ventôse, Nippy; Germinal, Showery; Floréal, Flowery; Prairial, Bowery; Messidor, Wheaty; Thermidor, Heaty; and Fructidor, Sweety.

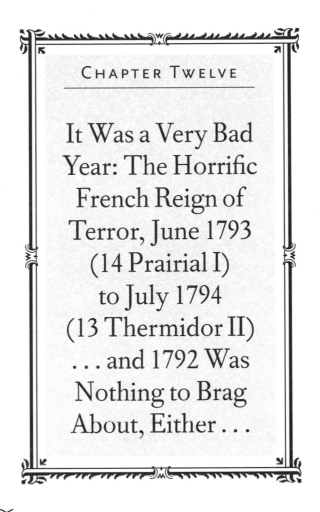

CHAPTER TWELVE

It Was a Very Bad Year: The Horrific French Reign of Terror, June 1793 (14 Prairial I) to July 1794 (13 Thermidor II) ... and 1792 Was Nothing to Brag About, Either ...

*P*hilippe Égalité, despite his best efforts to be identified with the revolutionaries, was one of the many victims of the Reign of Terror. Now Grace Elliott was about to become a victim; once her lover Philippe was gone, there was no one—no one at all—who could save her.

The Reign of Terror was initiated to destroy suspected enemies of the Revolution, both inside and outside France. It's often dated from June 2, 1793, when the Girondist deputies (more moderate republicans) were arrested by the Montagnards, the radical faction headed by Georges Danton, Jean-Paul Marat, and Maximilien Robespierre.

Horrific acts of terror had been occurring, however, from the onset of the

Revolution: the storming of the Bastille on July 14, 1789; the siege of the Tuileries, August 10–13, 1792; the killing of the Swiss guards and the capture of the royal family; the September Massacres (September 2–7, 1792), when Royalist prisoners were butchered; the execution of Louis XVI on January 21, 1793; and the brutal suppression of Royalist regions in the country, notably the Vendée, where thousands were slain. Upwards of forty thousand people may have been killed.

Some date the Terror from the actions in September 1793 of the French National Convention (formerly the National Assembly) that led to brutal enforcement of what were considered the guiding principles of the Revolution and included the elimination of individuals or groups whose ideas were considered moderate; the administration of justice became a joke. In March 1794, the Girondist deputies were arrested; less than a month later, they were all executed.

In April 1793, after General Charles-François du Périer Dumouriez deserted to the Austrians, the Committee of Public Safety was installed to run the country. On October 16, 1793, Queen Marie-Antoinette met the kiss of the guillotine's blade, and on November 8, the respected Madame Roland, brilliant essayist and wife of Jean-Marie Roland de la Platière, a leader of the Girondists, was executed. On June 10, 1794, a decree made execution without a trial legal. Though the so-called trials that had been held for the past year were a joke, this was a chilling proclamation.

It is estimated that between eighteen thousand and forty thousand people were executed during the period when the Terror held sway in France. No one will ever come up with a number that will satisfy scholars. At the height of the killing frenzy, people—foreigners along with French citizens—were scooped off the streets and guillotined for no reason. In the single month before the bloody spree ended, at least thirteen hundred people lost their lives. There is no verifiable list of those who died during the Reign of Terror; only the most famous of the murdered are known, including, finally, in late July of 1794, the architects of the Terror, Robespierre and his faction. These executions brought an end to the horrific period known as the Reign of Terror.

The Revolutionary Tribunal, the Revolutionary Committees, the Committee of Public Safety, and the Revolutionary Army

- The Revolutionary Tribunal was established on March 10, 1793, as a special court to deal with "counterrevolutionary crimes" against the Republic. The first Tribunal was a jury, five judges, and a public prosecutor.

- Twelve-man revolutionary committees were set up in localities throughout France, in the departments and in Paris. They were the regional and local eyes and ears of the National Convention. Grace Elliott appeared before one such committee.

- The Committee of Public Safety was installed on April 6, 1793, after General Dumouriez, a Girondist, defected to the Austrian army. It was a nine-man committee under the leadership of Danton that was in control of the country during the Terror.

- The Revolutionary Army—not to be confused with the Army of France—operated as groups of vigilantes sanctioned by the government to spy on the twelve-man revolutionary committees and to invade homes and businesses. The groups were dispersed to specific areas, and how well or badly they behaved toward citizens depended on who led them. Grace Elliott had several run-ins with the ones operating in her area.

Who Were the Girondists and the Montagnards?

The Girondists (whose first leaders hailed from the Gironde region) were moderates and intellectuals who wanted a republic but would have been satisfied with moderate reforms of the existing system; they were characterized as men of theory and principle. The Montagnards (mountain men, from *la montagne*, the mountain, because they sat on the topmost benches of the National Convention chamber), led by Robespierre, Marat, and Danton, were a smaller but more extreme group; these radicals controlled the National Convention, the country's ruling body, during the Reign of Terror. They were men of action who'd brook no compromise. The Montagnards controlled the Jacobin clubs, and the English newspapers used the term "Jacobins" when referring to them.

British Images of the French Revolution

Life was brutal in the aftermath of the Reign of Terror, and the political cartoonists wasted no time satirizing what they saw as a failed revolution. Gillray, Rowlandson, Isaac Robert Cruickshank, and many others churned out images. The print below is by Isaac Robert Cruickshank. Gillray had another, *French Liberty / British Slavery,* also with the food motif of the French and English at table. In Gillray's take, a depraved, skeletal Frenchman is munching some dried-up bulbs of garlic, while an obese, ruddy-cheeked Englishman scarfs down a huge roast of beef. Rowlandson, in a piece titled *The Contrast,* drew two medallions, showing a female symbol for British Liberty and another for French Liberty, and asking, "Which Is Best?" Under the British symbol are listed "Religion; Morality; Loyalty; Obedience To The Laws; Independence; Personal Security; Justice; Inheritance; Protection; Property; Industry; National Prosperity; Happiness." "Happiness" is underlined. The female French symbol holds sway over "Atheism; Perjury; Rebellion; Treason; Anarchy; Murder; Equality; Madness; Cruelty; Injustice; Treachery; Ingratitude; Idleness; Famine; National & Private Ruin; Misery." "Misery" is underlined. Subtlety, begone!

The satirists got serious when they condemned the executions of many good and noble-minded French people who wanted an end to the mass murder. Among these was the instant heroine Charlotte Corday (Cruikshank calls her Charlotte de la Corde).

French Happiness   *English Misery*

The heroic Charlotte la Corde, upon her Trial, at the bar of the Revolutionary Tribunal of Paris, July 17th 1793, for having rid the World, of that monster of Atheism, and Murder, the Regicide MARAT, whom she Stabbed in a bath, where he had retired on account of a Leprosy, with which, Heaven had begun the punishment of his Crimes.

"The noble enthusiasm with which this Woman met the charge, & the elevated disdain with which she treated the self created Tribunal, struck the whole assembly with terror & astonishment."

Publish'd July 29th 1793, by H. Humphrey N° 18 Old Bond Street.

Wretches —

— I did not expect to appear before you. — I always thought that I should be delivered up to the rage of the people, torn in pieces, & that my head stuck on the top of a pike, would have preceded Marat on his state bed, to serve as a rallying point to Frenchmen, if there still are any worthy of that name. — But happen what will, if I have the honours of the guillotine, & my clay cold remains are buried, they will soon have conferred upon them the honours of the Pantheon; and my memory will be more honoured in France than that of Judith in Bethulia.

ABOVE: *The Heroic Charlotte de la Corde at Her Trial.* Drawing by Isaac Robert Cruikshank. The English considered Charlotte Corday a heroine for knifing the insane Montagnard leader Marat to death in his bath; the French vilified her. Corday was guillotined for her action. (Library of Congress)

FACING PAGE: Satirical print by Isaac Robert Cruickshank on living the good life in France—in contrast to England—during the Reign of Terror in 1793. *French Happiness and English Misery* shows, on the left-hand side, four ragged and starving *sansculottes* fighting over a tiny frog; in the foreground a cat has dropped dead at their feet and on the wall in the background are horrific scenes of death. On the right-hand side, it shows a scene in an English tavern centered on a table groaning with food—roasts, plum puddings, etc.—and four Englishmen stuffing their bellies; a dog as fat as the men lies on the floor under the table and a happy cat has caught a mouse. Published by Samuel William Fores, January 3, 1793. (Library of Congress)

Grace Elliott's lover Philippe Égalité may have had a couple of defining moments; Grace had at least one, and it was a biggie.

When Philippe cast his lot with the revolutionaries and voted for the death of his cousin the King, he condemned himself forever in the eyes of many Frenchmen. This was a defining moment. He may have had another defining, and somewhat redeeming, moment, however, when he aided Grace in saving the life of a man he despised, the Marquis de Champcenetz. The saving of Champcenetz (which Grace phonetically spells "Chansenets") was clearly Grace's defining moment.

Grace Elliott's type was the brave, resourceful Englishwoman, a type that surfaces in works of fiction as well as throughout history. (Who can forget the wonderful Miss Froy, the elderly governess-spy in Alfred Hitchcock's *The Lady Vanishes?*) When Grace answered an urgent summons from a widowed friend, Mrs. Meyler, to come to Paris immediately, in the aftermath of the bloody massacre at the Tuileries, she didn't hesitate for a moment.

Most would agree that it was a foolish thing to do, given the turmoil and danger in the Paris streets and the bloodlust of the crowds. Even before that, however, the signs were clear that Grace would be targeted. She was an outsider, a foreigner, and she was closely allied to the ancien régime; she stuck out among the *citoyens* and the *citoyennes* for exactly who and what she was. Grace was already being watched owing to her ties with Philippe, whom the radical elements of the Revolution did not trust, despite his new pro-Revolution name of Citoyen Égalité. Philippe himself was warning her to be wary of her servants.

The siege of the Tuileries Palace took place over three days, August 10 to 13, 1792. The royal family had resided there with a handful of devoted servants since the march of the market women on Versailles on October 5, 1789, two months after the fall of the Bastille. The Tuileries was a far cry from the splendors of Versailles; it was unwelcoming, musty, and cavernous, though the gardens were beautiful. The royal family had attempted to flee in June 1791, only to be stopped at Varennes, near the German border, when a peasant supposedly recognized the face of Louis XVI from a coin and alerted authorities. (Grace Elliott witnessed their ignominious return; it prompted her to flee to the more hospitable environs of Spa for several months.)

On August 10, 1792, a little more than a year after Varennes, the rabble stormed the Tuileries. The royals meanwhile had fled to the General Assembly Hall near the place de la Concorde, leaving their loyal Swiss guards to face the anger and brutality of the mob. The governor of the Tuileries was a controversial character named Jean-Louis Quentin de Richebourg, the Marquis de Champcenetz.

The Marquis was in charge when the Tuileries was overrun by the mob and almost a thousand Swiss guards defending the royal family were killed. Champcenetz escaped by pretending to be dead, hiding under the bodies of his butchered guards. Here is where his life intersects with Grace Elliott's, who, incidentally, was the same age as he was and would die only a year after he did.

Grace receives a message at Meudon from her friend Mrs. Meyler (some sources call her Mrs. Miglia). The friend gives her instructions for getting in and out of the city so that she can come to the aid of an unfortunate person. Without hesitation, Grace sets out for Paris and when she arrives finds that this person is none other than the supposedly murdered governor of the Tuileries—she knows *of* him, but does not know him personally—and that he is not dead, as most of the Swiss guards are, but alive, though barely hanging on.

Mrs. Meyler took him in and has been hiding him in her attic. Now, however, she fears that the domiciliary visits made by the Revolutionary Army will result in his discovery. After a good deal of effort—and walking, for the coach Grace has secured refuses to take them any farther—Grace gets him to her house on the rue de Miromesnil, as she cannot get back to Meudon safely.

Servants! Here's where it gets sticky. Some of Grace's servants are intensely loyal to her, but others support the Revolution and have no love for people like the governor of the Tuileries and all that he represents. Grace has to maneuver him into—and then out (but not really out) of—her house so that the republican servants, especially her Jacobin cook, will think he's gone and can answer honestly and forthrightly when the searchers arrive to turn Grace's house upside down. (She gets her cook out of the way by pretending she is hungry and insisting that the woman go to buy a chicken.)

Grace has learned a good deal since Dr. Eliot's servants testified against her at her divorce hearing; she's learned who is to be trusted and who is not, she's become more careful in her dealings with servants. Her porter helps her devise the plan of hiding the sick, exhausted Champcenetz between her mattresses. Then Grace she gets into her nightgown and pretends to go to sleep, in the hope that she can prevent the revolutionaries from bayoneting her bed . . . and her. As she recounts the episode in her *Journal:*

My cook I had managed to get rid of, but she might soon return. M. Chansenets [she always spells it thusly] was almost in fits, and in a deplorable state from extreme weakness. . . . My porter thought that he might be hid between the mattresses of my bed, which were very large, and in an alcove. We accordingly pulled two of the mattresses out further than the others, and made a space next the wall, and put him in. When he was there, we found that the bed looked tumbled, and of course suspicious. I then decided upon getting into bed myself, which prevented any appearance of a person being hid. I had all my curtains festooned up; my chandeliers and candelabra lighted, which in all formed about twenty candles. . . . My cook soon came home, and I made her sit by my bedside the rest of the night. She abused Monsieur Chansenets, and said that she was sure he would be guillotined; that she hoped I had turned him out directly; in short, she had not the most distant idea of his being in my house.

A nice touch, having that fierce Jacobin cook sit at the side of the bed where Champcenetz is hidden! Clever Grace. Meanwhile, the female servant Grace trusts has just come back from visiting her son. She's missed the hiding of the Marquis; as far as she knows, he was turned out by Grace. Another nice touch. Neither of these servants will be lying when the expected domiciliary visit is paid and they are quizzed as to Champcenetz's whereabouts. Grace continues:

I passed a most miserable night, surrounded by my servants, and almost in fits myself at the idea of the horrid visit I was going to receive. I trembled so much, that I could hardly keep in bed, and the unfortunate man, who was the cause of my misery, I thought perhaps lay dead near me, for I could not hear him breathe.

The Marquis de Champcenetz, Jean-Louis Quentin de Richebourg (1754–1822)

The surname in the title of the "Marquis de Champcenetz"—a name that barely seems French—is taken from a little village in the Seine-et-Marne a dozen kilometers north of the ancient Roman town of Provins in north-central France. The Marquis was named Jean-Louis for his father and was the firstborn son of his father's first marriage. His father (1723–1813) had been first valet of the bedchamber to King Louis XV (Louis XVI's grandfather), the semiofficial governor of the Tuileries since 1770, and officially its governor after 1775.

There were two younger de Richebourg half-brothers from his father's second marriage. Louis-René, a fervent monarchist, was guillotined in 1794. It was said of him that in the face of death he was the perfect gentleman. The younger brother, Edmond-Ferdinand, was a captain in the Noailles-dragons and lived to 1849; he succeeded to the title after Champcenetz's death in 1822. Jean-Louis had a career in the military that included a stint in the American Revolu-

tion, and upon returning home was named *gouverneur des Tuileries en survivance,* succeeding his father—*en survivance*—in the office. From the remarks of his contemporaries as described by Bernard Delahaye in "L'Ecossaise, le Duc . . . et Champcenetz dans la tourmente révolutionnaire (1792–1794)," in the *Bulletin de la société d'histoire et d'archeologie de l'arrondissement de provins,* number 156 (2002). Champcenetz appears to have been an annoying, nasty, even hurtful individual. He was called indolent *(lache);* treacherous *(traître);* envious *(envieux);* a shabby little man *(villain petit monsieur),* and two-faced *(dissimulé).* One biographer observed that he was endowed with a certain toughness or flexibility of spirit, but with a total lack of character *("doué d'une certaine souplesse d'esprit, ou à proprement parler, d'un manqué total de caractère").* He'd earned the strong enmity of the Duc d'Orléans on a number of occasions.

At 4 A.M., the cook answers the door and bursts in to tell Grace that the municipal officers have arrived. So has the moment of truth. Grace despairs:

No pen or words can give the smallest idea of my feelings at that moment. I felt that I was lost . . . but a very deep groan from my companion roused me in a moment, and God inspired me with more courage than I had ever felt in my life. So strong was my abhorrence of the horrid acts which were being committed, that I am certain I could have mounted the scaffold with pleasure. . . . I was determined to brave every danger.

The men pull apart all of the servants' beds, "running their bayonets into the mattresses and feather-beds, swearing that they would not leave the house until they had found Chansenets." The cook and maidservant are "very bold" and fear nothing, because they are sure the Marquis has been sent away, but the ruffians insist that Champcenetz was not seen to leave the house, only to go in.

This is where Grace reconsiders her "deplorable situation." Her adrenaline is surging, but she realizes she must stay in control of her emotions:

> *This long search gave me time to cool. . . . Although my own life was of little value, still I had no reason to suppose that the unfortunate man near me did not value his. . . . I had no right to commit any act of desperation, as the life of a fellow-creature depended on my conduct.*

Grace feels herself go "perfectly calm, full of presence of mind, and . . . inspired with a courage equal to anything earthly." She looks around and muses that the many candles are still burning, day is breaking, and her bedroom looks more like a ballroom than the possible setting for acts of horror. The men—she estimates there are forty of them—come up to her bed and ask her to get up, but she's caught the eye of an individual "less hard than the others." He tells her there is to reason to get out of bed, as she "could not dress before so many men."

She plays with them, saying that of course she'll get up if they require it, that she had expected them much earlier and had passed a bad night, waiting for them. The seasoned courtesan can handle men, and now she's being put to the test of her sisterhood. She flatters them:

> *I owned that I had been much alarmed at the idea of such a visit in the dead of the night, but that now I saw how considerate, kind, and good they were, I was not the least alarmed, and if they pleased I would get up and conduct them about my house myself. . . . I was sure they must be much fatigued, and proposed wine or liqueurs and cold pie to them.*

It works. The leaders of the group are "delighted" with her, "cut some very indecent jokes," and comment that no one that night has been half so civil to them. They insist that she stay in her bed and they search only the top of the bed, under the bed, and the foot of the bed. They take an hour to look into her boudoir, dressing room, and bath, and to undo all the sofa cushions.

A couple of them are dissatisfied; she hears grumbling that they had good information that Champcenetz was in the house. She fears that she will be asked to get out of bed again and see the bayonets doing their worst to the mattresses—and to the poor unfortunate hiding between them—but here her feisty cook interrupts and states that "she was certain I would not have harboured so great a foe of the Duke of Orléans."

Grace is only chastised, then, for not calling the guards the minute Champcenetz turned up at her house; she is, they tell her, "a bad *citoyenne.*" She lies, explaining that though she disliked the man she did not like to denounce anyone. She lies further, saying that Champcenetz had said he was returning to his home. At this point, she almost loses it as one of the guards sits down on her bed.

Grace can hardly breathe, wondering if Champcenetz has breathed his last. Then the guards abruptly leave her bedroom, wishing her a good night, but from the sounds she hears, they linger in the house for a while longer. When she hears the gates shut, finally, she asks all of her servants except for her personal maid to leave. When she tells her who has been hiding in her bed, the maid "scream[s] with dread," saying she would never have had the courage to get through what had just happened if she had known the truth.

Grace herself has an attack of hysterics, but she recovers quickly, for she and her maid have to free poor Champcenetz:

> *We now got our prisoner out of the bed with great difficulty. . . . [He had] been so smothered he was as wet as if he had been in a bath, and speechless. We laid him on the ground, opened the windows, and . . . made him drink a large glass of brandy.*

When Champcenetz recovers, he is "full of gratitude." He had been "both frightened and surprised" at her courage, especially when she offered to get out of bed. He is put into Grace's boudoir, which the maid then locks. When they look in on him later in the afternoon he is "in a high fever and almost delirious, and crying." Now she and the maid fear he will die.

As they are pondering their options—how are they going to rid themselves of a dead body without anyone noticing?—the Duc d'Orléans pays Grace a visit. He is concerned for her welfare and has come to ask her to keep her opinions about the Revolution to herself and to be careful what she says in front of her servants. He cautions:

> *"We are all surrounded by spies, and if you get yourself into a scrape I*

cannot save you; so, for God's sake, keep your politics to yourself, and plague me no more on this subject; it will be of no use."

Grace decides that perhaps now is not the best time to tell him she has the governor of the Tuileries—a man Philippe despises—ill with fever in her boudoir. Philippe advises her to go back to Meudon as soon as the city barriers are opened and she can pass through. She will be safer there, he says, adding that she must not show anyone how eager she is to leave Paris, as "they might suspect something."

Champcenetz, who has heard the discussion between Grace and Philippe from behind the boudoir door, tells Grace later that he will leave, so as not to endanger her further, but she insists that he stay and says all will be well. The next day, Philippe arrives for breakfast and now she tells him what she's done.

Philippe takes the news surprisingly well and together they plot the next move. What's been done is done, is his attitude, and now they must get her out of this scrape she's gotten herself into. In short, he is concerned for her, but not judgmental. But poor Champcenetz! He has to hear—from behind that door—what Philippe really thinks of him:

He told me that "I had exposed my life for a very bad purpose, for that Chansenets was a good-for-nothing creature; that many better people had been taken up and executed; that he wished I had saved anybody else; and that it would be cruel if I was to lose my life for such a poor miserable being."

He leaves her, saying that he wishes she "had been more prudent." As Grace's *Journal* notes, he also said that "he would see what he could do to get this man out" of her house, and added that he also "wished to God" that she was "safe in England, for he thought something would happen" to her where she is.

When Champcenetz recovers and speaks to Orléans a few days later he apologizes to him, and receives a dressing-down for getting Grace into this mess. Orléans will not, however, betray either of them, despite his low opinion of the former governor of the Tuileries.

When the city's barriers are reopened, Grace smuggles Champcenetz out of her Paris home to her cottage in Meudon.

The revolutionaries have still been searching for him in Paris but are now beginning to think that he died in the massacre after all. Meanwhile, Grace gets wind of the rumor that domiciliary visits are going to be paid to areas outside of Paris, and she fears for their lives, but Philippe comes through:

[Philippe] sent me one of his old valets-de-chambre, who was a royalist, to deliver me a letter from him, telling me that the mail-cart which stopped at St. Denis, would, for fifty louis, take Chansenets to Boulogne, from whence he might soon get to England. The Duke also sent me a note for the master of the inn at St. Denis, called the Pavillon Royal. I did not tell Chansenets whence this information came, for he would have been alarmed, and would not have gone; but I assured him that Meudon was dangerous, and that I could now get him to Boulogne.

The deed is soon done. Champcenetz is dispatched in a cabriolet, accompanied by Grace and her old Royalist neighbor in Meudon, a gentleman whom she can trust; they arrive in Saint-Denis at 3 A.M., and the mail cart comes for the Marquis the next hour:

I saw poor Chansenets, in a deplorable condition and much disguised, set

off. There were other emigrants in the cart also. It was in January, and quite dark. . . . Some years afterwards I heard that Chansenets got safely to England.

Postscript: Grace must have harbored the Marquis in her home for at least three months. In his epilogue to her *Journal,* Richard Bentley writes, "Mrs. Elliott had the satisfaction of seeing the Marquis de Chansenets (whose life she had saved at so great risk to her own) reinstated as Governor of the Tuileries."

Philippe's role in this amazing story is not insignificant; Grace might not have been able to pull off another of her bedroom coups at Meudon as she had done in Paris. Things were going from bad to extremely bad, and the Duke had warned her to watch her step. He knew what was going on and was telling her the plain truth, that he would no longer be able to protect her.

What Grace did, in the Champcenetz incident, was to lay her life on the line. In similar situations people will behave differently. Questions of innate character arise, and nowhere is this more marked than in the experience of another English eyewitness of the Reign of Terror, the poet Helen Maria Williams.

A TALE OF TWO WOMEN: GRACE ELLIOTT AND HELEN MARIA WILLIAMS

Grace Elliott and Helen Maria Williams traveled in different circles; they probably did not know each other but may have heard of each other. No way, though, could they ever have been friends. The similarities between them were these: Both of them lived in Paris during the Revolution and the Reign of Terror; both were intelligent Englishwomen who were staunch believers in their respective causes, monarchy and republicanism; both were imprisoned during the Reign of Terror and had good reason to fear for their lives.

The major difference between them—beyond the fact that Grace was a courtesan and Helen Maria a pious single lady—emerges when we notice that Grace found the courage to save the life of a stranger, whereas Helen Maria failed to save papers entrusted to her by a good friend about to be executed. It's a question of mettle—and perhaps Darwinism, too.

Jeanne-Marie née Phlipon Roland de la Platière, or Madame Roland (1754–1793), French Heroine

Madame Roland and her husband had stood against the excesses committed in the name of Liberty-Equality-Fraternity and had become pariahs. It was clear that they and the rest of the Girondists were in the way of the radical Jacobins and others of that ilk.

Madame Roland was arrested in June 1793 and (like Grace Elliott) kept in several prisons in succession, among them the Abbaye, the Sainte-Pélagie, and the Conciergerie. In prison, Madame Roland wrote a number of essays and her memoirs; she was allowed visitors, among them stalwart English republican friends and sympathizers like Helen Maria Williams. She was incarcerated and executed after a typical mockery of a trial; she's now heralded as a heroine of the early Revolution and famous for the last words she uttered as she faced the statue of Liberty on the place de la Révolution: "O Liberté, que de crimes on commet en ton nom!" (O Liberty, what crimes are committed in your name!) Two days after word of her execution on November 8 reached the countryside, her husband (who'd been in hiding) committed suicide. (Her young lover, François Buzot, committed suicide in June 1794.) Grace Elliott was the same age

Madame Roland in prison. Engraving by Pierre-François Delannoy. (Library of Congress)

as Madame Roland, was imprisoned in some of the same jails, and narrowly—and miraculously—escaped the Frenchwoman's fate. Roland entrusted some papers, among the last she wrote in prison, to her friend Williams for safekeeping. Williams said they were left behind when she herself was taken prisoner, but that may not be the whole truth.

"Doesn't natural selection favor the selfish, those who maximize their own life . . . at the expense of others?" asks Richard C. Lewontin in his 1998 essay "Survival of the Nicest?" This natural selection—also known as the survival of the fittest—means that only the most successful individuals get to pass on their genes to future generations. Was Williams acting instinctively to protect her gene pool and Elliott—contrary to all natural instinct—

acting against it? Is selfishness, reduced to biological terms, good for the genetic group, as some biologists believe?

If so, why be unselfish? Why risk one's own life when there is no payoff either in one's own survival or in the future of the genetic group? Saving those in one's family can be understood in the first model, because family members have genes in common, and if one has to be sacrificed so that others can be saved, the gene pool stays largely intact. But why risk all to save a stranger, someone with whom one may have nothing at all in common but the fact of one's humanity?

On the face of it, both Grace Elliott and Helen Maria Williams were involved with "group" members—Grace with a fellow monarchist (though not a friend or even an acquaintance) and Helen Maria with a fellow republican (who had the added virtue of being a good friend). Was that enough to risk one's own survival? Evidently it was for Grace, but not for Helen Maria.

Why? Grace Elliott explained it by saying that although she had no qualms about losing her life—with the implication that it was not that important to her—but she had no reason to believe that the life of a man she could save wasn't important to him. She assumed he wanted to live, and that was justification enough for her.

Helen Maria, on the other hand, knew for a fact that Madame Roland would be executed and there was nothing she could do about it. She had just as much to lose as Grace did; Helen Maria's harboring of her friend's papers could have led to her arrest and death as surely as Grace's harboring of Champcenetz, the fugitive, could have led to Grace's.

Are mere papers worth as much as someone's life? Of course they are, and Helen Maria Williams, as a writer, someone dedicated to words and their power to move people and to influence events, surely had to realize that at the deepest level of her understanding. Was Williams more of a survivor than Elliott? Was her wish to live stronger? Possibly, but the fear factor has to enter into this discussion, too. Grace Elliott seemed free from fear, whereas Helen Maria Williams seemed consumed by it. Grace Elliott asked herself, Is it good for me to do this? and got the answer, Why not? Helen Maria Williams's ego resolved the question for her quickly; it wasn't good for her; ergo, she didn't do it.

_H_elen Maria Williams (1762–1827), False Friend or Just Plain Scared?

The writer Helen Maria Williams was born in the north of England, the daughter of a Welsh army officer and a Scotswoman. Wordsworth's first published poem (1787) was the sonnet "On Seeing Miss Helen Maria Williams Weep at a Tale of Distress." She was a brilliant woman: a poet, essayist, writer of hymns, translator of French literature, and novelist. Her _Poems,_ in two volumes, had been published in 1786; her _Letters from France_ in 1790. Her sister was married to a French Protestant minister and lived in France, and Williams had other friends in France as well when she left England to go to Paris. A Francophile and sympathetic to the cause of the Revolution, she was a habitué of Madame Roland's salon and got to know the Girondists, becoming close friends with them. She was briefly imprisoned upon the order of Robespierre—probably because of her friendship with the Rolands—but escaped execution. Williams, who lived with a married Englishman, John Hurford Stone, was vilified in England as immoral for her relationship with Stone and traitorous for her liberal republican views; not a heroine in her own country, she never returned home, and died in Paris.

The manuscripts Madame Roland entrusted to Williams were destroyed because "Williams became frightened that if they were found in her possession, she would be executed as an enemy of the republic. Rather than risk that, she burned them," according to Jack Fruchtman Jr. in his introduction to _An Eye-Witness Account of the French Revolution by Helen Maria Williams: Letters Containing a Sketch of the Politics of France_ (1997), which he edited. Williams is arguably one of the best of the eyewitness chroniclers of the Revolution and she had a unique viewpoint, as she was a foreigner in the inner circle of the Girondists who saw the Revolution turn from idealism—liberty, humanity, and justice for all—into chaos and murder. That she remained an optimist in the face of all the suffering she witnessed—and experienced herself—is open to various interpretations, including, undeniably, the great power of denial.

Henrietta Maria Williams. Engraving by an unknown artist, 1816. (National Portrait Gallery, London)

Grace Elliott acted out of unselfishness, or altruism, by looking out for the good of her group: the small group, monarchists, and the larger group, humanity. She put aside her natural survival instincts, whereas Helen Maria Williams never got that far. The two women's reactions don't make one of them a better person than the other, not inherently. Altruistic behavior is certainly not that well understood and it seems to go counter to impulses of survival and natural selection, but it does indicate who might have been a better person to have as a friend or neighbor when the going got rough.

Another explanation is possible, though it may seem way out there at first: hedonism. It makes some people feel really, really good when they help others, even taking into account the serious personal risks. The pleasure, the high, can be worth it. Feeling good about oneself can have value for an individual so wired, genetically or socially. Grace Elliott—no more than a mere woman of pleasure to many—may have understood the pleasure principle far better than Helen Maria Williams, the committed republican, did.

IMPRISONMENT: EIGHTEEN MONTHS OF SUFFERING, A MIRACULOUS REPRIEVE, AND A WORLD CHANGED FOREVER

The proof necessary to convict the enemies of the people is every kind of evidence, either material or moral or verbal or written. . . . Every citizen has the right to seize conspirators and counterrevolutionaries and to arraign them before magistrates. He is required to denounce them when he knows of them.

Law of 22 Prairial Year II (June 10, 1794)

One of the serious criticisms of Grace's *Journal* is that she fabricated the anecdotes she related, that they actually happened to others and she simply went ahead and cast herself as the heroine of the lot. It is also charged that she was never imprisoned at all.

If Grace embellished her part in the accounts she writes in her *Journal,* she is to be credited for her storytelling ability and her writing skill. The book reads beautifully and the narration is gripping. The reader is drawn into the tale of one woman's survival in a horrific situation, and what she recounts has the ring of authenticity. At this late date, quibbling about the content is pointless. There are few records to substantiate or to discredit her story; insanity is the defining motif for this period of French history and it behooves one to be skeptical even of eyewitness accounts.

Bentley's prologue and epilogue to the *Journal* leave a good deal to be desired in the way of accuracy. Bentley relates anecdotal information about Grace as if it were fact. Where did this information come from? Who was around in 1858–1859 to tell him these stories? It's obvious that a good deal came from Grace's granddaughter, Georgina Cavendish-Bentinck, who was then almost fifty years of age. These were stories she'd heard in the family—not from her mother, who'd died when she was two years old, but from other family members. It had to be third- or fourth-hand information by the time it got to Bentley.

To return to the last days of the Revolution and to that awful year called the Reign of Terror: Grace says she was imprisoned in four different jails beginning in 1793, for a total of eighteen months: Sainte-Pélagie; the Recollets (at Versailles); Plessis; and the Carmes (Carmelites).

Things had come to a head between Grace and the Duc d'Orléans after the adventure with the Marquis de Champcenetz. Philippe was having his own great problems, exacerbated by the fateful vote he'd cast for the death of the King in January 1793. Straining relations with Grace was his promise he would not cast a vote. Then Philippe's eldest son defected to Austria with General Dumouriez and condemned his father in a farewell letter in which, according to Grace's *Journal*, he "upbraided him much with the King's death." Grace goes on, "I perfectly remember the letter, for I had it two days in my possession. The Duke burnt it in my room, the last time in his life that he came to my house."

Ever the realist, Grace finally begins to acknowledge she's stayed too long at the fair. Clearly, Philippe—who's come to her house accompanied by gendarmes—is in great danger. He has a last discussion with her concerning finances:

> *[He said] he did not feel at his ease about the money I possessed, which I*

The Mysterious Friend

Who was this mysterious friend of Grace's, whom Bentley refers to as "the lady who has kindly contributed much of the information collected here [and who] resided with her"? Was it the Mrs. Naylor at whose home Bentley says Grace was a lodger? Could it have been that widow, Mrs. Meyler/Miglia? Or was it another of those phantoms who glided through Grace's life? The real Mrs. Meyler must have been long dead. If not Meyler or Naylor, then who was the lady? This unnamed woman will remain unknown. Here's what Bentley says, shedding no light whatsoever:

> For a short time she [Grace] resided at Brompton, at the house of a Mrs. Naylor, where lodgings had been procured for her, by her direction, by her maid, Madame La Rue. . . . Mrs. Elliott remained in England until 1814. . . . During the whole period of her residence here, from 1801 to 1814, the lady who has kindly contributed much of the information here collected resided with her, and she also accompanied her to Paris, and remained with her ten weeks.

Horace Walpole mentions a Mrs. Naylor in a 1760 letter to George Montagu; the reference is to a known house of prostitution run by this woman. This would have been forty years prior to Grace's return to England in 1801. Same person? Doubtful. Would Grace have resided in a house of ill-repute? Equally doubtful! Or was this the Mrs. Sarah Naylor—another woman of the same surname—who lived in Prospect Road, Brompton, circa 1800, according to a local history pamphlet at the South Kensington Public Library? It is known—from the London ratebooks—that Grace resided at Brompton Park House from 1808 to 1813, and she may also have been there in 1798, living next door to her friend Lady Seymour Dorothy Fleming (who used to be Lady Worsley), but there's also mention of her living in Twickenham circa 1801, when she's supposed to have written the *Journal*.

Even the biographer Bleackley is at a loss; he says that "the rest of Grace's life [after 1798] is veiled in mystery." Perhaps the only option is to leave it at that. The sole eyewitness to Grace in England after 1800 is her niece Frances, Lady Shelley, who describes a remarkable meeting at her mother's deathbed, but she gets the dates wrong, too. Her mother, then known as Jacintha Barrington, reportedly died on January 7, 1802, and Lady Shelley sets the meeting between Jacintha and Grace a year later, in 1803.

had placed on his estates. He thought, in case of his death, he could make an arrangement for me which would secure the payment of my annuities in England; that he would arrange all the business and give me effects, which would be money to me when I could get to England. He assured me that I should be far from being a loser, and that if they paid his creditors after his death so much the better, for I should then be so much the richer.

All during this period, a lady—Madame de Périgord—has been hiding out in Grace's house. When Philippe leaves, Grace has barely enough time to get her into a closet when another domiciliary visit takes place. It's midnight, and there are as many men in the group as before; they ask for her keys and tell her they want to look at all her papers. Not good, for they find an incriminating letter addressed to Charles James Fox. She cannot charm them this time.

> *They thought that I should be sent the next day to the guillotine; and they were enchanted at the discovery they had made. They told me that they had long suspected me, but that now they had found out that I was in correspondence with the enemies of the Republic, and that I should pay dearly for it.*

Grace tries in vain to assure the men that Fox is a friend of the Revolution and in correspondence with the Committee of Surveillance, their tribunal, but they are woefully "ignorant men" who are eager to arrest her:

> *They stated that they had orders to put me under arrest that night; and they put their echarpes over their shoulders, and arrested me in the name of the Republique Française. They took all the papers they pleased, and hardly allowed me time to put a shawl over my shoulders, though it was very cold; and put the seals on my cabinets. . . . It happened however, that they were so pleased at getting me out of my own house, and leading me, as they thought, to the scaffold, that they left my house without seals.*

(Everyone knew it was certain death to break a seal put on one's doors; if one of Grace's loyal servants had broken a seal to free Madame de Périgord, Grace's own fate would have been sealed.)

Grace is taken to a guardroom located only one street from her home. There she spends a cold and terrifying night, taunted by the drunken guards that she'll soon "dance the Carmagnole in the Place Louis Quinze," i.e., face the guillotine. The room is full of other prisoners, none of whom she knows, and she is the only woman in the place. She tries to explain that the letter they found was innocent, but soon gives up.

In the morning, one of her manservants brings her tea and bread; she has a headache from the smells of cheap wine and strong tobacco and is exhausted. She describes her jailers:

The members of the Comité Révolutionnaire of my Section, who had come to my house with the guards to arrest me, were various tradesmen, and the president was a barber, who had been a zealous actor in the prisons on the 2nd of September [the start of the bloody September Massacres, in which so many Royalist prisoners had been killed], and of course was a monster."

She is walked to the *mairie,* the town hall, where the state prisoners are examined, at 8 A.M., and stands on her feet from 9 A.M. until the next day at noon. A young soldier who recognizes Grace (his sister "used to wash my laces," she says) hands her a chair, but she gives it to two elderly countesses instead. She has an interesting conversation with the two women, who seem to know that she had helped Champcenetz.

When she is finally brought before the presiding magistrate, Mayor Chambronne, he tells her that she must go before the Committee of Surveillance, that hers is "a grave business." She's taken to the Feuillants, in the Tuileries Gardens, and witnesses wrenching scenes of "poor men and women coming out of the Comité in tears, papers having been found upon them; everyone whom I saw was ordered for imprisonment . . . to be tried by the horrid Tribunal Révolutionnaire."

Now she begins to panic, more so as she realizes she has no idea of what's in that letter. As she worries, the door opens and "who should come out, attended by guards, but the Duke of Orléans!" They have no chance to talk, except for him to say he is "very sorry indeed" to see her there.

FIRST INTERROGATION: LA COMITÉ DE SURVEILLANCE

She's taken into the room where she will be questioned and sees members of the Committee of Surveillance; of them all, Vergniaud, Guadet, Osselin, and Chabot are those she remembers. She writes that they "all sat along a green table, and a chair was placed facing them." To get to the chair she has to mount some high steps. The room is crowded with people and she is frightened. The cynosure of all hostile eyes, she tries to concentrate on not tripping up those steps.

François Chabot, a Capuchin friar who is a deputy to the National Assembly, is openly hostile. He accuses her of being a Royalist, engaging in conspiracy, and "intriguing in England to make D'Orléans's daughter marry an English prince." He demands that she be sent to the prison of La Force. (Chabot was guillotined with the Montagnard Danton on April 5, 1794.)

From bad cop Chabot to good cop Vergniaud. The orator and lawyer Pierre Vergniaud, considered one of the most brilliant of the Girondist leaders, defends Grace, saying that she should not have been arrested for having a letter for Fox in her home. He adds, "Mr. Fox is our friend; he is the friend of a free nation; he loves our Revolution. . . . We will keep the letter, and send it safely to Mr. Fox." (Vergniaud was eventually to be guillotined with the rest of the Girondist deputies.)

Chabot doesn't give up and insists upon the letter's being opened and read, but there's one catch: none of them can read English, and their interpreter is busy elsewhere. Charles-Nicolas Osselin, the president of the committee, asks Grace to rise and come read the letter to them, adding that some of them understood enough English to know if she is providing an accurate translation. (Like Chabot and Vergniaud and the fourth man recognized by Grace, Marguerite-Elie Guadet, Osselin was later executed. Guadet hid for almost a year before being captured; Osselin attempted suicide. Shed no tears for these men: the blood of too many they questioned was on their hands as they met their own demise.)

The letter from Charles James Fox turns out to be full of praise for the French. It comments favorably on Admiral Latouche-Treville's (the name is not "Freville"—Grace gets this name wrong, too) manifesto to the King of Naples urging him to stay the course of the French Revolution and not lose faith. Grace writes that "the letter greatly delighted them." But Chabot persists, asking her now what words she exchanged with the Duc d'Orléans in the corridor before she was examined. His brutal questioning style unnerves her and she breaks down in tears, while he sneers at her evident distress.

As Chabot continues to hammer away at her concerning her friendship with Orléans, and Orléans's desire to be king, Grace is defended by some twenty or so of the fifty men present, who rise in protest; but she is truly saved by the bell (as she will be later, as well) when Robespierre arrives and interrupts the proceedings for more urgent business. A shattered Grace is allowed to return home, but she's soon to be arrested.

Prisons

There were at least fifty places of detention for the unfortunate prisoners in Paris during the Revolution and Reign of Terror. These are a few of the better known:

LA FORCE. In Dickens's *A Tale of Two Cities,* the character Charles Darnay is consigned to the prison at La Force. Originally the private residence of the Duc de la Force, it was converted into a prison in 1780. La Force was located above the rue Saint-Antoine to the west of the Bastille on the rue Pavée. (The prison was destroyed in the nineteenth century.) Princesse de Lamballe was the most famous of the hundreds of prisoners murdered at La Force during the September Massacres.

THE ABBAYE. The Abbaye was a house of detention within the precincts of the abbey of Saint-Germain-des-Prés. It was considered the gloomiest of all jails in Paris. The first mass killing of the infamous September Massacres took place here, that of nineteen priests who were hacked to death in a garden by killers armed with knives, axes, hatchets, sabers, and a carpenter's saw. Later, two-thirds of the prisoners at the Abbaye were killed. It stood on what is now the boulevard Saint-Germain between street numbers 135 and 137. Before its demolition in the mid-1850s, it served for a while as a place of military detention. Grace was never here.

THE RECOLLETS. The monastery of the Recollets, at Versailles, was transferred to the French National Assembly in November 1789 and the monks removed. The religious order, with its emphasis on piety, poverty, and service, was a minor branch of the

Portrait of Madame du Barry by Élisabeth Vigée-Lebrun. (Corcoran Gallery of Art, Washington, D.C.)

Franciscans; its members were also referred to as Capuchins. Grace Elliott was sent to the Recollets not long after she was released from Sainte-Pélagie; it was her second time in prison. She shared a room with a Dr. Gem—an elderly Englishman—and her pet dogs. From here she went for one night to the Plessis prison and was then sent on to the Carmes.

SAINTE-PÉLAGIE. Grace Elliott's first incarceration was at Sainte-Pélagie, which she describes as "a most deplorable, dirty, uncomfortable hole." It had been a house of correction. She mentions one "miserable supper" there as consisting of "ham, eggs, and dirty water." Men and women were kept to different sides of the building. Grace stayed there for only a couple of months, from May to June of 1793. She was released to give testimony before the Committee of Public Safety and wasn't sent back. She relates meeting the doomed Madame du Barry, the mistress of King Louis XV, during her stay at Sainte-Pélagie.

THE CONCIERGERIE. The Conciergerie was originally a part of a palace built in the fourteenth century for King Philip IV of France. It was the section controlled by the *concierge,* or keeper, of the royal palace. Around the beginning of the fifteenth century, the royal family moved out and it became a prison. During the Revolution, the Conciergerie became known as death's waiting room, the last step before the guillotine. About twelve hundred prisoners could be housed at one time, and during the Reign of Terror the Revolutionary Tribunal held court here. During April 1793 and May 1795, more than twenty-five hundred were sent to their death from this infamous place, among them Queen Marie-Antoinette, Charlotte Corday, André Chénier, the Girondist leaders, Madame Roland, Lavoisier, Danton, and Robespierre. En route to the tumbrels, the condemned prisoners walked through what became known as the Salle de les Perdus (Room of the Doomed). Marie-Antoinette's cell was converted into a chapel in her honor in the nineteenth century. Today, the building is one of the city's major tourist attractions; most of it houses the Paris law courts. Grace was not imprisoned here.

THE CARMES. This former Carmelite convent on the rue Vaugirard, near the Luxembourg Gardens—now the church of Saint-Joseph-des-Carmes—holds in an ossuary the skulls and bones of more than one hundred members of the clergy who were massacred in its gardens on September 2, 1792. In April 1794, Joséphine de Beauharnais—who was to become the Empress Joséphine, wife of Napoléon—was arrested and jailed at the Carmes, where her husband, Alexandre, was already incarcerated. It was a noxious place and there were vermin everywhere. The walls, cobblestones, ceilings, and stairs were still stained with the blood of the martyred clergymen, even after two years and some attempts at cleaning. Prisoners were kept in cramped dormitories that slept a dozen or more to the room. Joséphine de Beauharnais shared this prison with her friends the Duchesse d' Aiguillon, Delphine de Custine, and Grace Elliott, among others; Grace's friend Mrs. Meyler was there. It was probably Grace's last incarceration.

THE BASTILLE. Here's where it all started. More people by far died storming the Bastille than were liberated by the storming. Only seven prisoners were found inside—and none of them was the Marquis de Sade. Though legend has it he was the sole prisoner there, he had been removed and transferred to the Charenton asylum after screaming out the window early in July that the guards were killing the prisoners. The governor of the prison, the unfortunate Marquis de Launay, who'd promised not to fire on the crowd coming to free the prisoners unless attacked, panicked and went back on his word. He was killed, beheaded, and his head was paraded around Paris on a pike. The Bastille was never more than a symbol, but the Revolution had begun. Grace Elliott and the Duc d'Orléans heard about the storming while dining at Orléans's country home outside Paris. Although the fortress was demolished, the area known as the Place de la Bastille is one of the most visited places in Paris. July 14, the anniversary of the storming of the Bastille, is the French national holiday.

First Imprisonment: Sainte-Pélagie

The nature of that urgent business is apparent the next day, when Grace learns that Philippe has been arrested, along with his eleven-year-old son, the Comte de Beaujolais. Later, at the Sainte-Pélagie prison, where Grace is incarcerated, she meets the Duc de Lauzon, who tells her how Philippe's other young son, the Duc de Montpensier, joined him in his prison at Fort Saint-Jean. She is never to lay eyes on Philippe again. She writes, "When he was brought back to Paris to be tried and executed, I was myself a miserable prisoner."

Second Interrogation: La Comité du Salut Public

Released from Sainte-Pélagie in or around June, Grace has to undergo another round of intense questioning, this time by the newly constituted Committee of Public Safety, whose head is the feared Danton. The committee wants to know from her if a letter they've found in the confiscated papers of her ex-lover, Philippe, is written in code. It is from a man named Vernon (whom she calls "old Mr. Vernon") and it discusses "horses and bets and Newmarket, &c., all of which they thought had a double meaning." Grace notes in her *Journal* that "that unfortunate letter was once more produced at the Tribunal on the poor Duke's trial, and was one of the pretexts for condemning him to death."

It was probably an innocent letter, but apparently the racing jargon—unfamiliar to the members of this committee—raised suspicion. Philippe had many friends among the English gentlemen of the turf, among them Richard Vernon and his nephew Henry. Richard Vernon owned the great Thoroughbred known as the Vernon Arabian. (The reference to someone who is "old" in the 1790s makes it more likely it was Richard, who was born before 1735.) But what an interesting idea—a letter coded in racing jargon—that's brilliant, really. Or, it could just have been a letter about horses . . . sometimes a cigar is only a cigar.

The members of the Committee of Public Safety who examined Grace on that day were formidable and terrifying. They were Bertrand Barère de Vieuzac (Grace calls him Barrere—he's later known as Barre de Vieuzac);

Jacques Nicolas Billaud-Varennes; Philippe-Antoine Merlin (she calls him Merlin de Douay); and Robespierre himself. Grace notes that the questioning took place in "the King's fine room in the Pavillon de Flora," and that Robespierre did not sit with the others, but walked in and out of the room. (Barere was imprisoned later for his role in the Terror, reappearing as a Bonapartist spy and coming to an ignominious end. Billaud-Varennes was transported for his crimes to Cayenne, French Guiana, and died in Haiti. Merlin retired peacefully into public life. Robespierre was executed, which effectively ended the Terror and indirectly saved Grace's life.)

Grace's next prison adventure is set off by her maid awakening her at 6 A.M. with the news that she is about to be arrested:

> [She said] "Madame, get up directly. There is no time to lose. You are to be arrested at nine o'clock; and your death-warrant is signed! I had this information last night from your grocer, who is one of the members of the Section, but he wishes you well, and advises you to make your escape. I was to have told you this last night, but I had not the heart to do so; you looked so happy, and I have not seen you so for a long time."

Grace grabs her diamonds (!) "and other things which might be put into my pocket. I did not even wait to tie my petticoats on . . ." and runs, wandering about the fields and new boulevards until she gets help from Royalist acquaintances in getting to her cottage at Meudon. She asks the mayor for advice, saying that if she is arrested in Paris, she will be doomed. The mayor agrees that she is out of the jurisdiction of the Paris Section at Meudon and would now fall under the Versailles Section. But the Paris Section soon shows up, with the Section from Sèvres, and they taunt her with the guillotine for trying to escape:

> They made me get up . . . and searched my things; upbraided me for making my escape, and said, "Ah! Ma mignon, vous nous n'échapperez pas *this* time. You will make a good appearance on the Place Louis Quinze. We will all go and see you make your exit: it will be quite a fine sight."

It's almost like a Marx Brothers farce, as who should come now but the Committee of Versailles:

> They were furious at those of Paris for having dared to come into their department . . . [and] also very angry with those of Sèvres for joining them without the leave of those of Versailles. Both were for having me, and

I anticipated that they were going to fight, had not the gensd'armes *interposed.*"

A mounted soldier is sent to Versailles to settle this territorial issue and the order comes back that Grace is to be delivered up to the Committee of Versailles immediately, "to the prison there called the Recollets." She grouses, "They kept me on my legs the whole day, and they drank and cooked their own dinner in my rooms, and stayed till nine o'clock at night."

SECOND IMPRISONMENT: THE RECOLLETS

She's conveyed in the rain to the Recollets in a cart laid with wet straw; she's allowed to take a few things. When she gets to the prison there is no place prepared for her and she has to stay in the prison guardroom, where there is a bed. She's tired, weepy, and wet through to the skin, but the jailer's wife brings her cold beef, salad, and warm wine, and she dries herself at the fire. The guards assure her that she will be safe and promise they will neither smoke nor allow anyone into the room to bother her. "Accordingly," she writes,

I lay down with my damp clothes on, and I slept till seven o'clock. I really believe that in the whole course of my life I never slept so soundly, though God knows that I was not happy; but complete misery had stupefied me.

Grace finds her new quarters "better than Ste. Pélagie." There are no other prisoners, just felons, and she is placed by herself in a very large room, "room for at least forty beds." Though she says that the room was "offensive and dirty," as it had previously been "occupied by about three or four hundred rabbits," there is "an immensely large fire," where she imagines a good-sized ox could be roasted easily. In one corner there is "a miserable truckle-bed, with two old chairs and a dirty old table . . . [and] a candle and candlestick."

She's interrogated by one of her captors, but is "fortunate enough not to displease him." There's a condemned man next door with the felons, who'll be executed the next day, and his lamentations through the night unnerve her so that she is unable to eat or drink anything, "though," she writes, "as I had money in my pocket I might have anything I pleased to eat or drink." She vows to herself that she will never carry on as this poor unfortunate did.

She learns that she will have a roommate, an elderly man named Dr. Gem, the doctor from the British embassy and uncle of William Huskisson. Gem is eighty years old and has spent half his life in France. He is "much shocked and surprised" to see Grace, for the word was that her fate was soon to be decided. This odd couple in age, personality, and beliefs rubs together tolerably well, but Grace worries about the man's health and manages to get him released and confined into his own home at Meudon.

Dr. Gem weeps at their parting, expecting that they will never see each other again, Grace says, but she adds, "We did both live to meet again, and I saw him the day before he died. . . . When I came out of prison [he] used to walk a mile to see me every day." But that's in the future. For now, the Recollets fills up with ever more Royalist prisoners, and she writes, "We were then deprived of every comfort. . . . The little money which we had was taken from us, and our silver spoon and fork." (She is surprised to get her silverware returned years later, along with her money, thimble, scissors, etc.) The episode with the elderly doctor was questioned by critics of the *Journal;* neither Gem nor Grace, alas, was around to dispute or support her account.

In November 1793, while Grace is at the Recollets, her servant brings her word of the execution of Philippe; the next month, she hears of that of the Duc de Biron, who'd been with her at Sainte-Pélagie. Though Philippe met his death with the steady determination required of an aristocrat, Grace hears that Biron "was much affected at his own situation, and showed some weakness in his last moments." Meeting one's death with dignity was important to these prisoners.

AN UNPLEASANT ARGUMENT AND ITS CONSEQUENCES

Grace is removed from the Recollets after an ill-advised argument with a "deputy named Crasseau [who] came to be the head of the department of Versailles [and] was a great friend of Robespierre." (According to the *Journal,* Crasseau, who cannot be identified, accused Grace of having "too much luxe" and being "very much perfumed," qualities leading to the inescapable conclusion that she "was a royalist." Grace explains later that she always wore a sweet-scented sachet in her corset, and this led Crasseau to think she was using perfume.) When she answers back that she certainly is a

Royalist, "or I should not now be in prison," Crasseau says that she "should go and join [her] friends in the Cimetière de la Magdalene," as that is "the only place for royalists." Grace counters that she often wishes herself there, to be put out of her misery, and he says that he will "take care that [her] wishes should be soon accomplished." Not good! She really is being a smart-mouth, and the Montagnards now running the country have no tolerance for back talk.

Removal to Plessis Prison: A Short Stay in Jail Number Three

The unpleasant exchange leads to her transfer three weeks later to the Plessis prison, "a terrible prison"; the Duchesse de Duras, incarcerated there, had said of it that "one had the impression that considerable attention had been paid to everything that could cause disgust. . . . The smell was awful, the dishes were filled with hairs, . . . pigs trotted in the dining hall during meals." But Grace is in luck. There's no room there for her and so she goes the next day to her last incarceration at the Carmes in the rue Vaugirard.

Grace is transported with cartloads of prisoners from Nantes, in the west of France. Fierce battles were being waged in that region by supporters of the monarchy against the revolutionary army. Of all the death sentences pronounced in France during the Revolution, Paris accounted for only 15 percent; 19 percent were dealt in the southeast and 52 percent in the west, where the worst of the civil war was being waged. Incredible excesses were being committed in Nantes and Lyons with the massacre of men, women, and even children.

Grace notes that on the road from Versailles to Paris

the populace of Sévres pelted us through the bars of our wagon with mud, dead cats, and old shoes. They were very violent, and called us dogs and aristocrats. . . . We met with ill-usage all the way. I regretted having left the Recollets; there at least the air was better than in Paris, and many good, respectable people were there, such as poor farmers and old labourers, who could not make up their minds to the Republic, and who had in their own villages expressed too freely their abhorrence of the new system. Many of these truly good and pious people were executed.

Final Incarceration: The Carmes

The first person she encounters is the popular and handsome young general Louis-Lazare Hoche, who will become involved in a month-long affair with another soon-to-be-famous prisoner at the Carmes, Joséphine de Beauharnais. (Hoche was a hero of the Republic but had been accused of treason in the aftermath of General Dumouriez's defection to the Austrians. He escaped execution, even after he was transferred to the Conciergerie, and went on to greater military successes, pacifying the whole of rebellious western France. He died mysteriously in 1797, supposedly of consumption, or tuberculosis, to which so many former prisoners succumbed, but there were rumors that he'd been poisoned.)

In *The Rose of Martinique*, Joséphine's biographer Andrea Stuart notes that

> *the atmosphere at Les Carmes, like that in the other revolutionary prisons, was a kind of "amorous frenzy." "Everywhere," reported one witness, "the sound of kisses and cries of love resonated around the somber corridors." At Les Carmes this was made possible by the lax security within the prison. There were no bars to separate prisoners; the jailer simply locked the access to the corridors. With minimal effort or a little bribery it was easy to arrange an assignation.*

Grace is surprisingly silent on this aspect of prison life, though she comments that she thought Beauharnais, Josephine's soon-to-be-executed husband, became involved—the implication is, sexually involved—with another man's wife. She finds General Hoche civil and kind, despite his republicanism, and says he was "a very handsome young man, with a very military appearance, very good-humored, and very gallant," and adds, "I believe that he was an excellent officer." She quotes him as saying that he had been "cruelly slandered" but that he hoped he would not have to be imprisoned for long.

Hoche and Grace "became afterwards very good friends," and they found many people at Les Carmes whom they'd known, "such as the Duchess D'Aiguillon, Madame Lamotte, Madame Beauharnais, now Madame Bonaparte, Madame de Custine, . . . Madame de Jarnac, my friend Mrs. Meyler, and Madame de D'Araij." Despite the circumstances, she says, they all "bore their misfortunes with courage and good humor."

She describes Joséphine de Beauharnais as "one of the most accomplished, good-humored women I ever met with," and writes, "The only little disputes we had when together were politics . . . but she was not in the least a Jacobin, for nobody suffered more by the Reign of Terror and by Robespierre than she did." The prisoners sleep eighteen to a room, and her bed is closest to those of Joséphine and Madame de Custine. Those two women, whose husbands are also at the Carmes, will shortly become widows.

The horror of being at the mercy of these radical revolutionaries and their robotic minions, the prison jailers, is reminiscent of the Nazi concentration camps. It's not such a stretch. Consider this scenario described by Grace after Barère de Vieuzac, one of the madmen on the Committee of Public Safety, announces that there is a conspiracy at the Carmes—a plot to set fire to the prison—and it will be punished by the public execution of fifty prisoners. It's something out of a film about the Nazis, like *Schindler's List* or *Sophie's Choice*. As Grace describes it:

> *Fifty were led out of our prison to the scaffold for that same conspiracy. Amongst the number, who were all men, was poor Beauharnais; the Chevalier de Chansenets, brother to him whose life I saved; the young Duke de Charost; the Prince of Salms; a General Ward, an Irishman in the French service, and his servant; and a young Englishman of the name of Harrop, who had been sent to the Irish college for his education, and whose parents had never sent for him home. He had been imprudent, and had abused the Republic in some coffee-house, in consequence of which he was arrested. He was only eighteen years old. [His first name was Charles and he was said to be twenty-two.] Two other young men, in going down the prison-stairs, which were formed like a well, took hold of each other's hands, and leaped down. They were dashed to pieces; but as the number was to be fifty, they took two other people to make up the number.*

Grace remarked that Champcenetz took his leave of her and "showed great courage, more than his poor brother did with me." Grace relates other horror tales of life in the Carmes, saying that

> *the scenes became so dreadful, . . . it was impossible to exist much longer in such a state of constant woe, to see husbands forced from their wives' arms, children torn from their mothers, their screams and fits, people when they could get a knife even cutting their own throats! Such were the horrors going*

on in the Carmes, and we expecting, and indeed being told, that every day might be our last. This was what I believed we all wished, yet the idea of the means was dreadful.

An understatement.

THE LAST DAY IN THE LIFE OF A CONDEMNED PRISONER DURING THE REIGN OF TERROR, PARIS

MORNING

Roll Call

—The names of prisoners to be executed that day, the condemned, were called out at the jail. Only the highest-ranking political prisoners, like the Duc d'Orléans and the Duc de Lauzun, had the privilege—this was in the early days—of an elaborate last meal or of receiving the last rites from a priest.

—At the Carmes, where Grace resided for a time with Joséphine de Beauharnais, the ritual was this, according to Andrea Stuart in *The Rose of Martinique:*

> *It was during . . . periods of recreation that the Revolutionary Tribunal sent its representatives to collect fresh victims. When the Tribunal's cart entered the forecourt, the entire prison was alerted. Once the victim's name had been called, it was the tradition that they should raise an arm, compose their face, make a simple goodbye and depart with the minimum of fuss. Those left behind wished them good luck and waved goodbye with as little display of feeling as they could manage. . . . This grisly ritual took place every day, with the exception of Décadi, the tenth day—the revolutionary calendar's equivalent of Sunday, when the guillotine took a day off.*

Last Toilette

—If not done previously, the condemneds' hair was cut to allow the blade of the guillotine to slice neatly through flesh and bone. Some noblewomen were made to change into rough linen shifts—as was the case with Queen Marie-Antoinette. Notches were cut into the necks of men's shirts. (In England, aristocratic women sympathizing with the plight of their French sisters would have their hair shorn in a very short style, *à la victime;* some would wear thin red silk ribbons around their necks. In France there would later be outlandish balls to which the admission requirement would be a relative who'd fallen victim to the guillotine.)

LATE MORNING AND EARLY AFTERNOON

Conveyance to the Place of Execution

—The prisoners were crowded into plain, uncomfortable wooden carts called tumbrels. At the height of the frenzy, nearly one hundred prisoners a day would be taken to the scaffold; as many as could be loaded at one time were crowded into these carts. Their hands tied behind their backs, they were jostled together as they bounced over the uneven cobblestone streets, on their last journey.

—Jeering *citoyens* and *citoyennes* lined the streets leading to the place of execution. The crowds would scream insults, curse, and throw refuse at the prisoners; this mob behavior was intended to unnerve and frighten them.

—The length of the ride to the scaffold varied, depending on which prison sent the condemned (there were some fifty of them, all over the city), where the guillotine was set up for that day, and the behavior of the crowds. When Robespierre was taken for beheading, there was such a mob along the way that it took the tumbrel a full three hours to get to its destination.

The Executioner

—The last contact the condemned would have with any human being would be with Henri Sanson, also called "Young Sanson," who inherited the job of chief executioner from his father, Charles-Henri Sanson, in 1793. Young Sanson followed in his father's bloody footsteps: Charles-Henri executed King Louis XVI and Henri executed Queen Marie-Antoinette. The executioner had three or four assistants, other family members, who would strap down victims and hold severed heads up to the crowd. In France the role of executioner was a hereditary post, and from 1688 to 1847 it was held by the Sanson family. At the peak of the Terror Young Sanson guillotined three hundred men and women in three days. There was a gruesome exchange between Grace Elliott and Young Sanson (whose name, in her typical way, she spells "Samson") in the fall of 1793 when Grace was in the Recollets prison at Versailles:

> I was much shocked one day on going into the gaoler's room, where we used sometimes to go when we wanted anything. He was sitting at a table with a very handsome, smart young man, drinking wine. The gaoler told me to sit down, and drink a glass too. I did not dare to refuse. The young man then said, "Well, I must be off," and looked at his watch. The gaoler replied, "No; your work will not begin till twelve o'clock." I looked at the man, and the gaoler said to me, "You must make friends with this citizen, it is young Samson, the executioner, and perhaps it may fall to his lot to behead you." I felt quite sick, especially when he took hold of my throat saying, "It will soon be off your neck, it is so long and small. If I am to dispatch you, it will be nothing but a squeeze." . . . I was in hope that I should have remained long at Versailles.

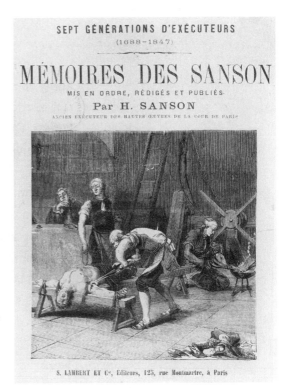

The Sanson family memoirs; in six volumes, published 1862–63. The grisly subtitle is *Seven Generations of Executioners*. (Bridgeman Art Library)

At the Scaffold

—The condemned were taken out and lined up on the stairs leading to the platform. The executions were mostly over swiftly, but some of the condemned addressed the crowd. A certain sangfroid was de rigueur for the occasion, and there were good deaths and bad deaths. The death of Madame du Barry, Louis XV's mistress, was considered a bad death by her peers. She cried and screamed in the tumbrel, asked onlookers to take pity and save her, and struggled with the executioners on the scaffold as she begged for more time. She was pathetic. Grace Elliott wrote that du Barry "showed very little courage on the scaffold. . . . [Her] screams, they told me, frightened and alarmed the mob." Yet though it seems that Grace was a proponent of going stoically to the guillotine, she speculates that "had every one made as much resistance as she did, Robespierre would not have dared to put so many to death."

You are going to hurt me, please don't hurt me, just one more moment, I beg you!" (Said to be the last words of Madame du Barry, King's courtesan)

A little-known procedure was the tying of the condemned's full body length to a sturdy board before his or her neck was placed in the mouth of the guillotine. This restricted movement of the body, especially any uncontrolled kicking of the legs. The moment of death, as everyone knows, releases bodily wastes and other fluids; the voiding of excrement, urine, and semen, as well as menstrual and arterial blood, added to the horrific smells and underfoot slime. The men had trousers to catch solid waste, but their urine would stain, wet the wooden planks, and convey the sharp smell of fear. Women were messier. Underwear was not widely used by them—wearing pantaloons was a nine-teenth-century fashion—and Marie-Antoinette was menstruating when she was brought to the scaffold. The severed heads were held up and shown to the crowd and sometimes displayed on pikes before burial if the victims were well known, or were hated, or had been feared.

Note that in the illustration below, there's no railing around the scaffold platform. The executioner's working conditions were all but impossible during the Reign of Terror, with so many victims and so much blood soaking the platform. Old Sanson and his assistants were easily liable to the old

La Guillotine, with her victims being bundled out of the tumbrel and up the stairs to the scaffold, where they were bound to a board that held them immobile. The autumn of 1793 saw a horrific staged witch hunt. This image is of Marie-Antoinette's execution. (Bridgeman Art Library)

slip-and-fall. The blood pooled into a pond underneath the scaffold, a horrendous sight that also caused a disgusting stench, and actual rivers of blood ran down the cobblestone streets. In 1792, Old Sanson saw his son Gabriel tumble to the ground and sustain fatal injuries after skidding on the bloody scaffold. After this accident, railings were put up around the scaffold to safeguard the executioners.

Late Afternoon / Dusk

The Guillotine Moves On

—Originally meant to be stationed permanently at the place du Carrousel in the Tuileries Gardens, the machine of execution was afterwards disassembled and reassembled and taken from place to place. The crowds, the stench, the noise—not to mention the horror—brought complaints from area residents.

Dusk / Nightfall

Burial

— The heads and bodies were put into a deep pit with the head between the legs, and the remains were covered with quicklime. The heads of certain famous individuals were sent first to young Marie Grosholtz (later to be known as Madame Tussaud) for wax impressions to be made. The site in Paris where the Chapelle Expiatoire now stands marks the mass pit that held the bodies of more than three thousand victims.

Release!

Was the Carmes the last prison inhabited by Grace Elliott? There was talk that she was sent to the Conciergerie when her hair was cut for her imminent execution, but if she was released with Joséphine Beauharnais, it was from the Carmes. Robespierre was arrested by his own people on July 27, 1794, when he'd encouraged the execution of more than seventeen thousand individuals he called "enemies of the Revolution." Incredibly, enough was finally enough, this excess sickening even those in charge of the ongoing

A Brief History of the French Killing Machine, the Guillotine

It was called "the national razor," "the hungry lady," "the she-wolf," "Madame Guillotine," "Louisette" or "Louison" (after its promoter, Dr. Antoine Louis, secretary of the Academy of Surgery), and "the widow."

Dr. Louis was looking for a quick, painless, decapitation machine; a version of a machine like this was already in use in Europe and the Near East. His design was perfected by a German piano maker named Tobias Schmidt and it was first tested on animals and corpses. It consisted of two fourteen-foot uprights joined by a crossbar, whose grooved internal edges were greased with tallow; the weighted blade was either straight or curved like an axe. The system was operated via a rope and pulley, while the whole construction was mounted on a high platform. Metal trays to collect blood were added, a blade angled at 45 degrees was substituted for the original cutting piece, and the high platform was replaced by a standard scaffold.

Dr. Joseph-Ignace Guillotin (1738–1814), whose name became linked to this infamous machine as Dr. Louis's disappeared, was actually part of a reform movement that was in favor of completely banishing the death penalty in France. The guillotine, he thought, would be a compromise on the way to the eventual abolition of capital punishment, as it treated all the condemned equally, regardless of wealth, status, age, or sex, and as such embodied that second ideal of the French Revolution, equality. Decapitation had previously been a special, respectful means of execution reserved for the rich and the powerful. (Dr. Guillotin had also thought that the carrying out of any death penalty should be a private event, not one meant for public voyeurism and spectacle.)

Simon Schama, in *Citizens: A Chronicle of the French Revolution* (1990) writes that members of the viewing public were initially turned off by the guillotine; they preferred the drama attached to a hanging:

> *For crowds accustomed to the prolonged and emotionally rich ritual of penitential processions, loud public confession, the climactic jump of the body on the gibbet, the exposure of the hanging remains, even in some rare cases the prolonged ordeal of breaking on the wheel, the machine was a distinct disappointment. It was too expeditious. A swish, a thud; sometimes not even a display of the head; the executioner reduced to a low-grade mechanic like some flunkey pulling a bell rope.*

The bloody mass spectacle to come was soon to change their minds.

Some Facts about the Guillotine

- Total weight: 1,270 pounds
- Weight of blade (with attached ballast): 88.2 pounds
- Height of posts: 14 feet
- Blade drop: 88 inches
- Rate of speed of falling blades: 21 feet per second
- Actual beheading time: 2/100 of a second

The first execution by guillotine in France was on April 25, 1792, and the last on September 10, 1977. One reason for the guillotine's retirement from use—aside from the global feeling that the state should not engage in murder—was that people believed that the victims might live on for several seconds after their heads were severed and it was thus an inhumane punishment. When the chemist Lavoisier was to be executed, he arranged for a friend to count how many times his eyes blinked after his head was severed. It was said to be eleven.

bloodbath. Robespierre escaped and, cornered, put up a fight; he was shot in the jaw and recaptured. The next day, July 28, Maximilien Robespierre, called "the Incorruptible," was guillotined in front of a cheering mob. Thus endeth the most deplorable chapter in French history.

Robespierre's arrest and execution brought about the release of many Royalist prisoners, among them Grace Elliott. As Richard Bentley puts it in his epilogue to Grace's *Journal:*

> *Madame Beauharnais, . . . Madame de Fontenaye, . . . [and Grace] very narrowly escaped destruction, for they were ordered for execution, and their locks shorn, on the very day that France was delivered by Providence from the monster Robespierre.*

In *The Rose of Martinique,* Andrea Stuart says that Joséphine de Beauharnais was released ten days after Robespierre's execution, on August 6, 1794, "amongst the first batch of prisoners to be released from Les Carmes." Grace may have been among that group with Joséphine, as may have been her friend Mrs. Meyler, although she would have been imprisoned less than the eighteen months she claimed.

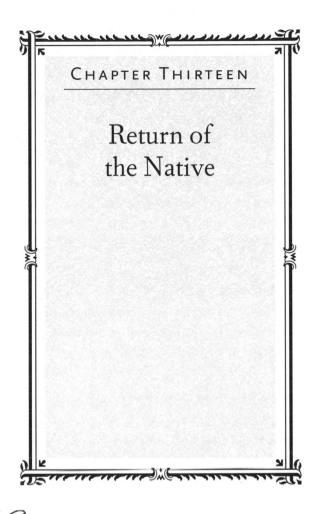

CHAPTER THIRTEEN

Return of the Native

$\mathcal{W}$hen did Grace Elliott return to England? The few sources indicate that she may have turned up in England circa 1802, during the period known as the Peace of Amiens, but one newspaper report has her arriving in London in 1798 with a "certain diplomatic agent," who is unidentified. That agent may have been one Henry Swinburne (1743–1803), a wealthy man from Bristol, whose hobby was writing about his extensive travels on the Continent, and who'd been sent to Paris in 1796 to negotiate an exchange of prisoners. Grace may have traveled to England, gone back to France, and returned again to England, during the period in question, 1798–1801.

Swinburne was recalled to England in December 1798 when difficulties arose with the escape of Sir William Sidney Smith from the Temple prison, and it appears that Grace hooked up with him to return home. (An interesting sidelight is that there may have been a connection between Swinburne and the British secret service. If so, it is of even more interest that he perhaps got together with Grace—a possible agent for the secret service herself—and was the one who took her back to England.)

What other proof is there to support this return in 1798? There's a letter from Grace dated only February 14 (no year) to Admiral John Payne, private secretary to the Prince of Wales, in the collection of King George IV's papers at Windsor Castle that may substantiate this claim. The registrar at the Royal Archives in Windsor, Pamela Clark, refers to this document as "from Mrs. Elliott" and notes that "the watermark on the paper is 1798." The letter reads:

> *Mrs. Elliot presents her Compliments to Admiral Payne and she will take it as a very great favor if he will inform her to whom she is to apply for the payment of the last quarter of her annuity from His Royal Highness The Prince of Wales, as Admiral Payne told Lord Melbourne when he waited on the Admiral at her request that it would be pay'd early in January and she has heard nothing more about it, she is very sorry indeed to be so troublesome to Admiral Payne but she is on the eve of leaving England, and very much [unintelligible—distressed? pressed?] for Money.*
>
> *Mrs. Elliot had some hopes of seeing the Admiral before her departure and if it was possible she wou'd be extremely obliged to him for five Minutes conversation with him before she goes. She hopes he will be kind enough to send her an answer to this note as soon as possible. Mrs. E. was very sorry to hear that Admiral Payne has been unwell.*
>
> *Portman Street*
> *No. 3*
> *Febr. the 14th*

Since Grace was resident at Brompton Park House, the return address of her letter—3 Portman Street—is puzzling. A likely explanation is that she was using the mailing address of the offices of her solicitors, the firm of Morland Ransom. The street is a short one right around the corner from Portman Square, and that address was recently found to be a construction site for a high-rise office building. Across an alley, there's a row of small Georgian houses—numbers 7 to 11—probably from the same era as the group that contained number 3, or so it seems from an old map.

Along with this letter from Grace is another from Lord Cholomondeley, also in the possession of the Royal Archives, dated September 5, 1800, and sent from his residence at 94 Piccadilly to the Prince of Wales:

> *Piccadilly, Sept. 5, 1800*
>
> *Sir:*
>
> *I am persuaded your Royal Highness must recollect, that you were graciously pleased to promise that Mrs. Elliott when she returned to Paris, should receive an annuity of Three Hundred Pounds a Year. It was paid quarterly from that Time when I had the Honor of being in your Royal Highness' Family [not family per se, but referring to a servant to the Royals] untill the Fifth of January last.*
>
> *I conceive it would be disrespectful to your Royal Highness if I was not to enclose a Letter from the Banker at Paris, by which it appears that he has paid her at His own [unintelligible—Person? Pocket?] the two last Quarters, in Consequence of your Royal Highness' Promise to Mrs. Elliot. I have the Honor to be*
>
> *Sir*
>
> > *Your Royal Highness'*
> > *Most Obedient*
> > *Humble Servant*
> > *Cholmondeley*

It appears from these two letters that Grace's letter to Admiral Payne, along with the personal entreaty from Lord Melbourne on her behalf, bore no fruit. Her banker in Paris, anticipating (hoping?) funds would be forthcoming, had been paying her out of his own pocket for two quarters, according to the letter from Lord Cholmondeley directly to his friend the Prince. This letter from Cholmondeley brings results. (The letter from Grace is similar to that sent by her rival Mary Robinson to the Prince's previous secretary, Colonel Hotham, asking for her annuity payment in 1785, as cited in Paula Byrne's biography of Robinson, *Perdita* (2004).

When did the payments begin, and when did they end? Mistresses who'd

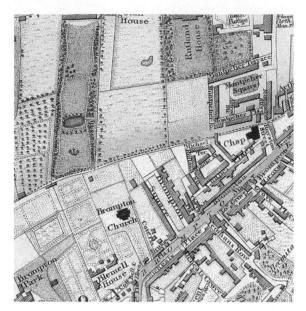

This is from the *Greenwood Map of London*, 2nd edition, 1830. It shows Brompton Park in the lower left-hand corner. Grace was said to be living in Brompton Park House circa 1798 and again after 1800 on her second return to London. The building was demolished in 1899 to make way for the Victoria & Albert Museum and the area is now known as South Kensington. Between the time of this map and the turn of the nineteenth century, this was an undeveloped leafy suburb of London between Knightsbridge and Kensington, surrounded by parks and nursery gardens, with occasional cottages and inns between the gardens and a few large houses set into their own grounds. The nursery gardens included Harrison & Bristow, Brompton Park, and a small plot between Caroline Place and Green Lane. Many of these streets are no longer there, as the entire area was redeveloped after the Great Exhibition of 1851. The Brompton Church—shown to the right of Brompton Park—was not built until 1826. Grace also lived on Micheal's Place, just below Brompton Road, directly south of Brompton Square and very close to Brompton Park House, and with a Mrs. Naylor in Prospect Row. One of the large houses set into their own grounds was Brompton Park House, which in 1784 had been converted into three separate dwellings. Grace Elliott lived in the middle of the three houses; her friend Lady Seymour Dorothy Fleming (who had been the notorious Lady Worsley) and her second husband lived in the westernmost house, known as Fleming Villa; and a gentleman named Charles Greenwood, who was a close friend of the royal dukes, lived in the easternmost house. (Lady Fleming's father had owned extensive nursery properties in the area.) With these two women in residence, it was no doubt a happening spot. (Mark Annon, Bath Spa University College, http://users.bathspa.ac.uk/greenwood/map_g2u.html)

borne children said to be the Prince's usually began to receive their annuities upon the birth of said children. This suggests that Grace Elliott might have been receiving income from the Prince since 1782, when her daughter, Georgiana, was born and when Lord Cholmondeley, as he writes, "had the Honor of being in your Royal Highness' Family." Miss Clark, however, stated the following to the author:

> *The first payment of the annuity is recorded in a list of the Prince's annuities and pensions under warrant dated 16 October 1800 and is for the quarter ending 5 April 1800. . . . We do have a list of the annuities paid in the previous quarter, ending 5 January 1800, and Grace's name is not given there, so I think this must be the very first payment made to her. The last payment is recorded in*

a list of pensions paid in the year ending 5 January 1824 and records that she is deceased and that £150 was paid for the first year up to 5 July 1823. I am afraid that no envelope has survived for Grace's letter, so all I can tell you is that the watermark on the paper is 1798.

In another letter from Miss Clark, it is noted that

there might have been earlier payments—our set of accounts for the Prince is not complete. . . . Receipts [were] signed on Mrs. Elliott's behalf by an employee of Messrs. Morland Ransome.

No conclusions can be drawn from these records other than Grace Elliott began to receive her £300 annuity—paid in quarters to her Paris bank—in 1800, and that the payments continued until her death in May 1823, when only a half year of the annuity was doled out. It makes sense that Grace might have been receiving monies from the Prince before the Revolution and that the wartime conditions in France made it impossible for her to receive the annuity, so it was stopped until she surfaced and requested it again. People had not heard from her, according to the newspapers, and may have believed she was dead, a victim of the Terror. The registrar at the Royal Archives, Miss Clark, admits that some records of the Prince's are lacking.

The scenario, then, seems to be that Grace somehow did make it back to London in 1798, but left shortly after petitioning the Prince's private secretary for the resumption of her annuity. It could have been a condition of the annuity's reinstatement (or commencement) that Grace return to France. Note that Lord Cholmondeley is reminding the Prince that Grace kept her part of the bargain—if one was indeed made—to return to Paris. This fits in with the statement in an article that appeared in the *Morning Herald* in March 1798 that

Mrs. E——tt . . . is said to have since received a settlement of four or five hundred a year from a young Gentleman of high rank, on the express condition that she shall for the future reside out of the kingdom. This establishment has taken place in consequence of an amorous attachment that formerly subsisted between them, and which the Gentleman, being now married, is desirous of concealing from his amiable spouse.

The implication in the newspaper article is that it's Lord Cholmondeley who is providing the annuity, not the Prince. This may not, however, be contradictory. Multiple annuities were not uncommon; Mary Robinson was col-

Grace's Salary and Prospects for Future Income

How much did Grace Elliott collect from the Prince for those hours of bliss? If only 22 1/2 years (1800 to mid-1823) at £300 per year: £6,750 (today £405,000/$810,000). Not bad compensation. If the payments were from 1782, double the above amounts: well over $1.5 million is excellent. Add to this the £200 annually from Dr. Eliot, multiplied by forty-seven years (dating it from 1776, her divorce); and possibly £400–£500 more from Lord Cholmondeley, multiplied by twenty-five years (dating this from 1798), and she's not exactly destitute, though

she is living at a level much below what she was used to in her toastiest days on the town.

The truth is that Grace no longer has the fabulously wealthy Duc d'Orléans to pay her bills—and unfortunately he died before he could set her up better financially. She had to sell her *hôtel particulier* on the rue de Miromesnil after she got out of prison in 1794 and has had to adjust to a lower standard of living. She's past forty-five years of age, her prime long gone by eighteenth-century standards.

lecting from Lord Malden and the Prince of Wales at the same time. Grace could have come back to negotiate collecting annuities from Lord Cholmondeley as well as from the Prince, as in the modern-day scenario of the title character played by Gina Lollobrigida in the 1968 film *Buona Sera, Mrs. Campbell* who's getting support payments from three ex-GIs, each of whom thinks he is the father of her child. There's nothing new under the sun.

A CHILD OF THE MIST: GEORGIANA ELLIOTT, THE GIRL WHO MIGHT HAVE BEEN QUEEN OF ENGLAND

In the second decade of the nineteenth century, according to Christopher Hibbert in *Queen Victoria*, it was reckoned that King George III had at least fifty-six illegitimate grandchildren, or, as they were called, "children of the mist." Georgiana Augusta Frederica Elliott (1782–1813), had been one of them. If her mother, Grace Elliott, had been the legal wife of George, Prince of Wales, when the girl was born, she might one day have had a shot at becoming queen of England, but as only one of Prinny's many alleged natural children, she did not stand a chance.

The children supposedly fathered by George, Prince of Wales, can be

A portrait of Maria Fitzherbert by Sir Joshua Reynolds. (National Portrait Gallery, London)

grouped as follows: those he apparently acknowledged, those he somewhat acknowledged, those he did not acknowledge at all, and those he "adopted" with his secret wife, Maria Fitzherbert. (In the late Georgian era adoption was an informal process, not at all as we know it today; it was not codified until the second half of the nineteenth century.) This last group, the adoptees, thought by many to be his natural children with the Roman Catholic widow Mrs. Fitzherbert, were all girls: Marianne Smythe (d. 1859); Mary Seymour (1798–1848), known variously as Minny, Minnie, or Minney); and one or two others about whom little is known.

Marianne was said to have been the natural daughter of Jack Smythe, Maria Fitzherbert's brother, who'd died unmarried, and thus a blood relation only of Mrs. Fitzherbert's. There's overwhelming proof, however, that Minney was never the natural child of the Prince of Wales and Mrs. Fitzherbert. She was the youngest child of Admiral Lord Hugh Seymour and his wife, Lady Anne Horatia Waldegrave, who'd apparently placed the child into the safekeeping of Mrs. Fitzherbert for a short time when they'd left the country. Unfortunately, both parents died suddenly, and within a month of each other.

An ugly legal battle with Minney's guardians threatened, but the Prince intervened with all his considerable power, and—while the named guardian was, on paper, the Marquess of Hertford (head of the Seymour family)—the girl remained in Mrs. Fitzherbert's care. When Minney turned twenty-one she received a huge payment of £10,000 plus interest from King George IV. In 1825, Minney married the Colonel Right Honourable George Lionel Dawson-Damer (1788–1856), a younger son of the Earl of Portarlington.

The dashing cavalry officer was a Regency dandy, part of Beau Brummell's clique at White's.

Mrs. Fitzherbert and King George IV vehemently opposed the match. According to her biographer Shane Leslie, Mrs. Fitzherbert scorned Dawson-Damer as "a penniless soldier." The King and Mrs. Fitzherbert couldn't prevent the marriage, but they arranged it so that Minney's husband was cut out of her settlement, which had grown to £20,000 with accumulated interest.

There were rumors about a third girl about whom very little is known, and, in 1839, there was a story about an odd claimant named Mrs. Sophia Elizabeth Guelph Sims. This woman sought to petition the Lord Mayor of London for money she said was owed her, as she was born the daughter of Mrs. Fitzherbert and the Prince of Wales. Her argument was that Mrs. Fitzherbert had been unaware of her existence because the midwife had lied and told her that the baby she'd just delivered was stillborn. Her claims were summarily dismissed.

According to M. J. Levy, in *The Mistresses of King George IV* (1996), Mrs. Fitzherbert never denied having had children by the Prince. A 1991 book, *Mrs. Fitzherbert and Sons*, by Philippa and Jim Foord-Kelcey, relates the oral

THREE WEEKS AFTER MARRIAGE.

tradition in the Payne family that the Paynes were descendants of King George IV. The case remains open as to whether or not the Catholic widow and the Prince ever had biological children. (Mrs. Fitzherbert, twice a widow, had had no children with either of her previous husbands; she may have been sterile.)

As to the group of putative children apparently acknowledged by the King, there are a number of cases, perhaps the most interesting being that of George Seymour Crole (sometimes spelled Crowe), who's actually listed in *The Complete Peerage* as King George IV's illegitimate son. Crole's mother was one Elizabeth Fox, a former mistress of Lord Egremont: She was also known as Mrs. Crole.

George Seymour Crole was born on August 23, 1799, and was educated at the Royal Military College at Sandhurst. He had a fairly successful career as a soldier in India. (Ironically, as a young man King George IV had yearned for the military life.) Crole was an ensign in the twenty-first Dragoons, then a lieutenant, and subsequently aide-de-camp to the governor of Bengal. From there he made captain of the Forty-first Foot, advancing to major in that division. He died unmarried in Chatham on June 13, 1863, and was buried in Highgate Cemetery. He was not thought to have had children.

Crole received substantial amounts of money from the King, as did his mother. Mrs. Crole was awarded an annuity of £500 on the boy's birth; the annuity stopped in 1823, which was probably when she died. In 1831 George Seymour Crole received a bequest of £10,000 from King George IV's will, somewhat less than the £30,000 the King had mentioned he might leave him in a discussion with Lord Eldon in 1823.

King George IV is thought to have acknowledged another son, William Francis, born in 1806 to an adventuress known as Mrs. Davies. William Francis was educated at a London school in Parsons Green, and Mrs. Davies received an annuity of £400 from the King. At her death in 1817 that

FACING PAGE: Etching by J. Nunn, Queen Street, April 10, 1786. The print shows a man offering portraits of "new passions" to Prinny. The Prince is seated on a sofa beneath paintings of "The Perdita" and "The Armstead." The salesman says, "The originals have been carefully tried, and are in fine order for your H——s, as for Fitz—she must put up with my Comfits, for you know, your H——s, you may have twenty such wives." George holds the portraits of these "new beauties" and a "list of com[. . .]able wives widows and crackt maids." On the sofa is an open copy of *"Uncle Morgan's Frolics,* second edition," while a sheet stating "variety is charming" has fallen to the floor. Mrs. Fitzherbert is castigating her new husband, exclaiming, "Confusion! have I been [. . .] up with a mock-marriage. . . ." At her feet is the title page of a booklet, "Who's the Dupe." Mrs. Fitzherbert wouldn't sleep with the Prince outside of marriage. (Library of Congress)

Miniature of Princess Charlotte as a child by Abraham Daniel, 1798–1799. (National Portrait Gallery, London)

sum was halved to a £200 annuity for the boy. In 1820 there were doubts raised about William Francis's parentage, and, three years later, the annuity was discontinued.

Putative children mentioned but unacknowledged included tales of a James Ord, who left England for America; a boy born in 1793 in Lille, France; another boy, who was adopted by Sir James Harris; a daughter by a Weymouth woman, Mrs. Mary Lewis; and Georgiana Elliott. Georgiana fell between the cracks of King George IV's acknowledged and unacknowledged children. He never said she wasn't his, but he never said she was, either. This coyness is reminiscent of Maria Fitzherbert, who would never put down on paper whether she did or did not have children with her secret husband, the Prince.

Will anyone ever know just how many children King George IV fathered? It's unlikely, but he did instruct the Privy Purse to pay out a good number of annuities to former mistresses and their offspring. As we have seen, Grace Elliott was paid such monies from the Privy Purse from 1800 until her death in 1823. (The book is kept at Windsor Castle and is a matter of public record.) There is no official record showing that Georgiana Elliott (or Seymour, as she later called herself) received any money or annuity from the King.

In contrast to all these wannabe children, George IV's only recognized legitimate daughter was Princess Charlotte of Wales (1796–1817). She was the issue of his disastrous marriage to the German princess Caroline of Brunswick. Princess Charlotte most definitely would have been queen of England—if she had lived.

Maternal Deaths in Childbirth and Infant Mortality in the Georgian Era

Estimates of maternal mortality in the late eighteenth century ranged from five to twenty-nine deaths per one thousand women, according "Deaths in Childbed from the Eighteenth Century to 1935," an article published in 1986, by Irvine Loudon. In 1779–1788, records kept by hospitals in London showed deaths of mothers in childbirth to be one in sixty. Alarming mortality figures involved children under five. Between 1730 and 1749, records show that three out of four baptized children died. In her book *History's Midwives* (2003), Joan E. Grundy, herself a nurse-midwife, writes, "With limited knowledge of anatomy and physiology, the structure and function of the human body, and no knowledge at all of bacteriology and anaesthesia, it is perhaps surprising that more mothers did not die in childbirth."

Georgiana's forthcoming birth was heralded in the scurrilous press of the day and her mother, Grace Dalrymple Elliott, was targeted and taunted by cruel and anonymous gossip columnists. It was in January *1782* that the pregnancy became common knowledge. Those who believed themselves to be in the know reckoned that the Prince's bastard would be born in April.

On March 30, the Saturday before Easter Sunday of *1782*, Grace Elliott gave birth to a daughter, two days before the know-it-alls had predicted. The temperature that Holy Saturday in March was 48 degrees Farenheit and the wind was from the southwest. A mild rain fell and the general forecast was fair, according to *The Gentleman's Magazine* of April *1783*.

She was apparently a healthy infant, as there was no rush to baptize her until four months later, and, too, mothers were customarily given a long time to recover from childbirth. The secretive ceremony took place at fashionable St. Marylebone Church, on London's Marylebone Road.

Charlotte and Georgiana—an almost-queen and the perhaps-daughter of a king—were women who suffered the same fate, that of dying while still very young. Princess Charlotte died giving birth to a stillborn child when barely twenty-one, and Georgiana—ten years older than the Princess at her demise—might well have shared the same fate as her possible half sister, dying in childbed. Deaths of young women in childbirth were common in the eighteenth and early nineteenth centuries. Mortality rates for children were also very high. Surviving childbirth was the first hurdle; surviving past the first five years of life was an even greater one.

July 30, 1782, the day of Georgiana's christening, a midsummer day, was

King George IV, dark-haired in middle-age, in a portrait by Sir
Thomas Lawrence. (National Portrait Gallery, London)

recorded by the June 1783 *The Gentleman's
Magazine* as only slightly warmer than the day
of her birth. (Ah, English weather!) It was 54
degrees Fahrenheit, a chilly wind blew from the
north, and there were clouds in the sky.

The parish register—"Baptisms in the Year
of our Lord 1782 . . . July"—for July 30
recorded the baptism of "Georgina Augusta
Frederica Elliott, Daughter of His Royal Highness George Prince of Wales & Grace Elliott
30th March."

According to Richard Bentley's prologue in
Grace's *Journal,* only "Lord Cholmondeley and one or two other persons"
were present at the ceremony. Bentley states unequivocally a few sentences
prior to this that Georgiana was "the result of [the] intimate connexion" between the Prince and Mrs. Elliott.

Illegitimacy was becoming more the norm in the latter part of the Georgian era, as the Economic History Society notes on its Web site:

> *Illegitimacy rose, accounting for about 2% of all births at the beginning of
> the 18th century and 6% at the end. There was a very significant increase in
> conceptions occurring outside marriage which resulted either in illegitimate
> births or in shot-gun weddings.*

The pretty child with the solemn face was painted by the eminent portraitist and royal academician Sir Joshua Reynolds in 1784, when she would
have been about two years old. Reynolds was the preeminent painter of children in his time; little Georgiana was painted by the best, as befit her purported lineage. This small but perfect painting—once belonging to the
Marquess of Cholmondeley, according to Richard Bentley—is now owned
by the Metropolitan Museum of Art but is not often on display.

Miniature of Georgiana at age 10. Artist either Andrew Plimer or Samuel Shelley. (Private collection)

What became of this pretty child, this possible royal bastard? What sort of life did she have, growing up in the late Georgian/early Regency period, the offspring of a demimondaine mother and an aristo-cratic, possibly royal father?

Although the Prince of Wales—who became Prince Regent in 1811 and King George IV upon the death of his father in 1820—as noted previously, never publicly acknowledged Georgiana as his daughter, he seems never to have made a public state-ment that she wasn't his child, despite the comment he supposedly made upon being shown the baby that he would have to be convinced that black was white before he could be con-vinced she was his.

That story goes on to say that Grace, in desperation, bleached Geor-giana's eyebrows in order to convince the Prince of his paternity. In the Reynolds portrait, however, the child's brows are dark brown, as is her hair. It's hard to believe, too, that any loving mother would use a dangerous sub-stance like bleach on a child's eyebrows.

Georgiana grew up at Cholmondeley Castle (formerly Cholmondeley Hall), near Malpas, Chester; at the Cholmondeley town house at 94 Pic-cadilly (across from Green Park and a stone's throw from Buckingham Palace); and later at Houghton Hall, Norfolk, when that prized Palladian-style property came into the hands of the Cholmondeleys from Horace Wal-pole. There were two other children besides Lord Cholmondeley's legitimate offspring brought up with Georgiana Elliott in that household, Susan Priscilla Bertie and Harriet Cholmondeley.

Susan Priscilla's father had been a good friend of Lord Cholmondeley's, and Cholmondeley had married her aunt, Ancaster's sister Charlotte (her

Just How Close Was the Royal Family to the Cholmondeleys?

They were very close, indeed, *thisclose*, close enough for the young ladies in both families to go visiting together. Just how close is illustrated by the account of the tragic death of Lord Cholmondeley's first cousin, Mary Henrietta, the eldest of the three daughters of his late uncle, the Reverend Robert Cholmondeley. It was reported for several days in the *Times*; this is the summary of the incident that appeared in the newspaper on October 6, 1806:

There are but few particulars to add to those we have already stated, relative to the fatal accident which happened at Leatherhead on Thursday last. Her Royal Highness [Princess Charlotte of Wales, the future King George IV's daughter and heir to the throne] accompanied by Lady Sheffield and Miss Cholmondeley, left Blackheath about eleven o'clock that day, in a barouche and four, driven by her own servants. [A barouche was a type of open carriage, a four-wheeler with a fold-up hood at the back, two inside seats that faced each other, and a seat on the outside for the driver. It was by far the fanciest carriage of the early nineteenth century.] On their arrival at Sutton, they took post-horses, and were driven by the post-boys belonging to the Cock Inn. Her Royal Highness's horses and servants were left to refresh, in order to take her home that evening. Her Royal Highness proceeded to Leatherhead, when, on turning a sharp corner to get into the road which leads to Norbury Park, the carriage was, according to the coachman's expression, "swung off her legs," directly opposite to a large tree, against which Miss Cholmondeley was thrown with such violence, as to be killed on the spot. She was sitting on the front seat of the barouche alone. Her Royal Highness and Lady Sheffield occupied the back-seat, and were thrown out together. The Princess received a very trifling bruise on the shoulder, and a small cut on the upper part of her nose; one of her hands was also slightly wounded, and was saved by her glove, which was cut through. Her Royal Highness and Lady Sheffield went into the Swan Inn, at Leatherhead. Sir Lucas Pepys, who lives in that neighbourhood, and had not left Leatherhead, where he had been to visit a patient . . . was immediately followed, and brought back; and a servant was sent to Mr. Locke's, with an account of the accident. Mrs. Locke arrived in her carriage with all possible expedition, and conducted

given Christian name was Georgina Charlotte, but she preferred Charlotte), on April 25, 1791. Charlotte was a black-haired beauty, known among the gallants of the day by the nickname "Black Bess," and as elevated from Georgiana's mother in rank and status as it was possible to be.

MARRIED

Yesterday afternoon, by Special licence, the Right Hon. Earl Cholmondeley, to Lady Charlotte Bertie, second daughter to the Dowager Duchess of

the Princess to Norbury Park, where Sir Lucas Pepys attended her Royal Highness, and, as no surgeon was at hand, bled her himself. On the following day, the Princess returned to Blackheath. The answer to numerous enquiries all day yesterday was, that her Royal Highness was very well; Lady Sheffield was also very well.

A Coroner's Inquest was held on Saturday, at the Swan Inn, Leatherhead, on the body of Miss Cholmondeley: it sat a short time to examine the servants who saw the accident. The Jury returned a verdict—

Accidental Death. Amongst the numerous enquiries at Blackheath yesterday, was the Lord Mayor of London. Miss Cholmondeley was the daughter of the late Hon. and Rev. Robert Cholmondeley, Rector of Hartingford-Bury, and St. Andrew's, Hertford, who was son of the third Earl of Cholmondeley, and uncle to the present Earl. . . . Her mother is living, and resides in Jermyn-street.

A barouche. (Bridgeman Art Library)

*Ancaster. The ceremony was performed at the Duchess's house in Berkeley-square, by the Rev. Mr. Bowier, of Lincoln. (*Times, *April 26, 1791)*

It was a privileged existence, in the very best English aristocratic tradition, and Georgiana was very well protected by this family. Richard Bentley says in his prologue to Grace's *Journal:*

Her little daughter was left in charge of Lord and Lady Cholmondeley, but was occasionally permitted to visit her mother at Paris. On those occasions she

Queen Marie-Antoinette of France, "as amiable and good a princess as ever lived." Portrait by Élisabeth Vigée-Lebrun. (Bridgeman Art Library)

was always accompanied by a nurse and a footman of Lord Cholmondeley's; but she never resided any length of time with her mother.

There's a sweet anecdote in the *Journal* concerning the fondness of Queen Marie-Antoinette for Georgiana:

I used frequently to meet her Majesty when I was driving my curricle. Of course I showed her every mark of respect in my power, at which she expressed herself much pleased. Indeed she had the condescension to send one of her equerries, M. de Chatiers, after me, to ask me how my daughter was, as her Majesty had been good enough to think her a beautiful child, and to take great notice of her when she was about three years old [this would have been around 1785–1786], at St. Cloud, and had sent the Duke de Liancourt for her, and kept her upon her knee all the time their Majesties were at dinner. From that moment I always felt myself obliged to the Queen for her kindness to my child.

Very little is known of Georgiana as she grew to adulthood, save the occasional anecdote that's survived in a few contemporary journals and letters. Georgiana's quiet life was not fodder for the press, but a picture emerges of a beautiful and accomplished young woman well liked by her peers. This charming entry from the diary of her cousin Frances, Lady Shelley, written in 1803, gives an interesting insight into Georgiana and into Cholmondeley family life as well:

I used to go almost daily to Cholmondeley House [94 Piccadilly]. . . . We used to go to Fragard's riding school together. . . . But to return to Houghton. Georgiana Seymour and Harriet Cholmondeley were the bright stars in that firmament. The latter was the daughter of Lord Cholmondeley, and after-

wards married the great parti [a parti is a highly eligible bachelor] of the day, Mr. Lambton. She and Priscilla [Susan Priscilla Bertie, six years older than Georgiana], afterwards Lady Tarleton [she married Banastre Tarleton, ex-lover of Mary Robinson], were adopted daughters of the Cholmondeleys, and were brought up with Lady Cholmondeley's own children. They certainly made Houghton the pleasantest house I ever stayed at. Its society was that of an old French château, where every lady laid out her best accomplishments to please the assembled guests . . . [who] submitted to old Cholmondeley's atrocious wines in order to enjoy the agreements of Houghton.

I saw a great deal of the beautiful Georgiana Seymour here, and in London. She was always wishing to have me as a companion, and as we lived close to the corner of Down Street and Piccadilly, I was often at Cholmondeley House, which was afterwards the residence of the Duke of Cambridge. . . . The parentage of this beautiful girl was claimed both by the Prince of Wales, and by Lord Cholmondeley (who were equally devoted to her).

This is not only charming, it is a telling description that confirms the closeness of the Cholmondeleys and all of their children—natural as well as legitimate (the Cholmondeleys had three legitimate children, two boys and a girl). It also gives insight into the pleasing personality of Georgiana Seymour, who seems to have been a popular as well as a lovely girl. Note, too, that well into the early nineteenth century there were still questions as to who her father actually was.

If Grace Elliott did come back to England in 1798, one has to imagine how awkward and embarrassing it must have been to the sensitive teenager to have her notorious demirep mother show up on the doorstep, disrupting a cosy family circle. For disruption it surely had to be, as Georgiana was now at a vulnerable age: sixteen. Could the timing have been worse? Though no details come down to us of this family reunion, Grace's arrival had to impact on her daughter's chances of marrying well, and marrying well was what the ton was all about.

Sixteen was a perfectly marriageable age for the period. Georgiana may not yet have been presented at Court, but she no doubt attended balls and socialized within the innermost circles of the ton. The telling action at this time is that Georgiana dropped her mother's surname of Elliott for Seymour.

There appears to have been a "Seymour" precedent among those reputed to be offspring of the Prince of Wales, and Georgiana's taking it could be significant. Or it could just be that this was the surname of some Cholmondeley relatives with whom Georgiana was very well acquainted.

The promise of beauty Georgiana showed as a young child had blossomed into fine good looks, from the evidence of surviving portrait miniatures by Andrew Plimer and Anne Mee in the collections of the Duke of Portland and Windsor Castle, so it was not unlikely that she was already receiving attention from young bucks and that this attention brought good offers of marriage. It would have been unusual if it had not been so. Her beauty was a lure, and surely Lord Cholmondeley—if not the Prince of Wales himself—was prepared to provide a reasonably adequate dowry.

Meanwhile, during this eventful year of 1798, Georgiana's sixteenth year, her childhood companion Susan Priscilla Bertie, now twenty-two, married Colonel Sir Banastre Tarleton. Georgiana was one of her bridesmaids, but it was to be some time before she'd walk down the aisle herself. Another ten years would pass before Georgiana married, at the age of twenty-six. For marriage in late Georgian times the norm was to be a teenage bride or in one's early twenties.

One has to wonder and speculate—and wonder and speculate is all one can do, for no documentation exists—that perhaps good offers of marriage were aborted owing to Grace Elliott's sudden reappearance on English soil. Unkind gossip can present itself at the wrong time and place and destroy anyone's reputation.

Georgiana, who had not made an appearance in the tabloids since her own scandalous birth, now saw her name bandied about for the ton to savor with their morning coffee:

Mrs. E——tt, ci-devant Miss D——le, who lately returned to England from France with a certain diplomatic Agent, is said to have since received a settlement of four or five hundred a year from a young Gentleman of high rank, on the express condition that she shall for the future reside out of the kingdom. This establishment has taken place in consequence of an amorous attachment that formerly subsisted between them, and which the Gentleman, being now married, is desirous of concealing from his amiable spouse.

A daughter by the above connection, who is a young Lady of great beauty *and considerable accomplishments, is expected to be shortly presented at Court, under the name of Miss S———r. (*Morning Herald, *March 15, 1798)*

Although Grace Elliott's reaction to the name change goes unrecorded, it had to be devastating.

Was Georgiana ever presented at Court? It's doubtful she'd have been presented when Queen Charlotte was in charge of presentations, but it might have been possible during the regency or reign of George IV, Georgiana's putative father. Her guardians the Cholmondeleys were so close to George IV, it's very possible. If Georgiana was to marry into the peerage, she surely had to be presented at Court.

Georgiana's female contemporaries could be snippy, even when their own families could not stand up to close scrutiny. The scandal-ridden Devonshires and their close relatives—whose various adulteries, scandals, and illegitimate children were public knowledge—evidently still felt themselves superior to young Georgiana Seymour. In a letter to her older sister, Lady Harriette Cavendish, or "Hary-O"—who was to later marry her aunt's lover, the father of the aunt's two illegitimate cousins—could remark (meow!) that as much as she admired Susan Priscilla Tarleton, who had grown up as a sister with Georgiana:

> *The only flaw in her [Susan's] character is her great admiration of Miss Seymour, but that I am doomed to meet with." (Letter to Lady Georgiana Morpeth, December 30, 1803)*

In 1808, ten years after the marriage of Georgiana's chum Susan Bertie, an offer of marriage was received and accepted, and Grace Elliott's daughter did exceedingly well: she married

Frontispiece from *La Belle Assemblée*, volume 13, number 85 (June 1816): "The Princes Charlotte of Wales and Prince Leopold of Cobourg returning from the altar, after the Marriage Ceremony." There are no images extant of Georgiana's wedding to Lord Charles, but this image of the Prince and Princess gives a good idea of what the other young couple might have looked like on their day. Lord Charles probably wore his uniform. Georgiana, a girl from a wealthy family, would have worn a dress especially made for the occasion but not a wedding dress as we know it today. (City of London Museum)

Lord William Francis Charles James Augustus Cavendish-Bentinck, the son of William Henry Cavendish-Bentinck, third Duke of Portland. (Her husband, Lord Charles, is sometimes referred to by his military rank of lieutenant-colonel).

Lord Charles was equerry to the Prince of Wales. Like Lord Cholmondeley, he was close to the royal heir, and, indeed, he might have been his son-in-law. (These Cavendishes were not the same Cavendishes as the Dukes of Devonshire, but were related to them.) It was a distinguished family—the third Duke was briefly prime minister, from 1807 to 1808—and the title was one of the most prestigious ducal titles in all of England. It was, in the parlance of the times, a family very "high in the instep," though Lord Charles himself, it must be noted, was not particularly distinguished.

{What's an Equerry? The noun refers to a personal attendant of the British royal family and/or an official charged with the care of the horses of princes or nobles. As a former cavalry officer and a friend to the Prince of Wales, Lord Charles Bentinck was an admirable fit for this position.}

It could well have been a love match and not one made for dynastic reasons. Though there was probably a good dowry, Georgiana brought no land to Lord Charles. Lord Cholmondeley—always so good where money was concerned—must have had a strong hand in negotiating the settlement made by the groom's family on Georgiana. The Cavendish-Bentinck papers at the University of Nottingham show that a settlement of £5000 was made by them a year later on Georgiana Seymour as a marriage portion. It's a tidy sum.

This amount was released to her surviving child some years after the death of the child's father. Though a husband had control of a wife's money, if she predeceased him it was hers. Or, depending on the way the marriage settlement was written, it could go to her children. Lord Cholmondeley was looking out for Georgiana's children.

Illegitimate offspring of princes and kings did not lack suitors. These individuals were by no means unmarriageable, but a duke's son—even though he was not the duke's heir—was an excellent catch for Grace Elliott's daughter. And it could indeed have been one of those rare occurrences for that time and place, marrying for love, not fortune, acreage, rank, or status.

Though having no substantial fortune of his own, Charles could as easily have married a wealthy heiress from a family much like his, or a daughter of rich landed gentry, rather than a quasi-acknowledged royal bastard. He was also only two years older than his bride, another unusual circumstance in age when grooms were customarily ten, fifteen, even twenty or more years older.

Charles and his brother Frederick were two of the many gallants named in the infamous *Memoirs* of the courtesan Harriette Wilson. Though, like all of Harriette's one-night stands and her longer liaisons, they were given the opportunity to buy themselves out of her tell-all tome, these two men did not do so. Charles probably did not have the money required by Wilson; he was always lacking funds. According to the courtesan's *Memoirs,* Charles made light of the whole thing, saying:

> *We are all in for it. . . . My brother Frederick and I are in the book up to our necks; but we shall only make bad worse by contending against it; for it is . . . true.*

What sort of man was Lord Charles Bentinck? Physically, he was a very handsome man, as one can observe from the portrait painted by Sir Thomas Lawrence and the portrait miniatures that survive. Like many a former cavalry officer, he was described as dashing. Alas, he may not have been terribly bright. Hyacinthe Littleton, who became his sister-in-law in 1816, when he remarried, wrote to her brother Gerald in the spring of 1817 that Charles was "abominably stupid." He was never particularly plump in the pocket; in fact, he spent a good deal of time in the last years of his life scrambling to get trusts set up for the children he had with his second wife.

Like Lord Cholmondeley, he was a man-about-town—a gallant—who spent his time at clubs and other hangouts of the young and titled. (Think eighteenth-century club kid.) He paid court to actresses and ladies of the night and was enough of a name to be mentioned with his brother in the forementioned Harriette Wilson's *Memoirs*. Although he was in the set of the Prince of Wales and Lord Cholmondeley, he lacked Lord Cholmondeley's considerable financial resources. He'd done well to ally himself with the wealthy Cholmondeleys by marrying Lord Cholmondeley's ward—and possible daughter. It was an excellent trade-off.

The beautiful couple married at beautiful Cholmondeley Castle in Chester, near Malpas, not far from the Welsh border, on September 21, 1808:

> Births and Marriages of Remarkable Persons . . . 21. At Chester, Lord Charles Bentinck, son of the Duke of Portland, to the Hon. Miss Seymour . . . (Gentleman's Magazine, September 1808)

The child with no acknowledged father and a demirep mother was now to be addressed as Lady Charles Bentinck. (Her husband preferred to be styled Lord Charles Bentinck rather than use the longer form of his name.) Her Ladyship! It was a designation that had eluded her mother, Grace, her entire life.

Was Grace Elliott at that wedding in 1808? No record remains, but it's highly doubtful her name was on the guest list, though we know that she was still living in England at the time of the happy event. The presence of Lord Cholmondeley's ex-mistress would have taxed the most amiable spouse, even the accommodating Lady Charlotte. It just wasn't possible.

It's interesting that the wedding announcement styles Georgiana as "Hon.," standing for "Honourable," which is how the daughters and sons of viscounts and barons are termed. A true daughter of an earl would be called Lady Georgiana; the younger sons of an earl are termed Honourables. The daughter of a king, as everyone knows, is a princess. Adopted children and/or illegitimate children, however, have no right to titles. If, though, the Earl of Cholmondeley wished to have Georgiana addressed in a particular fashion, who was to stop him?

Showing respect to Georgiana Seymour was tantamount to showing respect to the Earl, who was a rich and powerful man. It is also entirely possible that the writer of the wedding notice in the *Gentleman's Magazine* knew that Georgiana Seymour was not entitled to the "Honourable" designation but simply wanted to curry favor with the Earl. Sucking up to the rich, and to peers and royalty, is not a rare phenomenon. The age had a disparaging phrase for those who did it: "toad eaters."

There's a curious entry in the *Journal of Thomas Raikes* concerning the Seymour-Bentinck wedding, having to do with crests on one's carriage:

> George, Prince of Wales, . . . showed great interest in her [Georgiana's] welfare; she married Lord Charles Bentinck; but when in consequence of this royal

protection, an attempt was made on the marriage to quarter the royal arms with the bar of bastardy, a royal veto was immediately issued to prevent it.

Quartering one's arms was often done on marriage, and the quartered shield became the arms of the new family, though technically it only applied to the children. As a younger son, Lord Charles Bentinck was entitled to a variation of the Bentinck coat of arms. When he married, he would be able to quarter his arms with that of his spouse. Bastards, however, had no claim to any arms.

The term "quartering" means dividing the shield into four quarters—husband's arms on the dexter (right) side, wife's arms on the sinister (left). If Georgiana Seymour had been the descendant of an arms bearer, the arms of her family would have been "impaled" on the same shield as those of Lord Charles, i.e., placed side by side. Apparently someone—the Cavendish-Bentincks or the Cholmondeleys—wanted to have the royal coat of arms with the "bar of bastardy" placed on the sinister side of the shield on the coach carrying Georgiana to her wedding.

{Toad Eater. From the *1811 Dictionary of the Vulgar Tongue*: a poor female relation, and humble companion, or reduced gentlewoman, in a great family, the standing butt, on whom all kinds of practical jokes are played off, and all ill humours vented. This appellation is derived from a mountebank's servant, on whom all experiments used to be made in public by the doctor, his master; among which was the eating of toads, formerly supposed poisonous. Swallowing toads is here figuratively meant for swallowing or putting up with insults, as disagreeable to a person of feeling as toads to the stomach.}

But only a personal grant of arms to a bastard would allow him or her to carry any arms at all. The "baton sinister," that "bar of bastardy" was used mostly by males whose fathers recognized them as their offspring. When the Duke of Clarence, King George IV's younger brother, became King William IV, he made his illegitimate eldest son the Earl of Munster, entitling him to carry arms.

Those arms of the Earl of Munster carry the baton sinister. In other words, they are the arms of King William IV without the escutcheon of the treasurer and the crown of Hanover, debruised by a baton sinister azure charged with three anchors or. (This is heraldic language; "or," here, is the Latin word for gold, not the grammatical conjunction.)

Obviously the Prince of Wales did not want Georgiana Seymour to use his arms alongside those of her husband. It would have been a tacit acknowledgment to the world that he accepted her as his daughter, and that was never to happen.

Lady Charles Bentinck did not present her husband with a child until 1811, when their daughter, Georgina, was born. This was within the fourth year of their marriage, and it raises some question about Georgiana's fertility, or—more likely—the possibility that she'd suffered miscarriages and/or stillbirths. No other children were to come from the marriage, and Lady Charles Bentinck died when her baby was only two years old.

In an ironic replay of the affair between Grace Elliott and Lord Valentia that set the direction for the rest of Grace's life, her son-in-law, Lord Charles Bentinck, at the age of thirty-six, seduced an unhappily married twenty-five-year-old woman and eloped with her.

Lady Abdy, née Anne Wellesley, was the daughter of Richard, second Earl of Mornington, later Marquis Wellesley, and Hyacinthe Gabrielle Roland, a beautiful Frenchwoman who'd been her husband's mistress before she became his wife. Anne's uncle was Arthur Wellesley, first Duke of Wellington. Anne was noted for a fine complexion and enormous dark eyes and she was an excellent amateur musician.

Anne's musical talents on the harp and the piano were of very high quality,

Georgiana and Charles. Portrait miniatures set in a tortoiseshell locket. Artist unknown. (Private collection)

Who's Your Daddy? Redux

In *A Regency Elopement* (1969), Hugh Farmar, a descendant of the Wellesleys, weighs in with his opinion on Georgiana Seymour's parentage. Bear in mind that Farmar as a small boy knew individuals who knew these Regency personages when they themselves were young and who talked family stories in his presence, so he was not so far removed from those actual events. Farmar writes, "The parentage of Georgiana must remain undecided. Mr. Roger Fulford, the foremost authority on George IV [or considered such at the time Farmar was writing—there have been several well-received biographies of George IV since Fulford's 1935 work], while discounting exaggerated reports of children fathered by the King in his young days, allows Georgiana Seymour as a possible exception. The balance of the evidence, however, tends to show that Lord Cholmondeley was in fact her father. Nevertheless, the possibility must remain that Lord Charles, [who] in addition to his post as the Regent's Equerry, was in fact . . . also his son-in-law, and the only child of the marriage, also named Georgiana [see below] the Regent's grand-daughter."

What's in a name?

GEORGINA OR GEORGIANA?

Spelling goes back and forth on the names of Georgiana (Grace Elliott's daughter) and Georgina (Georgiana's daughter, Grace's granddaughter). It can lead to confusion, but "Georgina" seemed to have been the preferred spelling for Grace's granddaughter. The obituary and will of Miss Cavendish-Bentinck verify the spelling as "Georgina."

and people said that she'd inherited her skill in music—as well as her lovely eyes—from her grandfather, the first Lord Mornington. There was no question that she ranked high among the beauties of Regency London. Few of those who knew her, however—beyond her immediate family members, who suffered in typical well-bred English silence—were aware of her volatile temperament. Anne Wellesley was a handful.

Like Lord Charles's mother-in-law, Grace Elliott, Anne Wellesley had also married a man older than she, as was the norm. Sir William Abdy, the seventh Baronet Abdy, was born in 1779, and so was probably about ten years older than Anne when they married on July 3, 1806, whereas the age difference between Grace and Dr. Eliot was more than double that. It seems, however, that the couple was as ill suited as Grace and Dr. Eliot had been. (There's some confusion about Anne Wellesley's date of birth—anywhere from 1780 to 1795—but the most probable date is 1788; thus she could have been about eighteen when she married Abdy, and he would have been about twenty-eight.)

Lady Abdy engaged in flirtatious behavior—and perhaps more than merely innocent flirtation—with at least two of her husband's male friends. One of those with whom her name had been linked was the notorious rake Frederick Lamb (he of Harriette Wilson infamy). The other was Lord Charles Bentinck, who was a lonely thirty-six-year-old widower on the prowl. Anne's mother and sister apparently knew of these intrigues and openly disapproved of her behavior with unattached gallants, but, with that temper, she was not a young woman who was easy to reason with, not ever.

Unlike Lord Valentia, who was an ignoble seducer and a thorough rake, Lord Charles may have fallen deeply in love with Anne Abdy. Adultery, however, is not honorable, nor is insinuating oneself inside the household of another to gain access to the desired one, as Lord Charles did. Though Sir William's family and friends were adamant in testifying in the Abdy divorce action that Sir William and Anne had a love match—thus placing the blame on her vile seducer—the Wellesleys knew better. In *A Regency Elopement*, Hugh Farmer quotes from a letter in which Anne's brother Gerald, writing to his sister Hyacinthe Littleton in 1817, a year after the divorce, remarked:

> *I always considered it Anne's misfortune that her marriage with Sir William was hurried over and pressed on her, as certainly it was. . . . You had time and freedom allowed you for a choice. Indeed you had your entire will in that important affair of your life, and I recollect you used to express yourself on the subject to me with great prudence and independence. Your union has consequently been attended with happiness, while the circumstances of Anne's were I think an extenuation of her late misconduct. After all, she and Sir William were ill-assorted to each other, for although he is a good man, he was not the person adapted to Anne.*

It seems that Lord Charles may have fallen in love with Lady Abdy. The affair probably began sometime in 1813, a couple of years after the first Lady Charles died. In her haste to elope, Anne unfortunately left behind incriminating letters that testified there'd been a relationship of long standing between them.

Charles and Anne ran off together early on the morning of September 4 or 5, 1815, and hid out in Greenwich and other locations in and around London. Charles had simply appeared at Lady Abdy's Hill Street house in his brand-new gig and picked her up—and off they went.

It was a very public elopement, and there were witnesses. It took no time at all for the *St. James's Chronicle* to report an *Elopement in High Life*

Oil painting of Georgiana Lady Charles Bentinck, by James Northcote. (Private collection)

> *A young married Lady of rank and highly distinguished in the fashionable circles by her personal attractions, absconded from the neighbourhood of Berkeley Square, a few days since, in order to throw herself into the arms of a noble gallant, the brother of an English Duke. The fair inconstant had shewn a restless disposition for some time before her departure, which took place by her going out immediately after breakfast, and walking to a street adjoining the new Road where Lord——awaited her arrival in his gig, ascending which, she was instantly driven off to their amorous retreat, which the afflicted husband, Sir—— had not yet been able to discover. Lady——, either from hurry or singular design, went off without a single article of apparel besides the dress she wore. Her Ladyship is only in her 25th year, and in the full bloom of beauty; and the only palliation that can be offered for this indiscreet transfer of her charms, is that "her mother did so before her."*

Sir William, the deserted, cuckolded husband, had been away for two days, shooting partridge in the country at the start of the hunting season. Parliament had closed its doors in August, and the London "Season" closed with it. Nothing—neither parliamentary sessions nor the social whirl and marriage mart—

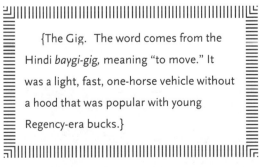

{The Gig. The word comes from the Hindi *baygi-gig*, meaning "to move." It was a light, fast, one-horse vehicle without a hood that was popular with young Regency-era bucks.}

Book cover illustration by Osbert Lancaster. (Photo by Ray Wadia)

was allowed to compete with the chasing and killing of animals and birds throughout the English countryside in the early fall. The ton had established its priorities. Sir William was a hunter, in the best English tradition. (And note, too, the article's snide reference to Anne's mother, making sure readers knew that Hyacinthe Roland had been her father's longtime mistress before he'd made her his wife.)

Only a few days prior to the planned elopement, Lord Charles, who had been a friendly acquaintance of Sir William's, had come by to show off his new conveyance, this very same gig, to the gentleman he was about to cuckold publicly. Anne's husband secured a divorce on June 25, 1816, by an act of Parliament. It usually took two or three years to get a divorce; this was extremely fast. Obviously, influential family connections made it happen quickly.

Anne Wellesley's father, the Marquis of Wellesley, and her three brothers, who held the private opinion that poor Sir William was a "nincompoop," nevertheless considered Lord Charles's behavior to be "infamous"; they never became terribly fond of him. Wellesley wrote to his eldest son, Richard, upon being told the gig story, "I have never heard any anecdote of such complicated treachery, impudence, insults and low profligate humour, as your history of the Gig."

The quickie divorce was granted—not a moment too soon! Lord Charles and the former Lady Abdy were married on July 23, 1816 at St. Martin-in-the-Fields in

St. Martin-in-the-Fields. (Photo by Simon Tibbs)

The Special Licence and Lord Hardwicke's Marriage Act of 1753

A 1534 statute gave the Archbishop of Canterbury the right to issue a Special Licence under which a couple could marry at any time or place (whether a consecrated place—such as a church—or not). The Special Licence, which was far costlier than the Common Licence, made up a tiny percentage of all marriage licenses issued and remained a prerogative of the aristocracy. The fee for a Common Licence in 1808 was 10 shillings and that for a Special Licence was £4; in 1815, the cost of the Special Licence was increased to £5. (George III, Anno 55, Cap. 184, has the text of the law.) The equivalent today in English currency would be £300, and in U.S. currency, $600. In the Regency period, that put the Special Licence out of the reach of all but the wealthiest. The Special Licence could be bought on the day of the marriage and it eliminated the public notification of the proposed marriage that was required by the banns. The marriage could thus be conducted privately or in secret. Some 99 percent of all marriage licenses issued before 1900 were of the common variety. The state's requirements for marriage licenses were codified in Lord Hardwicke's Marriage Act of 1753. (See *Marriage Laws, Rites, Records & Customs,* by Colin R. Chapman, with Pauline M. Litton, 1996)

The Marriage Act of 1753—which is also referred to as Lord Hardwicke's Marriage Act—was introduced to eliminate irregular, unlicensed marriages among all social classes and to protect the rights of the wealthier classes. It did away with the popular but unregulated "Fleet marriages," conducted in and around the environs of the Fleet Prison in London. Among the law's many provisions were the prohibition of marriage for those under twenty-one without parental consent; the requirement of a paid license for marriage, whether Special or Common; and the publication, or broadcasting, in the parish church of the engaged couple's banns for the three Sundays preceding the marriage.

Westminster. They had time to call the banns, but the marriage could also have been by that prerogative widely used by the wealthy, the "Special Licence." No one was in attendance but the couple and their lawyer, the eminent Henry Brougham. The age difference between bride and groom was the same as the one between Lady Anne and Sir William, ten years. It was as secretive a ceremony as the baptism of Lord Charles's first wife, Georgiana.

Their first daughter, Anne, was born on the first day of September 1816, less than two months—oops!—after the wedding took place. She was followed, in rapid succession, by their sons Charles William, born in 1817, and Arthur, in 1819; their second daughter, Emily, was born circa 1820–1823.

Portrait of the very beautiful Frenchwoman Hyacinthe Gabrielle Roland, Marchioness Wellesley, 1791, by Élisabeth Vigée-Lebrun. She was Anne's mother. (Museum of Fine Arts, San Francisco)

FACING PAGE, TOP AND BOTTOM: Is this Anne Mee portrait of Lady Anne Abdy, née Wellesley, or is it Georgiana Cavendish-Bentinck? The Windsor Castle catalogue identifies her as Georgiana, while the caption for Hugh Farmar's frontispiece in *A Regency Elopement* identifies her as Lady Anne. The women looked very much alike, almost as if they were identical twins. (The Royal Collection © HM Queen Elizabeth II)

(Their first son, Charles, may have been a twin whose brother died soon after birth.)

There was another curious coincidence relating to this marriage. Anne Wellesley—like her predecessor Georgiana Seymour—was born illegitimate. Her mother, Hyacinthe Gabrielle Roland, had been Richard Wellesley's mistress for many years before they became man and wife. (Another minor scandal: Hyacinthe Roland's mother was said to have been an actress, Hyacinthe Gabrielle Varis, and her father not Pierre Rolland, her mother's husband, but her lover, an Irish cavalry officer in the service of France named Christopher Alexander Fagan.)

All of the children born to Richard Wellesley and Hyacinthe Roland—including Anne—were born outside of the bonds of holy matrimony. Though Richard and Hyacinthe later married, becoming legitimate man and wife, this did not legitimize their children under English law. Ironically, both of Lord Charles Bentinck's wives were "children of the mist."

Another interesting coincidence was that both Georgiana, as Lady Charles Bentinck, and Anne, as Baroness Abdy, were painted by the miniaturist Anne Mee for the Prince of Wales's Gallery of Beauties at Windsor Castle. And there's an irony here as well: the portrait of Anne Abdy was confused with the portrait of Georgiana in Hugh Farmar's *A Regency Elopement*. The confusion is not hard to understand, since the women look incredibly alike. Was Charles attracted to his second wife because she so much resembled his deceased first wife? This is something that does happen.

One has to wonder what Grace Elliott thought of the whole affair, of this scandalous elopement and marriage that once again made her family the cynosure of the ever-curious, ever-ripe-for-gossip ton. By now, Dr. Eliot was long deceased and past caring, but did Lord Valentia, Grace's old paramour, hear of this? Were fond memories rekindled of his own scandalous and passionate affair with her?

Arthur Annesley, Lord Valentia, died on July 4, 1816, at the age of seventy-one, exactly two months before this fateful elopement of Grace's son-in-law and another man's wife. Of the trio most intimately involved in Grace's story, only Grace was still living to muse upon all that had happened—if, that is, this strong and pragmatic lady was wont to muse upon those long-ago events that had changed the course of her life so dramatically. If she weakened momentarily and did so muse, one wonders if indeed she ever pondered . . . What if? There was such a thin line between respectability and notoriety, but once it was crossed, the pattern of one's future life was set irrevocably.

After 1800, the tabloids were no longer concerned about the affairs of the previous century's courtesans. Mary Robinson, Elizabeth Armistead, and Grace Elliott were old, tired news. There were sporadic mentions (as when Robinson's old lover Tarleton married the young woman who'd been raised by Lord Cholmondeley), but there was markedly less interest. Basically, no one cared. However, there is one sighting of Grace that came to light when the *Diary* of Frances, Lady Shelley, was published more than a hundred years later.

It's known because of an entry in the *Diary* indicating that Grace Elliott paid a surprise visit to her sister, Jacintha—who was then Jacintha Barrington, married to her third husband—as she lay dying in the winter of 1802 (or 1803, the date is disputable).

Cause and Effect

A butterfly flaps its wings in the Amazon . . . and there's a tornado in Oklahoma. Lady Anne Abdy elopes with Lord Charles Bentinck in 1815 and Charles, Prince of Wales, is born in 1948. It is interesting to note that Lord Charles and Lady Anne's descendants include Charles, the heir to the throne of England, through the second marriage of their first son, Charles William Frederick Cavendish-Bentinck, to Caroline Louisa Burnaby. Their child Nina Cecelia Cavendish-Bentinck married Claude George Bowes-Lyon, fourteenth Earl of Strathmore, the direct ancestor of the late Queen Mother Elizabeth, mother of Queen Elizabeth II, the present Queen of England. Without Charles and Anne's impetuous actions that day in September—the flapping of those butterfly wings—there would not have been this Queen Mother, nor this Queen Elizabeth II, nor this Prince Charles.

This was the first time Grace had seen her sibling since her own scandalous divorce. Jacintha had kept any word of Grace from her daughter Frances. Ironically, Frances, born in 1783, was only a year older than Grace's Georgiana, and the two were bosom buddies. They did not know that they were related, much less that they were first cousins.

As Frances wrote, her mother, already so ill, was extremely distraught at seeing her sister again. Showing up at a relative's deathbed takes courage; one has to face the humiliating possibility of being turned away. That Grace went ahead anyway is to her credit.

Unfortunately, as Frances put it, her mother's third marriage was to "an Irish Major Barrington, of good family certainly, but of most disgusting vulgarity." Jacintha and Major Barrington had evidently married in secret, and he, a gambler and drunk, abused her physically and took her money. Frances witnessed the abuse firsthand and blamed her stepfather for her mother's death:

> *Often have I averted the blows which that brute leveled at her, and often have I seen the marks of his violence when I was not present to protect her! A faithful old servant . . . told me of my mother's sufferings, and said that it would not be possible for her to live long, under such treatment. We both lamented the fatal infatuation which had brought my mother to this dreadful pass.*

Jacintha, married to an abusive man, was no one to cast stones at what another woman had made of her life, but her sense of propriety seems to have been overwhelming. Abusive treatment by husbands is to be borne, endured, not spoken of, but a sister who is a courtesan is forever a shame and a disgrace and to be cast out of one's sight. Poor Jacintha! Grace might have been able to give her some good and sensible advice about men.

The scene Frances describes is poignant, and the snapshot of Grace memorable, even if the date Frances gives contradicts other information. Jacintha died on January 7, 1802, according to some sources, but Frances says this happened in 1803, while at another point she says that her mother died in about 1804. A good guess is that the meeting took place late in 1801, upon Grace's second return to England after 1798. Frances writes:

Flattering portrait of Lady Abdy, by Thomas Lawrence. (Private collection)

> *One day, it must have been in 1803, I came back unexpectedly to my mother's sick-room, and saw, sitting at her bedside, the most beautiful woman I had ever beheld. She was dressed in the indecent style of the French republican period. Tears were rolling down her cheeks; this heightened her beauty without defacing the rouge which had been artistically applied. Her sleeves were of the finest embroidered muslin, and transparent drapery lay over a bust of ivory.*
>
> *When the lady saw me, she rose to her feet, rushed towards me, and cried out impulsively: "Do let me kiss my darling niece." She did so, of course, and the odour of musk enchanted me.*
>
> *This was the first and only time that I saw my mother's unhappy sister, Grace Dalrymple Eliot. Her story is full of romance. . . . Of course I knew nothing then of my aunt's history, and could not understand why my poor mother burst into tears and afterwards regretted this accidental rencon-*

The house at rue de Miromesnil. Note the medallion over the gate. (Photo by Kristina F. Hickey)

tre. . . . *Although this misfortune had caused my mother much pain, she did not refuse to allow me to visit and play with my cousin.*

Grace may have wanted to remain in England the first time she came back in 1798; she'd sold her *hôtel particulier* on the rue de Miromesnil in 1794, immediately upon her release from prison, and she may have disposed of the cottage at Meudon as well.

The house in Paris was sold to a General Murat. Joachim Murat (1767–1815) was a cavalry officer who supported Napoléon and rose from obscurity to become his brother-in-law and later the King of Naples. Richard Bentley notes that the house "was afterwards sold to General Lannes, Duc de Montebello." Archival records in Paris show that at different times the Swedish ambassador (and lover of Queen Marie-Antoinette) Count Hans Axel Fersen and François-Auguste-René, Vicomte de Chateaubriand, the writer and diplomat, resided there. César Gabriel de Choiseul (1712–1785), the Comte de Chevigny, may also have lived there at one time.

The land—one hectare—was purchased in 1769 by the Duc de Chartres (later the Duc d'Orléans) and is situated in the fashionable faubourg Saint-Honoré. This description is from *Le 8e Arrondissement . . . ,* by Béatrice de Andia et al. (Mairie de Paris, no date):

#31—Dans la cour, petit hôtel avec bâtiment central à colonnes et fronton et avec galerie à colonnes doriques sur la côte, propriété avant la Révolution de Miss Elliot, amie de Philippe Égalité. Fersen l'habita en 1790 et Chateaubriand et sa femme en 1804.

The 1963 edition of the *Dictionnaire historique des rues de Paris,* by Jacques Hillairet, confirms that this was Grace Elliott's home and describes it similarly, except that it notes Chateaubriand lived next door:

Le bel hôtel neo-classique du No. 31, bâti peu avant la Révolution, fut pro-

priété d'une maîtresse de duc d'Orléans Philippe-Égalité, Miss Grace Elliott;
François de Chateaubriand et son épouse en occupent en 1804 la partie voisine
du No. 33; côte cour, le corps sur rue est supporte par des arcades sur colonnes
doriques.

The house is still there, incongruous in its surroundings of shops and office buildings; in 2003 it was the headquarters of a French telecommunications company. As in the description above, it is a large, elegant white building in the neoclassical style, with Doric columns; it is protected by imposing wooden doors reminiscent of castle gates that, when opened, lead into a cobblestone courtyard. One can imagine splendid carriages entering from the street and turning up to the front doors. Over the gates is an elaborate blue enameled medallion with the initials *G* and *E* intertwined quite prettily in a circle.

The building—a Classified Historical Monument—is not wholly accepted as Grace's Paris residence, though the evidence is strong. The film director Eric Rohmer was at first certain it was hers, but then changed his mind. However, there is no other house on the street that comes as close to this description as the house that belonged to Grace Elliott. Until firm evidence to the contrary emerges, this has to be the place. The sources quoted above (seen at the City of Paris Archives) both identify it as such.

In the *Journal*, Grace talks about buying another property, her cottage at Meudon. It, too, was a substantial property, hardly what one would describe as a cottage. Meudon, like Ville d'Avray, is not far from Paris. This cottage was close to the Parc Monceau, where Philippe owned an elegant home in the midst of an exquisite property landscaped in the English style, "un magnifique parc anglais." The park was acquired in 1852 by the state, then in 1870 by the town. Grace sold her Meudon property through Joseph-Marie Lecoq, the town notary, probably circa 1800. It is currently in private hands.

CHAPTER FOURTEEN

The Trail Goes Cold: Grace's Final Return to France and Those Last, Lost Nine Years of Her Life

Grace Elliott returned to France in 1814 after her daughter's death and the restoration of the Bourbon monarchy. She seems to have preferred life in France, where her profession was not regarded with the disdain she met in England, and it was where she had close personal ties that had been forged before, during, and after the Revolution. Georgiana had died the year before, at the age of thirty-one, and her death may have been a factor in Grace's decision to uproot herself. One likes to imagine that things might have gotten better between them, with Georgiana's days of teenage rebellion safely behind her upon marriage to Lord Charles Bentinck in 1808 and motherhood in 1811.

There may have been nothing left for Grace in England. Bentley hints at a renewal of her acquaintance with the Prince of Wales—the Prince Regent, beginning in 1811—but that's extremely unlikely. Except for some on-again, off-again with Mrs. Fitzherbert, he was not inclined to look up old girl-friends, Grace is not mentioned by any of his biographers as one of the ladies he was seeing at that time. If she had further exploits, they were not recorded in the press. No one seemed interested in her anymore, and she may also have been in ill health.

Grace may have hoped to reclaim some of the old glamour of her past life in France, but here is where the trail goes cold. It's known that her good friend and next-door neighbor at Brompton Park House, Lady Seymour Dorothy Worsely—who was now going by her former name of Fleming— returned to Paris at about the same time; they could well have decamped to-gether, along with Lady Fleming's Swiss-French husband Jean Louis Couchet (1779–1836).

From 1814 to 1823, though, Grace Elliott fades from public view as she moves into her sixties. Where she resided is unknown, and the last that's heard of her is the news of her death on May 15, 1823, at Ville d' Avray.

Georgina Cavendish-Bentinck (1811–1883), Victorian Spinster

There's a saying that the name of a proper lady appears in the newspapers only three times, on the occasions of her birth, marriage, and death. Note, too, that only *one* marriage is presumed proper.

Georgina Cavendish-Bentinck lived according to those terms more prop-erly than most. Her birth seems to have passed unnoticed and, as she never married, there was no marriage announcement, either. Only her obituary made the newspapers. The *Times,* of course. It could not have been more proper.

She was neither titled—though from a titled family—nor a fabulous heiress, but she'd accumulated enough wealth by the time of her demise to garner that bit of attention. All of Grace Elliott's direct descendants, alas, died out with the passing of this woman, her spinster granddaughter Geor-gina, at the age of seventy-two, on September 12, 1883:

Deaths

On the 12th Inst., at her house, in Chester, aged 72, Georgina Cavendish Bentinck, eldest daughter of the late Lord Charles Cavendish Bentinck. (Times, *Saturday, September 15, 1883*)

There are a number of questions that simply cannot be answered. Georgina lived and died in comfortable, genteel obscurity and left neither husband nor children. No letters or journals are known to exist. She passed out of this world like a sigh. She'd been a living, breathing Victorian lady not so far removed from females of the two centuries to come, a human being who ate, drank, talked, had good gossips with her friends, read newspapers and books, and enjoyed leisure-time activities familiar to us, among them, perhaps, croquet, tennis, riding, or archery. It's inconceivable that she did not write letters to family or friends or keep a diary of her activities, banal though they might have been.

The dukedom in her father's family, that of Portland, disappeared in 1990, when the title became extinct. What happened to humble family artifacts like letters, journals, and photographs is unknown. They were dispersed somewhere, most likely among friends and other relatives. Only the important family papers—primarily the papers dealing with the Bentinck men and their affairs—have been noted and collected. The University of Nottingham, the largest academic institution near Welbeck Abbey, the Portland country seat, is the place where deeds, financial documents, records of lawsuits and business transactions, and the wills and letters of the important men in the family, the peers and politicians, are stored. These are of little use to biographers of the female relatives of these illustrious individuals—those mere wives, sisters, daughters, et al.

Not even one photograph—much less a portrait—of Grace's granddaughter has been located, neither in the public record nor in private archives. It's hard to believe that no photographs of Georgina exist. She was no recluse overcome with shyness like her cousin, the fifth Duke of Portland, and she was twenty-eight years old when the daguerreotype was invented. Is it possible that no one—no one at all—took her photograph in the intervening forty-four years? That no portraits are known is in itself hard to imagine—but no photographs? Photographs were becoming commonplace, and this was a wealthy woman from a wealthy family.

Wealthy people still have their portraits painted, and there are still portrait painters on the art scene, though perhaps not as many now as there were in the eighteenth and nineteenth centuries, prior to the advent of photography. (Horace Walpole estimated in a 1759 letter to a friend that there were two hundred thousand painters of portraits—just of portraits—in London alone.) Somewhere, a painting of Georgina Cavendish-Bentinck must surely exist. Rich people had their portraits painted; it was a given. If not a full-size painting, then surely a portrait miniature must have been painted. Miniatures, those tiny portraits suitable for a brooch, locket, snuffbox, or ring, were very popular and were widely exchanged as keepsakes and tokens of friendship. But if not paintings, then there surely have to be photographs . . . somewhere.

So, trying to picture this woman is a challenge from the very start. Was she a beauty like her mother and grandmother? The Dalrymple genes carried beauty, as did the Bentinck genes. Lord Cholmondeley was an attractive man; the Prince of Wales, before he grew so corpulent and gross, had been attractive as well. The Earl of Portland, Lord Charles's ancestor, was a notably handsome gentleman, one of the best-looking men, it was said, of his time, and Lord Charles was handsome. Good looks ran in these families.

What do we know of Georgina's sheltered life? Not much. She was born in 1811 to Georgiana Seymour Bentinck and her husband, Lord Charles Bentinck. We can state with some certainty that Bentinck was her father. Georgina lost her mother when she was two years old. She was an only child for five years until her father's remarriage to Anne, Lady Abdy, and the birth of her half sibling Anne in 1816. She was to have three more half siblings: Charles William, Arthur, and Emily. Her father died in 1826 at the age of forty-six. There was an ugly battle for her custody between her father and stepmother, on the one hand, and the Marquess and Marchioness of Cholmondeley, on the other.

Georgina must have had guardian-trustees ("protectors," Grace Elliott called them in her will) during her infancy. (Infancy was defined then as the period from birth to adulthood at age twenty-one.) They were most probably individuals from her large extended family and included Cholmondeleys as well as Bentincks. This is known from one of the few documents bearing her name in the Portland collection at Nottingham. What cannot be ascer-

The Handsome Earl of Portland, Royal Favorite, and His Heirs

Hans Willem Bentinck (1649–1709) came to England from Diepenheim, in the province of Overyssel, the Netherlands, in the late seventeenth century. He was a close friend and longtime favorite of William of Orange. Made Earl of Portland in 1689 by William, now King William III of England, Bentinck was the King's most trusted adviser, serving as his groom of the stole and ambassador to Paris. The Earl acquired magnificent estates in Buckinghamshire and Hertfordshire as well as substantial properties in Cumberland and London. *The Complete Peerage* states, "His personal beauty . . . was great and not improbably was the cause of his early favour with the King, whose appreciation of its existence in the male sex resembled that of . . . James I." There was a story that Bentinck had saved the future king's life, risking his own, when he nursed William through smallpox.

Bentinck's son Henry, the second Earl, (1682–1726), was made Duke of Portland in 1716, in token of his sire's services to the Crown. Henry lost

Portrait of Hans Willem Bentinck, by Hyacinthe Rigaud (1659–1743). Rigaud and his school painted several portraits of him. (National Portrait Gallery, London)

much of the family wealth in the South Sea Bubble, but his son William, second Duke of Portland (1709–1762), mended the family fortune by marrying the heiress Lady Margaret Cavendish-Holles-Harley, daughter of Edward Harley, second Earl of Oxford. (From this marriage came the formidable double-barreled name of Cavendish-Bentinck.) William Henry Cavendish-Bentinck, third Duke of Portland (1738–1809), made Welbeck Abbey the principal family seat. Lord Charles Bentinck, Georgina Cavendish-Bentinck's father, was a younger son of the third Duke and brother to the fourth Duke. The fifth Duke was a noted eccentric who never married nor was seen in public. The title passed to a distant cousin upon his death. The ninth Duke, Victor Frederick William Cavendish-Bentinck (b. 1897), who died heirless, was the last titleholder. When the title became extinct in 1990 the line was traced back to the original letters patent for the earldom. Though there was no direct "tail-male" heir to the dukedom, there was one to the earldom, so the earlier title was still viable,

sans, alas, money or property. The twelfth Earl of Portland is the actor Tim Bentinck, who portrays David Archer in the popular and long-running BBC Radio 4 soap opera *The Archers*.

Tim Bentinck, twelfth Earl of Portland. (Tim Bentinck)

tained, however, are the names of these guardian-trustees—though they were certainly all men—as this particular document is so water-damaged it's unreadable.

On November 6, 1817, when Georgina was six years old and her mother had been dead four years, a sum of £5000 (or two sums of £5000 each—again, the document is barely readable) was settled upon her by the Marquess of Cholmondeley and Grace Elliott. A year before, Lady Charlotte, the Marquess's wife, had asked for the guardianship of Georgina, who was now living with her father and his second wife, Anne. The Cholmondeleys had taken care of Georgina after the death of her mother, Georgiana

Bentinck—whom they had raised—and now they wanted her returned to them. The following excerpts are taken from Hugh Farmar's revealing book, *A Regency Elopement:*

> *[The little girl] . . . now became the centre of a distasteful wrangle. Anne had taken a violent fancy to her. . . . Lady Cholmondeley had to a great extent cared for the child since the death of the first Lady Charles. She now proposed to adopt her, and her husband to settle money for her benefit. This suggestion, in the present circumstances of his finances, seems to have appealed to Lord Charles; but Anne had other views.*

The volatile Lady Anne complained bitterly about Lady Cholmondeley's suggestion in a letter to her elder brother, Richard Wellesley. Anne was very close to Richard, an even-tempered man who had the natural instincts of a peacemaker and a problem solver. He'd seen her through the scandalous days of her affair with Lord Charles and her ugly divorce from Sir William Abdy. She wrote to him sometime in 1816, probably just before giving birth to her first child, Anne, in early September:

> *I should very much like to see you tomorrow if you could call on me. I have been so harrassed about Ld. C's child, I don't know what to do. It makes me miserable the idea of giving it up, that I have been quite ill about it.*

"It"? How callous and impersonal. The child is a "her," not an "it." One shudders at the thought of any child in the custody of this Lady Anne! An intermediary and friend of Lord Charles's, John Walker, stepped in and wrote to Wellesley at about the same time, giving the Cholmondeleys' side of the issue at hand:

> *I wished to have had a few minutes conversation with you upon the subject of a daughter of the late Lady Charles Bentinck.*
>
> *Since the death of the late Ly. Charles she had resided principally at Lord Cholmondeley's. Lord Cholmondeley is very desirous that she should continue to do so and in that instance has proposed to settle £5,000 upon her. This was acceded to by your Sister and Lord Charles upon the condition of occasional visits at all times etc. However this arrangement was broken up by Ly. Charles saying that she could not part with the child. Both Ld. Wm. and Ld. Frederick and Lord and Lady Charles Bentinck have done me the Honour to talk over the subject upon which, altho' I have a strong opinion, yet as it was decided upon and is also a matter of much delicacy I spoke very delicately—And it also oc-*

curred to me that when Ly. Charles had children of her own she might possibly view the affair differently. I therefore thought it better to reserve myself until after her laying-in and also to request your aid who can as a brother urge those points which I cannot. I also perceive that Lord Charles's family will take it ill if Ly. Charles should not accede to Lord Cholmondeley's proposal. This is written in great confidence.

Wellesley sensibly tried to take himself out of the situation, replying that it was not his place to take sides in this personal family matter. It is, however, a fascinating issue that sheds light upon the various relationships in these noble families and upon the characters of those most intimately involved.

First, it shows that Lord Cholmondeley very naturally stepped in to take Georgiana's child when the young woman died, assuming once again his role as guardian and protector to anyone in Grace Elliott's immediate family. Second, it shows the great power and influence of Lord Cholmondeley. He has the Bentincks—Lord Charles's two brothers—agreeing with him as to who should be raising this child, even over their brother's legal right to her. Third, it shows a singular lack of affection, or just plain carelessness, on Lord Charles's part toward his child with his first wife that is disturbing. Fourth, it indicates a willingness and love on Lady Cholmondeley's part to care for the granddaughter of her husband's former mistress. If Lady Charlotte really wanted to do this—and had not been unduly influenced by her husband in the matter—she was indeed a remarkable woman. Last, it casts an extremely bad light on Georgina's stepmother, Anne Bentinck, giving one cause to wonder at her mental stability, personal character, and overall fitness as a mother.

Richard Wellesley was drawn into the family imbroglio despite his strong wish to steer clear of it. As Hugh Farmar says, "the Bentincks no doubt realized" that her elder brother "was the only person who was capable of influencing the wayward Anne." The Wellesleys were well aware of Anne's personality problems, having had to put up with her erratic behavior all their lives. Lord Charles called in his elder brother, Lord William Bentinck, third Duke of Portland, to work together with Anne's brother to sort out the delicate matter between him and the Cholmondeleys.

Obviously upset, Anne expressed her fears as to the outcome of the matter to Richard in another letter that late summer of 1816:

I dare say it will be some time now before we have Ly. C's answer to Lord Wm. . . . It is very provoking as we don't know what plan to fix upon and deranges everything we had settled. All our chance of happiness depends upon having the child and the more we think of it the more we are convinced of it. I tremble for fear Ly. C. should accept the offer [custody of Georgiana in return for a settlement by Lord Cholmondeley] which, however, I must abide by if she does.

The wrangle over the little child continued well into the next year. One wonders what Grace Elliott thought of it. One assumes that she wanted the Cholmondeleys to take responsibility for her grandchild, as her name appears on the document in the Duke of Portland's papers at the University of Nottingham setting up the trust for Georgina Cavendish-Bentinck and naming her guardians. She trusted Lord Cholmondeley, who'd always looked out for her interests.

Hugh Farmar, his exasperation evident, writes:

And so, for month after month, this distasteful transaction, with little Georgiana as an innocent pawn of the contending Bentincks and Cholmondeleys, dragged on. Lord Charles was prepared to hand her over if, in addition to Lord Cholmondeley's proposed settlement on his daughter, arrangements could be made for some of the Bentinck trust-money to go to the baby Anne [born in September 1816] and any other children that Anne and he might have. But here the family lawyers found difficulty: since Georgiana was a minor, she could not consent to give up an inheritance in favour of her half-sister and, possibly, other children. For his part, Lord Cholmondeley was given to changes of mind. The peacemakers, in the shape of Lord William and Richard, were baulked rather than blessed.

Farmar comments further that

Lord Cholmondeley's relationship with Lord Charles remains, in one sense at least, equivocal. Was it in the capacity of father-in-law and grandfather of Georgiana or as the agent of the real grandfather, the Prince Regent, that he now proposed in effect to adopt the little girl? At this distance of time there can be no clear answer.

The moody, mercurial Anne held no warm feelings toward Lord Cholmondely. She wrote to her brother-in-law Lord William Bentinck that "Lord Cholmondeley is such a shabby fellow that he is capable of anything where *Money* is the question." (The word "money" is capitalized and italicized in the quoted letter.) But Lord Charles is not much better. Anne quotes her husband as saying "that he should expect the £5,000 *as was promised; and that the child should not return to the Cholmondeleys until it was paid as promised."* The phrases "as was promised," and "as promised," are all italicized by Anne in her letter.

So much for Anne's warm, tender, even maternal feelings toward her husband's firstborn child, the child she supposedly did not want to give up because she had become so attached to her/it. It does become rather repugnant to read of a child being held hostage for payment. One also has to feel for the mediators caught in the middle of a distasteful situation.

Lord and Lady Cholmondeley, too, appear to have argued and come to a disagreement over the adoption of little Georgina, as a letter from Lord William Bentinck to his brother and his sister-in-law sometime in 1817 attests:

> *I have not told you as yet that Lord Cholmondeley's disposition in this business is by no means as favourable as it was. He has strongly advised Lady C. not to take G. back. He says to her— "You have had a great deal of annoyance—you have got over the pain of the separation and don't expose yourself to further embarrassment." . . . I have only seen Ly. C. twice since she came to Town, but her wishes and affection for the child seem unaltered.*

The sticking point was the settlement Lord Charles wished to have made on his younger children by—it now appeared—his brother the Duke of Portland. Such an agreement was eventually made. The documents describing this settlement are in the Portland collection at the University of Nottingham, and they seem to go on forever. Lord Charles is to be commended for looking after his progeny, but apparently he did so at the expense of giving up any claim to his child with Grace Elliott's daughter. It seems that he could not have cared less about her; he did not even refer to her by her Christian name, but rather as "the child."

Lord Charles wrote to his brother-in-law Richard Wellesley complaining about the "long disagreeable negotiation" and asking him, rather coldly:

> *Pray have the goodness to let me know when the child is to be sent—that is—when she is actually ready to set out. Until she is actually gone I will make no move in the business.*

Late in 1817 Anne sent a letter to her brother Richard at Brighton, announcing that his diplomacy had achieved success. Farmar adds, "Typically, she had now suffered a complete reversal of opinion" with regard to young Georgina Cavendish-Bentinck. Anne wrote:

I received your kind letter which I thank you for very much and in consequence of its contents Lord Charles has written to his brother to say that whenever the Cholmondeleys choose to send for the child she is ready to go. For my part, I must say she has been a source of little comfort to me. I have had so much annoyance and unpleasant things to counterbalance the pleasure of her society that I think I shall not regret her loss as much as I should have done 5 months ago. I hope all parties will now be pleased tho' I daresay they will still find some new subject to complain of. . . . I suppose that in a week we shall hear something from the Cholmondeleys. I rather dread the thought of it [Georgina's departure], but one good thing is that I shall not feel a stronger feeling than that of missing *her when she is gone, for she is so devoid of affection herself and so difficult a child to what she was originally. Besides, knowing that she has to leave me, I have not allowed to attach myself to her. As for signing of the papers Ld. C. . . . said he left it to Ld. Wm. to do what he liked. I begged him to say, however, that in case he might have anything to communicate to you, that you were at Brighton, so perhaps he may write to you.*

At this point, Farmar is completely disgusted with Anne—and for good reason. He cites the "barefaced egotism and a complete lack of consideration for the feelings of little Georgiana [sic]" as shown in this missive, and further states:

It is to be hoped that, whatever sort of adoptive grandfather Lord Cholmondeley may have turned out to be, Georgiana found happiness in the childhood that she spent with a kind Lady Cholmondeley whose affection, we may trust, in Lord William's words, "remained unaltered." Of the four people chiefly involved in this unsavoury business, she alone remained steadfast and uninfluenced by worldly motives. If Georgiana's mother had been indeed Lord Cholmondeley's daughter by Mrs. Elliott, the determination of his wife to take the little girl permanently into her home is of infinite credit to her charity.

It's not a great leap to imagine that this six-year-old was confused over her stepmother's admitted withdrawal of affection. Did she not have more than ample cause to be "difficult" at this sudden rejection and coldness emanating from a mother figure? She'd lost her own mother; she'd lost a grand-mother figure (Lady Cholmondeley); now she was losing yet another mother as well as her own seemingly rather indifferent father.

Georgiana Seymour, Georgina's mother, appears to have been a happy child and young woman in the Cholmondeley household, according to various contemporary accounts, and the description of Georgina Cavendish-Bentinck in her middle age as a benevolent and generous woman leads one to surmise that both she and her mother were as different as it was possible to be in personality and temperament from Lady Anne, her mercurial step-mother. To any twenty-first-century observer with the slightest grounding in psychology, Lady Anne's behavior verges on the manic-depressive.

Lady Anne had a miserable old age—giving credence perhaps to the saying that the good die young—and gave her namesake daughter Anne, the poor soul who took care of her, a difficult existence. Visits to Lady Anne were described by her children and grandchildren as "ordeals," according to Hugh Farmar, and her bad temperament apparently got worse as she aged. A watercolor portrait by Sir Hubert von Herkomer seen in a private collection shows a disagreeable-looking old woman.

It is entirely to Georgina Cavendish-Bentinck's credit—and perhaps to that of the Cholmondeleys who raised her—that she kept in touch with her stepmother Lady Anne and stayed at her Park Lane house in London when she came to town. Lord Charles may have been lucky to have died relatively young, after eleven years with this difficult woman as mistress and wife, and Sir William Abdy may have been even luckier to have divorced Anne when he did.

Georgina's name appeared in connection with various wills and lawsuits connected with the Dukes of Portland / Cavendish-Bentincks over a number of years. Georgina was named in the will of her grandmother Grace Elliott in 1823; in a codicil to the will of her aunt Lady William Bentinck in 1842; and in the will of her aunt Lady Mary Cavendish-Bentinck in 1843. One aunt bequeathed her £2,000; the other, £1,000. Grace Elliott may have left her one of the Gainsborough portraits of herself, or it could have been Lord Cholmondeley who did so.

A wealthy, eligible heiress, a young woman of good family. Georgina was ripe for marriage, but it never happened. She would have been sixteen in 1827, in the seventh year of the reign of King George IV. She was possibly the King's granddaughter. It was widely noted that the King had taken an interest in her mother, Georgiana, Lady Charles Bentinck, and that he'd given her grandmother, Grace, an annuity. Her father was the King's equerry, later treasurer of the royal household, and a friend of his. But what of Georgina? That she—like her mother—was given the female form of "George" as her Christian name is significant, but did it mean anything to the King?

Unfortunately, George IV had a sad old age and deteriorated badly and rapidly. He was obese, ill, and prone to overeating and to overindulging in spirits. (It was reported that he drank gallons of cherry brandy and had delusions of taking part in—and singlehandedly winning—the Battle of Waterloo.)

Would he have cared even a little bit for the child of a possible natural daughter—his grandchild? His one-time paramour Grace Elliott, the child's grandmother, had died. The annuity he'd given her had terminated with her death and she'd been out of his sight and out of his mind for a long time.

Steel engraved print of Cholmondeley Castle by F. J. Havell, after T. Allom. Published in *The Counties of Chester, Derby, Nottingham... Illustrated*, 1837. (Collection of the author)

*G*eorgina Augusta Frederica Henrietta Cavendish-Bentinck's Will

In her will, written in 1866, Georgina identified George Horatio as the "Marquis of Cholmondeley." He died in 1870, predeceasing her. By the time of probate, George Horatio's brother, William Henry Hugh, held the title of Marquess of Cholmondeley. He died in December 1884, little more than a year after Georgina. George Horatio, the second Marquess, was born in 1792 and raised with Georgina's mother, who'd been ten years older than he. George Horatio, though married, had died without issue, so the title had passed from the heir to the spare, his brother William Henry Hugh, who became the third Marquess. In her will, Georgina gives what appears to be all the portraits of her mother, including miniatures, to the second Marquess of Cholmondeley. It's not completely clear if these instead went to the third Marquess, or, upon his death, to the fourth Marquess. She mentions "the two oil pictures of my mother"—possibly the Reynolds portrait of Georgiana, Lady Charles, as a baby and one other. She does not mention any Gainsborough that Grace Elliott may have left to her, nor any other paintings, miniatures, drawings, or whatever. That Georgina Cavendish-Bentinck did not go into more detail about these valuable paintings, oils and miniatures, not going to the trouble of mentioning the artists or the dates painted, while she went into almost absurd detail about pieces of jewelry, inkstands, boxes, vases, shawls, blotting books, buttons, et cetera, is very odd indeed, and no help to those seeking the provenance of the various paintings as they were dispersed through the family.

It's likely the King had no interest whatsoever in Georgina Cavendish-Bentinck.

But luckily there were others who did care that Georgina was happy and well. Her "protectors," those individuals named by Lord Cholmondeley and Grace Elliott, were there to advise and look out for her, and Lord and Lady Cholmondeley raised her as lovingly as they'd raised her mother before her. Grace Elliott died in 1823; the Marquess of Cholmondeley in 1827; Lady Cholmondeley in 1838. Georgina was twenty-seven years old when Lady Cholmondeley, her dear adoptive grandmother, died. Georgina's father, Lord Charles, died in 1826; King George IV in 1830.

Georgina herself passed away at the age of seventy-two at her home, Malpas Cottage, on the banks of the River Dee, in the county of Chester. It was noted in the probate document that she had previously resided at Cholmondeley Castle, the principal seat of the Cholmondeley family, and the will was apparently written while she was resident there.

The probate document, dated January 24, 1884, valued her personal estate at exactly £1,568, 2 shillings, 6 pence. (Today that would be over £90,000, or, in U.S. currency, over $180,000.) In Georgina's will the majority of bequests are to family members and neighbors, including the Cholmondeleys. Her executor is Hugh Horatio Seymour, Esq.

Documentation is paltry concerning the latter part of Georgina's life. She bequeathed item upon item to a great number of people, indicating that she had a wide acquaintanceship, though mostly in the Cheshire environs. Those named include Seymours, Heathcotes, Langdales, Williams-Wynns, and Willoughby d'Eresbys.

The Seymours—Hugh Horatio is her executor—come in for a fair number of bequests. This family is related to another branch of the Cholmondeley family, from Vale Royal in Cheshire. The Cholmondeleys of Vale Royal were later created the barons Delamere of Vale Royal. Hugh Cholmondeley was the second Lord Delamere. The Williams-Wynns were related to these Cholmondeleys by marriage. The relationship with the Willoughby d'Eresbys is through the Bertie family, the dukes of Ancaster. The Bertie who married the first Marquess of Cholmondeley, Lady Charlotte, was the mother of the second and third Marquesses of Cholmondeley.

Over the years, as noted, Georgina's name appeared in Cavendish-Bentinck documents, all of them items relating to trusts, wills, and settlements of cash. She was deeded a large sum by Lord Cholmondeley and Grace Elliott the year after her father's remarriage to Lady Abdy. In August 1860 she petitioned for, and received, the £5000 from her parents' 1809 marriage settlement, the sum that was settled on Grace's daughter by the Cavendish-Bentincks.

As to her marriage prospects, unless there was something terribly wrong with her such as a disability, a birth defect, some physical unattractiveness, or an unstable or repellent personality or character—Georgina would have been, as a young, wealthy heiress of good family, an excellent candidate for marriage into a prestigious upper-class or aristocratic family, or a well-to-do mercantile family looking for an infusion of blue blood to enrich its own.

Was there a shortage of male candidates for her hand? There was no major population-decimating war during Georgina's most eligible years, from 1827, when she was sixteen, through the late 1840s, when she would have been in her late thirties. Waterloo—which claimed the lives of at least fifteen thousand of Wellington's forces, almost five hundred of whom were officers—took place in 1815, when she was four years old. The Crimean War, the next great destroyer of the lives of young Englishmen, did not begin until 1853, when Georgina was long past what was considered marriageable age.

What did happen during Georgina's life, however, were a great number of terrible epidemics, spread, ironically, by modern and faster modes of transportation. Some of the epidemics were so threatening to life throughout the world that they were termed pandemics. From 1816 through 1819 there were outbreaks of typhus and smallpox. Prior to that, influenza epidemics raged in England. Living in an urban area or a port city increased one's chances of catching diseases like influenza, typhus, and smallpox.

Cholera was a major killer out of India. The first great cholera pandemic of the nineteenth century occurred from 1817 through 1823. It was thought to have originated in Calcutta and from there to have spread to Southeast Asia, China, and Japan. It hit Russia and the Middle East, but the cold winter of 1823–1824 kept it out of Western Europe. The second cholera pandemic (1826–1827) did find its deadly way to Western Europe, reaching England in 1831–1832, possibly on a ship sailing from Hamburg in October 1831. It was by far the most serious of these outbreaks. The third pandemic reached Europe between 1848 and 1849, the fourth between 1863 and 1865, the fifth went from 1881 to 1896, and the last major outbreak of the nineteenth century began in 1899 but did not impact greatly on Western Europe.

In 1831, Georgina was twenty years old, in 1848, she was thirty-seven; and in 1853, she was forty-two. By the time the third cholera pandemic had run its course, her childbearing years were over. That a suitor or suitors might have fallen prey to cholera or some other epidemic disease is not impossible. If large numbers of eligible males died from these diseases, it would seriously affect the marriage chances of even the wealthiest heiresses.

Another possibility emerges from the pages of *A Regency Elopement*, that retelling of the courtship and marriage of Georgina's father, Lord Charles, and his second wife, Anne, Lady Abdy, née Wellesley. Hugh Farmar based the book on his analysis of some seven hundred family letters that had passed down to his cousin, Richard Wellesley, who'd suggested the idea of a book to him for the pleasure of their family. (The letters are now preserved at the University of Southampton.)

Georgina might have been obese, perhaps even grossly so, given this nickname that Farmar recalls from family lore:

> Now a maiden lady of large proportions, a substantial income and a benevolent disposition, this generous and indulgent relation, another example of supreme Victorian respectability sprung from raffish and, in part, uncertain origins, was affectionately known in the younger generation as "The Old Hippopotamus."

Ugh! A large and unlovely animal, the hippopotamus . . . Not a pleasing image. If Georgina was grossly unattractive, it could explain the absence of portraits or photographs.

With regard to Georgina's possible biological ancestry, it should again be noted that King George IV became grossly overweight in his old age. Modern knowledge of heredity indicates that a tendency to fat can be inherited. Was she, then, George's granddaughter after all? (Lord Cholmondeley, whom many believed to be her father, was also a very large man.) Unless a family member undertakes to disinter her remains and ask for a DNA test, we shall never know. At this late date, though, does it matter?

Whatever explanation there may be for Georgina's unwed state, it is not outside the realm of possibility that she didn't want to enter into marriage at all. She may have been quite happy to be a spinster and for all we know may even have been a lesbian. But, lacking evidence from her letters or diaries, there's no clue as to what really happened in her life and why she remained a spinster.

What do we know of her character or personality? Her defense of her grandmother—a notorious lady by the standards of any era, particularly the Victorian—indicates Georgina was a brave, loyal woman who may not have cared what others thought. If she did, indeed, bring Grace Elliott's *Journal* to the attention of the British Museum and then perhaps to that of the publisher Richard Bentley over the objections of family, she was stubborn, single-minded, and not easily deterred from her goals.

Tough. She has to have been tough. Not many women would or could stand up to family pressures during the Victorian era, when patriarchal rule was the name of the game. Women still did not have the vote and were under the thumb of husbands if they were married and of fathers and brothers if they were not. One can safely assume from her determination to get her grandmother's memoir published that Georgina Cavendish-Bentinck was an independent lady. Yes, she was generous, benevolent, and indulgent, and was looked upon with affection by those who knew her, according to Hugh Farmar. But she was tough and independent-minded as well.

She must also have recognized that Grace Elliott's *Journal* was a brilliant piece of writing. Though short, it was a compelling read. The immediacy of the narrative and the winning personality of its author shine through its pages. Grace had been an educated woman; her daughter was probably clever; Georgina, in her assessment of the *Journal*'s literary merit, shows intelligence.

Was she a feminist, then, or a very early, budding suffragist? The woman's suffrage movement did not get started until late in the nineteenth century. The Women's Social and Political Union was founded in 1903, when Georgina had been dead for twenty years. She may, though, have had the character and personality of a potential suffragist, an individual who supported rights for women in all arenas, including the right to vote—but there's no concrete evidence.

Georgina, however, was aware that marriage was not necessarily an ideal state for women. She may well have been single out of her own deliberate choice. Marriage was not always desirable, even in the most privileged classes—especially if arranged, and if the woman was intelligent and strong willed and had a mind of her own. Women not only lost their independence upon marriage, they stood a good chance of losing their lives in childbirth. She certainly had enough examples in her family of the latter, including her mother.

Consider the pessimism in this revealing passage from Lady Louisa Stuart (1757–1851), who was roughly a contemporary of Georgina's, on woman's lot:

> The truth is, woman has a natural dependence on man, which, do what she will, she can never shake off. I believe (in earnest believe) it part of the curse originally laid on Eve, "Thy desire shall be to thy husband, and he shall rule

over thee," which she can by no means elude by taking no husband, or surviving one, or keeping her heart free from a tyrannical passion. A son or a brother takes the reins, or a clergyman, a lawyer, a physician, becomes her governor. If she can escape all and stand quite alone, quite independent of man, tant pis pour elle, *it only renders her existence uncommonly forlorn and desolate. I have seen a woman forced to endure treatment from her butler that would have been held just cause of complaint against a husband. . . . It seems a very fine thing to be utterly independent, but God almighty made no woman to be so.*

How true is this depressing picture? If a woman was unmarried, and thus not under the jurisdiction of a husband, there were plenty of other males who could and would place restrictions on her freedom. There's more than a suggestion of how Georgina may have felt about this when she states firmly in her will that her female beneficiaries are the beneficiaries, *not* their husbands:

And I direct that all bequests in favor of persons who may be married women at the time of my death shall be for their respective sole and separate use.

"For their sole and separate use." Yes, she understood the workings of her society and times very well.

A word about women's wills is necessary here. Very, very few wills of married women are to be found before the twentieth century. Prior to this time, most wills were those of widows, not wives, and most spinsters had little to leave. When a wife died, there were no formalities to go through: everything belonged to her husband. When a husband died (as can be seen in Lord Cholmondeley's long and detailed will, probated in 1827), the normal way of things was to give the widow a life interest in his estate, with the assets ultimately left to the children or other heirs.

From the early middle ages there were repeated attempts to render the wills of married women illegal. The dying Catherine of Aragon, spurned wife of Henry VIII, refusing to admit that she was divorced to the last, got her physician to write a "little bill . . . knowing according to English law a wife can make no will."

Catherine was not quite right. The Church had managed to salvage some women's rights and a wife was allowed to bequeath her personal savings, property given her for her own separate use, pin money, maintenance, and any assets which were "in action," such as money she had in hand as executrix or administratix of somebody else. She might also be empowered to make a will under the terms of the marriage settlement. Her husband had to approve the contents of the will and the appointment of an executor.

Georgina appears to have been luckier than most in her male relatives and guardians. Grace Elliott's blessing of the girl's "protectors" in her will seems to have been heartfelt. Georgina had been privileged to have Lord Cholmondeley looking out for her interests during her girlhood, as well as these other unnamed but caring individuals. It was not easy to be a female in the century into which she came of age.

Now imagine this middle-aged spinster just shy of fifty, Georgina Cavendish-Bentinck, this "maiden lady of large proportions," doing her research and selecting the best publisher in London for her grandmother's memoir; see her picking out a no-nonsense costume to conduct this business; envision her girding her substantial loins and getting herself psyched to stride briskly through the offices of said publisher, Richard Bentley & Son, on New Burlington Street, in the late fall of 1858. There she is, in the flesh, making her impassioned pitch! Grace Elliott, to her granddaughter, may have been the model of an independent woman, a survivor in a world dominated by men, a heroine.

It's not a difficult scene to evoke, though it may be rather fanciful. Georgina may have approached Bentley through an intermediary at the British Museum and they may never have met face to face. But, unquestionably, the lady had spirit. She may not have inherited her grandmother's willowy, sylphlike figure, her large-eyed, extraordinary beauty, but she had her indomitable spirit, her bravery, her strong sense of loyalty, her passion.

It was in her blood and sinews, straight from Grace Elliott herself.

CHAPTER FIFTEEN

"De Langueur"

Ville d'Avray is a picturesque French village of twelve thousand people on a hilly site in the region called Hauts-de-Seine, just outside Paris, near the town of Sèvres. Among the many artists who painted this beautiful place many times were Alfred Sisley and Camille Corot.

Grace spent the final two years of her life as a lodger in the home of Ville d'Avray's mayor, a Monsieur Dupuis. The mayor—who served for ten years, 1816–1826—had acquired some land in 1790 and 1818 and had a house built at what is now lot 57 on rue Saint-Cloud, at the hilly end of the street. (The house has since been demolished, so no photos are available.) Accordinging to *Ville d'Avray—Its Roads and Its Streets,* written for the Société des

Amis du Músee de Ville d'Avray by a Madame Matheron in 1992, Dupuis was an *intendant*—a district administrator—for the noble family of Baron Thierry of that area. Thierry was a *valet de chambre* for the King. Grace's network of friends in Paris may have located this lodging for her.

Despite her comments in the *Journal* that her eighteen-month stay in French prisons had not been detrimental to her health, the effects of that imprisonment, with its bad food and inhumane living conditions, coupled with the stress of not knowing if she'd survive from one day to the next, seem finally to have caught up with her. Grace put a brave face on it, but that year and a half had bad consequences:

> *But even in all these moments of distress my health was perfect; and God Almighty never forsook me, as I bore my misfortunes with calm and resignation. I found all my comfort in religion.*

Perhaps so, but she contradicts herself and says in various passages that she suffered from severe sore throats and fever. But even when very ill, Grace counted her blessings that she was not "perishing by the hands of the executioner, and being made a show for the horrid crowds which followed the poor victims to the scaffold." In those terrible days, one had to consider the alternative.

She must have been constantly hungry, and she notes her gratitude for the occasional gifts of food she received, even from people like General Antoine-Joseph Santerre (the man who'd conducted the King to the scaffold, and who himself had been jailed briefly during the Terror), whom she did not respect:

> *He used to send us little trifles for our comfort, and I will say that he never lost an opportunity of serving us. When he was at liberty he sent me a pound of the finest green tea I ever drank, and some sugar. He also sent us a pie; but the gaoler liked that too well to give us any of it.*

Grace states in her *Journal* that she'd been fed mostly on a diet of "pickled herrings [the Dutch had sent great quantities of the fish to France to pay off a debt] at the rate of two pence a-day, with one bottle of water for all purposes." The state was paying for the prisoners' sustenance:

> *The gaoler was allowed about eight pence English a day for our food, and God knows he did not spend six pence. We had for constant food boiled haricots [green beans], sometimes hot and sometimes cold; when hot they were dressed*

with rancid butter, when cold with common oil; we had also bad eggs dressed in different ways. A favourite thing was raw pickled herrings. Sometimes we had what was called soup and bouilli but we were always sick after eating it. Some of the prisoners thought that it was human flesh . . . but I really think that it was horses' or asses' flesh, or dead cows. . . . Our bread was made of barley, and very dirty, and used to make our throats sore.

She comments that a number of the prisoners had problems with their teeth, but that she never did, as she managed to wangle a few drops of brandy from one of the jailers every day and gargled with it. She said it kept her teeth and gums healthy, though she hated the taste. Alcohol is a major component of some modern-day mouthwashes, so it makes sense that the brandy would have helped to maintain oral health.

Whatever the ultimate cause of her death—her incarceration, her genes, a disease, old age—Grace was in a weak state those last two years in France and she died slowly, possibly from tuberculosis. If her health and finances had been better, she probably would have been no one's lodger. The diagnosis given, *"de langueur"* (from wasting away), can cover a variety of ailments, including tuberculosis and even depression, a sad condition that affects many elderly people alone in the world.

Her will was begun on September 19, 1822, and completed on March 26, 1823. She died two months later. On the earlier date, she stated that she was "very ill," so she was in a bad way for at least eight months.

In concluding his two-part essay on Grace's *Journal,* the *Times* reviewer chillingly notes:

[Mrs. Elliott] died quietly and almost obscurely at Ville d'Avray. "Starvation and neglect" are hinted at, and they were probably her fate, from which neither the remembrance of her beauty or courage procured her immunity.

One is suddenly reminded of the scene in the film *Zorba the Greek,* when the aged French courtesan Madame Hortense's impoverished Cretan neighbors descend upon her like scavengers on a sick animal as she's dying. They strip her room of all its furniture and belongings, even to the linens on her deathbed and the bedclothes in which she's wrapped.

That's not so far-fetched a scenario for an elderly person at the mercy of caretakers—strangers, really—far away from family and friends. (Many of us can add stories of such things occurring our own times—abuses in nursing homes and even in swankier settings.) But the reviewer's phrase is repeated from the very last sentence of Richard Bentley's epilogue to the *Journal*—and anything Bentley says is suspect, as it is merely hearsay. Moreover, the expression could not be more vague. What on earth is he saying? (He also remarks that she'd lived to see the expulsion of the Bourbons in 1830, when she'd already been dead seven years.) Bentley writes:

> *Thus ended the life of this remarkable woman; at one time cherished by the Princes and nobles of the land—at another, the miserable companion of nobles and peasants, reduced to one common level of wretchedness, expecting one moment to be led away to the scaffold, amidst the yells of an infuriated and brutal mob, and at another to perish from starvation and neglect.*

If the date of her birth—1754—was correct, she would have been about sixty-nine years old when she died on May 15, 1823. The death certificate is dated May 16, which has erroneously been used as her death date. The certificate, however, says she was *"décédée d'hyer six heures du soir"* (deceased yesterday at six in the evening). The certificate—in the original bound volume at the city hall in Ville d' Avray—states that she was sixty-three when she died. This would make the year of her birth 1760; thus she would have

Alfred Sisley, *The Hill Path, Ville d'Avray*, 1879. (Bridgeman Art Library)

been eleven when she married Dr. Eliot and not yet fourteen when she began her affair with Lord Valentia—which is absurd.

Bleackley says that she had almost reached her "allotted" Biblical time span, i.e., three score and ten, or seventy years of age, which is more likely. She's listed on the death certificate as *"Dame Georgette née D'alrymple en Écosse, veuve Elliotte,"* that is, Dame (or Madame) Georgette born Dalrymple in Scotland, the widow Elliott. Why her Christian name is given incorrectly is not known; it could have been a slip of the pen or it could be that some called her by that other name.

Grace received the last rites from a Roman Catholic priest, the Ville d'Avray curé, Père Courtin, who served in that capacity for ten years, from 1819 to 1829. Had Grace converted to Catholicism during the many years she spent in France? Had her Scottish family been secret Catholics? She'd gone to a French convent school when she was eleven years old and stayed there for at least four years. Or was Père Courtin the only cleric in this French town and for miles around who was available to come to Grace's deathbed?

It's possible Grace had been—or became—a practicing Roman Catholic. She was a Francophile and monarchist and she fit the profile. The church in Ville d'Avray was constructed between 1789 and 1790. During the French Revolution, when Catholicism was abolished, this church, Saint-Nicolas-Saint-Marc, briefly became a *"temple de raison"* (temple of reason). The historic marble church is situated in the middle of the village on the rue de Sévres.

Contrary to a rumor that Grace was the mistress of Mayor Dupuis, or was the mayor's wife, she was but a paying guest. It would be a stretch to imagine the once-glittering Grace as a mere municipal employee's mistress when she'd numbered royals, nobles, and distinguished men among her conquests; Grace's men were always at the very top of the food chain. She was also old and ill, not in the best shape to be anyone's bedmate.

She was probably very lonely. Her daughter Georgiana was dead ten years; her friend Lady Fleming, five years, her former lovers, too, had begun to die off. Only the Prince of Wales and Lord Cholmondeley would survive her, and not by much. She'd moved to Ville d'Avray—perhaps from her Meudon cottage, perhaps from somewhere else—to die. The only English people she mentions in her will are the Reverend Joshua Greville (true to form, she calls him Josiah); his wife, Sophia; their child (Grace's godson) Peniston; and a Mary Curtis, who witnessed her will and of whom nothing else is known. (The Anglican priest Greville was for forty years the vicar of St. Luke's, Duston, Northamptonshire.)

Georgina Cavendish-Bentinck was twelve years old when Grace died. There's no record of any visits, but much affection shines through in Grace's will for her beloved granddaughter. Grace had made sure, with Lord Cholmondeley, that the girl would be provided for, loved, and protected. The girl, too, must have had affectionate feelings toward Grace, as exemplified in her drive to get her grandmother's *Journal* published.

There are records of two other children, both girls, in Grace's story. J. G. Alger, the author of the *DNB* article, makes a sly reference to one of them, whom Grace adopted, comparing this "adoption" to that of a mistress of the Duc d'Orléans—Madame de Genlis—and the so-called adoption of the girl, Hermine, born of her liaison with him. Bleackley takes his cue from Alger and also hints that this girl is Grace's biological child.

The girl Grace adopted on March 20, 1794, before the Municipal Assembly in Meudon, was the daughter of a former groom of Philippe's named Guillaume Staunton, an Englishman; the girl was nine years old and had been born on French soil. The latter is important because Grace needed to adopt a French citizen in order to remain in France after she left prison. She took responsibility for this child after Staunton's death, and the girl would have been Grace's legal heir under French law. All that's known of her, according to Bleackley, is that she had musical talent; he states that she would have inherited all of Grace's goods. The girl is not even mentioned in Grace's will.

Sometime in 1793, a friend of Grace's named Madame de Périgord entrusted her with her two young children, a girl, Melanie, who was nine, and a son who was five. Amazingly, the woman planned to flee to Calais and leave these children behind. Says Grace in her *Journal*, "She entreated me to adopt them as my own." This adoption did not take place, but Grace kept them with her for six weeks, sending them for safekeeping when she was about to be arrested to another woman, Madame de Jarnac, who in turn sent them to a former maid of Madame de Périgord's. The children apparently survived all this shuffling around and Grace noted that Melanie eventually became a Madame de Noialles.

Later that year, on December 9, 1793, Grace signed her name as witness for two of her servants in Meudon, Nicolas Giguet and Elizabeth Dourdan, on the birth certificate of their daughter, Georgina Françoise. Nothing more is known of this girl.

". . . My Blessing Is All I Can Leave Her": Grace Elliott's Last Will and Testament

There can be few wills extant that read more sadly than the one Grace Dalrymple Elliott dictated to a scribe on March 26, 1823. In it she says:

> *I fear when my lawful Debts are paid little will remain for my dear Grand Daughter but I in my last moments pray for her happiness and for that of her kind and respectable protectors and if my blessing is all I can leave her may she ever be good and grateful and may God Almighty protect her and all the Cholmondeley Family and may we all meet in heaven if our blessed Lord forgives my sins and disobedience to his Commandments. These shall be my last Prayers.*

In contrast to that great blowhard Sir John Eliot's will, which rambles on for seven pages, and to Lord Cholmondeley's massive will, which is standard for a very wealthy peer with a lot of money and property to dole out and a good number of beneficiaries, Grace's will is half a page. The hand it's written in is small, cramped, and hard to read, with many unintelligible words. (The copy sent to Lord Cholmondeley in England for safekeeping is, thankfully, readable.)

Most of what is left is directed to go to Georgina Cavendish-Bentinck, but it is somewhat undefined and seems paltry, consisting of

> *all my Laces and Trinquets that I may have at my death . . . also all my clothes . . . to give to who she pleases . . . as I have none to whom I wish to leave them also all my plate . . . All the effects Monies and other things I may possess . . . shall belong to my dear Grand Daughter.*

In contrast to this, there is a rather astonishing spelled-out bequest for a large amount of money to someone whose name has not appeared before connected to Grace Elliott, with a surprising statement that Grace expects to be receiving money from a settlement:

> *As I hope to receive Money from the settling of the Queensbury Cause I*

shall expect all my lawful Debts to be paid which there is £1,000 to Sophia Greville Wife of the Rev. Joshua Greville which was lent to me in lawful Money and also £100 to her son Peniston Greville my God Son I also leave him my Gold Watch.

There is no information whatsoever about this "Queensbury Cause." What on earth was Grace talking about? Note that no jewelry—copious amounts of which she must have owned at one time—is mentioned; nor are the Reynolds or Gainsborough portraits. No property at all. Village lore has it that the Dupuis family took the furnishings of Grace's quarters, having purchased them from Grace's heirs, but what heirs? Furniture is not mentioned in the will, though laces, "trinquets," plate, and old clothes are. It is unclear who bought the furnishings in the first place—Dupuis or Grace—but they were said to have wound up in the hands of the heirs of Mayor Dupuis. "These rumors," according to the author's local French researcher, Colette Pozzi-Barsot, "have been collected by a local historian, long deceased, and the sources are impossible to verify."

The will is witnessed by a Mary Curtis, who may have been a friend or Grace's servant, and signed by both her and Grace, who signs as Grace Dalrymple, not Grace Elliott. The will was probated by John Lovegrove of 1 Pall Mall, a clerk in the banking firm of "Messrs. Ransom and Company of London" on December 16, 1824. (This firm of bankers connected with Grace is variously given as "Morland Ransom," "Morland Ransome,"or just "Ransom," and later in the nineteenth century as "Ransom Bouverie.")

Lovegrove states that Grace has had a twenty-four-year relationship with Ransom and that she was formerly of "Michaels Place, Brompton," which is on Brompton Road and only a few streets from Brompton Park. This confirms that she had been living in London in the Brompton Road area, whether at Brompton Park House, nearby, or at that Mrs. Naylor's in Brompton, and that she was resident there for a number of years after 1800.

Because Grace was an English citizen who died in a foreign country, her will was subject to probate in England, and verification procedures had to be carried out. Lovegrove states that Grace was a longtime client of Ransom's, that she was personally known to him, and that he can recognize her handwriting and signature. Lord Cholmondeley will have to pay £32, 10 shillings, 5 pence for various fees connected with the filing of her will in

In the Name of the Father the Son and
Holy Ghost amen this is my will and testament made at Ville D'Avray
this 19th of Sept in the year of our Lord 1822 my being very ill and not
leaving any other will either here in France or in England and
wishing that my beloved Granddaughter Georgiana Augusta Frederica
Dorothea Henrietta Cavendish Bentinck daughter to Lord Charles Wm
Bentinck 2nd Son to the late Duke of Portland and Brother to the present
Duke by my Granddaughter in lawful marriage Georgiana Augusta
Frederica Seymour commonly called Lady Charles Bentinck as I hope
to receive money by the settling of the Aumesbury Cause I shall expect
all my lawful debts to be paid of which there is one thousand pounds
to Sophia Orville wife to the Revd Jos   Orville which she lent
me in lawful money and also one hundred pounds to her Son Preston
Orville my Godson I also leave him my Gold watch all my Lace and
trinkets that I may leave at my death to my dear Granddaughter
Georgiana Augusta Frederica Cavendish Bentinck also all my Cloathes
at her disposal to give to whom she please which I suppose will be
Maria Williams her Maid as I have now to whom I wish to leave
them also all my plate to my said Granddaughter G. A. F. D. Cavendish
Bentinck all the Effects money and other things Proffitts after these Legacies
are paid and my lawful debts shall belong to my dear Granddaughter
Georgiana Augusta Frederica Dorothea Cavendish Bentinck this is my will
and I shall send one Copy to England to the Marquis Cholmondeley and
keep the other here they are both signed and sealed by me at Ville D'Avray
near Paris the 26th of March 1823 G Dalrymple Elliott
I fear when my lawful debts are paid little will remain for my
dear Granddaughter but I in my last moments pray for her happiness
and for that of her kind and respectable protectors and if my blessing is
all I can leave her may she ever be good and grateful and may God
Almighty ever protect her and all the Cholmondeley ffamily and may
we all meet in Heaven if our blessed Lord forgives my Sins and
disobeying to his Commandments these shall be my last prayers
G Dalrymple Elliot
This is my last and only will made at Ville d'Avray near Paris
Sept 1822 and finished March the 26th 1823 at the same place
signed and sealed by me witness Mary Curtis G Dalrymple
Mary Curtis

Appeared personally John Lovegrove of No 1 Pall Mall
East in the County of Middlesex and that he is a Clerk in the Banking
house of Messrs Ransom and Company of London and hath so been
for about twenty four years last past that during the last three
years of the said time Grace Dalrymple otherwise Grace
Dalrymple Elliot formerly of Michael's Place Brompton in the County
of Middlesex but late of Ville d'Avray near the City of Paris single
woman deceased kept a Cash account and was in the habit of
drawing Bills or drafts on the said Banking house for money at
different periods which often came under this deponent's inspection
when presented for payment and thereby he this deponent became
well acquainted with the manner and character of her handwriting
and subscription and he having now carefully viewed and inspected
the paper writings hereunto purporting to be the last will and testament
of the said deceased written in the English Language which begins
thus "In the Name of the Father Son and Holy Ghost this is my
will and testament made at Ville d'Avray this 19th of Sept in the year
of our Lord 1822" ends thus "This is my last and only will made at Ville
d'Avray near Paris Sept 1822 and finished March the 26th 1823 at the

(National Archives, Kew)

MY LADY SCANDALOUS 357

same place signed and sealed by me witness Mary Curtis" and is thus subscribed "E. Dalrymple" he saith he hath not the least doubt but doth verily and in his conscience believe that the whole body arms and contents of the said will and the names "E. Dalrymple Elliot and E. Dalrymple" thereto set and subscribed were and are of the proper handwriting and subscription of the said Grace Dalrymple otherwise Grace Dalrymple Elliot deceased J. Lovegrove 10th Augt 1824 the said mr John Dawson was duly sworn to the truth of this affidavit before me John Daubeny, Sur. Prof. Mark Morley Noty Pub ‑

On the 16 December 1824 admion (with the will annexed) of the Goods Chattels and Credits of Grace Dalrymple otherwise Grace Dalrymple Elliot formerly of Richards Place Brompton in the County of Middlesex but late of Ville d'Avray near the City of Paris single woman deceased was granted to the most Honorable Georgiana Charlotte Marchioness of Cholmondeley wife of the most Honorable George Marquis of Cholmondeley the Curatrix or Guardian lawfully assigned to Georgiana Augusta Frederica Dorothea Henrietta Camilla Seymour a minor the testamentary Legatee named in the said will having been first sworn duly to administer for the use and benefit of the said minor and until she shall attain her age of twenty one years no Executor being named in the said will the Right Honorable William Charles Cavendish Bentinck commonly called Lord William Charles Cavendish Bentinck the natural and lawful father of the said minor having first renounced the Curation or Guardianship to the minor aforesaid as by Court appear./

Thomas Dand

42

This is the last Will and Testament of me Thomas Dand of Little Walton in the parish of Monks Kirby in the County of Warwick Grazier I give and bequeath unto my Sons Joseph Dand and John Dand and my daughters Priscilla Dand and Maryann Dand the Sum of one thousand Seven hundred pounds apiece to and for their own use and benefit respectively I give and bequeath unto my Son Thomas Dand the Sum of one thousand pounds for his own use and benefit and I give and bequeath unto my daughter Sophia Deval the Sum of Seven hundred pounds for her own use and benefit all which said portions Legacies I will and direct shall be paid to my said Children respectively at the expiration of twelve Calendar Months next after my decease but without Interest in the meantime I give and bequeath all my household Goods and furniture implements and Utensils of household plate Linen and all my Stock of Cattle Crops of Corn Grain and hay Implements of husbandry and all other my farming Stock whatsoever and wheresoever together with the Tenant right and occupation of mine and to my farm at Little Walton aforesaid unto my Son Thomas Dand to and for his own use and benefit I give and bequeath unto Marston Buzzard of Lutterworth in the County of Leicester Banker and my Son in Law George Deval of Little Ashby in the said County of Leicester Grazier their Executors and Admtors the Sum of Six thousand pounds upon the trusts hereinafter mentioned and expressed concerning the same and all the rest and residue of my monies Securities for money personal Estate and Effects whatsoever and wheresoever not hereinbefore by me disposed of after payment of all my just debts ffuneral Testamentary Expenses I give and bequeath unto the said Marston Buzzard and George Deval and the Survivor of them upon trust that they the said Marston Buzzard and George Deval and the Survivor

France; for a copy of her will to be sent to England; for French lawyers, notaries, and couriers; for the payment of other duties; and for transportation expenses. There are also English death duties. (In a letter from W. E. Allen, of Grace's Paris bank, dated March 8, 1826, the £32 looks like £72. Did Allen make a mistake transcribing the original bills? Did Cholmondeley pay £40 more than he should have? Copies of all of these are at Houghton Hall.)

There is also an odd notation in the invoices from the banker referring to a sister of Grace's. That cannot be right, can it? If so, who is this person? Whoever this person was, she went to Sévres—a larger municipality close to Ville d'Avray and Meudon—to swear that the signature on Grace's will was actually hers. The sum of £1 (plus 5 shillings for the coachman) was paid "for a Carriage when Mrs. Elliott's sister went to Notary at Sévres with the intention of certifying to Mrs. E's hand writing . . . 25 f [francs] or . . . £1."

The will reads like that of an almost-destitute person, but was she, really? She lived on the annuities from the Prince, from Dr. Eliot, and possibly from Lord Cholmondeley, all of which brought in at least £500 annually (£35,000/$70,000 today) and might have been as much as £1,000 annually (£60,000/$120,000 today) Though she could not have been living in the grand and extravagant style of her salad days, she did have substantial monies coming in just from the annuities alone.

For some moralists it satisfies a certain schadenfreude to picture a former courtesan who lived an immoral life dying in poverty, alone and neglected. The reviewer of the *Journal* in the *Times* in 1859 made just that point, saying that "as an illustration of Princely gratitude, her lot was . . . commonplace." Though one hates to disappoint such people, who get off on seeing women of dubious virtue get their comeuppance with an ignominious end, it may not have been the case at all.

Living with the mayor's family was not exactly like living in an almshouse; Grace was a paying guest who needed care. She made a will. Poor people, especially females, did not make wills. Making a will implies something to leave. Grace had things to leave, as it turns out, but her expenditures and debts may have outstripped what she had in the bank and was receiving as dividends from various kinds of stock, including "India Bonds" and "Bank Stock."

Letters between Lord Cholmondeley and the banker W. E. Allen go back and forth, as they attempt to straighten out Grace's financial affairs. It seems a mess, further complicated by the claim of her adopted French daughter, referred to only as "formerly Miss Staunton," to Grace's estate. There seems to have been no resolution, that is, there are no letters indicating the issue was resolved, but all matters were laid in Lord Cholmondeley's hands.

Interestingly, Grace's last dressmaker's bill was sent to Lady Cholmondeley (who may have been—of all things—Grace's executor, according to a note appended to the probated will). An undated letter, in the same group as the dressmaker's detailed invoice, is at Houghton Hall. Written in a charming, clear, girlish hand, it's signed "G.A.F.H. C Bentinck," and can only be young Georgina, Grace's granddaughter, who is passing on the bill, per Lady Cholmondeley's instructions, for payment. She writes:

> *Sir*
> *I am desired by Lady Cholmondeley to send the enclosed Papers relative to Mrs. Elliott for your inspection.*
> *I remain Sir*
>
> > *Your obliged and humble*
> > *Serv. G.A.F.H. C Bentinck*

The bill is in two parts, dated 1821 and 1822, and was forwarded from Paris on the seventeenth (of September?), 1824, by someone named Hobby, on the porte Saint-Honoré. This Hobby asks that the payment be sent to a Mrs. Campbell on Charles Street, No. 3, Grosvenor Square. A second letter from Hobby was sent to Lady Cholmondeley on September 15, 1825. On October 5, 1825, Lord Cholmondeley sent it to his solicitor. (Whether or not Hobby or Campbell ever received payment of this invoice is not known, but that was one of the drawbacks tradespeople faced in dealing with the ton: getting paid for goods and services provided.) Whatever transpired, the costly goods show that Grace Elliott was still interested in keeping up a good appearance:

August 20th, 1821:

Six Ells of fine flannel at 6/	36
Six Pair of Silk Stockings at 9/	54
Ten Ells of fine Scotch Cambric at 7/10	75

Ten Ells of Nett at 5/	50
A Fancy Dress	50
July 5th, 1822:	
Two Pounds of Windsor Soap	12
Nine Gauze handkerchiefs at 3/10	31-10
A Fancy Shawl	30
Total:	338-10

(An ell is an old English measurement, equivalent to about forty-five inches, or the length from the elbow to the middle finger's tip, used mainly for measuring fabric.)

Grace comes off as heavily religious in this document. The phrase "if our blessed Lord forgives my sins" is, yes, typical of the times, but for such a short document, a lot of space is taken up with entreaties to God, prayers for her soul and for the welfare of young Georgina. Did Grace experience a religious conversion during her time in those French prisons or in her last years? Did she repent a life she may have come to recognize as sinful? Was she religious all along? Did the French nuns at her convent instill in her a deep piety that no one ever knew was there? In the *Journal* she makes references to God's giving her courage and strength, particularly through her incarcerations, and that may have been what she genuinely felt.

A courtesan may be a sinner, but that doesn't mean Grace didn't believe in God. Her expression of hope that "our blessed Lord forgives my sins and disobedience to his Commandments" may mean she recognized she'd sinned—one can easily speculate on the number of Commandments she'd broken—and she was looking for salvation. The sentiments seem sincere, and she comes off as a true believer, whether or not she actually was.

One hopes, though, that the good Lord did forgive Grace her sins. That reunion in heaven . . . it must have been something else.

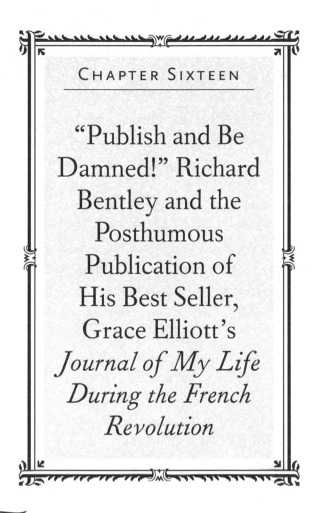

"Publish and Be Damned!" Richard Bentley and the Posthumous Publication of His Best Seller, Grace Elliott's *Journal of My Life During the French Revolution*

The eminent Victorian publisher of Grace Elliott's *Journal*, Richard Bentley, was not a flamboyant man. One cannot imagine him or any of those with whom he dealt uttering anything like that famous phrase "Publish and be damned!"

That often-quoted remark—attributed to the Duke of Wellington—first surfaced in the memoirs of the courtesan Julia Johnstone. Her *Confessions: In Contradiction to The Fables of Harriette Wilson* was a rebuke to her former demimondaine friend, whom Johnstone felt had maligned her.

What Johnstone said was that Wellington had scribbled the phrase on the back of an envelope, and it was actually "Write and be damned!" This occurred in 1824, when Wellington (the distinguished hero of Waterloo and later Prime Minister under George IV) was being solicited, along with scores of other men, for a payment in cash of at least £200 to be left out of Wilson's kiss-and-tell memoirs, which were to be published beginning in 1825.

The publisher of that notorious tome, *The Memoirs of Harriette Wilson, Written by Herself,* was a dodgy fellow named John Joseph Stockdale, a publisher and pornographer with few scruples—not unlike the dissembler Wilson—whose activities led to frequent arrests, convictions, and time behind bars. Though Wellington may never have uttered or written either version, it remains one of the great quotes of all time.

But Richard Bentley was no John Joseph Stockdale, and Grace Elliott, though also a courtesan, was no mere strumpet like the tell-all memoirists Harriette Wilson and Julia Johnstone. Grace's *Journal* is discreet, and the respectable publisher Bentley was as far as one could get from someone like Stockdale the pornographer.

Bentley's publication of Grace Elliott's polished memoir of the French Revolution was not a matter of damning, but of confusing. There's a lot of confusion in what he writes about Grace's personal life and how he came by the manuscript. His editorial comments in the prologue and epilogue to her book have misled readers and perpetuated gross inaccuracies, causing many to doubt the veracity of her narrative.

Bentley served up the anecdotes and apocryphal tales he got from Grace's granddaughter, Georgina Cavendish-Bentinck, and others (alas, unnamed) who claimed to have known Grace. It's perhaps not fair to come down on the publisher, who was following the wishes of Miss Cavendish-Bentinck and, for want of any way of confirming her information, trusting what she—or her intermediary—told him. There may also have been a class issue as subtext. The forty-seven-year-old spinster who brought Grace's manuscript to him in 1858—after it was supposedly rejected by the British Museum—was cousin and niece to the prestigious dukes of Portland. How could Bentley—a plebeian tradesman, a cit, really—dare to challenge this aristocratic lady's version of events?

Bentley's firm was suffering large financial losses at about this time owing to the loss of American copyrights that had previously been the firm's exclu-

Richard Bentley's List

Excerpts from Mr. Bentley's 1859 list, as advertised in the *Times* on March 23, 1859. This included Grace Elliott's memoir of the French Revolution. Note the mix of fiction and nonfiction:

> *The Ingoldsby Legends* . . . illustrations of Cruickshank and Leech . . . 5 shillings
>
> *Buckland's Curiosities of Natural History* . . . 6 shillings
>
> *Simmonds' Curiosities of Food in all Countries* . . . 6 shillings
>
> *Mrs. Webb's Works:—The Martyrs of Carthage* . . . 5 shillings
>
> *Debit and Credit.* From the German of Freytag . . . By Mrs. Malcolm . . . 6 shillings
>
> *Lieut.-Col. Graham's History of the Art of War* . . . 7 shillings 6 pence
>
> *Passages from My Autobiography.* By Sydney, Lady Morgan . . . 14 shillings
>
> *The Polehampton Letters and Diaries* . . . 10 shillings 6 pence
>
> *The Three Clerks.* By the Author of "Barchester Towers" . . . 5 shillings

The advertisement for Grace's book reads:

Now ready, 8vo., with three beautiful Portraits from a Painting by Gainsborough, and from a Miniature by Cosway, 10s. 6d., Journal of My Life During the Great French Revolution. By Mrs. Grace Dalrymple Elliott. *Written at the express desire of His Majesty King George III. Richard Bentley, New Burlington-street, publisher in ordinary to Her Majesty.*

---

sive domain, and he was no doubt eager to print a book by a once-notorious woman who'd been a celebrated demirep and mistress to royalty. If it sold well, he could recoup some needed income. Nevertheless, as a conscientious publisher, he should have done some research.

Richard Bentley (1794–1871) went into the publishing business in 1829 with a partner named Henry Colburn, a publisher of fashionable novels; their company's premises were on New Burlington Street in Westminster. This was a good address. Bentley had previously owned a printing establishment with his older brother Samuel on Shoe Lane. According to an 1898 issue of *The Bookseller*, Bentley "was too enterprising and too energetic to be content with the ordinary routine of a printer's office. He was ambitious to become a publisher."

New Burlington Street was a big step up from Shoe Lane. Despite its name, the street had nothing to do with cobblers; the north end of the street had been the site of an ancient well called the Sho. The area was best known for its seventeenth-century cockpit and for broadsheet and sign shops. Richard and Samuel's father, Edward Bentley, had been part proprietor, with his brother-in-law John Nicholls, of the *General Evening Post*, on Red Lion Square. Printer's ink ran in the Bentley blood, and R. Bentley and J. Nicholls were considered among the best of their kind, excelling particularly in the rendering of woodcuts.

Colburn retired in 1832 and Bentley later took his own son George into the business, renaming it Richard Bentley & Son. In 1837 Bentley initiated his popular *Bentley's Miscellany* series, which was edited until 1840 by Charles Dickens. Bentley also published Dickens's second novel, *Oliver Twist*, coupling it with illustrations by George Cruikshank. With the huge success of this popular novel, Bentley offered a generous sum to Dickens for another of his books, *Barnaby Rudge*, but by that time the two of them had had an unfortunate falling out and the disgruntled author took his work elsewhere.

Beware the author who bears a grudge against his publisher! Dickens, who felt Bentley had taken advantage of him, skewered the man in his masterpiece, *Great Expectations*, modeling a villainous character—a wife beater named Bentley Drummle—on him. Writing in the *Guardian* in 2003, John Sutherland comments, "Everyone in literary London got the point. Most painfully, Bentley—right between the shoulder blades."

Despite the loss of Dickens, Richard Bentley & Son had a respectable list and the company was one of the major nineteenth-century English publishing houses, a solid Victorian firm handling both nonfiction (travel, autobiography, and history) and fiction. In 1860 they published that perennial favorite, Mrs. Henry Wood's *East Lynne*.

When Georgina Cavendish-Bentinck took her late grandmother's memoirs to Richard Bentley & Son she made a good and educated choice of publisher.

A special and elaborate edition of Grace's *Journal* showed up recently on eBay, the auction Web site. The seller, from the United Kingdom, presented an "Extra Illustrated" 1859 edition, described as "Grangerised [booksellers' jargon for "extra-illustrated"] with 39 extra engravings including ten coloured by hand. The subjects are mainly portraits and views." There is an "inlaid portrait" of Grace copied (badly, if one compares it to the original) from a Cosway miniature now in a private collection. This portrait is described as "a hand coloured print on (probably) vellum" and "under glass." The book's binding is "full morocco, ornately gilt, spine with 5 raised bands, silk end papers." The book sold for a mere $182 in early 2004 to a gentleman more interested in the beautiful Cosway binding than in the contents.

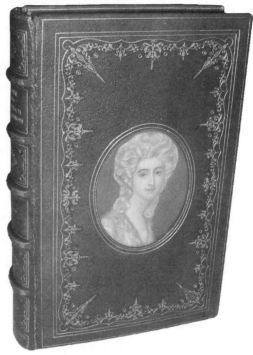

(Paul S. Smith)

There are several things to note in the ad for Grace Elliott's *Journal* in Bentley's 1859 list. One is the price, 10 shillings, 6 pence, which places it among the most expensive on the publisher's list. Another is the title, which varied in later editions, one of the variations being the omission of the word "Great." The book was quickly translated into French and issued in Paris by several publishers, going into a number of editions there.

An 1864 edition published by Michel Levy Freres titled it the *Mémoires de Madame Elliott sur La Révolution Française* (Mrs. Elliott's Memoirs of the French Revolution). A later edition ran this title: *Sous la Terreur: Journal d'une amie de Philippe-Égalité,* which translates as *Under the Terror: The Journal of a Friend of Philip-Equality.* (In this context, *amie* could also indicate lover, as *chère-amie* was a Regency term for mistress.)

Concerning the advertised illustrations, several editions of the *Journal* in both English and French were examined and were found to have a colored rendering of a Cosway miniature of Grace, and two engravings, one of the Duc d'Orléans, and the other from the Joshua Reynolds portrait of Grace's daughter Georgiana as a baby. Engravings of the two paintings of Grace by Thomas Gainsborough were not included in the *Journal.* The Reynolds portrait of Georgiana as a toddler, however, was lent by the Cholmondeleys to facilitate the engraving that appeared in the *Journal.* The engraving of the Duc d'Orléans presumably was made from a snuffbox (with a miniature portrait of him on the lid) that was supplied by Georgina.

Richard Bentley wrote both a prologue and an epilogue to the 1859 En-

Cosway Bindings

Cosway bindings are named after the English miniaturist artist Richard Cosway (1742?–1821). They were the invention of Henry Sotheran & Company, London booksellers, or their firm's manager, J. Harrison Stonehouse (1864–1937), in the first decade of the twentieth century. The books were bound by Robert Riviere of the firm of Riviere & Son in Levant morocco, finely tooled, gilt-stamped on the leather, gilt inner dentelles and all gilt edges, with exquisite watered-silk endpapers and glazed miniatures painted on ivory set into the front—and sometimes the back—covers. The volumes usually came with elegant slipcases. The painting of the miniatures was the undertaking of a Miss C. B. Currie (?–1940), who was responsible for the rendering of over nine hundred bindings during her career as a copier of miniatures. Grace Elliott's *Journal* predates these Stonehouse/Riviere/Currie Cosway bindings by decades, but the style in which Richard Bentley pre-pared the costlier editions of her memoir is very much in the tradition that this Cosway-style binding represents. The miniatures are not always on ivory, but they are always glazed and set below the level of the leather, which is Levant morocco, i.e., kidskin. Paul S. Smith, the purchaser of the Grangerised edition of the *Journal* recently sold on eBay, bought it for this special binding. He says of it that the Cosway binding "is simply a style of binding and any handcrafted, full-leather bound book with a hand-painted miniature inset into the front board would be referred to as a Cosway binding, despite the fact that Cosway had nothing to do with it. This is a not uncommon phenomenon in this rather obscure branch of art history." He adds, "It is just coincidence that the portrait of Grace Dalrymple Elliott that you have been trying to track down is also by Cosway."

glish edition of the *Journal,* though there is no credit line indicating he did so. These were carried verbatim—and uncorrected—into all subsequent editions of the book.

The statement that the memoir was "written at the express desire of His Majesty King George III" would have been a great selling point for the publisher, giving the tome added dignity and a touch of class, but it's doubtful that King George III (already slipping into mental illness at the time Grace wrote the memoir circa 1803) would have had any interest at all in a memoir by one of his profligate son's many mistresses. The notion is laughable.

Moreover, King George III and Queen Charlotte had been especially fond of Dr. John Eliot, who'd been the injured party in his scandalous divorce from Grace. By all accounts they had sympathized with Eliot. George III, dead thirty-nine years, could not contest the publisher's statement, nor could his son George IV, Grace's ex-lover, who'd been dead twenty-nine years when the book appeared.

Georgina Cavendish-Bentinck supposedly brought the manuscript to Richard Bentley because she'd been turned down in her attempt to donate it to the British Museum. Bentley reiterates this in a letter he sent to the editor of the *Times* on January 27, 1859, printed on January 28. He stated that a Mr. Levien of the British Museum "thought it not to be of sufficient extent to be entertained" for addition to the collection.

This may not be the whole story. Edward Levien worked in the manuscripts department of the British Museum and had been involved in at least one other transaction with the Bentley publishing firm. He appears to have acted as an intermediary between Georgina Cavendish-Bentinck and Richard Bentley. The letters they exchanged are tantalizing. It's possible that it was this Edward Levien, not Georgina herself, who answered all the questions Bentley asked.

Up to September 3, 1858, it seems, Miss Cavendish-Bentinck had not communicated directly with Richard Bentley, and perhaps she never did, so what's said in the prologue and epilogue by Bentley may be second- or even third-hand information. Miss Cavendish-Bentinck may have been far more removed from the publishing process than the writer of the *DNB* article on Grace Elliott realized. It's questionable how much of what Bentley wrote is valid, but what's contained in his prologue and epilogue is what has been repeated over the years.

Clearly, the manuscript had been in Georgina's keeping, or available to her. But the circumstances—how long she had it and who might have had it previously—are a mystery. The memoir is not mentioned in the will Grace Elliott completed in 1823, so one might assume that the manuscript did not leave England with Grace in the early 1800s when she returned to France. She may have left it with her daughter, who died in 1813. It could easily have been passed on to Grace's granddaughter. This seems the most logical explanation of its provenance.

Note, too, that in that September 3 letter Bentley remarked, "I observe the Manuscript is torn off at the end. Can the remainder be recovered? It ends with her escape from prison." The manuscript was in a calf-bound folio and it would have been very clear if anything was "torn off." How many pages were gone? Why had they been removed? What did Grace Elliott write that someone saw fit to censor? This is yet another mystery that will probably never be resolved, but those Victorians did so love to censor! The memoir ends too abruptly.

According to J. G. Alger, in his *DNB* article on Grace Elliott, Georgina Cavendish-Bentinck came to Bentley's offices with the manuscript and "offered" it to him "against the wish of her family," who'd also objected to her taking it to the British Museum. There is already the question of whether she actually showed up in person—ever. And which family is Alger talking about? The Cavendish-Bentincks / dukes of Portland, her father's family, or the Cholmondeleys, now raised to the rank of marquesses, who brought her up and with whom she maintained a close relationship all of her life? This is not clear.

The *Times* ran that January 27 letter from Bentley explaining how he came by the manuscript and how he verified its authenticity immediately after a favorable two-part review of the *Journal* appeared on January 26 and January 27, 1859. In addition to repeating the story of the British Museum's refusal to take it, Bentley asserted:

> *Miss Bentinck kindly sent me the miniature of Mrs. Elliott by Cosway, allowed me to have the picture of Lady Charles Bentinck (Mrs. Elliott's daughter), by Sir J. Reynolds, from Lord Cholmondeley's in Carlton-terrace, for the purpose of engraving, and the miniature of the Duke of Orléans on a snuffbox, presented to Mrs. Elliott by that prince. . . . I owe you [the editor of the* Times*] thanks . . . [for giving me] the opportunity of establishing the authenticity of this MS., which remains in exactly the same state it was when written . . . and is published without addition whatsoever, or any alteration than that of dividing into chapters and paragraphs.*

The *Journal* went to several reprints and editions by Bentley, and, though copies of these are rarely seen today and are not inexpensive to purchase, it was bought by hundreds of libraries at the time of publication and can be seen today in rare books rooms, in archives, and on open circulation shelves. It was a best seller for Bentley, selling well until 1863. According to a Bentley ledger now in the Bentley Archive at the British Library, as of June 30, 1859, alone, six months after its publication, he'd made a profit of £594, 8 shillings, 8 pence (roughly £36,000/$72,000).

Editions of the work do vary; some have better bindings than others, and there was the special Grangerised edition with that hand-painted miniature. As noted, titles also vary. An edition in the Library of Memoirs series, published in London in 1908 and annotated by Helen Kendrick Hayes, bears the title *In the Shadow of the Guillotine* and refers to the author as an "intimate friend of Philippe Égalité."

In 1955, a reprint was published by the Rodale Press. It appeared in a series called Story Classics, conceived by the iconoclastic American publisher J. I. Rodale in the 1940s. The following excerpt from *J. I. Rodale—Apostle of Nonconformity,* by Carlton Jackson, was supplied by the Rodale family's archivist Mark Kintzel:

> *Story Classics . . . were reprints of some of the world's most famous literature.*
> *They included such selections as Longfellow's* Continental Tales, *Chekhov's*
> The Beggar *and* The Seagull, Selected Stories of Alphonse Daudet,
> *Pedro Antonio de Alarcón's* Tales *from the Spanish,* Prosper Mérimée's *Tales*
> of Love and Death, *and Molière's* The Doctor in Spite of Himself.

It's interesting that almost a hundred years after the publication of Grace Elliott's *Journal,* an editor would consider the book valuable enough to include with "the world's most famous literature." (The fact that it was out of copyright, however, could have been an additional impetus for the publisher. Publishers are eternally aware of the bottom line.) But along with whatever else she excelled at, Grace Dalrymple Elliott could write beautiful prose, and her memoir is proof of this.

As to Bentley, he continued to be a successful publisher, doing well with another series, Standard Novels, which ran to 127 volumes. In 1859, however, at the time he acquired *Journal of My Life During the French Revolution,* he'd unfortunately lost his right to publish American novels. The decision of the House of Lords that took away his copyright claims was a serious blow to the company's finances and one from which Richard Bentley & Son may never have fully recovered.

Less than ten years later, in 1867, Richard Bentley, a giant among Victorian publishers, suffered a serious accident at the Chepstow railway station that left him incapacitated.

Eminent Victorian publisher Richard Bentley (National Portrait Gallery, London)

Injuries owing to this marvel of new technology, the railroads, were to become more common as the years went on. At least he was luckier than the unfortunate statesman William Huskisson, who holds the dubious distinction of being the first railway fatality. Huskisson was struck by another car while attempting to get back into the car from which he'd just alighted. He was killed on the opening day of the Liverpool–Manchester Railway, September 15, 1830. In *The Last Journey of William Huskisson* (London: Faber & Faber, 2002), Simon Garfield writes:

> *There were a great many witnesses to the terrible accident which befell William Huskisson, but none could agree precisely what occurred. Some said his left leg fell on the track in one way, some quite another, and some said it was his thigh. A few observed a "fiery fountain" of blood, but others saw only a trickle. Some claimed there was shrieking, but the rest believed he was rendered mute by the shock. Yet there was one thing on which everyone agreed. They all said that the accident was the worst thing they had ever seen, and the one thing they would never forget.*

In the great interconnecting circles that made up British society in the eighteenth century—their version of today's six degrees of separation—the unfortunate William Huskisson and Grace Elliott had known each other. Huskisson was for a brief while private secretary to Lord Gower (later the Marquess of Stafford), the British ambassador in Paris and the grandnephew of that Dr. Gem who shared part of Grace's imprisonment. According to the 1949 edition of *The Dictionary of National Biography*, "after the attack on the Tuileries [August 10, 1792], he was instrumental in enabling its governor, M. de Champcenetz, to make his escape from the populace."

Grace Elliott tells a different story. With all the challenges made over the years to her *Journal of My Life During the French Revolution,* one thing that has not been challenged is that it was owing to her great courage—and that of her friend, Mrs. Meyler—that Champcenetz was able to survive after the horrific massacre at the Tuileries. The Duc d'Orléans—at considerable risk—was actually the one responsible for smuggling Champcenetz out of France. Huskisson's part, according to Grace's narrative, seems to have consisted merely of being "very kind to him" and lending him clothes; Lord Gower was no help at all. After Champcenetz made his slow journey, exhausted, sick, and desperate, to the British Embassy on the faubourg Saint-Germain, this is what Grace says happened:

> *On Chansenets' arrival there he saw Mr. Huskisson, Lord Gower's secretary, who was very kind to him, and went to inform Lord Gower of his being there. Lord Gower, however, as a public man, and not knowing what was to become of himself, could not receive him, as a strong proclamation had been published that night, and read by a man on horseback in the streets, prohibiting everybody, on pain of death, to receive or give any aid to the proscribed people who were with the King in the Tuileries, and thus pointing most at Monsieur de Chansenets as governor. Mr. Huskisson lent him clothes. When he left Lord Gower's he hardly knew what to do; nor had he any idea where to go.*

Simon Garfield spins the *DNB* story in more detail. In this version, Champcenetz goes to see Huskisson at his ambassadorial suite at the Hôtel de Monaco:

> *Huskisson knew de Champcentz slightly, and realized that he was in a difficult situation. If he threw him out he would become his murderer; if he sheltered him he could embarrass the Ambassador and create a perilous situation between England and France. Keeping his guest's presence a secret from Lord Gower, he hustled him out to the custody of a trustworthy laundry woman, and instructed that he receive money and a safe passage. Within a week, Huskisson learnt that he had successfully escaped from Paris, and a while later that he had been returned and restored to the government of Louis XVIII.*

Unfortunately, Huskisson died in 1830, and Grace's *Journal* was not published until twenty-nine years later, so we have no idea if he would have challenged her version of that event.

Alas, after a distinguished public career, Huskisson's fame now resides in the fact that he was the first railroad fatality. Bentley was much luckier, thirty-seven years later, to have survived his accident. Though he lived four more years, he was not well, and had to pass on the management of the business to his son, George (1828–1895), in 1867. Richard Bentley died in 1871 at Ramsgate, Kent. Bentley's grandson, another Richard Bentley (1854–1936), nicknamed "Richard II," took over in the last decade of the nineteenth century, but only for a few more years. As the new century dawned, the company waned, and by 1898, Richard Bentley & Son was no more.

Mr. Bentley's retirement after more than a quarter century of unbroken work, is due, we believe, mainly to the circumstance of having no brothers or sons to share in the direction of the business, and the combined work of publisher and editor growing too onerous to be carried on longer by one person.

Richard Bentley & Son still stands as the model for an enterprising, successful nineteenth-century publishing company, a distinction owing primarily to Richard Bentley's efforts and vision. The grand old firm was absorbed by a newer kid on the block, Macmillan & Company—founded in 1844 by the Scottish brothers Daniel and Alexander Macmillan.

It is romantic to speculate that the original manuscript of the *Journal*, written in Grace's own precise penmanship, was carried by the hand of her forceful spinster granddaughter on a day sometime in the fall of 1858 directly to Richard Bentley & Son. But it might simply have arrived by courier from the British Museum after Bentley had laid out £25 for its "Entire Copyright," per that entry in the Bentley ledger. That's why the original manuscript does not appear in Georgina's will: she'd sold it outright to Bentley. Under such an arrangement, there were usually no advances and no royalties as part of the publishing agreement; Bentley would have absorbed all costs of publication and received all profits.

Richard Bentley and Georgina Cavendish-Bentinck may never have met face-to-face, and Grace Elliott's manuscript may never have been offered to the British Museum at all. Miss Cavendish-Bentinck may have been aware that Edward Levien sometimes acted as an intermediary with Richard Bentley, and she may have used his services as such. The truth may never be known, but the fanciful image of the spinster—bound folio in hand, determined to see her grandmother's memoir in print—meeting the publisher is more pleasing to this writer. What happened to that manuscript? The mysteries surrounding the life of Grace Dalrymple never end, as more bits turn up to tantalize.

When Richard Bentley died in 1871, there was a three-day auction of his private library, handled by Sotheby, Wilkinson & Hodge (the original name of Sotheby's auction house), from December 18 to December 20 of that year. The *Catalogue of the Valuable Private Library, of the Late Eminent Publisher, Richard Bentley Esquire* describes "Lot 1108" as the "Original Manuscript of Mrs. Dalrymple Elliot's Story of her Life during the First Great Revolution / half calf / folio." The material in the sale had been divided into several parts, and this item was in the last part of the sale, the part that contained only manuscripts. This was apparently, then, *the* original handwritten manuscript of Grace's *Journal* that Richard Bentley had kept in his personal library. It makes sense that he would have had it.

Someone annotated the sales catalogue in the Bentley Archives at the British Library, and so we know that the manuscript sold for a mere £1, 9 shillings, the equivalent today of about £62/$125, far less than the £25 (£1,800/$3,600) that Richard Bentley paid for it. One wonders why it sold

so cheaply. Perhaps the later criticism concerning the veracity of the document played a role in reducing its value.

Sotheby's—whose policy is not to reveal client information—had none to reveal upon inquiry by this author. The name of the buyer at this auction 134 years ago was not set down in the auction record books. There was no documentation of that sale. Therefore, who might have bought the manuscript, and why, are queries that cannot be answered at this time.

In fact, the Sotheby's representative questioned whether this item was indeed the original manuscript of the *Journal,* commenting that it might simply have been a copy of the 1859 published book. This is highly questionable, as it was described in the sale catalogue as a "folio." A folio is not necessarily a book; if this was a book, it would have been described as one. There *were* some copies of the book sold in the three-day auction, but this wasn't one of them.

It's difficult, at this point in time and lacking more complete documentation from Sotheby's, to get an answer that is 100 percent satisfactory. But that this folio was simply a copy in one of the many published editions of the *Journal* that anyone could have bought in 1859—and that was probably still available from bookstores in 1871—is difficult to believe.

Lacking any more definitive documentation from Sotheby's, one has no choice but to go along with the firm's own description of that manuscript, the one that the booksellers themselves wrote in 1871, and trust that they knew what they were talking about. They should have known what a manuscript was, and what it wasn't, and whether or not they included *only* manuscripts in their "Lot 1108," which was supposed to have been made up entirely of manuscripts and nothing else. Once again, here is their description:

> *Original Manuscript of Mrs. Dalrymple Elliot's Story of her Life during the First Great Revolution / half calf / folio.*

LITERARY MERIT OF *JOURNAL OF MY LIFE DURING THE FRENCH REVOLUTION,* BY GRACE DALRYMPLE ELLIOTT

Whatever its author's problems with names, dates, events, and places, the *Journal* is a beautiful and moving piece of writing. Grace Elliott knows how to tell a story, and her eyewitness account of the major events of the French Revolution and the Reign of Terror is compelling. Her story has—to use writers' jargon—"march." It moves forward with determination and is a good read.

Grace plunges right into the story—as all good writers do. She opens with events in Paris leading up to the dramatic fall of the Bastille in mid-July of 1789. The Revolution, unbeknownst to her, has begun, and life for Grace and her privileged circle will never again be the same. She begins:

> In the year 1789, July the 12th, which was on a Sunday, I went, with the Duke of Orléans, Prince Louis D'Aremberg, and others . . . to fish and dine at the Duke's château of Rainey, in the Forest of Bondy, near Paris. We returned to Paris in the evening, meaning to go to the Comédie Italienne. We had left Paris at eleven o'clock in perfect tranquillity; but on our return at eight o'clock at the Porte St. Martin . . . [we found that] the theatres were all shut by orders from the police; [and] that Paris was all in confusion and tumult.

The reviewer in the *Times*, in his essay of January 26 and 27, 1859, first attacks the credibility of the *Journal*, then, after giving all the reasons it is not to be believed, castigating among others the editor who doesn't give his name—i.e., Richard Bentley—states:

> The [editor] must bear the discredit . . . of issuing for public acceptance a most important work without any of the tests or criteria of authenticity. It is simply a disgrace to literature that it is so put forth that we should have these aliunde [from the Latin, a legal term meaning "from another source; from elsewhere"] . . . and but for the intervention of the critic the public would be warranted in treating the book as spurious, in almost doubting if there was a Mrs. Elliott at all—at least, in suspecting and discrediting this version of her story as wholly or substantially a pure fabrication.

It is interesting to note that the reviewer calls the *Journal* "a most important work" and goes so far as to classify it as "literature." He goes on to state:

> Nevertheless, the conclusion to which we tend is almost as extraordinary,—that this narrative, allowing for feminine exaggerations [Ouch! Talk about sexist polemic!], is, or may be wholly or substantially true. . . . Our literary contemporaries have accepted it as trustworthy throughout; and, guarding against the presumption that we do so ourselves, we shall treat it with the attention due to its possible importance.

Even the ever-critical-of-Grace Horace Bleackley comments positively on the literary merit of the *Journal:*

There can be no doubt that Grace Dalrymple was a clever woman. Her book shows that she had inherited some of her father's talents. Although often sketchy the descriptions throughout her narrative are full of life, and impressions of actual people are vivid and convincing. Whether true or false it is the story of a gifted writer and presents a spirited picture of the period.

Here, Bleackley's correct. The descriptions of people are indeed lively and engaging, the narrative is compelling, and the conveying of character is succinct and on the mark. Likewise, the events Grace lived through are written with the forceful march that's essential in carrying any story forward. It's a disappointment when the book ends, for it has presented the reader with a vivid, up-close and personal portrait of those exciting times and people. Grace's depiction of the Duc d'Orléans's fall from power has the makings of a Greek tragedy. His downfall is brought about, as she says, by his own innate weakness of character—his tragic flaw—yet she manages to make him not altogether unsympathetic. She rescues what there is to rescue about the man considered so appalling by his class and by historians, and it's a job well done.

It's too bad that J. G. Alger, the author of the error-filled piece on Grace Elliott in *the Dictionary of National Biography,* is so negative and biased. The *DNB* is an important reference work, shelved in libraries all over the world. Alger's evaluation of Grace and her *Journal* has been too easily accepted by many as gospel truth, whereas it's highly subjective and inaccurate, and sexist as well, just like those written by other of Grace's male critics in Edwardian and Victorian times. Alger speaks of "inaccuracies" and says that the "very title is a misnomer, for the work is confessedly a narrative written seven or eight years after the experiences it relates." He also harps on the fact that her name does not appear on the French prison registers.

Let's discuss this latter criticism, as it is serious. Alger and other critics say that Grace was a very great liar and had never been imprisoned at all, that she took the tale of her incarceration at the Carmes from her friend Mrs. Meyler, and that she never knew Joséphine de Beauharnais. The critics also discount as pure fabrication the story of the old physician Dr. Gem, who shared a room with her at the Recollets.

How to respond? For one, reliance on the accuracy of prison lists made up by the *greffiers* (recorders) at the individual prisons is problematic. From Grace's narrative we should have a good idea of what sort of people were in charge and what could be expected from them. Mistaken identities abounded throughout the Reign of Terror; the wrong people were arrested and summarily executed all the time.

It was chaos at the prisons for months, with constant moving and removal of prisoners, hundreds of executions daily, and uneven, incomplete record-keeping. It's possible that Grace's name was on some of these lists, but in unrecognizable form. (Remember that on her death certificate her name was spelled "Georgette.") It was a time of great confusion, and it's not enough to say that if Grace's name was not on a list, then—ergo—she could not have been in that particular jail.

There is also the possibility that Grace used an assumed name to fool the jailers, ignorant as they were. Though the various committees knew who she was, the illiterate company who manned the prisons may not necessarily have known her by her correct name. The reviewer of the *Journal* in the *Times* in 1859 comes to exactly this conclusion. Commenting on her imprisonment at the Carmes, he writes that it's "possible that she was there under another name." He notes a Monsieur Cottant, who was there and also wrote of his experiences, saying that while Cottant enumerated *"nos prisonniers les plus remarquables,"* he managed to omit several very prominent people who'd been there.

Grace does get names and dates wrong—dyslexia, Georgian inconsistency in spelling, perhaps, or proof the *Journal* was written long after the events?—and she may have exaggerated what she'd seen and added bits she'd heard from others. Should these discredit her entire narrative and her claims of having been imprisoned? Perhaps there are some falsehoods, but to label it *all* false is overreaching.

If Grace Elliott was not in prison during those eighteen months, can anyone come forward and say where she was? Safe and secure in Meudon or on the rue de Miromesnil? Hiding in the countryside? She could not leave France, and she was considered an enemy of the state at worst, an abhorred foreigner at best. Where on earth would she have been safe, with her ties to the Duc d'Orléans and the Queen? In prison people seemed to know she'd aided Champcenetz in his escape. There was no way that such a high-profile woman as she would not have been picked up—as she says she was—and arrested.

The French have always been kinder to Grace Elliott than her own nitpicking and biased countrymen. The *Journal,* which was written in English, was translated into French and sold in France a couple of years after it was published in England. No less a literary luminary than Charles-Augustin Sainte-Beuve (1804–1869), the foremost French critic of the nineteenth century, published a commentary in the periodical *Moniteur,* May 27, 1861.

The essay was reprinted in a French edition of the *Journal* titled *Mémoires de Madame Elliott sur la Révolution française* (Paris: Michel Lévy Frères, 1861), which carried the note *suivi d'une "appréciation critique" par Sainte-Beuve, Membre de l'Académie Française.*

Sainte-Beuve gives Grace Elliott a good deal of credit, not least for having written the memoir herself, unlike certain Frenchwomen who also lived through the terrible times of the Revolution and published narratives about them. The *Journal,* he implies, was not ghostwritten, as he suspects those might have been:

> *We do not have to fear any of this inconvenience with Mrs. Elliott;—M. de Baillon [the translator] limited himself to translate her, and he did it in good taste, showing intelligence by doing so, leaving her so much herself and natural, that the book seems to have been written and told in its original version in French.*

(Lucy Russell, the British actress who played Grace in *The Lady and the Duke,* reads and speaks French fluently and would disagree with the venerable literary critic; she said—in a conversation with this writer—that the French translation, though good, was a bit too flowery, and not really the Grace of the English edition.)

Sainte-Beuve likes Grace's passion and indignation and finds these sentiments expressed as if she were herself French, and were writing as if "to one of her friends in France. This is the way the words would have come out from her heart to the paper." The emotions are real, and they are emotions, he claims, that anyone who is French would understand.

He comments on her characterization of that slippery fellow Philippe, Duc d'Orléans, turncoat Philippe Égalité, giving her high marks for her insight:

> *We cannot ask for mature judgments about people from Mrs. Elliott, we have to look for impressions with her; and because hers are so honest, they are priceless—what she tells us about the Duke of Orléans . . . is really quite sim-*

ilar to what the greatest minds of her time have said about this deplorable prince.

Noting that Grace describes Philippe as simply "a man of pleasure," not a plotter, Sainte-Beuve agrees with her estimation of him, saying that "she shows us even more his lack of firmness and his weak character"; this lack of moral fortitude, he explains, left Philippe easy prey for the schemers and traitors who manipulated him. He quotes her as saying that if Philippe "had ever thought the Revolution could last longer than six months, he would never have wanted it."

He relates the crucial disagreement Grace had with Philippe over the death of King Louis XVI. If you will recall, Philippe had promised her he would not attend the session in which the vote would be taken, but he did go and he voted for his cousin's death. This is a moving part of the narrative. When Grace learns what Philippe has done, she is distraught and emotional, giving him no room to make excuses. Sainte-Beuve's opinion is that Philippe tried to hide his head in the sand and ignore what the eventual consequences would be for him; he feels that Grace has given a historically accurate and moving account of Philippe's weak personality and character and he understands her frustration with him.

The rest of the essay is taken up with many of the prison anecdotes related earlier in this biography. Sainte-Beuve calls the anecdotes "vivid" and "well-told," "contrasting with the well-known background of horrors" that set the Reign of Terror apart. He remarks that the narrative—for whatever reason—is unfinished and that it is difficult to accept all of the editorial copy written by Richard Bentley, "the English editor who has continued this narrative." He also disputes the anecdote that Bentley repeats, that General (and soon-to-be-emperor) Napoléon proposed marriage to Mrs. Elliott. He writes, "to take it seriously we would need to hear it from Mrs. Elliott herself."

Saint-Beuve ends by paying tribute to Grace's beauty, noting the hand-colored engraving of Grace that illustrated the *Journal,* calling hers a "delicate beauty," a slim, long-necked loveliness— *"cette beauté fine au col long et mince"*—that he felt was worthy of being painted by the foremost artists. The image he refers to is the engraving of a miniature portrait of Grace Elliott perhaps painted by Richard Cosway that is not the same as the miniature copied for the Grangerised editions. It shows a somewhat weak-chinned, conventionally pretty woman, her hair loose and blond, her cleavage deep. Nothing more is known about this image, which was used in the Rodale Press edition.

The *Times* reviewer has the last word. He calls Grace Elliott "remarkable" but says that "her story is otherwise romantic and worthy of historical investigation." Oh, yes, he underscores "the slovenliness of the publisher," Richard Bentley, and castigates him for foisting the *Journal* upon the public with his inadequate editing and his reliance on the dubious anecdotes with which he brackets Grace's text. The reviewer—who's uncredited himself, by the way, and may be the editor of the *Times* but perhaps is not—states that the narrative *"may* be true in the main; this is all we can say."

The word "may" is italicized, but one has to remember that this reviewer also termed the narrative "literature" and said it was "an important work." That may (unitalicized) be enough to make the *Journal* respectable and worthy of note, "true in the main" or not. Whatever it is, it provides an exciting picture of the French Revolution, as true and as worthy of reading as Dickens's classic *A Tale of Two Cities*. In fact, they could be read together.

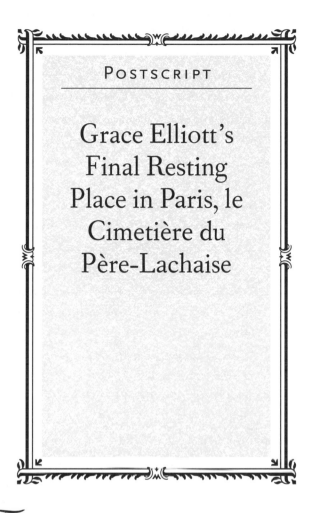

Grace Elliott's Final Resting Place in Paris, le Cimetière du Père-Lachaise

The Père-Lachaise Web site specifies who may be buried at that cemetery in the form of the following frequently asked questions:

QUESTION: *Qui peut se faire enterer au Père-Lachaise?* (Who can be buried at the Père-Lachaise Cemetery?)

ANSWER: *Tout le monde ne peut pas se faire enterer au Père-Lachaise. Seules auront ce droit* (Not everyone can be buried at Père-Lachaise. Those who have the right to be buried there are):

* *Les personnes habitant Paris et décédées à Paris* (Residents of Paris who've died in Paris);

The 118-acre cemetery was founded in 1804 and named after Père François de La Chaise, the Jesuit priest who was confessor to Louis XIV; he lived in a house the Jesuit order had built on the site in 1682. It was the first of the major landscaped cemeteries in modern Europe. It's set on a hill to the east of Paris in a bucolic, faux-Arcadian milieu, with serpentine paths, rolling hills, mausoleums, ponds, classical monuments, and statuary. It's said that the design of the cemetery owes much to English landscape mod-els seen at stately homes and public parks. The cemetery is a tourist attraction only a short distance from the center of Paris; maps are provided in order to locate graves more easily. People of note who have been buried there are: Honoré de Balzac, Sarah Bernhardt, Frédéric Chopin, Jacques-Louis David, Isadora Duncan, René Lalique, Amadeo Modigliani, Edith Piaf, Marcel Proust, and Gertrude Stein. The tomb of the Marquis de Champcenetz is also at Père-Lachaise. Grace Elliott's grave is unmarked.

* *Les personnes décédées à Paris quelque soit leur domicile* (People who've died in Paris, no matter where their permanent residences might be);

* *Les personnes habitant Paris, quelque soit leur lieu de décès* (Residents of Paris, wherever their deaths have occurred).

Grace Elliott, who died in 1823, almost twenty years after the cemetery was founded, qualified for burial. She'd been a longtime Paris resident, though she'd moved to Ville d'Avray, just outside Paris, two years prior to her death. (Jim Morrison, of the 1970s rock group the Doors, is perhaps the best-known modern inhabitant of Père-Lachaise; he was living in Paris when he died, so he met one of the three criteria for inclusion.)

Grace Elliott's tombstone was removed on June 11, 1992, by "prefectoral order" and may have been part of a so-called burial-renewal process that cemeteries undertake in relandscaping their oldest areas. Why it was done in this case could not be established, as the cemetery's administration was unavailable to answer queries put to them since 2003.

It is a safe guess, though, from walking through other French and European cemeteries contemporary with Père-Lachaise's oldest sections, that the stone may simply have lost its integrity; there are many deteriorating tombstones from this period and, sadly, no attempt is made by administrators to let visitors know who's buried where when the headstones have gone.

The approximate site of the grave—plot 4005P of 1823, located in section 43, the English Cemetery—was located, however, thanks to the persistence of a French researcher. It's a shame that there is no surviving tombstone and that no record of it is forthcoming from the Service des Cimitières; the inscription would have been of great interest. It is worthy of note that Grace is buried near the grandmother of Honoré de Balzac. Grace always did have a knack of sleeping with the rich and/or famous.

We don't know what the weather was like in France the day Grace was interred—as we don't know the date of her interment at Père-Lachaise. In England, though, on the day of her death, May 15, the temperature hovered between 50 and 62 degrees and the weather was fair; a trifle chilly for May, but "fair" indicates the sun had been shining. Grace's last day on earth was sunny, which is good to know.

What's also known is that the Marquess of Cholmondeley paid for the funeral and the erection of the tombstone. It cost him £100 and there was much discussion back and forth between His Lordship and Grace's law firm Morland Ransom as to whether or not her annuities would cover the expenses. They didn't. As Grace died before the next quarterly payments were to be sent out, neither King George IV's Privy Purse nor Sir John Eliot's estate would contribute, despite Lord Cholmondeley's persistence in trying to get them to do so. At the end, as was always the case in her lifetime, Lord Cholmondeley came through and was there for her.

People die, but love may not.

L'Anglaise et le Duc

The Lady and the Duke

The Eric Rohmer film *L'Anglaise et le Duc,* or *The Lady and the Duke,* based on Grace Dalrymple Elliott's memoir of the French Revolution, was released in 2001. It starred the English actress Lucy Russell as Grace and the French actor Jean-Claude Dreyfus as the Duc d'Orléans. The 128-minute film received worldwide praise for its sensitive direction and fine acting. It premiered at the Venice Film Festival, where director Eric Rohmer received a lifetime achievement award for his work in cinema.

In an interview with Aurélien Ferenzi in 2001, Rohmer related how he came across the story of Grace Elliott:

While on holiday about ten years ago, I came across a digest of the memoirs of Grace Elliott in a history magazine. This English lady had been the mistress of the Duke of Orléans, King Louis XVI's cousin, and had written an account of her life during the French Revolution. The article mentioned that her town house was still standing at such-and-such a number [31] on rue Miromesnil. I have always been interested in places and was particularly struck by the idea that this house could still be seen at a certain address. That gave me the idea of making a film that would be set in that particular spot in Paris and would play on the relationship between the peaceful apartment, which served Grace as a kind of hideout, and the rest of the city in the throes of revolutionary turmoil.

Grace Elliott's *Journal of My Life During the French Revolution* has always been available, in one edition or another, in France. The French consider Grace a Royalist heroine of the Revolution.

Eric Rohmer, now eighty-five years old, has had a long and distinguished career of more than fifty years as a director, screenwriter, professor of French literature, critic, and magazine editor. He's contributed to many prestigious film journals, among them *Les Cahiers du Cinéma,* and cowrote a book on Alfred Hitchcock with Claude Chabrol. Rohmer was part of the New Wave movement, alongside François Truffaut, Louis Malle, and Jean-Luc Godard. This group were the forerunners of today's independent filmmakers.

Rohmer made his mark with a series of talky, relationship-centered films that he gathered into a series—*Six Moral Tales, Comedies and Proverbs,* and *Tales of the Four Seasons*—and that are perhaps better known by their individual titles, such as *My Night at Maud's, Claire's Knee, The Aviator's Wife, Love in the Afternoon,* and *Pauline at the Beach.*

He's a shy, withdrawn man who rarely gives interviews. While his work does not have universal appeal, he has a dedicated fan base that finds delight in his subtle comedies about love and the human condition.

What are Rohmer films about? Almost voyeuristic, they

are about people in relationships, contemplating relationships, or trying to get out of relationships. (And talking about it!) Rohmer's actors are young and attractive, his stories slight; something may happen, but often nothing does. His films explore relationships between small groups of people, issues of the heart, and his camera plays no special effects tricks. He likes deep-focus, static camera work, and use of the zoom lens; sometimes he does location shooting, but most of his tales take place in a single room. His is an elliptical narrative style. People talk. And talk and talk and talk. His characters reveal who they are by what they say, and most times they have a good deal to say. Oftentimes what they say can be overly philosophical and off-putting to the average filmgoer; even devoted Rohmer fans can be turned off by the lack of action. (From a review by the author.)

The Lady and the Duke, a stylized and sumptuous costume drama based on a real-life eighteenth-century courtesan's memoir, may seem a stretch for a director who is identified with small movies dealing with realistic, contemporary urban themes, but Rohmer had previously directed two other period pieces, *The Marquise of O,* in 1976, and *Perceval* (based on the Arthurian legend), in 1978. He shot *The Lady and the Duke* in digital video, often incorporating his players into exquisitely painted backgrounds that give an unusual cinematic effect; they are actually more like elaborate stage sets against which the actors move.

Stuart Jeffries, in an interview with Lucy Russell published in the *Guardian* in 2002, commented on the "technicalities of the filming process" Rohmer employed, calling them "tricky," but "wonderful":

Rohmer commissioned artists to oil-paint backdrops of Paris in revolutionary times and used digital technology to insert the actors into the projections. . . . And the finished effect is wonderful. In close-up shots of Elliott trying to elude the revolutionaries by fleeing Paris at night, we can see the brushstrokes of the magnified paintings of the countryside behind her. It's a magical, sometimes distracting effect: at the start of the film, when the characters first move through the painted canvas of the revolution, we are instantly taken to another, visually and emotionally heightened world.

The Lady and the Duke has considerably more action than Rohmer's signature films; there are mob scenes and scenes where secondary characters fill the screen, but it is primarily a verbatim retelling of Grace Elliott's *Journal*. The dialogue between Grace and the Duc d'Orléans, her former lover, arguing their divergent philosophies of monarchy vis-à-vis revolutionary anarchy, is at the core of the movie, as it is at the core of Grace's memoir. In this respect, the film is not so very different from the typical

Grace Elliott (British actress Lucy Russell) and her maid witness—via telescope—the execution of King Louis XVI against an elaborately painted background of 1793 Paris. (Pathé)

argument-based films Rohmer has written about characters from our own time.

In the Ferenzi interview, Rohmer addressed how powerfully Grace Elliott's memoir struck him:

Over and above its undeniable historical interest (it contains a few minor errors in dates, but most of it has the ring of truth), there is something striking about it, as though it had already been written as a script, with scenes, sequences, and even dialogue. It has a very different tone from the other journals I have read. Memoir-writers mostly tend to write about themselves, their fears and hopes, but Grace Elliott includes herself in the picture, though always maintaining a certain detachment and distance. We see her acting and moving around, but the other characters also live in a very powerful way, especially the Duke of Orléans, of whom we have very few first-hand reports.

As for Grace Elliott's fierce loyalty, Rohmer addressed it when Ferenzi asked him, "Was it her loyalty to her commitments that touched you?" Rohmer replied:

No, it was more her British stiff upper lip: a certain modesty and self-control, a completely unaffected way of talking about herself and, above all, a way of looking at events that makes her the heroine of a novel. Perhaps this is how it happens when History overturns the lives of individuals. Few other historical characters have ever seemed so close to us, and

so moving. . . . The details of her private life that appear in the book, which I kept in the film, create an effect of reality.

Rohmer cast Lucy Russell over several other English actresses who spoke French—his primary criterion for the role of Grace Elliott—via taped auditions. The actress, whose fluent French is flawless, told me that she prepared herself for the audition by going to her local London public library and finding a copy of Grace's *Journal*.

She read it, was taken by it, and thus was able to do what none of the other actresses vying for the part did, discuss it intelligently on the tape: "I read it in two hours in one sitting. It's a wonderful, immediate story."

Later, according to Jeffries, she added:

I made a cassette and sent it to Rohmer. "Hello, my name is Lucy and I've just read the memoirs and I think they're fabulous." And I gabbled on for three or four minutes and sent it off.

Rohmer's method of selecting actors is unusual. In the Ferenzi interview, he described the process and how he chose Lucy Russell to play Grace Elliott:

By intuition, as always. I audition one person, he or she reads the lines, and that's it! I had difficulty casting the Englishwoman. A casting director known to Margaret Menegoz sent me photos of actresses and an audio tape of their voices. The only tape I liked was of an actress who said she knew

Jean-Claude Dreyfus as the Duc d'Orléans and Lucy Russell as Grace Elliott in a still from *The Lady and the Duke*—an example of perfect casting. (Pathé)

Grace Elliott's book and wanted to play her. Her voice appealed to me before her photo did, and when I met her, I found the actress even more attractive than her picture!

Oddly, Rohmer did not think that Jean-Claude Dreyfus resembled the Duc d'Orléans! (This writer respectfully begs to differ.) He told Ferenzi:

As for Jean-Claude Dreyfus, I didn't think of him at first, but I was looking for a strong personality. I needed somebody big and stout, even if he didn't physically resemble the Duke of Orléans all that closely.

Rohmer places great trust in his actors to get it right and gives them space along with sensitive direction. Lucy Russell said he was

unfailingly polite and considerate. In rehearsal, we had great discussions about everything, but on set, he concentrates on the technical side and lets you get on with it. Some of the dialogue scenes are pages long and he doesn't like to do more than one or two takes. But if you were really unhappy, he was quite open for you to ask for another take.

Perhaps choosing the perfect actor for the role is what makes all the difference in a Rohmer film. Rohmer told Ferenzi:

I am very pleased with the cast. My directing of actors, as usual, went no further than giving them technical instructions. Feelings are the actor's business. All I did was tell them to enunciate clearly so that they would be understood. They didn't let me down.

Rohmer can be over-the-top in his obsession with detail, for example finding the perfect color for the lining of an actress's raincoat in one of his early films. He was concerned that the color of the lining complement the other colors he was using in the scene. The film was shot in black-and-white. Only Rohmer was aware of the lining's color. To make the story even more bizarre, the audience never saw the lining.

Likewise, the fastidious Frenchman insisted that the inside lining of Lucy Russell's handmade shoes had to be embroidered—according to the fashion in the late eighteenth century—and that there had to be embroidery on her handmade corsets and hosiery as well. Though the audience never sees the inside of her shoes nor the elaborate clocking on her hose, Rohmer knows it's there, and so does the actress. Rohmer is meticulous in his pursuit of authenticity and detail, and never more so than in this period drama.

In her interviews with the author and with Stuart Jeffries, Lucy Russell commented that this obsessive attention to detail worked for her in creating the role of Grace Elliott, though she could not see its value to her portrayal at first. Wearing the very clothes Grace would have worn, down to the last piece of embroidered fabric, made her character even more real to the actress portraying her. Russell was—literally—in Grace's shoes:

Every single stitch on my costumes was hand-sewn. Rohmer said that clothes that are machine-made do not hang the same way. How many people who see that film are going to appreciate that? But that's not even the issue. He [Rohmer] sets such a high standard. All my shoes were handmade too, but you never see them in the film. I wanted to hold them up to the camera and go, "Look!"

The result was that the twenty-first-century actress Lucy Russell fit nicely into the skin of the eighteenth-century courtesan she described as "elegant, stubborn, spoiled, and insistent on having her own way." In the Tom Charity interview in *Time Out*, she said, "Grace . . . sometimes she's just a silly cow, but she's a wonderfully brave, snobby Englishwoman, very human and warm."

As Lucy Russell discovered, the historical woman was real, a genuine human being. She told Jeffries:

I fell in love with Grace. I've got a lot of sympathy for her because I can't imagine she had anybody who educated her at all about how one should behave in society.

NOTES

FRONTISPIECE

Grace Elliott, Mary Robinson, and Gertrude Mahon primping prior to going out on the town. This somewhat prurient engraving shows a lot of leg but is highly imaginative. Grace Elliott would never have shared her space with her greatest rival, Mary Robinson; she loathed her. Gertrude Mahon, however, was a good buddy.

INTRODUCTION

Research for this biography was undertaken in primary and secondary sources at libraries and archives (including newspaper archives), museums, public record offices, private societies, stately homes, and from interviews. The only surviving letter from Grace Elliott is at Windsor Castle, but she's mentioned in the letters and diaries of contemporaries. Detailed curatorial files for the two Gainsborough portraits of Grace, one at the Metropolitan Museum of Art and the other at the Frick Collection in New York City, provided the most rewarding information on her life.

Recent biographies on the courtesan contemporaries of Grace Elliott as well as scandalous ladies of fashion are: Hester Davenport on Mary Robinson, *The Prince's Mistress* (Stroud, Gloucestershire: Sutton, 2004); Martin Levy on Martha Ray, *Love & Madness* (New York: HarperCollins, 2004); Susan Nagel on Mary Nisbit, *Mistress of the Elgin Marbles* (New York: William Morrow, 2004); Paula Byrne on Mary Robinson, *Perdita* (London: HarperCollins, 2004); Claire Gervat on Elizabeth Chudleigh, *Elizabeth* (London: Century, 2003); Katie Hickman on Sophia Baddeley, Harriette Wilson, and Elizabeth Armistead, among others, *Courtesans* (London: HarperCollins, 2003); and Frances Wilson on Harriette Wilson, *The Courtesan's Revenge* (London: Faber & Faber, 2003).

Older works worthy of mention are: Robert D. Bass on Banastre Tarleton and Mary Robinson, *The Green Dragoon* (Orangeburg, SC: Sandlapper, 1957); Harriette Wilson's memoirs, edited by Lesley Blanch, NY: *The Game of Hearts* (Simon & Schuster, 1955); I. M. Davis on Charles James Fox and Elizabeth Armistead, *The Harlot and the Statesman* (Abbotsbrook, Buckinghamshire: Kensal Press, 1986); Elizabeth Foster on another Elizabeth Foster, *Children of the Mist* (New York: Macmillan, 1961); Carola Hicks on Diana Beauclerk, *Improper Pursuits* (New York: St. Martin's Press, 2002); M. J. Levy on a bevy of beauties, *The Mistresses of King George IV* (London: Peter Owen, 1996); James Munson, *Maria Fitzherbert* (London: Robinson, 2001); Valerie Grosvenor Myer, *Harriette Wilson* (Haddenham, Cambridgeshire: Fern House, 1999); Angela Thirkell on Harriette Wilson, *Tribute for Harriette* (London: Hamish Hamilton, 1936); Claire Tomalin on Dorothy Jordan, *Mrs. Jordan's Profession* (New York: Knopf, 1995), and Amanda Foreman, *Georgiana, Duchess of Devonshire* (NY: Random House, 1998).

These were not the only accounts consulted; new books appear every year. Courtesans and their coteries and scandalous ladies have always been an endless source of fascination. The original editions of Harriette Wilson's infamous *Memoirs* (circa 1825) and the 1787 biography of Sophia Baddeley written by her companion, Elizabeth Steele, *The Memoirs of Mrs. Sophia Baddeley* (London: Literary Press, 1787), are invaluable primary sources for the life and times of these glorious creatures, whose letters—like Grace Elliott's—do not survive.

There are many biographies of that skirt-chasing monarch King George IV, including: Roger Fulford, *George the Fourth* (London: Duckworth, 1935); Christopher Hibbert, *George IV, Prince of Wales, 1762–1811* (London: Longman, 1972) and *George IV, Regent and King, 1811–1830* (London: Allen Lane, 1973); Lewis Melville, *The First Gentleman of Europe* (Hutchinson, 1906); Steven Parissien, *George IV* (London: John Murray, 2001); J. B. Priestley, *The Prince of Pleasure and His Regency, 1811–1820* (London: Heinemann, 1969); and another *Prince of Pleasure* (New York: Little, Brown, 1998), by David Saul. George IV has at least two female biographers, of whom one is Cynthia Campbell, author of *The Most Polished Gentleman: George IV and the Women in His Life* (London: Kudos Books, 1995). Charles Cavendish Fulke Greville's *Memoirs* (New York: Scribner, Armstrong, and Company, 1875) is a must-read primary source for the later life of this king; it's an intimate, scathing look by an insider, his clerk of the council, that was published after Greville's death in 1865.

Those who could be called Grace Elliott's biographers are only three, and there has never been a full-length biography. The first was Richard Bentley in his notes to Grace's *Journal of My Life During the French Revolution*. Unfortunately, Bentley neither checked his facts nor named the sources for the anecdotes he repeated. The second was

John Goldworth Alger, in his *Dictionary of National Biography* profile of Grace. (She made it into this who's who of Dead Notable Brits as a writer, because of her *Journal*.) Alger takes much of his material from Bentley and compounds the misinformation. Her last biographer was Horace Bleackley, a self-styled literary polymath who penned novels, accounts of famous trials and hangings, and books on sports (at least two on cricket) and world travel.

Grace is one of the several courtesans covered in Bleackley's 1909 collective biography, *Ladies Fair and Frail: Sketches of the Demi-Monde in the Eighteenth Century;* there were other editions, including a 1926 U.S. edition (New York: Dodd Mead). It was by far the fullest and most ambitious account of her life.

The colorful terms for courtesans and prostitutes come primarily from the *1811 Dictionary of the Vulgar Tongue*. This dictionary is augmented by phrases from newspapers such as the *Morning Post, Morning Chronicle,* and *Daily Advertiser;* periodicals like *The Town and Country Magazine* and *The Gentleman's Magazine;* and correspondence and novels.

Historical information on newspapers was provided in part by Dr. Jeremy Black's essay, "The 18th century British Press," in *The Encyclopedia of the British Press, 1422–1992,* edited by Dennis Griffiths (Macmillan, 1992); additional background can be found in K. John Westmancoat's *Newspapers* (British Library, 1985). All the newspapers personally consulted are to be found on microfilm or online at the British Library's Newspaper Annex in Colindale, North London.

Two gritty, unsentimental, and well-written novels with a fine sense of time and place featuring prostitute protagonists are Emma Donoghue's *Slammerkin* (Harcourt, 2001) and Michel Faber's *The Crimson Petal and the White* (Harcourt, 2002). Donoghue's book is set in the mid-1700s, Faber's in the Victorian period.

The quotations on the writing of biography come from various and many Internet sources, some of which have disappeared. The opening definition of "courtesan" was found on the Web site www.hyperdictionary.com; the Laurel Thatcher Ulrich quote was from quotes.prolix

.nu/History/002317/html; the others are from www
.entplaza.com.

Amanda Foreman (biographer of Georgiana, Duchess
of Devonshire), James Gleick (biographer of scientists
Richard Feynman and Isaac Newton), and Laura Hillen-
brand (who wrote about the life and times of the racehorse
Seabiscuit) have all spoken about the perils, pitfalls, and
pleasures of writing biographies. Gleick's article "Known
to Everyone and No One," *New York Times*, August 16,
2003, compared how it was to write about a contemporary
versus someone long dead:

> *Contemporary biography is not the same genre at all. My
> own previous adventure in biography might as well have oc-
> curred in a separate universe. . . . Feynman . . . left a great,
> smoldering trail of oral history, videotape, and friends with
> vivid memories. Newton, secretive and withdrawn, lived in a
> time of isolation and information scarcity. The 17th century
> was nearer the 7th century than the 20th.*

A note about British titles and naming protocol, which
can be confusing: Upper ranks of peers are known by their
titles as well as by their family names. Only rarely, as in the
case of George James Cholmondeley, Earl of Cholmondeley (and later Marquess of Cholmondeley), are the family
name and the title one and the same name. Knights and
baronets use only their family name.

CHAPTER ONE. "DALLY THE TALL"

Courtesans were given sobriquets by the tabloids that exaggerated some facet of their personality, style, or physical
looks. Thus Gertrude Mahon was dubbed the "Bird of Paradise" for her colorful plumage; her rival Mary Robinson
was forever "Perdita," after her most famous stage role;
and Grace was "Dally" after her maiden name, Dalrymple,
and "the Tall" after her most distinguishing physical feature, her height. The Sir Walter Scott quote disparaging
Harriette Wilson's looks comes from Angela Thirkell's
Tribute for Harriette, page 248.

Masquerade balls were profitable arenas for these ladies
of the night, the club scenes of their day. They took place
at the Pantheon, the Opera House, and private venues.

There were also so-called courtesans' balls—where these
ladies and the men they sought as protectors held sway—
and something pretty low-down called the *balum rancum*,
in which all the women were prostitutes and everyone present danced naked.

Frances, Lady Shelley—Grace's niece—is the source
for the remark on the "Dalrymple brow," and it is she who
furnished the most complete contemporary description of
Grace's looks, dubbing her the "most beautiful woman"
she'd ever seen. The quote from Lady Craven comparing
Grace to the young giantess in *Gulliver's Travels* should be
understood in the context of Lady Craven's possible relationship with Lord Cholmondeley.

Dress was daring. Necklines plunged so low that nipples
were often exposed. Victorians covered the revealing portraits of their Georgian and Regency forebears with "modesty drapes," as can be seen in the miniature of Grace that
appeared on the Grangerised editions of the *Journal*. Of all
Grace's portraits, the Gainsborough owned by the Metropolitan Museum of Art (1778) is the most striking; the one
owned by the Frick Collection, the most beautiful; the
miniature (possibly by Richard Cosway) in a private collection in Britain the sweetest; the supposed Gainsborough
portrait with no provenance at the Lady Lever Art Gallery,
the most puzzling. That odd arrangement of ribbon attached to Grace's earrings was explained to me by British
historical novelist Lynne Connolly.

Gill Perry's essay "The Spectacle of the Muse: Exhibiting the Actress at the Royal Academy" appears in *Art on the
Line: The Royal Academy Exhibitions at Somerset House,
1780–1836*, edited by David H. Solkin (Yale University
Press, 2001), pages 115–116. Somerset House is now the
home of the Courtauld Institute of Art, and the RA exhibitions are now held at the Royal Academy of Arts building
on Piccadilly.

The women's magazines contain gorgeous hand-
colored fashion plates that have become prized collectibles
and can be purchased at online auction sites. A number of
these plates and an account of Madame Lanchester can be
viewed at the romance novelist Candice Hern's Web site,
www.candicehern.com.

CHAPTER TWO. THE PROUD SCOTTISH DALRYMPLES

Grace Elliott, née Dalrymple, was a Scot. A piece by Tracey Lawson, "Return for Courtesan's Auld Alliances," in the *Scotsman*, November 19, 2001, took issue with the film adaptation of her *Journal*, saying it should better have been not *L'Anglaise et le Duc (The [English] Lady and the Duke)* but *L'Ecossaise et le Duc (The Scotswoman and the Duke)*. French director Eric Rohmer should have known better.

The Dalrymples were an old Scots family who claimed a close relationship to the wealthy earls of Stair. The few facts about the family of Grace's father, Hew/Hugh Dalrymple, come from Scottish legal sources, among them volume 76 of the Scottish Record Society, *The Faculty of Advocates in Scotland, 1532–1943 with Genealogical Notes*, edited by Sir Francis J. Grant (J. Skinner, 1944). (Horace Bleackley said he got his information on the family from a Dalrymple descendant, Hew H.

The document called the Special Licence attesting to Grace's age at the time of her marriage and the Eliot–Dalrymple marriage certificate are both signed by Hugh Dalrymple, and are on file at, respectively, the Guildhall Library and the Metropolitan Archives in London.

The annotated volume of *Some Old Families: A Contribution to the Genealogical History of Scotland*, by Hardy Bertram McCall, published in 1889, was happened upon by accident at the Genealogical Society in London. That it was annotated (see pages 33 to 34) by an unnamed genealogist taking issue with the information about Hew's siblings and his offspring was serendipitous. It should be noted that Hew Dalrymple, contrary to the J. Goldworth Alger article in the *DNB* so admired by Bleackley, wasn't the Dalrymple involved in the celebrated case called the Hamilton–Douglas Cause; that Dalrymple was the distinguished jurist Sir Hew Dalrymple, who was many years the senior of Grace's father. (It's a common name.)

Librarians at the Faculty of Advocates in Scotland and the Middle Temple kindly supplied information on the legal profession in Scotland and England during the eighteenth century and confirmed that a Scottish lawyer wishing to practice in England had to go through a period of study and take up residence at the Inns of Court. The quote from *The Prime Ministers: An Irreverent History in Cartoons*, by Kenneth Baker (London: Thames & Hudson, 1995) is on page 42 of that book.

Alison Mowat, a Scottish genealogist hired by me, could not turn up anything in the printed records in Scotland concerning Grace's mother's family or the date of Grace's birth. The conclusion was that her birth was simply not registered. The convent school Grace attended was said to have been either in France or in Flanders, but no specific name is mentioned.

CHAPTER THREE. GRACE DALRYMPLE'S UNHAPPY MARRIAGE TO THE "CORNUTED" DOCTOR, JOHN ELIOT

John Eliot's obituary in the *World & Fashionable Advertizer* was consulted on microfilm at the British Library's Newspaper Annex in Colindale, North London, and his will at the Public Records Office database (available on microfilm at two locations, in London and Kew at the National Archives, and also online). *The Dictionary of National Biography* is found on the reference shelves of most large libraries.

The pedigree Eliot had commissioned is on file with the College of Arms in London. Henry Gray kindly supplied a copy, working with the Richmond Herald, Patric Dickinson. Mr. Gray stated that much of the pedigree is questionable; he also photographed Eliot's memorial plaque for me at St. Etheldreda's Church, Hertfordshire.

Divorce was becoming more of an escape from marriage among the wealthy upper classes in the late Georgian period than it had been in the past. In Scotland, when Hew Dalrymple and his wife Grizel parted company (probably circa 1753–1754) marital separation and divorce was at a fairly constant rate (fewer than twenty cases a year since the seventeenth century) and remained so until about 1800. Divorces in Scotland, however, outstripped marital separations by great leaps after 1761, as happened in England, and by 1811 there were ten times that number of divorce proceedings.

Lawrence Stone's *Broken Lives: Separation and Divorce*

in England, 1660–1857 (Oxford University Press, 1993) offers detailed case studies among the wealthy (mostly) and is considered a seminal work in the field. Other books on the same subject (or related ones) are *Affection Defying the Power of Death: Wills, Probate and Death Duty Records*, by Jane Cox (Lancashire: Federation of Family History Societies, 1993); *Alienated Affections: The Scottish Experience of Divorce and Separation, 1684–1830*, by Leah Leneman (Edinburgh University Press, 1998), which uses the same case study approach, and *Family Ties: English Families 1540–1920*, by Mary Abbott (Routledge, 1993). (Abbott's book deals with a wide range of family issues besides separation and divorce.)

In 1820—the first year of the reign of King George IV—the journalist Pierce Egan began issuing monthly installments of his *Tom & Jerry: Life in London, or The Day and Night Scenes of Jerry Hawthorn Esq. and His Elegant Friend Corinthian Tom* (published as a book in 1821); the illustrations are by George and Isaac Robert Cruikshank; and "to tom and jerry," means to get into drunken brawls.

It's possible that Mrs. Steele got it wrong in the biography of her friend, Sophia Baddeley, and that it was George Hanger (1751–1824), not Gaby Hanger, who was the cause of that laudanum overdose. If Gabriel Hanger—the name of George's father, Lord Coleraine—was the culprit, more power to his abilities as a lover, as he would have been seventy-two at the time of the 1769 incident. George Hanger was a hell-raiser at university and preferred the company of Cyprians at a very early age; he would have been eighteen when this happened.

Abuse of laudanum was a problem; it was a drug too easily available. Other abusers/addicts may have been Mary Robinson; like her friend Samuel Taylor Coleridge, she was said to have once written poetry under its influence, according to Paula Byrne's new biography, *Perdita*.

The quote from the charter of the Royal College of Physicians is taken from its Web site www.replendon.ac.uk/college.

Lord Hardwicke's Marriage Act of 1753 codified marriage laws in England, and the Special Licence was a perk of wealth well out of the price range of ordinary folk.

St. Pancras Old Church is one of thousands of churches in England that are barely operational these days. On the three occasions I tried to get inside it for a firsthand look it was closed to visitors.

The quote from Lillian S. Robinson is from "Why Marry Mr. Collins?" in *Sex, Class, and Culture*. NY: Methuen, pages 178–199.

CHAPTER FOUR. THE LOVE RAT
Reading the articles in both *The Complete Peerage* and *The Dictionary of National Biography* is essential for the background of the Valentia family, whose truth is stranger than fiction.

Cindy McCreery's essay "Keeping Up with the Bon Ton: the Tête-à-Tête series in *The Town and Country Magazine*," in *Gender in Eighteenth-century England: Roles, Representations, and Responsibilities*, edited by Hannah Barker and Elaine Chalus (Longman, 1997), pages 206–229, gives a complete history of this popular gossip feature in *The Town and Country Magazine*. Prints in the series were cataloged by Mary Dorothy George in volume 5 (covering the years 1771–1783) of the *Catalogue of Political and Personal Satires Preserved in the Department of Prints and Drawings of the British Museum* (Trustees of the British Museum, 1978).

CHAPTER FIVE. THE DIVORCE
The text of the Eliot divorce bill is from the 1776 public record at the House of Lords, the *Journals of the House of Lords*. Other quotes are from Lawrence Stone's *Broken Lives*, Leneman's *Alienated Affections*, and Abbott's *Family Ties*, titles discussed earlier.

CHAPTER SIX. BED-HOPPING AND SOCIAL STATUS
The 1999 BBC dramatization of Stella Tillyard's *Aristocrats: Caroline, Emily, Louisa, and Sarah Lennox, 1740–1832* (Chatto & Windus, 1994) her joint biography of the four Lennox sisters, caught the milieu in which Grace Elliott moved, though she never moved in the company of proper aristocratic women like the Lennoxes (unless she was encased anonymously in a domino at a masquerade ball they might also have attended).

Contraception was of paramount importance given the indiscriminate bedhopping of the era. Enlightening background reading is: A. D. Harvey, *Sex in Georgian England* (London: Phoenix Press, 1994); Roy Porter and Lesley Hall, *The Facts of Life: The Creation of Sexual Knowledge in Britain, 1650–1950* (Yale University Press, 1995); Julie Peakman, *Lascivious Bodies: A Sexual History of the Eighteenth Century* (London: Atlantic Books, 2004); John M. Riddle, *Eve's Herbs: A History of Abortion and Contraception in the West* (Harvard University Press, 1997); and Sian Rees's *The Floating Brothel* (London: Hodder, 2001). (Rees's book, while not as specifically targeted as these others, supplies interesting information on how prostitutes suppressed conception.)

And who would omit that little seventeenth-century gem *Aristotle's Masterpiece*, first published in 1684, which served as marriage, sex, and conception manual to generations, going into hundreds of printings in England and colonial America as well as on the Continent? Although there was speculation that the anonymous author (not Aristotle!) was the English physician Dr. William Salmon, whose best-known work was the three-volume *Synopsis Medicinal, or A Compendium of Astrological, Galenical, and Chymical Physick* (1671), he (or she) still remains unknown.

The material on condoms comes in part from the British Museum's exhibition catalog *London 1753* (British Museum Press, 2003), page 144; I saw these amazing artifacts—in remarkably fine condition—on display in the fall of 2003. There are two exuberant prints (see pages 142–144) of the 1749 Penlez riots (named for sailor Bosavern Penlez, who was later hanged for inciting them) that show boxes of condoms hurled out of windows in the general mayhem: *The Tar's Triumph, or Bawdy-House Battery,* by Charles Mosley, and *The Sailor's Revenge, or The Strand in an Uproar,* by Louis Philippe Boitard. Eric J. Dingwall's detailed and descriptive article "Early Contraceptive Sheaths," in the *British Medical Journal,* January 3, 1953, pages 40–41, is of interest on the subject of condom manufacture and the materials used.

There was a fascinating exhibition on Georgian medicine at Dr. Johnson's house on Gough Square, September 18, 2003 to January 31, 2004. The accompanying exhibition booklet, *The Tyranny of Treatment: Dr. Samuel Johnson, His Friends, and Georgian Medicine,* edited by Natasha McEnroe and Robin Simon (*British Art Journal,* 2003) contains an essay, "Boswell's Complaints," by Adam Sisman, that chronicles what happens to a man like Boswell who indulges too freely in frequent and indiscriminate whoring; it's a sobering and tragic story. Imagine, too, all the women he infected along the way:

His later medical problems were all self-inflicted. Drinking and whoring hurtled him towards an early grave, as his body collapsed in middle age under the combined weight of alcoholic excess and repeated venereal infections. In his journals . . . [he] recorded numerous encounters with prostitutes and their consequences: 19 manifestations of venereal attack, over a period of more than 30 years. . . . And he may well have contracted yet more infections during those periods when his journals lapsed, or recorded infections in journals . . . subsequently lost. Boswell contracted his first venereal infection while he was still in his teens.

Herbal medicine has come back into its own in the twenty-first century, and although official government agencies may regard it with skepticism, modern medicine has always relied on drugs and other treatments based on botanicals. Aspirin comes from the willow tree; the heart medicine digitalis from foxglove; morphine/opium (in laudanum) from the poppy. Even for people who could not read, information contained in the herbals was passed on through word of mouth by women.

CHAPTER SEVEN. GEORGE JAMES CHOLMONDELEY

The motto of the Cholmondeley family is from *The Complete Peerage.* A full-color coat of arms can be accessed at www.hereditarytitles.com/Page46.html. The College of Arms, based in London, is the self-supporting fee-based authority on peerages and the granting of titles. Heralds are members of the royal household and are directly appointed by the Sovereign upon recommendation of the Earl Marshal.

There are thirteen officers of arms, styled "Heralds in Ordinary," and their wonderfully medieval titles are:

Garter Principal King of Arms; Clarenceux King of Arms; Norroy and Ulster King of Arms; Richmond Herald; Chester Herald; York Herald; Lancaster Herald; Windsor Herald; Somerset Herald; Rouge Dragon Pursuivant; Blue Mantle Pursuivant; Portcullis Pursuivant; and Rouge Croix Pursuivant. The Richmond Herald, Patric Dickinson, provided the Eliot pedigree, and Clive Cheesman, Rouge Dragon Pursuivant, answered a question for me concerning extinct titles. Their Web site is www.college-of-arms.gov.uk.

Information on the quartering of arms came from Nancy Mayer and Regency romance author Emily Hendrickson. Mrs. Hendrickson is the author of *The Regency Reference Book* (now on CD-ROM).

The quotation from Lady Sarah Napier (née Lennox) on the perils facing rich young lords in the wicked city of London is from *The Life and Letters of Lady Sarah Lennox, 1745–1826* . . . , volume 2, edited by the Countess of Ilchester and Lord Stavordale (J. Murray, 1901). Winston Churchill—not THE Winston Churchill—was an American historical novelist who wrote *Richard Carvel* (1899). The full text is available free on the Project Gutenberg site, www.gutenberg.net.

Statistics on London's population can be found in many places. The first national (though incomplete) census was taken in 1801. Popular works such as Fergus Linnane's *London: The Wicked City* (London: Robson, 2003) and Giles Emerson's *Sin City: London in Pursuit of Pleasure* (London: Granada, 2002) attest to a capital where anything went, and often did.

Thomas Raikes was one of those diarists and letter writers of the late eighteenth and early nineteenth centuries to whom, along with Mary, Lady Coke (1727–1811), Charles Cavendish Fulke Greville (1794–1865), Frances, Lady Shelley (1787–1873), Captain Rees Howell Gronow (1794–1865), and Horace Walpole (1717–1797), biographers owe much. Though not always accurate, they painted unparalleled pictures of their times and contemporaries. Greville and Raikes have been published by the Library of America; only parts of Lady Coke's journals are in print. *The Reminiscences and Recollections of Captain Gronow, Being Anecdotes of the Camp, Court, Clubs & Society, 1810–1860* appeared in several editions; one is abridged by John Raymond (New York: Viking Press, 1964). Lady Shelley's *Diary* is widely available. There have been several editions of Walpole's complete and selected letters. The most popular are *The Letters of Horace Walpole*, edited by Mrs. Paget Toynbee (Clarendon Press, 1903–1905), and supplementary volumes edited by Paget Toynbee (1918–1925); and the highly regarded forty-eight-volume *Horace Walpole's Correspondence*, edited by W. S. Lewis and known as the Yale edition (Yale University Press, 1937–1983).

Money, money, money. It made the Georgian world go round. . . . How much was it worth then, compared to now? Was a £200 fee for a portrait a lot or a little? The rule of thumb is to multiply the amount by 60, then adjust to national currencies. Currently (2004) the pound is worth two U.S. dollars. So, a painting costing £200 then would cost a Briton £12,000 now and an American $24,000. The information on what painters charged comes from Marcia Pointon's study *Hanging the Head: Portraiture and Social Formation in Eighteenth-Century England* (Yale University Press, 1993). There was definitely a pecking order dictating which artists charged what prices, and at the top were Reynolds and Gainsborough. George Romney gained their lasting enmity—and exclusion from the Royal Academy—because he consistently undercut their fees, thus poaching more frugal clients from them.

The London men's clubs, as per the Brian Wheeler article "If Anybody Wants Me, I'll Be at My Club," in the BBC News online magazine, November 24, 2003, are flourishing. It was big and important news when Prince William joined White's, the oldest men's club in London.

British-born historical novelist Jean Ross Ewing contributed the first part of the sidebar on British names (p. 142). Cholmondeley is perhaps the most widely known example of a British name pronounced markedly different from its spelling. It's a classic shibboleth, in that if one pronounces it incorrectly, one is clearly identified as not ton, but a mere outsider.

What Lord Cholmondeley thought about the two

satiric poems, *The Female Jockey Club* and *The Torpedo,* is not known. Everyone, from gallant to dotty old woman, was fair game for these merciless satirists. The other individual to whom *The Torpedo* was dedicated was John Hunter (1728–1793), a famous anatomist and surgeon. There are several biographies of Hunter, among them S. R. Gloyne's *John Hunter* (Baltimore: Williams & Wilkins, 1950) and John Kobler's *The Reluctant Surgeon* (Oxford: W. Heinemann, 1960). Recently, he has come under criticism by social activist writers for what they believe was his too-morbid fascination with the dissection of deformed human beings such as the Irish Giant (Charles Byrne/O'Brien) and the Sicilian dwarf. See Hilary Mantel's *The Giant O'Brien* (Doubleday Canada, 1998), a novel exposing the unscrupulous methods Hunter used to obtain O'Brien's corpse and a new play by Garry Robson, *The Irish Giant* (2003), about a disabled group who break into the Hunterian to rescue O'Brien's skeleton.

CHAPTER EIGHT. THE EARL'S MISTRESS AND THE UNSUITABLE MARRIAGE

The Walpole letters quoted are from the Yale edition.

Strawberry Hill, Walpole's beloved piece of Gothic Revival architecture and style, is in the London borough of Twickenham. In 1923 the house and its forty-six acres were bought by the Catholic Education Council and became the campus of St. Mary's, a teacher-training college, now part of Surrey University. The house is on the World Monuments Fund's list of the world's "100 Most Endangered Sites." The organization Friends of Strawberry Hill is trying to raise public awareness and looking for funds to restore it. Their Web site is www.friendsofstrawberry hill.org.

Highwaymen—think Mack the Knife, from *The Threepenny Opera* . . . and then disabuse yourself of that romantic notion. They were thugs and robbers who carried pistols, shot to kill, and raped female victims. Occasionally one would come across one of these gentlemen at leisure at one of the lesser London pleasure gardens like Marylebone. See David Brandon's *Stand and Deliver! A History of Highway Robbery* (London: Sutton, 2001).

The most famous lover's eye of all was probably the one the Prince of Wales gave to Mrs. Fitzherbert in 1785, according to a 1786 letter from the Dowager Countess of Devonshire to her daughter-in-law Georgiana. Novelist Candice Hern has examples of these tiny tokens of enduring affection—which were also popular as mourning jewelry—on her Web site, www.candicehern.com.

CHAPTER NINE. MRS. ELLIOTT'S EXCELLENT ADVENTURES, VOLUME ONE: GRACE GOES TO PARIS AND BAGS HER FIRST PRINCE

Get off the Piccadilly Line Tube at Green Park, stay on the side opposite the park and walk toward the higher numbers on the street. (This is in the opposite direction from the Royal Academy, which is across from Fortnum & Mason.) You will spot a dingy white mansion that's seen far, far better days. This is 94 Piccadilly, once the home of Lord Cholmondeley; the house had been designed in 1756–1760 by Matthew Brettingham, when His Lordship was a young boy. Brettingham—who also worked at Euston and Holkham Halls and Petworth House—was an assistant to William Kent, designer of the Houghton Hall interiors.

It's been the home of far, far more famous men than Lord Cholmondeley; there is one of the almost eight hundred to date of English Heritage's blue memorial plaques—the English equivalent of our "George Washington slept here" signs—on the side of the nearer gate post stating that Lord Palmerston (1784–1865), prime minister and foreign secretary, lived here; it was then (circa 1850) called Cambridge House, as the Duke of Cambridge had been a previous resident.

The building also housed at least two men's clubs, the Canning Club and the much better known Naval & Military Club. (Other nearby clubs were the American Club at 95 Piccadilly, the St. James Club at 106, and the Cavalry & Guards Club at 127; the nightclub Pangea, site of a recent scuffle involving Prince Harry and the paparazzi, is at number 85.) The Naval & Military Club was founded in 1862 on Clifford Street, and moved to 94 Piccadilly in 1865. It was familiarly known as the "In & Out," from the instructions on the gateposts; the club is famous for having set down the rules of bridge.

There's a gentleman who styles himself the Diamond Geezer who has a Web log (blog) that describes his favorite places in London (http://diamondgeezer.blogspot.com), and 94 Piccadilly is one of these places. Here is what he says about the house and its original owner: "This rather impressive building set back from the road is (or was) Cambridge House, built in 1760 for some dull Earl." (Lord Cholmondeley, dull?!) He goes on to talk about the Naval & Military Club, noting that it cost £1500 to join, plus an annual subscription of £810, and that "the club moved out to St. James's Square five years ago." Here is where it gets interesting. "The building was subsequently snapped up by an Arab buyer, and there are now plans to transform it into a 100-room hotel. Not quite so classy now, alas." When I last saw it, in November 2004, it seemed to be functioning as a party venue. A year earlier, in the fall of 2003, I was kicked off the premises by a surly watchman for presuming to ask if he could tell me who the owner was, and if I could view the interior of the building. It was being gutted, but traces of wallpaper and molding still remained and it appeared quite handsome inside.

Louis-Philippe-Joseph, fifth Duc d'Orléans, is a controversial figure to the French, depending on whether one is a monarchist or a republican. His major non-French biographer, Evarts Seelye Scudder (*Prince of the Blood*, London: Collins, 1937), tried hard to find positives, but was realist enough to know he'd set himself a difficult chore. To quote Scudder, "The task of lifting his faults from him is hopeless; he is swamped in them, bogged forever in history." The distinguished diplomat Talleyrand "called him the cesspool of the revolution," and the monarchist Mirabeau "declared that he wouldn't have him for his valet," according to Scudder.

A note here about the solidarity of the courtesan sisterhood—of which Agnes de Buffon (Orléans's last mistress), merely an adulterous wife, was not a part—and how these ladies stuck together to protect their territory. In true French roué tradition, Philippe's father had introduced him to his first mistress, the fifteen-year-old Rosalie Duthé.

She spent as much time across the Channel as she did in France and was said to have been involved with Lord Egremont as well as others in the ton. She was among the cleverest courtesans, as she saved her money and was smart enough to leave France when the Revolution began. In London, she was friendly with Elizabeth Armistead and Grace Elliott; an often repeated story (see the two recent biographies of Mary Robinson) tells how Elliott, Armistead, and Duthé, arms tightly interlocked, bore down on Robinson, who was alone one night at the theater, intimidating her so much she fled the premises. Sisterhood was powerful . . . when the women were not in competition for the same man.

CHAPTER TEN. MRS. ELLIOTT'S EXCELLENT ADVENTURES, VOLUME TWO: GRACE BAGS HER SECOND PRINCE . . .
Grace Elliott was in the right place at the right time to bag the Prince of Wales, her next high-profile conquest. The quote on page 195 from his biographer Cynthia Campbell (*The Most Polished Gentleman*, page 28) puts his tendency to fall in love succinctly.

Annuities. What were they and who got them? The Prince of Wales had a good number of them paid out from the Privy Purse to ex-girlfriends and bastards. Records of these payments can be found—though they are incomplete—in the papers of King George IV at Windsor Castle. Miss Pamela Clark, the registrar, will happily look up how much was paid and to whom over what period of time. In the end, it was the English people who paid for Georgie's fun. Annuities separated the smart courtesans from the not-so-smart. Harriette Wilson claimed she refused them, and so that's why she resorted to blackmail when high-ranking men were no longer interested in sampling her favors. (That was her story and she stuck with it, but Harriette had a coronet in her sights and so annuities were not uppermost in her mind. Unfortunately for her, the young heir's father thwarted her.)

Elizabeth Armistead, one of the smartest courtesans, secured annuities from all her clients. Grace Elliott would have done better if the Duc d'Orléans had survived the Reign of Terror. She received income from John Eliot,

King George IV, and probably Lord Cholmondeley (though there's no record in his papers).

Having the bastard of the future monarch put Grace into a different category from her courtesan sisters; she was now a force to be reckoned with, and she no doubt worked the advantage. Though the majority of respectable women still would not receive her, others who sought favor from the monarch-to-be no doubt did, as Frances, Lady Shelley, attested in her *Diary*. The years from 1782 to 1784 were heady times for Grace. In September of 1783 she appeared prominently in a cartoon, *The Aerostatick Stage Balloon*, in the company of her rival Mary Robinson and the woman who was to be one of her best friends, Lady Seymour Dorothy Worsley.

The translation of the Latin phrase *"Tentanda via est qua me quoque possim tollere humo,"* from the ballooning cartoon that featured Lord Cholmondeley, is from the third book of the poet Virgil's Georgics: "I, too, will strive o'er earth my flight to raise / And wing'd by victory, catch the gale of praise." It's a resolution to make oneself celebrated.

Chapter Eleven. "It Was the Best of Times, It Was the Worst of Times" . . .

The full text of *A Tale of Two Cities* can be found on many Internet sites; it's worth reading again. Between Dickens's novel and Grace Elliott's *Journal*, one comes away with a full and rounded image of these terrible times. Idealism gone wrong is always tragic. The Whigs in England at first applauded the republican ideas expressed by the revolutionaries, only to be disillusioned along with many other intellectuals and philosophers. Edmund Burke, who supported the ideals of the American Revolution, was soon repulsed by the excesses of the French Revolution. His *Reflections on the French Revolution* (1790), attacked the rabid pro–French Revolution cleric Richard Price for his sentiments. (See cartoon on page 265; it depicts Reverend Price in the bedchamber of Queen Marie Antoinette.) It was a highly charged political arena.

The National Archives, Office of National Statistics, and other agencies that hold public records (of births, marriages, deaths, wills, etc.) in the United Kingdom stock a number of aids—most are inexpensive booklets costing less than £5—in their on-site bookshops for genealogists and researchers to help them interpret these old documents and to sort out issues such as illegitimacy. Among these are several by Eve McLaughlin: *Illegitimac* (Haddenham, Bucks, UK: Varneys Press, 1999); *Modern Wills from 1858* (Haddenham, Bucks, UK: Varneys Press, 2001); and *Wills before 1858* (Ramsbottom, Lancashire: Federation of Family History Societies, 1989). Others are: *Marriages and Certificates in England and Wales,* by Barbara Dixon (Burnham, Berkshire: Dixon, 2000); *Marriage Laws, Rites, Records & Customs,* by Colin R. Chapman with Pauline M. Litton (Dursley, Gloucestershire: Lochin Publishing, 1997); *Using Wills After 1858* and *First Avenue House,* by Audrey Collins (Ramsbottom, Lancashire: Federation of Family History Societies, 1998); and *Affection Defying the Power of Death: Introduction to Wills, Probate & Death Duty Records,* by Jane Cox (Ramsbottom, Lancashire: Federation of Family History Societies, 1993. The National Archives journal, *Ancestors,* has solid research articles. For example, a current issue, number 28, has the timely article "Licensed to Wed."

Here are where the principal agencies (both public and private) dealing with wills and genealogical matters can be found: National Archives, Ruskin Avenue, Kew; London Metropolitan Archives, Northampton Road; Guildhall Library, Aldermanbury; Family Record Centre, Myddleton House, Islington; Principal Probate Registry, New Register House, High Holborn (also referred to as First Avenue House); Society of Genealogists, Charterhouse Buildings, Goswell Road.

The National Archives Family Record Centre in London has the same information as the National Archives' in Kew, but I found Kew easier to get to and easier and more pleasant to work in; it's a new building in a lovely location. (You can visit Kew Gardens afterwards.) The wills of Sir John Eliot, Grace Elliott, and Lord Cholmondeley are available on-site on microfiche; they are also downloadable for a fee from any remote location. Georgina Cavendish-Bentinck's will, a late nineteenth-century will, was at First Avenue House at the Principal Probate Registry. The London Metropolitan Archives had Grace Elliott's marriage license and Georgiana's baptismal certificate; the Guildhall Library had the annotations for the Special Licence applied for by John Eliot. As you can see, there are a number of places one must go to secure this kind of information, but reproduction costs are nominal. Digitization may one day deliver all this to one's home.

Grace Elliott was probably an amateur spy for England—recruited by the British secret service—and we know from the *Journal* that she acted as a courier for both Philippe and his cousin Queen Marie-Antoinette. There were too many trips to Spa and other places with mention of letters and boxes carried to and fro across the Continent for this activity to be innocent, though she is too discreet to out her spymaster(s).

That there was material that could possibly be compromising might be deduced by the pages that were torn from her manuscript. But finding hard proof in print—much less a list of amateur spies—is patently impossible. A revealing article on the workings of the British secret service during this period is "The British Secret Service and the Escape of Sir Sydney Smith from Paris in 1798," by Michael Durey, in *History,* volume 84, issue 275 (July 1999) pages 437–457.

Grace Elliott probably was back in England in 1798—note that date—and her traveling companion might have been Henry Swinburne, who himself could have been spying for England. It's all too much of a coincidence not to be suspicious.

Chapter Twelve. It Was a Very Bad Year . . .

This is not a book on the French Revolution or the Reign of Terror except as those events impacted upon the life of Grace Elliott, and it was a struggle to include what was necessary for historical background while keeping the focus on Grace and not miring the reader down in history and personalities. Grace's eyewitness accounts of events in the *Journal* have been a source for a number of histories and biographies (for one of the latest, see Andrea Stuart's *The Rose of Martinique: A Life of Napoleon's Josephine* (Lon-

don: Macmillan, 2003), a biography of Josephine de Beauharnais). Other contemporary sources on the Revolution are commentary in the English press, political cartoons, and other eyewitness accounts as in *English Witnesses of the French Revolution,* edited by J. M. Thompson (Port Washington, NY: Kennikat Press, 1938; 1970). Sympathetic accounts of the victims of the Revolution include Evarts Seelye Scudder's biography of the Duc d'Orléans, *Prince of the Blood;* Antonia Fraser's *Marie Antoinette: The Journey* (London: Weidenfield & Nicholson, 2001); and Simon Schama's *Citizens: A Chronicle of the French Revolution* (New York: Knopf, 1990).

Helen Maria Williams's *Letters from France* gives the viewpoint of an expatriate Englishwoman sympathetic to the revolutionary cause (for which she was reviled at home). There are several biographies of the Girondist heroine Madame Roland, such as *The Life of Madame Roland,* by Madeleine Clemenceau-Jacquemaire (London: Longmans & Green, 1930), and *Madame Roland and the Age of Revolution,* by Gita May (New York: Columbia University Press, 1970). A 20-franc postage stamp of Madame Roland was issued in her honor by the French government in 1989. *An Eye-Witness Account of the French Revolution* by Helen Maria Williams can be found in volume 19 of *The Age of Revolution and Romanticism* (Frankfurt: Peter Lang Publishing, 1997).

Chapter Thirteen. Return of the Native

The letter on page 294 is the only one we have in Grace Elliott's hand; it is in the Papers of King George IV at Windsor Castle. It was addressed to an Admiral Payne, who was private secretary to the Prince of Wales. John Willett Payne (1752–1803), known as Jack, served England in both the American Revolution and the Napoleonic wars. He resigned his command owing to ill health and served for a time as comptroller of the Prince's household, where his main duties were delivering *congés* (bye-bye, sweetheart) to royal mistresses and negotiating annuities and settlements with them.

The letter from Grace Elliott, which Payne obviously did not answer, is so respectful to a man infamous for his lack of respect to women and his foul sailor's mouth that it's groveling—she apparently really needed the money—the reader is embarrassed for her. Payne died at Greenwich Hospital, where he'd ended his days as treasurer.

I viewed the portraits of Grace's daughter Georgiana in November 2004. As a toddler Georgiana sat for Sir Joshua Reynolds, the premier painter of children; as a ten-year-old, she was drawn sporting a pixie haircut and wearing a coral necklace by Andrew Plimer, a foremost miniaturist; another miniature supposedly in the collection of the Earl of Jersey shows her as a young woman (the Earl did not respond to letters); and there are miniatures (one just of her, another a copy of it set into a locket facing a miniature of Lord Charles) and a large (26 x 21 inch) portrait bust of her as Lady Charles Bentinck by the pupil and biographer of Reynolds, James Northcote. All these but the Reynolds are in a private collection I have been asked not to disclose.

I am in agreement with Hugh Farmar, who wrote *A Regency Elopement* (M. Joseph, 1969), and with the biographer of George IV whom he quotes, Roger Fulford, that no one will ever know if Cholmondeley or the King was Georgiana's biological father. The quote from Farmar on page 317 is from page 22 of his book.

The information about Grace's real estate in Paris comes from the City of Paris Archives, a modern building situated in the wilds of the nineteenth Arrondissement, a long Metro ride from center-city Paris. The sources consulted were: Beatrice de Andia, et al., *Le 8e Arrondissement . . . .*, (Mairie de Paris, no date); Félix and Louis Lazare, *Dictionnaire Administratif et Historique des rues et monuments de Paris* (Maissoneure et Larose, 1994; reprint of 1855 edition), and the 1963 edition of Jacques Hillairet's *Dictionnaire historique des rues de Paris* (Editions de Minuit historique). (See pages 131–132 in Andia and page 104 in Hillairet.) The National Archives were undergoing renovation at the time I went to Paris and had moved to another location from its longtime site in the Marais; the personnel were so unhelpful—in fact, downright snippy—that the trip was an exercise in aggravation. A stringer from a U.S. newsmagazine based in Paris who's also been burned by the lack of professionalism shown by French librarians and archivists told me in all sincerity that the only conclusion he could draw, after years of encountering bad attitude, was that the government policy had to be to hire aliens only, aliens "who despised all carbon-based life forms." While I think this judgment might be a tad harsh, I have to go along with the underlying sentiment.

I went to the rue de Miromesnil to see the building that could have been Grace's *hôtel particulier,* as these town houses are called. My bet is that it's number 31—though it may not have been 31 in Grace's time, nor even had a number. The great big blue-enameled medallion—the intertwined *G* and *E*—over the front doors have got to stand for "Grace Elliott." Eric Rohmer, the director of *The Lady and the Duke,* thought so too, at first, but later was not so sure. I'm sure, and looking in the real estate record books for the period at the Paris Archives confirmed it. In fact, according to that 1855 Lazare brothers' dictionary of Paris streets, it might have been among the first buildings on Miromesnil, as *"il n'existant, en 1778, qu'une seule maison dans cette rue."* (only one house existed in 1778 on that street). Grace moved in circa 1779.

The Meudon cottage is still there. Photos were taken from the side streets and are not very good. The walls around the house and the shrubbery are too high. But it's a sizable edifice, in excellent condition.

CHAPTER FOURTEEN. THE TRAIL GOES COLD . . .

The double circumstances of the death of her daughter Georgiana in 1813 and the restoration of the Bourbon monarchy in 1814 doubtless contributed to Grace's decision to return to France. Though Georgiana had a baptismal certificate, no notice of her death could be found in the newspapers, and I don't know where she was buried.

The only public announcement of any kind concerning Grace's granddaughter Georgina Cavendish-Bentinck was the brief notice of her death in the *Times;* there was no proper obituary. She's presumably buried in Malpas, Cheshire, where she'd lived all her long life. Except for Hugh Farmar's book about her father and stepmother and her extraordinary will—and that's "will" as in fortitude and determination to get Grace Elliott's memoir published, as well as the document known as her last will and testament—we would know nothing about her. As with most turning points in this story of Grace and her life and family, the discovery of Farmar's *A Regency Elopement* was serendipitous—a chance search on Google—and answered questions about Georgina's childhood and subsequent spinsterhood.

Years ago, when I was a mere slip of a girl myself and interested in biology, I read a popular book on human genetics by Amram Scheinfeld called *The New You and Heredity* (Philadelphia: Lippincott, 1950). I have never forgotten the illustrations that showed how it was possible for a homely couple to have a beautiful child—"A Beauty Contest Winner"—and for a beautiful couple to have a homely child—"An Ugly Duckling." Georgina Cavendish-Bentinck, alas, may have been a prime example of the latter.

For more information on the eccentric 5th Duke of Portland, see these booklets, available from the Harley Gallery at Welbeck Abbey: Derek Adlam, *The Enigmatic Fifth Duke of Portland* (Pineapple Press, 2002) and *Miss Butler Remembers: A Laundrymaid's Recollections of the Fifth Duke of Portland, 1869–1879* (Pineapple Press, 2003). Two books on the fascinating dukes of England are: E. S. Turner, *Amazing Grace: The Great Days of Dukes* (Sutton, 2003; first published in London by Michael Joseph, 1975), and Brian Masters, *The Dukes: The Origins, Ennoblement, and History of Twenty-six Families* (London: Pimlico, 2001; first published in London by Blond & Briggs, 1975).

All quotes from the letters of the Wellesley family are from Hugh Farmar's very helpful book, *A Regency Elopement* (London: Michael Joseph, 1969) and I thank his son, the artist Francis Farmar, for speaking with me about this family, from whom the Farmars are descended. The letters are now stored in the Special Collections Division at the University of Southampton Libraries.

The quote from Lady Louisa Stuart is from pages 17–18 of *The Letters of Lady Louisa Stuart*, edited by R. Brimley Johnson (Oxford: Bodley Head, 1926). The quote about the wills of women is from pages 9–10 of Jane Cox's *Affec-*

tion Defying the Power of Death (Lancashire, UK: Federation of Family History Societies, 1993), fully cited in an earlier section of these Notes. The extensive Portland papers are in the collection of the University of Nottinghamshire.

Chapter Fifteen. "De Langueur"

Information on beautiful Ville d'Avray (a favorite of painters Camille Corot and Alfred Sisley) comes from time spent in that village in the fall of 2003 with my friend and translator Kristina Hickey; we saw the bound register for 1823 containing Grace's death certificate, kept on the open shelves of the *mairie* (town hall) with other registers. (I'd tried to get the information by snail mail and e-mail but received no response; when I showed up in person, I was told that someone had looked but there was nothing there. However, Ms. Hickey went to the book, opened it, and found Grace's death certificate right where I'd thought it should be.)

My French researcher Colette Pozzi-Barsot was a great, great help in tracking down additional information about Grace Elliott. She herself lives in the area where Grace spent her last years and was able to speak with local historians; she found the Madame Matheron source, *Ville d'Avray—Its Roads and Its Streets* (Société des Amis du Musée de Ville d'Avray, 1992) and was able to confirm Monsieur Dupuis's status in the village. She said that local lore categorically rejected any suggestion that Grace could have been his mistress; she was simply an elderly lodger in his family home. The circumstance of lodging the elderly with nonrelated caretakers is not unknown, even today.

All the quotes from Grace are to be found in her *Journal*.

Chapter Sixteen. "Publish and Be Damned!" . . .

My London-based researcher Barbara Rosenbaum sorted through the voluminous files of the Bentley Archives, which are owned by the British Library, to try to find the original manuscript of Grace's *Journal*. It's not there, but other worthwhile information on the print runs, what Bentley paid for the manuscript, and so on, turned up. Serendipity surfaced again in the form of a Sotheby's sales catalog for the auction of Bentley's personal library—Sotheby's itself no longer had a copy—that had been annotated by (my guess) one of the Bentley family or staff. There was nothing in the Bentley Archives that shed any further light on Richard Bentley's sources for the biographical material he wrote for the *Journal*.

The literary merit of the *Journal* is, to the French, a given. The essay by Sainte-Beuve is in a French edition of the *Journal* and also appeared in other sources at the time of the *Journal*'s publication. Thanks to French-born Daniele Perez-Venero for her excellent translation and also to Mark Kintzel of Rodale Press for his comments on the press's 1955 edition, and for sending a copy of the image of Grace which appeared in that book.

POSTSCRIPT. GRACE ELLIOTT'S FINAL RESTING PLACE IN PARIS . . .

When I searched in vain for Grace's grave on a hot day in the hilltop cemetery of Ville d'Avray—where there are no records of who's buried where and tombstones are crumbling all over the grounds—I realized what a fruitless task it was and tried to think more logically about where she could be buried. (Later I was to learn that this cemetery dated from years after her death.) The answer was clear: It had to be the celebrated Père-Lachaise. Grace met all the qualifications, it befit her status, and the time frame was right. I was, of course, eleven years too late to view her tombstone, which had been removed in 1992, probably because it had crumbled into pieces, as had so many at the Ville d'Avray burial ground.

My French researcher tried to find any information she could about the gravesite: Was there, for instance, a record of the inscription on the tomb? What Lord Cholmondeley had chosen to place on it in memory of Grace would have been interesting. It was, however, the same old story of endeavoring to light a fire under entrenched French bureaucrats. The man in charge of all the French cemeteries was on extended medical leave—or so he told my researcher in a letter—and he could not provide any help. He apparently had no deputy or underling who could help, either, or, more to the point, anyone who was interested in helping. He himself obviously wasn't interested in facilitating the matter. The gentleman is probably still on medical leave—or, *tant pis,* has passed away—as we have yet to hear anything from that quarter. Alien recruitment must be at an all-time low in France.

APPENDIX. *L'ANGLAISE ET LE DUC* . . .

One of the highlights of this research was interviewing the English actress Lucy Russell, who gave valuable insights into creating character and working for Eric Rohmer. She was kind enough to have lunch with me at the Maison Blanc in Chiswick on October 17, 2003, two years after the film's premiere. Russell was named a European Film Shooting Star in 2002. Her latest English-language films are *Tristan & Isolde* and *Batman Begins* (both 2005), and her most recent French films are *L'Ennemi Naturel* and *Pour le plaisir* (both 2004).

The film, one of the few historical dramas in Rohmer's oeuvre, was an international hit. Lucy Russell traveled the globe on the publicity tour and was interviewed by a number of journalists, among whom two should be noted: Stuart Jeffries in the *Guardian* (February 14, 2002) and Tom Charity in *Time Out* (February 13, 2002).

The entire 2001 Aurélien Ferenzi interview with Eric Rohmer can be found at the online journal Senses of Cinema (www.sensesofcinema.com/contents/01/16/rohmer.html). The full review by Jo Manning of the videotape *Eric Rohmer: With Supporting Evidence, Parts One & Two* is on the University of Buffalo's electronic journal site, Educational Media Reviews Online: (libweb.lib.buffalo.edu/emro/emroDetail.asp?Number=1170).

INDEX

Note: Page numbers in *italics* refer to illustrations.